Gwen John

By the same author

Fiction
Estella, her Expectations

Non-fiction
Writing and Gender: Virginia Woolf's Writing Practice

Poetry
The Spitfire Factory

Edited
Women Reading Women's Writing (ed.)
The Cambridge Companion to Virginia Woolf (co-ed.)
Virginia Woolf: *Jacob's Room* (ed.)

Gwen John
A Life

Sue Roe

Chatto & Windus
LONDON

Published by Chatto & Windus 2001

2 4 6 8 10 9 7 5 3

First published in Great Britain in 2001 by
Chatto & Windus
Random House, 20 Vauxhall Bridge Road,
London SW1V 2SA

Random House Australia (Pty) Limited
20 Alfred Street, Milsons Point, Sydney,
New South Wales 2061, Australia

Random House New Zealand Limited
18 Poland Road, Glenfield,
Auckland 10, New Zealand

Random House (Pty) Limited
Endulini, 5A Jubilee Road, Parktown 2193, South Africa

The Random House Group Limited Reg. No. 954009
www.randomhouse.co.uk

A CIP catalogue record for this book
is available from the British Library

ISBN 0 7011 6695 9

Papers used by Random House are natural,
recyclable products made from wood grown in sustainable forests;
the manufacturing processes conform to the environmental
regulations of the country of origin

Printed and bound in Great Britain by
Mackays of Chatham Ltd.

for my family

Contents

Illustrations ix

Acknowledgements xi

Preface xv

1 Childhood 1

2 The Slade 14

3 Interior with Figures 23

4 The Waif of Pimlico 29

5 The Road to Rome 37

6 Rodin 47

7 La Chambre sur la Cour (7 rue St Placide) 68

8 Ida 82

9 The Artist's Room (87 rue du Cherche-Midi) 90

10 Osez! osez! 109

11 29 rue Terre Neuve 127

12 The 'Nun' 137

13	War	150
14	17 November 1917	166
15	The Château Vauclair	181
16	Jeanne	191
17	Recovery	210
18	God's Little Artist	223
19	The Chenil Show	232
20	Véra	250
21	The Hangar	263
22	For Dieppe	287
	Notes	307
	Bibliography	345
	Index	349

Illustrations

Colour Plates

1. *Portrait of Mrs Atkinson*, c. 1897–8 (Metropolitan Museum, New York)
2. *Self Portrait*, c. 1900 (National Portrait Gallery, London)
3. *Dorelia in a Black Dress*, 1903–4 (Tate, London)
4. A *Corner of the Artist's Room in Paris*, 1907–9 (National Museum of Wales, Cardiff)
5. *Nude Girl*, c. 1909–10 (Tate, London)
6. A *Lady Reading*, 1910–11 (Tate, London)
7. *Mère Poussepin Seated at a Table*, mid-1910s (National Museum of Wales, Cardiff)
8. *Girl Holding a Rose*, late 1910s (Mellon Collection, Upperville, Virginia/Bridgeman Art Library, London)

Black and White Plates

1. Gwen John's mother, Augusta Smith
2. Gwen John's father, Edwin John
3. The four John children with their nurse, c. 1880
4. Augustus, Ida (holding David) and Gwen John
5. Rainer Maria Rilke (Musée Rodin, Paris)
6. Drawing of Ursula Tyrwhitt by Augustus John, c. 1897 (Private collection)

7. Gwen John, *Portrait study of Arthur Symons*, c. 1921 (Victoria & Albert Museum, London)
8. Jeanne Robert Foster and John Quinn (Collection of Cecily Langdale)
9. Gwen John, *Chloe Boughton-Leigh*, c. 1907 (Tate, London)
10. Gwen John, *Chloe Boughton-Leigh*, c. 1910 (Leeds City Art Galleries)
11. 87 rue du Cherche-Midi, photograph by Cecily Langdale
12. 29 rue Terre Neuve
13. Gwen John, *Breton Boy*, late 1910s (Private collection)
14. *The Child with a Polo*, late 1910s (Private collection)
15. The Château Vauclair
16. Gwen John, *The Victorian Sisters* (National Library of Wales, Aberystwyth)
17. Gwen John, *Madonna and child (in a Landscape)*, c. 1928 (Private collection)
18. The church at Meudon, photograph by the author
19. Gwen John, *Four little girls kneeling in church*, c. 1910 (Private collection)
20. Gwen John, *A Vase of Flowers*, late 1910s (National Library of Wales, Aberystwyth)
21. Gwen John, *Vase of Flowers with Ferns*, late 1920s to early 1930s (Davis & Langdale Co., New York)
22. Gwen John, *Rue Terre Neuve, Meudon*, c. 1920 (Cecil Higgins Art Gallery, Bedford)
23. Gwen John, *Cat* (Musée Rodin, Paris)
24. Auguste Rodin, *Danseuse Cambodigense* (Musée Rodin, Paris)
25. Auguste Rodin, photograph by Ernest H. Mills, 1909 (National Library of Wales, Aberystwyth)
26. Auguste Rodin, *The Whistler Muse* (Musée Rodin, Paris)

Acknowledgements

In writing this book I have been indebted to many people for their assistance, encouragement and support. I have been able to let Gwen John's voice speak throughout her story due to the generosity of her family, whose kind permission to quote from Gwen's letters and papers has enabled me to present her as I wished to. I am deeply grateful to Anna John, Ben John, Rebecca John and Sara John for their generous support, encouragement and trust. To the generosity of Ben John and Sara John I owe the privilege of quoting from Gwen John's own papers. I am grateful to Sara John for her close interest and constructive criticism of my treatment of Gwen's spiritual development in the writing of this book, for the loan of private letters, and her own writings on Gwen. Ida John's voice is freely heard due to the generosity of Rebecca John, as is Ada Nettleship's. Betty Cobb has generously allowed me to quote Winifred John's voice, and her own. To Julius White I owe the opportunity to present verbatim the voices of Dorelia McNeill and Augustus John.

My own family's support has enabled me to complete the project, and I am grateful for the encouragement of my parents, Pauline and Malcolm Roe. I also deeply appreciate the continuing encouragement and support of John Spiers.

My agent, Gill Coleridge and my editor, Jenny Uglow, have sustained me throughout the writing and re-writing of the book. Without their expertise and support it would not be the book it is. My copy-editor and friend Beth

Humphries also brought her expertise to bear. I am grateful to Jonathan Burnham for commissioning the book and to Alison Samuel, Publishing Director of Chatto & Windus, Jonathan Galassi, my publisher at Farrar, Straus & Giroux and Susan Grace Galassi, Associate Curator, The Frick Collection, for their advice and encouragement. I am also grateful to Cecily Langdale, author of *Gwen John* and to Alison Thomas, author of *Portraits of Women: Gwen John's Forgotten Contemporaries*, for their generous willingness to exchange ideas.

In pursuing my research the support of archivists, curators and technicians has been invaluable. My first thanks must be to Dr Ceridwen Lloyd-Morgan, Senior Assistant Archivist, The National Library of Wales, who was unfailingly generous with her time and her considerable knowledge of Gwen John during each of my extended visits to the Archive of the National Library of Wales.

I am similarly grateful for the kind assistance of Tony Askin, Chief Technician at the Metropolitan Museum of New York; also for that of Odile Barbier and Marie-Pierre Delclaux, archivists of the Gwen John Archive in the Musée Rodin, Paris, and for that of Claudie Judrin, *Conservateur en Chef* of the Musée Rodin and Alain Beausire, *Chargé des Archives et de la Bibliothèque du Musée Rodin*.

I also gratefully acknowledge the assistance of Andrew Barlow, Keeper of Fine Art at Brighton Museum; John Beynon, Hon. Curator of Tenby Museum; Jennifer Booth, The Archivist, Tate Archives, London; Mary Bowling, Curator of Manuscripts, the New York Public Library; Juliet Carey, formerly Assistant Curator at the National Museum of Wales, Cardiff; David Fraser Jenkins, Curator of Tate, London; Alex Robertson, Curator of the Leeds City Art Galleries. My thanks are also amply due to the staff of the Pictures and Maps Department and of the Sound and Moving Image Collection at the National Library of Wales, and to the staff of the Archives of the Museum of Modern Art, New York.

The descendants and executors of Gwen's friends have also been most generous and I am very grateful to Daniel Huws for kind permission to quote from Ursula Tyrwhitt's letters and to Brian Read, for kind permission to quote from those of Arthur Symons. Alexandre Roche generously gave permission to quote from the reminiscences and letters of his late mother, Louise Roche.

In Pléneuf, Monsieur and Madame Burquier de Germond showed

immense kindness in opening the doors of the Château Vauclair to me. I am deeply grateful for their welcome and for their interest. Michel Grimaud gave valuable assistance with my research into painters in Brittany. Madame Nathalie Morin Simorre kindly showed me inside no. 87, rue du Cherche-Midi.

To the encouragement and advice of Terence Blacker the idea for this book owes its survival in the early stages and beyond. I have also appreciated his critical responses to portions of the book as it emerged as well as those of Roger Deakin and Terry James. Robert Baldock gave invaluable help and support. Kate Hardy shared her practical knowledge of drawing and painting and Barbara Hardy gave ongoing encouragement and generous hospitality in Gower. Louise Murphy was always there in Paris, offering generous hospitality and help in Paris and accompanying me to Pléneuf.

Particular thanks are due to all those, family and friends, who regularly gave patient and enthusiastic personal support on a regular basis. In addition to those named above, I am grateful to Jehane Boden Spiers, Robyn Bolam, Marcella Evaristi, Adrian Fisher, Jennie James, Nina Martel, Shelley Roberts, David Roe, CBE, Alison Sharpe, Stephen Ward.

I was in grateful receipt of a grant from the Society of Authors. I also gratefully acknowledge permission to quote from the Foster-Murphy Papers, Manuscripts and Archives Division, The New York Public Library, Astor, Lenox and Tilden Foundations, and from the John Quinn Memorial Collection, Manuscripts and Archives Division, The New York Public Library, Astor, Lenox and Tilden Foundations, by kind permission of the New York Public Library. Quotation from *The Slade Animal Land* is by kind permission of University College London Library. Excepts from *Letters to a Young Poet* by Rainer Maria Rilke are translated by M.D. Herter Norton. Copyright 1934, by W.W. Norton & Company, Inc., renewed © 1962, 1982 by M.D. Herter Norton. Used by permission of W.W. Norton & Company, Inc. Gwen John's correspondence with Rodin and Louise Roche's reminiscences of Gwen John are translated from the original French by the author.

With regard to the illustrations, all works by Gwen John are © Estate of Gwen John 2001. All rights reserved, DACS. I would like to express my gratitude to Ben John and Sara John and to Janet Tod of the Design and

Artists Copyright Society, and to the Trustees and Boards of all the Museums, Galleries and Libraries noted in the illustrations list. Black and white plates nos. 8 and 11 are reproduced by courtesy of Cecily Langdale, no. 21, courtesy of Davis and Langdale, New York, and no. 15 by kind permission of Monsieur and Madame Burquier de Germond.

Every effort has been made to trace copyright holders. The publishers would be interested to hear from any copyright holders not here acknowledged.

Preface

'In about 1929 I saw coming into the church a woman in a felt hat with a wide brim, dressed in a long, dark cape, who slid discreetly to the end of the church, and there, without kneeling like the other worshippers, pulled out a sketchbook and began to draw.' The observer was Madame Louise Roche, who lived at 6 rue Babie, a suburban street in a residential area of Meudon, a village six miles outside Paris. The artist was Gwen John. Soon after Madame Roche had noticed her in the church, Gwen moved in next door, to a plot of land containing two wooden sheds on stilts: one was her home, the other her studio. She loved the garden, and though she immediately announced to Madame Roche that she was an artist, not a gardener, she soon had words with her about the way she disposed of the slugs in her vegetables, quoting Shakespeare's view that killing an insect was like killing a Caesar. What did she do with hers? asked Madame Roche. 'I collect them up carefully in a box and put it outside in the street,' replied Gwen.[1]

Gwen John, born in Haverfordwest in 1876, sister of Augustus, and Rodin's model and muse, has always seemed a mysterious and shadowy figure within the history of British painting. For a long time it was assumed that she lived the life of a recluse. Since little was known about her except that she lived alone with her cats and favoured attic rooms (she liked the sloping ceilings) perhaps she, like the figures in her paintings, was also a solitary figure in an empty room, a mystical creature who hid from the world and saw nobody. Perhaps she had moved to Paris to escape the influence of her charismatic brother, perhaps she had ended her life broken and beaten down by Rodin, like his earlier mistress, Camille Claudel; perhaps she had starved herself, perhaps . . . But in fact, Gwen regularly exhibited and sold her work during her lifetime, and lived a busy, daring and eventful life.

In 1895, she went to the Slade, encouraged by Augustus who had started there the previous year and quickly realised that she should be there too. She was taught by Henry Tonks and Frederick Brown, and her early drawings reveal her fine draughtsmanship. Shortly after leaving the Slade she went with Ida Nettleship (soon to become Augustus's wife) and Gwen Salmond to Paris, where she spent six months under the tutelage of Whistler. She returned to London afterwards, but was soon anxious to be off again. She decided to walk to Rome with Augustus's new lover, Dorelia McNeill and the two made their way along the River Garonne, weighed down with a large quantity of painting materials and their portfolios, singing for the locals to buy food and sleeping under the stars. They got as far as Toulouse, then decided to change direction and headed for Paris. Gwen was to live in Paris and Meudon for the rest of her life.

Her early years in Paris are compellingly documented by Gwen herself, mainly in her letters to Rodin. She lived in Paris during one of the most exciting periods in the history of modern European painting. She arrived in the winter of 1903 and lived there and in nearby Meudon until her death in 1939, modelling and painting, producing work whose unique qualities were recognised in her lifetime and which continue to haunt and fascinate. The sixth *arrondissement* at the turn of the century was busy and grimy, and the Hôtel Mont Blanc, the lodging house where she lived for two years in the rue Edgar Quinet, was full of strange people: the local *coquotte* (Gwen's spelling) and her lovers, the caretaker's mad husband, excited by the idea that lady artists saw men naked; the fat cleaning lady who swore she too had modelled for Rodin – 'like this' – head on one side, mimicking a pose. Domestic life was eventful since, as an artist, Gwen was the object of much curiosity. Her working life, as a model in turn-of-the-century Montparnasse, was just as adventurous. The lady painters she modelled for, most of whom were besotted with Rodin, became the subjects of similarly colourful anecdotes, with their temperaments, their obsessions, their stories: Miss Hart, shocked by the neighbouring Finnish men and their conquests, Miss O'Donel, resplendent in her fur-trimmed tea gown, complaining about her poverty and boasting about her ancestry; the 'man-woman' Mlle Roederstein. Gwen found them intermittently exasperating, but they enabled her to earn her living, and most of the time they were diverting and kind. One of the most serious lady painters, Isobel Bowser, was the sister-in-law of the Symbolist poet, Arthur Symons, and through her Gwen met him, becoming familiar with his work. He was enchanted by hers.

Rodin was a major influence, particularly on her drawings. He recommended freedom, instinct, drawing from 'nature', but knew that none of this could be achieved without study: 'on the contrary, it is necessary to have consummate technique in order to hide what one knows'.[2] He soon realised that Gwen was a gifted artist, and encouraged her to bring her drawings regularly to show him. He also encouraged her to study. She read literature, philosophy and religious tracts, selecting and copying out extracts for him to read and drafting critiques and letters to him many times so that the version he read would be perfect. She set herself the highest standards, telling herself, 'Unless you have the will to be great you will fall into mediocrity.'[3]

In 1911 she moved from Paris to Meudon, and began to sell her work to the well-known New York art dealer, John Quinn, who was recommended to her by Augustus. She knew that great art was never made by being seen at the right parties, but her private life was more sociable in Meudon than it had been in Paris. In Meudon she entered into the life of the neighbourhood, making friends among the local people. She also had illustrious friends – John Quinn and his companion the poet Jeanne Robert Foster; the poet Rainer Maria Rilke (secretary to Rodin); Arthur Symons; Maud Gonne. She kept her close friends from the Slade years, Ursula Tyrwhitt, Grilda Boughton-Leigh and her sister Chloe; and Constance Lloyd. But her early exuberance gradually gave way to a need for the privacy and solitude necessary to paint. She gave herself *retraits* – periods of time when she would go nowhere and see no one until she had solved a particular problem in her work.[4] At these times, no one succeeded in interrupting her, not even (on one occasion) Ezra Pound, who sat patiently in a nearby garden drinking tea while he waited (in vain) for her to emerge.

She painted women in rooms, lots of them, canvas after canvas, increasingly trying out the same subject in many variants, challenged by the differences, trying to produce one, from the series of versions, for exhibition and in the process making technical discoveries as she ceaselessly experimented with each new variation on her subject. Her early paintings have a depth-charge; her later work in oils is haunting, mysterious, oblique, as she pursued her technical search to express 'the strange form'. While her early figures are nerved-up, fragile, alert, her later ones are monumental, with elongated limbs, massed haunches, expressionist, big-boned hands holding enormous folds of cloth or paper, odd, misshapen flowers or open books. She used the same subject many times in order to explore the function of the room as abstract space, and to experiment with the relationship between figure and ground. Her female figures became gradually more expressionist as she ultimately moved towards abstraction. She was influenced by the work of her contemporaries – Cézanne, Rouault, Chagall, Lhote, Gleizes – and worked hard to incorporate new technical discoveries. She kept many notebooks in which she made jottings as she studied other painters' work and developed her own methods. Rodin called her a 'bel artiste'. Augustus, reading her notebooks after her death, found it 'Astonishing how she cultivated the scientific method. I feel ready to shut up shop.'[5] Both Rodin and Augustus were regularly supportive, and both encouraged her to exhibit and sell her work. The very men from whom she was alleged to have fled were those who took her most seriously as an artist. Just because little was known about her life, should we really have assumed that she was unaware of what she was striving for in her work? That it just crept up on her, haunting and arresting her in the way it haunts and arrests us, her viewers?

Nevertheless, Gwen continued to be an enigmatic figure. Her papers, gathered up by her nephew Edwin from the rue Babie after her death together with 'a mass of beautiful drawings',[6] were for a long time not in the public domain. Her letters to Rodin and all her literary, religious and philosophical extracts were in the archives of the Musée Rodin but though there are over a thousand documents they are largely undated and unattributed, and they create a necessarily partial impression. The papers in the Tate Archives tell another story, but that too is partial. In 1984 the National Library of Wales at Aberystwyth acquired the papers of Gwen John from Edwin John's son and daughter, Ben John and Sara John. Papers and documents have since been added, and the archive reveals the extent of Gwen's social connections and friendships and her regular contact with members of her family. Her letters to her Slade friend Ursula Tyrwhitt, acquired in 1975, were now supplemented by evidence of a broad range of connections – with women painters in early twentieth-century Paris, with Maud Gonne, Rilke, Arthur Symons – and of the nature of her relationships with members of her family: her father, Edwin William John, her brothers and sister – Augustus, Thornton, Winifred – and her nieces and nephews. These papers, together with those in the Musée Rodin in Paris, the John Quinn Memorial Collection and the Foster-Murphy Papers in the New York Library, and the Tate Archives in London, have enabled me to tell her story.

'I don't fancy strangers writing about her somehow,'[7] Augustus once remarked to his son, Edwin John, then Gwen's legatee. Anna John, Ben John, Rebecca John, Sara John and Julius White have been remarkably helpful and kind to me, the stranger who began to research a book about painting and ended up writing a new biography of their great-aunt. I am deeply grateful for their trust and encouragement. Understanding her as thoroughly as possible has been an honour and a responsibility. It has meant not only looking at all her available work but also studying all her letters, diaries and notebooks and perusing her correspondence with a range of her contemporaries. I travelled regularly to Aberystwyth, Cardiff, Haverfordwest, Tenby, London, Brittany, Paris and New York to study her papers and explore the places she lived and worked in. Given the allegedly solitary occupation of biography, I have accumulated an astonishing number of people to whom my thanks are amply due. People helped me wherever I went, and I am truly grateful. I have endeavoured to present Gwen as accurately as possible, without speculation or invention. I hope I convey in what follows something of her sense of humour and her daring, as well as her need for independence, her diligence and her perfectionism. The more she emerged in all her complexity, the more concerned I became to try to honour her memory.

The real mystery of Gwen John's life may turn out to have less to do with her own elusiveness than with the problem of why we find it so difficult to imagine the life-style and frame of mind of a woman artist living alone. Gwen lived in a focused, determined, ardent and exuberant way, with strenuous concentration and dedication. She once remarked that she could not understand why people wanted to have children: beautiful monuments were erected to artists who produced great works; nobody ever erected a monument to anyone for having children.[8] The work she produced and the way she lived mark her out as a woman with strength of character, sensitivity, daring and originality. Her papers reveal her as a great storyteller. She loved anecdotes and had an eye for detail, and an acute ear. Single woman, life model, female artist – these are all roles which challenge our imagination and our prejudices. Gwen John's story reveals her as a unique individual whose life challenges all our assumptions about women artists and about the distinctions between reclusiveness, eccentricity and hard-won independence. Her life was her own and she lived it in her own way. From time to time, Augustus urged her to return to Britain and abandon her reckless life in Paris. But she loved France, and had made it her home. 'If to "return to life" is to live as I did in London – Merci, Monsieur!' she told him. 'There are people like plants who cannot flourish in the cold, and I want to flourish!' [9]

1

Childhood

> . . . she would be rushed to the train and put aboard without a moment to spare, clutching her painting, still wet . . .[1]

The lanes surrounding Haverfordwest are leafy and high-banked, lit in spring and summer with the starry points of wild flowers. The path feels protected, with hedges on both sides, stretching up past South Parade (where you paraded your finery, and your family, on high days and holidays). You climb up to the Parade from the banks of the river just behind Victoria Place, where Gwen John lived as a child, and walk parallel to the River Cleddau until, very soon, you find yourself in the country. The hedgerows must have seemed very tall to a small child. She would have had to look up to see dapples of light through the trees as she made her way along the path, beaten into a track by walkers, drovers and horses, out on to the open road.

'When I was a child,' Gwen would say to a friend, years later, in middle age, 'I used to cry all the time, and they told me, "don't cry now, when you're grown up you'll have something to cry about." So I was afraid of growing up and I never expected any happiness in life.'[2] She had a melancholy streak, which afflicted her when she felt trapped or emotionally restrained, but when she was outside, running along the beach or walking in the open air she could be exuberant, dynamic; wild. The John children were experienced walkers – it was their father's favourite hobby, he liked to stride ahead and pick the primroses.[3] We can imagine Gwen as a small child, with pale skin, dark hair and serious, enquiring, penetratingly bright blue eyes, being led up the steep stone steps to the Parade with her two brothers – the dark-haired, pale-skinned, quiet elder brother Thornton and her younger brother Augustus (named after Augusta, their mother, and nicknamed 'Gussie' after her, too) – and their pretty little vibrant sister Winifred. Or sometimes they would continue along the river path (called the Frolic), down Scotch Wells past the mill where the miller used to come out all covered with flour; and on towards the old workhouse where the children had identical pinafores and blouses.[4] For walking in the Parade Gwen would probably have worn her black dress with its lace collar and tidy buttons, petticoats and her button boots – an outfit that marked her out as respectably middle class, in this prosperous market town.

A 'bustling, hilly town, centre of a rural and maritime community',[5] Haverfordwest was built on the Western Cleddau at a point where it was both fordable and accessible to the seagoing trade: until the railway came in 1853, this trade was what its survival had depended on. It was still the centre of the farming community and its market was one of the biggest and most abundant in Wales, known particularly for its wide varieties of fish and its large corn market. There was a large fair for horses and cattle every summer on 7 July. Traders came in from outlying areas: old photographs show women in traditional high, Welsh hats attending to donkeys laden with wares. The commercial traders were called bagmen, because they rode on horseback with saddlebags.[6]

Strict trading rules had been established. Back in 1835, Royal Assent had been given to an Act for paving, lighting and otherwise improving the town, one of its clauses stipulating, 'No animal is to be sold in the streets except at a market or fair.'[7] Victoria Place, built in 1837–9 and named after Queen Victoria, was part of a smart new project to repave the town: so many houses were out of alignment that all the awkward projections had to be removed before the pavements could be laid. The position of the town, at the foot and side of steep hills, gave it an irregular appearance, and it was felt that the narrowness of the streets, with their lack of proper pitching and paving, deprived it of an air of appropriate respectability[8] – all this had been ironed out, and the town boasted a prosperous appearance by the time Gwen was born into it.

The original layout of the streets had been determined by the river crossings. 'Old Bridge' had replaced the old medieval bridge in 1726, and in 1837 'New Bridge' provided a suitably imposing approach through the fine terraces of Victoria Place.[9] In 1885, when Gwen was nine, a drainage scheme was passed (at huge expense: £4,598 was granted) so that many houses would now have drains and plumbing.[10] Since 1840, the town had been 'principally occupied by shopkeepers, mechanics and merchants of moderately independent fortune'. By 1858 it had a Literary and Scientific Institution in Victoria Place, Potter's Library and Billiard Rooms in High Street, a police station on Tower Hill and a lunatic asylum on St Thomas's Green. Thirty-two houses were taverns or public houses; there were six auctioneers and appraisers, fifteen blacksmiths; thirty-five boot and shoe makers; twenty-three butchers (seven of the name of White); eight corn merchants; five lime merchants; nine straw bonnet makers and eight surgeons. From the 1860s onwards, Commerce House in Market Street was one of Wales's largest department stores; the street also boasted a branch of Ocky White's (it still does, at number 7 Bridge Street).[11]

Education at that time was primarily a matter for boys. It was still technically the responsibility of the state but the Grammar School, founded in 1813, had been set up for children of 'the poorest sort of people and not of any who were of great wealth and ability'.[12] The National School on Barn Street put the boys through examinations and there was also an imposing school on Heron's Hill where the better class of farmers and tradesmen sent their sons.[13] Schooling reflected the class and social standing of the parents, and the only prominent school for girls, Trasker's High School, had a reputation as a charity school. (In 1884, when Gwen was eight, it became Trasker's High School for Girls.)[14] The daughters of educated men such as Edwin John were taught at home, by their governesses or mothers, and as a child in Haverfordwest, Gwen would have been 'educated' at home, probably by Augusta.

Haverfordwest had considerable social and political standing. It was both town and county, as were Carmarthen, Chester and Bristol; but not even these had, as Haverfordwest had, its own Lord Lieutenant, who appointed the magistrates, and the magistrates of Haverfordwest appointed their own chairman of the quarter sessions, which was also unusual.[15] Respectability was the keyword. The *Pembrokeshire Herald* for 23 June 1876 reported the Pembrokeshire election, and reflected the prevailing views of the town: 'It is with the heartiest satisfaction that we announce that the canvass on the constituency on the part of the Conservative candidate has been a great success in all the divisions of the country, and there is no reason to doubt that he will be returned as the representative of Pembrokeshire by an overwhelming majority.' Just one birth was reported that week, on 17 June; only the professional classes announced private events in the newspaper. But in the *Herald* for 30 June there were four, including this one: 'On the 22nd instant, at Victoria Place, Haverfordwest, the wife of Mr. E.W. John, solicitor, of a daughter.'[16]

Six weeks later Augusta registered the birth, at Haverfordwest Register Office, of Gwendolen Mary John. It was usual for births to be registered more immediately, and by the father of the child, but the slight delay, and the registration by the mother, suggest nothing particularly untoward. Some items in the *Herald* for 23 June – the day after Gwen's birth – give a sense of the world she was born into. 'John Miller & Co's Reliable Cattle Food' was advertised: 'The Cost is Trifling, the Results Gigantic.' There was a notice to stock feeders: 'As LINSEED CAKE is extensively adulterated, we are doing all we can to put before our customers a Pure Article.' The Duke of Connaught's marriage was reported. The maxims for the day included, 'How to destroy flies – Encourage spiders' and 'A lock that burglars cannot pick – Wedlock.' The newspaper also supplied 'ADVICE TO MOTHERS: Are you broken in your rest by a sick child suffering with the pain of cutting teeth? Go at once to a chemist and get a bottle of MRS WILSON'S SOOTHING SYRUP. It will relieve the poor sufferer immediately.' The poem for the day after Gwen was born was 'Unsung', by T.H. Aldrich ('As sweet as the breath that goes / From the lips of the white rose / As weird as the elfin lights / That glimmer on frosty nights, / As wild as the winds that tear / The curled leaf in the air / Is the song I have never sung . . .')[17]

As a child herself, Gwen's mother Augusta had learned to paint, attending 'Mrs. Leleux's Establishment' at Eltham House in north Brixton, and she went on drawing and painting up to the time of her marriage.[18] Her painting, *Oranges and Lemons*,[19] showing children playing the childhood game, hung on the wall in Gwen's childhood home. Augusta painted in the conventional Victorian pastoral style; her *Figures in a Landscape*[20] show a peasant woman and her two children, their belongings in soft swag bags, pausing in their journey along the open road. The mother is putting the boy's bag on his head so that he can carry it and the painting is gentle but lively, done in good, strong colours. Augusta signed it 'Gussie'. Her *Landscape with Cows*,[21] which she signed 'A. John', hangs in the Dalton

Collection in Charlotte, North Carolina, among Constables, Rembrandts, Sickerts and Turners, and is attributed to Augustus.[22] She came from a long line of successful Sussex plumbers. Her father was the younger son of Thomas Smith, a village plumber, who was born in Chiddingly, in Sussex. When he inherited his father's business he moved to Brighton and in 1831, aged twenty-two, he married Augusta Phillips. They lived in Union Street. A year after Augusta died, he married again, the twenty-six-year-old Mary Thornton. They had at least ten more children, of whom four died in childhood. Mary's third child was called Augusta, after Thomas Smith's first wife.[23] (Augusta called her first-born son, Gwen's elder brother, Thornton.)

The man Augusta fell in love with, the solicitor Edwin William John, was the grandson of Welsh labourers living in Haverfordwest, though when his children later pressed him on the matter of their ancestry, he insisted that 'we come of a line of professional people'.[24] Edwin's father, William John, also a solicitor, had married Mary Davies, a local seamstress; Edwin was the fourth of their six children and the second son. Edwin brought his young wife to Haverfordwest where they set up home in Victoria Place (he practised from his office in nearby Quarry Street). He was evidently an immensely shy man, with few friends. If he saw a friend approaching in the street, he would hurry by as if late for an appointment. He stood very straight, with a commanding nose and a heavy moustache. When somebody once mistook him for a high-ranking officer, he was delighted.[25] He and Augusta were apparently very happy together. One of their common interests was music. She liked to play Chopin on the piano, while he played the organ, and preferred religious music.

Augusta was well liked. When she went about her business in Haverfordwest and nearby Tenby, which she liked to visit, she took her children with her as she made her way through the town, holding them by the hand. She painted all round the walls of the nursery to amuse them.[26] She taught them to paint by colouring outline pictures in drawing books.[27] In the summer holidays, she may have sat on the beach with her parasol while her children played on the sand. Perhaps she sometimes even went to the beach to paint, since Pembrokeshire was an area popular with artists and there were often painters on the beach. Augustus later remembered that 'Gwen and I, full of curiosity, would approach as near as we dared, to watch the mystery of painting. Even at that early age we were vaguely aware of Art and Beauty.'[28]

It was a long journey in pony and trap to Broad Haven, the seaside coastal inlet on St Bride's Bay just over six miles from Haverfordwest, where the family rented a large house with green gables, overlooking the sea, every summer. The pony and trap would have taken them down steep, narrow, winding roads towards the sea, and suddenly round the last bend, there it was: spread out and glittering ahead of them, the lion rock just visible, far out. Their house, Rocks Drift, was dour and imposing, right on the sea front, so they could lie in bed and listen to the sound of the sea all night. On the beach there was a large, dark cave, a safe but voluminous place for children to play. Out at sea are large, mysterious-looking rocks. The colour of the stone everywhere holds the light softly, so that it brushes against stone in patches and drifts, like watercolour washes. A primitive sect in the district practised baptism by total immersion: girls in skimpy dresses could be seen emerging from the water, making a lasting impression on Augustus, 'like Naiads from the ordeal'. At home, the day started with prayers, in which everybody joined. Those big enough to read were given improving tracts to follow: *Jessica's First Prayer*; *Christy's Old Organ*; *The Lamplighter*. Edwin John was a good churchman; his faith, Augustus later judged, was 'securely based on a shrewd estimate of its contingent rewards and penalties'.[29]

But Augusta was never well. She suffered from chronic rheumatism and travelled widely in search of a cure.[30] When her health began to fail, her sisters arrived from Brighton to take care of the children. Rosina and Leah Smith held positions of high rank in General Booth's Salvation Army, and travelled about in a wickerwork pony and trap, the 'Halleluja Chariot', preaching the word. Aunt Leah was by all accounts 'a lady of ruthless cheerfulness and alarming eloquence',[31] and 'already a notable saver of souls'. She had toured the US, successfully recruiting many new followers to the faith, and in the process polishing her platform technique.[32] Aunt Rose was, according to Winifred, 'a little whirlwind'. She had a face like a ferret, the children thought; they used to worry that one day she might get shot by mistake.[33] The aunts established their territorial rights by dismissing the children's nurse, who had encouraged them in wild habits. They used to like to go with her to her home in the Prescelly Mountains and be given cawl – the local soup – and listen to the local men, with their dark beards and brass-toed clogs, all chattering in Welsh. The John children had other shocking tastes: they were allowed to go to the circus and watch all manner of people and animals cavorting, and they were regularly in the audience at 'Poole's Diorama', a vast historical succession of pictures unrolled on endless canvas on a stage, to the accompaniment of music and other sound effects.[34] On market days they watched the gypsies, who came with their horses and carts and joined in the general noise, the 'lowing of cattle, the screaming of pigs and the loud vociferation of the drovers'.[35]

In 1884, when Gwen was eight, Augusta died, mysteriously and inexplicably among strangers, at Ferney Bottom, Hartington in Derbyshire. The cause of her death was given as rheumatic gout and exhaustion; she was thirty-five.[36] Edwin John had deeply loved his wife, and suffered very much from the tragedy of her illness and loss.[37] Much later, when Gwen was nearing the end of her own life, her elder brother Thornton referred to secrets their father had kept from them, he thought, to their great benefit.[38] Augustus always thought there was something secretive about him, too.[39] Perhaps he generated this atmosphere among his children simply by trying to protect them from knowing how ill their mother really was. Her death was not recorded in the *Pembrokeshire Herald.* The children ran about the house in a kind of baffled hysteria, chanting, 'Mama's dead! Mama's dead!'[40] – relieved, perhaps, that at last the tension and confusion of her strange absences had been resolved into something more accountable.

On Augusta's death, Edwin wound up his practice and removed his children to Tenby (in overdue deference to her wishes – would she have preferred life there? – or perhaps just to be somewhere larger and more anonymous, to escape the painful memories surrounding him in Haverfordwest). His life changed: he still practised a little, but he was not the pillar of society in Tenby that he had been in Haverfordwest. He led a quiet life from now on, with the occasional attempt to interest a new prospective wife, a habit Gwen and Winifred fiercely disapproved of.[41] He composed organ music, and his *Berceuse* for organ was published by the sheet music publishers, Boosey & Hawkes (there is a copy of it in the Tenby Museum). It is a spirited piece in G major, in 6/8 time, to be played *con moto.*[42] Every Sunday, he walked the mile and a half to the tiny church at Gumfreston to play the organ. When he died (not long before Gwen) aged ninety-one, he was buried in the graveyard there. He taught the local children to play the organ, and in the evenings he read aloud to his own children. It was he who planted in them, especially Gwen and Winifred, their great love of literature. (He may have read only to the girls, because when Augustus, much later, was rummaging among dusty books in the attic at Victoria Street, he came across a pile which surprised him, including Hamilton's *Memoirs of the Comte de Grammont*; Madame Blavatsky's *Isis Unveiled*; Richard Carlyle's *Key Arch*; some Smollett novels, Marlowe plays; Currer Bell's *Jane Eyre*.)[43] Winifred, years later, certainly remembered being read to by him; Gwen read literature all her life.

In Tenby they lived at 32 Victoria Street, a small, terraced street leading away from the South Beach end of the Esplanade, the last road at the end of the prom, with the sea at the bottom of their road. Round the corner at the end of the prom itself, there were more imposing, four-storey houses, in scale and atmosphere more like the architecture of Brighton than that of Haverfordwest. Tenby was very much a seaside resort, with palm trees and clear, blue skies. It was blander, wider, bluer, altogether more municipal than Haverfordwest, with ancient, crumbling high walls, a strolling fiddler and bathing machines on the beach. The Johns were aware of other families in the neighbourhood, including the beautiful and rebellious Swinburne children, descendants of the poet, and the Prusts, who lived in a big house on South Cliff, Major Prust resembling 'an ancient Elizabethan courtier qualifying for the block', according to Augustus. But strict rules of snobbery were observed, and families would exist side by side for years without acknowledging one another.[44] Gwen and Winifred now began their education, taught by the mother of one of their friends, a 'Miss Wilson', in a private, dame school for three pupils, Gwen, Winifred and Miss Wilson's own daughter.[45] Miss Wilson must have been diligent about deportment, one of the key lessons for young ladies, since Gwen seems to have spent some of her lesson-time on her back, her little sister Winifred lying loyally beside her. They would always be close. As an adult in Canada, married with three children of her own, she would write Gwen dazzling letters combining family news, hilarious anecdote and solicitousness, recognising in her the family tendency to melancholy and 'nerves'.

In the holidays, the children explored the wild, coastal places near Tenby. Their favourite haunts were Begelly, where in the company of 'only . . . a few cattle, geese and gypsies' they 'ran happily wild',[46] St Florence, and Manorbier, where you can follow the exposed, craggy cliff walk with its sheer drop down to the sea. In Manorbier they stayed with a German lady whose husband studied philosophy alone in his room. When he did emerge, he could be heard complaining about 'those turbulent Johns'.[47] They spent long days running in and out of the sea at Lydstep, Monkstone and other deserted spots along the coast. They sketched on the sand, and Gwen made rapid drawings of beached gulls, shells and fish on stray pieces of paper, or sometimes in the margins of the frontispieces of the book she was reading.[48]

The beach at Tenby was wide, pale; flanked on one side by a crescent of tall, typically Welsh terraces. In the evenings the lights were dotted round the curve of the bay, and people walked in the moonlight by the sea. By day their faces caught the light as children ran alongside parents, nurses, big sisters. One of Gwen's earliest known paintings, *Landscape at Tenby, With Figures*[49] depicts a willowy young lady, smartly dressed in long dark coat and high, elegant hat, walking by the sea, evidently at a brisk pace, holding by the hand a small girl who gazes up at her. The light falls on the upturned face of the child, and the figures are delicate and gently animated. All the lights of Tenby are studded along the coastline, it is twilight; and the sea is serenely, moodily blue. In the background a mother is busy with her two children and their dog. The model for the elegant lady was Gwen's sister Winifred, the little girl with the uplifted face may have been a friend or even a stranger.

There were always children on the beach. As they grew older, Gwen and Augustus began to choose models from among them to sketch. Gwen, in particular, had an eye for the beautiful ones. The local inhabitants of Tenby in the late 1880s and early 1890s thought the Johns very bohemian and wild. As small children they had played on the beach without shoes or socks; now they began to pay the local children to go with them to their attic bedrooms in Victoria Street, where they would paint their portraits.[50] One of Gwen's subjects, a wild, blond boy like an angel, came accompanied by his mother. This ran the risk of compromising Edwin, and they both had to be dispatched. On such occasions, however, Gwen would face her father down. One day, she and Winifred launched a comprehensive attack on him. He was mean, he could not stop embarking on embarrassing matrimonial adventures; he was plotting to ruin their lives. Papa, in the face of this passionate outburst, appealed in despair to Augustus; when he intervened with an equally passionate defence of their father, the three of them turned on him. Augustus later remembered it as an episode which illustrated 'Gwen's implacable nature when roused'. (Winifred, too, had suddenly displayed a 'fierce and unexpected intransigence').[51] Gwen would always stand up to her father, but it did not seem to diminish his love for her, even though as an adult she found his company impossible (she saw him only twice, both times briefly, after she moved to Paris in her twenties in 1903, though they corresponded regularly and with affection).

Gwen and Augustus always sketched and painted. It was what they shared, and it made them vivaciously close in their early years and affectionate and caring of each other all their lives, even though eventually it was her elder brother, Thornton, whom she confided in. The photograph of Gwen aged about eight, posing with her brothers and sister and their nurse, tiny, proud and ramrod straight in her hot-looking boots, hands gracefully clasped, shows someone already capable of displaying qualities of detachment and control, a self-possessed observer, with a strong sense of restraint.[52] Already she displayed pride, extreme seriousness, a strong regard for propriety and a capacity for defiance. When she joined Augustus at the Slade eleven years later in 1895, his remark, '*She* wasn't going to be left out of it' had the familiarity of an oft-used phrase.[53] Often, as her life unfolded, she displayed something in her temperament that went beyond mere determination. She was ardent in her opinions and in her wishes. She was astute and wise, but if integrity was the issue she could be ruthless.

In apparent contrast to this was her painful shyness, which later went hand in hand with a deep impatience with herself for allowing herself to feel intimidated by arrogant or opinionated people. As young women, Gwen and Winifred would speed through the streets of Tenby on their cumbersome Edwardian bicycles. On one occasion a crowd of soldiers had to part to let them through as they rode, heads down, 'blushing furiously' at their own recklessness.[54] It is not such a baffling contrast, though, given that both states signalled an ardent nature in the making. When, not long afterwards, she dived perilously off dangerous rocks, or posed nude for artists in bohemian Montparnasse, she was exploring her own nature, and enjoying a particular kind of protected exposure. It was social exposure that seemed more daunting: in provincial Britain, that could partly be dealt with by wearing the right clothes. Miss Wilson taught the importance of hats,[55] and Gwen was always fascinated by them. She drew and painted them inimitably: they are weighty, massed things, with a life of their own, in her paintings. (Later, in her thirties, when she moved apartments in Paris in 1907, she would let the drunk and belligerent removal men handle everything on their horse and cart, except her paintings and her hats.)[56]The John parents would also always have been impeccably turned out. In 1919, her father sent her an example of his 'self-photography'. It shows him standing stiffly to attention on the beach at St David's in his three-piece suit and bowler hat.[57]

Some of Gwen's earliest fully accomplished drawings are of Winifred in her hats. In *Winifred John in a Large Hat*[58] she painted her with hair curled untidily about her face, her hat alluringly tilted, the brim pulled down on one side. In *Winifred John in a Flowered Hat*,[59] the hint of wildness is in the hat itself. The figure, her hair now in a sophisticated chignon at her neck, sits in an attitude of dignified composure in a hat heavy with roughly sketched flowers piled high; the crown is suggested rather than drawn, the flowers elaborate and whimsical. Like Gwen, Winifred was an intriguing mixture of exuberance and restraint. In *Portrait of the Artist's sister Winifred*,[60] an early oil painting probably done in about 1898, the year Gwen left the Slade, she captured Winifred's grace and flair, wearing a bright, red scarf, caught in a moment of absorbed concentration, about to unbutton her glove. A drawing she probably did even earlier (perhaps during her Slade years) – *Portrait of Winifred John*[61] – captures her luminously fair complexion and the gentle, trustworthy gracefulness which also animates the figure modelled by Winifred in *Landscape at Tenby, with Figures*. But of the two sisters, it was Gwen who would become both more unconventional and more austere, the bohemian and the ascetic. Whatever they learned at 'Miss Wilson's Academy', they both developed a love of literature and an interest in spirituality (Gwen's interest eventually became more intellectual than Winifred's, which would always have more in common with the aunts'). Both sisters, particularly Gwen, read widely and seriously (in Paris, she would study Shakespeare and the Greek tragedies and read Verlaine, Rilke and Mallarmé; Richardson, Poe, Dostoevsky, Thomas Hardy, D.H. Lawrence and Katherine Mansfield, as well as lighter popular fiction).

While she was still in Tenby, Gwen painted her first self-portrait,[62] an early precursor of the *Self-Portrait* she was to do a year or two after leaving the Slade, in about 1900. She posed in the same brown blouse, her hair in the same chignon, though she displayed in it none of the fine draughtsmanship she would later learn at the Slade. The later portrait is the work of a professional painter; the earlier one is by an ambitious amateur. Already, in the early portrait, she achieved a special quality, a barely restrained nervous energy warring with absolute composure, stillness, control. Already she was alert in her work to a coexistence of indomitability and fragility, delicacy and strength, detecting it both in herself and others. Also already there was an awareness of being looked at, and the clearly detectable intention to show herself, if she must be looked at, as she actually was. It was a quality she often drew out, not only in her self-portraits but in her female sitters. Whatever their state of energy or repose, her figures seem to be saying to the viewer, look at me if you will, but see me as I am.

Gwen's life, from eight years old onwards, was a mixture of freedom, recklessness, respectability, culture, and the lack of it. As provincial childhoods went, it was cultured, despite her lack of formal schooling, since Edwin John recognised the importance of the arts, and went regularly every year to exhibitions at the Royal Academy.[63] He used to take his children to the theatre in London, and Augustus and Gwen took their sketchbooks, drawing furiously between the acts. She enjoyed an unusual degree of physical freedom, an impassioned sense of independence, a sense of organic connection with the landscape around her, and an intensity of experience. She quarrelled and ran and swam; she knew how to put her foot down; she could forget herself. Behind the smart black dress of the little motherless girl, with her clasped hands and her neat fringe, there was a relaxed, uninhibited child, wild and free, with a sensual awareness which she and Augustus acknowledged to themselves, early on, as a perception of beauty.

She also had other gifts. She could function happily both alone and in the company of others, and when she made friends, she judged them carefully. She was very close to each of her brothers and sisters. When Augustus came to write his memoirs, late in life, and referred implicitly to himself and Gwen, he employed an easy, effortless 'we'. When he described Thornton and Winifred, it became even clearer that 'we' usually meant Augustus and Gwen. She loved him, and he cared very much about her, though he could occasionally make her feel miserable and tended to play up the eccentric side of her nature when he talked to other people about her. Years later, he would tell people that Gwen 'utterly neglects herself for some bloody mystical reason' (in the same breath as 'borrowed a fiver off her').[64] They had serious rows about who was actually the elder.[65] If she sometimes felt he threatened to outshine her, he had had a head start, with his conventional schooling. She was intellectually ambitious, so her idiosyncratic spelling irritated her and she always felt, like many women who grew up in the Edwardian era, that she was insufficiently educated.

When she died, Augustus could not resist commenting that there were spelling mistakes in her will,[66] but it hardly mattered: she wrote the same way as she learned French, by ear; and she was learned as well as articulate.

The year she spent in Tenby with her father, after Augustus had gone up to the Slade in the autumn of 1894, must have been enough to convince Edwin of the wisdom of allowing her to study art in London too. She started at the Slade in 1895 and stayed for three years, making friends she would keep all her life. They were formative friendships, inspiring, reassuring, demonstrative and enduring. She also learned at the Slade methods and techniques which she would build on and develop throughout her life as an artist. She was an intense and responsive student. Winifred later told her own children the story of Gwen's intermittent visits home. 'The morning of her return day would be a wild skirmish of getting ready – until the moment to leave, when it would be discovered that she was missing. A frantic search would finally find her on the sands finishing a last painting. She would be rushed to the train and put aboard without a moment to spare, clutching her painting, still wet.'[67]

2

The Slade

. . . addicted to Diamonds and violets . . .[1]

When Augustus, in those days 'very quiet, polite, clean-shaven and neatly dressed',[2] began at the Slade in 1894, he quickly realised that Gwen should be there too.[3] So she left Tenby behind – as it turned out, effectively for ever – and with it, her identity as a young, unawakened Pembrokeshire girl, sketching and reading and trying to live with her stern, heart-broken father. In the autumn of 1895, she arrived at the Slade. London made a heady contrast with home, with its mahogany furniture, its shelves of devotional works and law tomes, stuffed doves beneath glass cases; and her father's sustained grief and gloom.[4] When she first arrived, she and Augustus lived in separate lodgings – Gwen, he was in the habit of saying, favoured 'slums and underground cellars',[5] for all the world as if his own habitations were palatial – but they still had a lot to do with each other. He had already made his mark on the largely female student coterie, and when Gwen arrived, her friendships gradually consolidated things socially. She was shy: one fellow student, Ethel Hatch, later remembered her as 'very fragile-looking and very quiet in her manners'.[6] But she was popular, and dearly loved by those in her immediate circle. According to Augustus, all the women were brilliant and beautiful; and they outnumbered and outshone the men. He later remembered that the Slade 'abounded in talented and highly ornamental girl students: the men cut a shabbier figure and seemed far less gifted'.[7]

One of the girls – the Slade's prodigy, Edna Waugh – looked set, at only seventeen, to outshine the rest. She had begun there aged only fourteen. She was vivacious, imaginative and gentle and she befriended Gwen who, though she was most of the time reserved and self-contained, was nevertheless prone to sudden bursts of exhilaration or despair. They used to go to lunch together – for which Gwen insisted on wearing her hat – and talk about life in Wales, Gwen remembering how she used to cycle for miles in spring to gather the first daffodils in the Pembrokeshire lanes.[8] The women's friendships were essentially demonstrative: these were Edwardian daughters most of whom had not even left home. Edna travelled back at the end of each day to her family in St Albans (her father was director and founder of the NSPCC). Ida Nettleship, Gwen's other close friend, was the daughter of Jack Nettleship, the renowned animal painter. Her mother was a theatrical dressmaker, and Ida lived with them at 58 Wigmore Street.

The girls treated one another as sisters. They conversed with each other in florid, Pre-Raphaelite vocabulary: Ida, said Edna, 'rises like a wild spirit and she comes to me but I cannot speak to her and she turns away. I can hear her saying "Oh Edna, my willow, you are too cold," and yet I feel I love as much as she loves.'[9] They were all affectionate and close, especially Ida and Ursula Tyrwhitt, who was to become Gwen's lifelong friend. She was an elegant, sophisticated girl five years older than the others. It had taken her five years to make her family relent and allow her to study art, so she was twenty-one when she arrived at the Slade in 1893, and twenty-five when Augustus ('the young fawn . . . dangerous breaker of hearts with his looks and ardour,' according to Will Rothenstein)[10] realised how beautiful she was and began a brief flirtation with her which more than confirmed her family's worst fears. In the summer of 1897 Augustus was almost to decapitate himself in a dramatic diving accident which changed his character for ever. He was absent from the Slade for a few weeks at the start of that autumn term; when he returned, with wilder hair and beard, more flamboyant dress and hoop earrings, Ursula had disappeared, magicked away by her family to Paris, out of harm's way. When she returned she transferred her affections, more safely, to Gwen.[11] Also at the Slade was Constance Lloyd, who had nine sisters and thought Gwen looked like a figure in a Puvis de Chavannes painting. Grilda Boughton-Leigh, a lean, elusive girl, would also become her friend.

In February and March of 1898, Gwen's final year at the Slade, a student aptly named Logic Whiteway made, with the help of her friend Dolly

Jeffreys, a book of illustrated caricatures of the tutors and students: '*The Slade Animal Land*, As seen by the Lo. With help in ideas from the Jeff and other friendly animals.'[12] It was an extension of Edwardian childhood reading, and may have been done to impress Ida Tonks, who was a skilled cartoonist; students and tutors both appeared in it, deftly and accurately illustrated, their remarkable characteristics exaggerated, their personalities affectionately caricatured. The animal personae included, in addition to the tutors Fred Brown, Henry Tonks and Wilson Steer ('The Fredd', 'The Tonk' and 'The Drafft'), Gwen, Augustus, Ida, Ursula, Louise Salaman and Grilda Boughton-Leigh. The interpretations were ingenious. 'The Tonk' was 'a voracious bird which lives on the tears of silly girls. Its sarcasms are something awful, but it generally says "All right, go on." (It only does it to be clever)'; 'The Fredd' was 'learned and kindly' with 'a big jaw, but it seldom bites'. 'The Drafft' was depicted with a continuous cold, dosing himself up with potions and pills. Augustus (by now dramatically bearded) was 'the Beardgion'; Ursula was 'the Peewit'. Ida ('the Nettlebug') was 'one of the "geniuses" the carroty Salamander [Louise Salaman] lives on'. Grilda was 'the Leen', a long-limbed, cadaverous creature, sitting with huge webbed feet and large hands, its knees drawn up. 'This drab coloured animal,' commented the Lo, 'haunts the Slade at intervals.'

Gwen, in Slade animal language, was 'the Gwengion', and she seems to have inspired an eloquent and fulsome commentary. 'This strange little animal is so artistic that if you say "Hooks & eyes" it faints and asks for "Hairpins," oh dear! It is addicted to Diamonds & violets.'[13] This was not the only comment on her diamonds; Augustus would mention them to Ursula in the summer of 1897, asking her, 'Have you seen my sister's diamonds? They must have caused a sensation.' (He drew a sketch of Gwen, depicted from behind. Brown and Tonks are facing her, with exaggerated poses and expressions of astonishment.)[14] The diamonds may have been family heirlooms; they may have been her mother's. Or perhaps they signalled a running joke, and were not actually diamonds at all. As for 'oh dear!' it seems to have been something she often said, characteristic of emotion spontaneously voiced, but with an edge of restraint.

Classes at the Slade ran from ten in the morning until five in the afternoon and consisted mainly of work in the Antique and then the Life Room, interspersed with lectures on anatomy, perspective and history of art. In the evenings, the students gathered in the cafés and cheap restaurants around Tottenham Court Road, Euston Road, Charlotte Street and Fitzroy Street,[15] or congregated in one of the local studios to model for and draw one another. Although in London life modelling was no job for a lady, and life models tended to be working-class women past their prime,[16] the importance of the modelling cannot be overestimated. Gwen was learning a skill which was to become a way of life, and it would soon be how she earned her living. (Even in France, things were only just beginning to change.[17] Modelling was traditionally strictly reserved for the lower social echelons, but lady painters and sculptresses tended to model for each other.) When they were not drawing or talking, the Slade students went to the theatre: Drury Lane or Sadler's Wells, where you could get a box for a shilling, or the Empire, where for the same price you could get a seat in the pit and see the ballet. At Sadler's Wells there was 'Variety', with a melodrama to follow: they saw Marie Lloyd, Herbert Campbell, Vesta Tilley and Victoria Monks. They would come home together in high spirits, Augustus waving his walking stick in the air, with unfortunate consequences, once, for the chandelier.[18]

Gwen's drawing, *Portrait Group*,[19] reflects the mood of that time. Painted in 1897 or 1898, it is flighty, whimsical, full of life. It shows an unstructured room, casually inhabited by students: a female figure to the left of the picture with a dancing step, skips about in her little pointed shoes and striped socks. The desk is casually draped with a cloth, as if it could be either eaten off or worked on; there is a second female figure at the desk, and two male figures – Augustus John and his friend, Michel Salaman. Outside, glimpsed through the window are two figures walking and talking (possibly Gwen and Ambrose McEvoy, another of Augustus's friends, whom she was gradually getting to know). It celebrates their sudden, heady loss of parental control. The animation, and the interaction of figures, establish the dynamic of the drawing; it depicts a fluid, flexible, communal world. Other work she did during her Slade years – especially the drawings of her sister Winifred – show the significant advances Gwen was making in her drawing: in *Portrait of Winifred John* (c. 1895–8)[20] she sketched her in a head and shoulders half-profile, head and eyes slightly inclined, taking her job as a sitter very seriously, but she nevertheless captured with great subtlety her sister's inner qualities: her youthful directness, her delicacy, her gracefulness.

There are drawings in the Museum at Tenby which date from before Gwen went up to the Slade: they lack the assurance of this drawing of

Winifred, and its authoritative draughtsmanship, which she now learned from her tutors, Professor Fred Brown and the younger, charismatic Henry Tonks. Gwen's friends drew her as she worked. Edna's drawing, *Gwen John*,[21] is a quick profile sketch with inclined head and raised hand, which gives an impression of her immense concentration and control. She worked hard. Tonks was an exacting tutor and she was a serious student. But life also had a lighter side. Augustus's glorious white chalk drawing, *Sister of Augustus John on a Day Bed*[22] shows Winifred, who came to London to study the violin in January 1897, decked out in Edwardian flounces, her hair piled up, her right leg resting on the day bed, her left splayed out on the floor in quite a dissolute, abandoned pose. She wears glamorous shoes, with cuban heels: a winsome mixture of Edwardian lady and coquette. They played fancy dress, they went to parties; they were at large in London, in theatre-land.

In January 1897 Gwen and Augustus moved – together with Winifred and her friend Grace Westray, who was also in London studying music – into the first floor of 21 Fitzroy Street, where Augustus's friend William Orpen, a 'monosyllabic' Dubliner with a carefully cultivated Oxford accent and an 'infinite capacity for avoiding pains', had the rat-infested basement. The property was owned by the extraordinary, ecclesiastical Augusta Everett, who dressed in widow's weeds and working men's boots, and carried a Gladstone bag containing a large bible, two gold watches, a figurine, religious tracts and some sandwiches. She later added a spirit stove and a large eighteenth-century treatise on art which she seems to have thought more dependable than Tonks's teaching. She read the Bible aloud in the hope of encouraging potential converts, and established at 21 Fitzroy Street, a former brothel, 'a house and a way of life that epitomised the bohemian student existence of the period'.[23] Augusta was herself a mature student at the Slade, the most spectacularly inept draughtswoman Tonks had ever encountered and 'the only completely primitive adult he had ever known'.[24] She also distinguished herself by being unprecedentedly capable of inducing in him a state of bewilderment: this she did by being nonplussed and unaffected by his criticisms, which seemed to have no impact whatever on either her equilibrium or her drawing skills. Tonks had been a qualified surgeon and demonstrator in anatomy at the London Medical School and senior resident medical officer at the Royal Free Hospital; he practised – and taught – precision. This was not Augusta's thing.

Tonks believed everyone could draw – it was simply a question of addressing the problems of conveying round objects on flat paper, or of suggesting three dimensions while working in two. Once achieved, a good drawing took on a transcendent lyricism: 'The drawings of great men are like lines in Shakespeare, the beauty of which are beyond explanation.'[25] Early on, then, Gwen would have been encouraged to think holistically, about drawing as a medium for expressing the poetry of the world. Perhaps it was Tonks who extended her love of literature. She always read and loved Shakespeare. She also clearly benefited from the kind of teaching that was incisive, but also expansive, articulate, marvelling. Tonks was charismatic to a fault and when critical, he criticised with great flair. Once a lady got to the Slade, she was an artist, and would be treated as one. 'Your paper is crooked, your pencil is blunt, your donkey wobbles, you are sitting in your own light, your drawing is atrocious,' he told one hapless girl, living up splendidly to his caption in *The Slade Animal Land*. 'And now you are crying and you haven't got a handkerchief.'[26] Steer, not Tonks, taught painting.[27] Like Poynter, his predecessor at the Slade, he believed that lighting, rather than line, was at the basis of good drawing. This was the generation of painters who believed that 'the ideas of touch know no contour'.[28] Augustus later summed it up: 'Tonks had a passion for teaching drawing, and the Slade was his mistress.'[29]

Students learned from Tonks by looking at his works, rather than by listening to him lecture. He showed them his own paintings, and taught them that they must 'observe the construction of the forms and then explain it'.[30] They learned 'stumping' with bits of bread used as erasers;[31] and he taught them to search for directions and egg shapes. By 'directions' he meant the direction of the bones: that is, the internal structure, as opposed to the contours, of the body. For Tonks, life drawing was the key. The two self-portraits Gwen was to do not long after she left the Slade show the extent to which this search for 'direction' within even clothed forms enabled her to detect and depict the essence or character of the figure, so that it was only one step from establishing the inner structure to evoking the inner life. Both *Self-Portrait* (1900)[32] and *Self-Portrait in a Red Blouse* (1903)[33] are very much in the style of the Old Masters – restrained, refined, with the paint built up in glazes. William Rothenstein said he thought *Self-Portrait in a Red Blouse*, particularly, had an air of grandeur,[34] and both portraits have a certain *gravitas*, but in both, the attitude of the sitter is essentially modern.

Tonks's teaching was mainly restricted to drawing; his teaching of painting was nowhere near as directive and he did not teach students how to handle, to mix or apply paint.[35] Gwen learned the methods of the Old Masters from Augustus's friend, Ambrose McEvoy, the 'Shelley of British Art', a talented painter whose other talents were sartorial excess and social flamboyance.[36] He was a great admirer of the American painter, James Abbott McNeill Whistler and, Augustus thought, the perfect advertisement for him. With his shiny black and white clothes, his gleaming, straight black hair and his monocle, he was 'an almost perfect "arrangement in black and white"'.[37] He was both energetic and exceptionally meticulous – very much a combination Gwen could respond to. From McEvoy she learned the painstaking method of building up colour in glazes, picking out the lights and darks; unifying them with a colour glaze, then layering up the paint with further tones and glazes. This way, brush strokes were not in and of themselves part of the painting, but served to contribute to the build-up of colour. The French Impressionists were discovering that the texture of the brush strokes themselves could constitute the surface of the painting, and Gwen would change her methods radically after her first few years in Paris, when her work became quintessentially French in method and mood.

But not yet. Tonks thought light should be conveyed through technical subterfuge and subtlety, not through the juxtaposition of unmodified colours in discernible brush strokes; that, he said, was 'tea-tray painting'.[38] He did not discount the Impressionists' influence on his own work and he recognised that he had learned from their discoveries. He too was concerned with the fall of light on skin or cloth. But by his standards, the Impressionists analysed only light, not form. Essentially, they seemed to veer off from 'the meaning of life'. For him, there were no ideas but in things: 'why I hate Post Impressionism or any form of subjectivity is because they, its followers, do not see that it is only possible to explain the spirit . . . by the things of the world, so that the painting of an old mackintosh (I don't pretend to explain how) very carefully and *realistically* wrought may be much more spiritual than an abstract landscape. There is no short cut to poetry . . .'[39] If only he had been tempted to immortalise Mrs Augusta Everett, in her widow's weeds and working men's boots. Or perhaps Gwen should have taken her on, though it is difficult to imagine her sitting still. But perhaps it was too early for her to tackle such monumental subjects.

She did, however, paint a poignant portrait, quite unlike the two self-portraits, of Mrs Atkinson, the cleaning lady. She used to greet her affectionately with a kiss, shocking Edna Waugh's sister Rosa into a rather dreadful outburst: 'All barriers of differing class and occupation were silently shattered by the sight of that simple act.'[40] *Portrait of* Mrs. *Atkinson*[41] is at first glance a conventional study: Mrs Atkinson is posed with the usual art student's props – the skull, the rich dressing-up clothes – modelling the dignity and solemnity of age rather than any quality more particular to herself. Gwen's close attention to detail brings out the cheap paint on the mantelpiece and there is a drawing, probably by Raphael, on the wall behind the figure, deftly suggested in a few strokes. Yet on closer inspection a quality of sublime awkwardness emerges, created almost wholly by the placing of the figure in space, and the painting's lack of perspectival clarity. The figure is positioned off-centre; so are her eyes. The hands are naive, compared to the hands Gwen was to highlight in later portraits, but they are definitely emphasised. The sense of balance is unclear and the three-quarter profile is awkward. The positioning of the figure – Mrs Atkinson has her back to the wall but also faces away from the adjacent wall – contrasts starkly with the basically Naturalist face, with which Gwen clearly took great pains. The awkward shifts of plane and perspective suggest that she was already playing some tentative technical tricks with pictorial space. Compared with *Self-Portrait* and *Self-Portrait in a Red Blouse*, *Portrait of* Mrs. *Atkinson* is subtly experimental, uncannily anticipating the qualities which would emerge in Gwen's later work.[42]

It is impossible to know what Tonks thought of *Portrait of* Mrs. *Atkinson*. He was essentially Naturalist. His insistence on seeing 'the meaning of life' in inanimate objects was arguably in one sense closer to the newly emerging agenda of Post-Impressionism than to the experiments of the Impressionists, but Tonks did not see it that way. He resisted Post-Impressionism, not so much for technical as for moral, or social reasons. He wanted, like Walter Sickert, above all to show up the magic of urban London and the intimacy of people in interaction; he was not interested in the new theories of the artist's subjectivity. A working man's boot was about the spirit of the working man, not an equivalent for the artist's emotion. This meant that his students used their Slade years to fine-tune their draughtsmanship. The Naturalism he defended is there in Gwen's early work but so, already, is a uniquely subjective instinct about the inner lives of her sitters and a subjective response, expressed with painstaking sensitivity, to their interior lives.

Not that Tonks was not, in his own way, inspiringly subjective: 'I want to have an art revival as they do in religion,' he used to tell his students, when he was not telling them, 'All right, go on', or making them cry. 'I feel I could go and weep and rave in Hyde Park and beg people to repent and turn to art before it is too late.' (It is easy to see why Augusta Everett was so devoted to him.)[43] By the time advances in French painting, with their emphasis on subjectivism and experiments with plane, perspective and colour, filtered through to the London art world, Gwen would already have discovered Paris. One of the catalysts for the gradual *rapprochement* of French taste with English style was Whistler, who had just opened an art school in Paris named after one of his students, the Académie Carmen. He had come to London to paint the river in 1898, the year Gwen left the Slade, and it was really Whistler who was the leading exponent of the new 'aesthetic' principles, discovering abstract harmonies in paint comparable with Symbolism in poetry, and Schoenberg's new twelve-tone harmonies in music. In Whistler's school, the students discovered synaesthesia: the fusion of all the senses in cross-currents between painting, poetry and music.[44] His *Symphony in White no.2: The Little White Girl* of 1864 had had Swinburne's sonnet, 'Before the Mirror' printed on the back of the original frame.[45] All the arts were being brought, in Paris, into a new, experimental fusion based on the discoveries of the Symbolists: Swinburne, Mallarmé and Verlaine in poetry, Puvis de Chavannes in painting, and in sculpture, Auguste Rodin. Gwen, when she finally found herself in Paris, turned out to be well prepared – in training, temperament, taste – for everything she would discover there.

3

Interior with Figures

sitting before a mirror carefully posing herself . . .[1]

In the summer of 1898 Gwen went back to Tenby and Papa, leaving Augustus in London, where he was taking a studio in Charlotte Street with McEvoy's brother Charles and other friends from the Slade.[2] That autumn, Ida and her friend Gwen Salmond set off for Paris, hoping to find an apartment together and study at the Paris Académies. It was Gwen Salmond's idea: she wanted to study at the Académie Julien (following in the footsteps of Bonnard, Vuillard, and Denis) and Ida was excited by the idea of Paris. Despite the lure of the Impressionists, the Symbolists and all the new revolutionary theories, the girls, fresh from the Slade in their long dresses, their hair still down, headed straight for the Louvre. They arrived in Paris in mid-September 1898, and found Montparnasse – then the heart of bohemian Paris – full of artists painting in the streets, and dark little shops well stocked with paints and artists' materials. They took rooms in a cheap hotel, and proceeded to look, in a state of high excitement, for an apartment like the first one Ida described to her mother, Ada: 'ever so high up looking down on a boulevard, lined with rather brown rustling plane trees – & cafés', where everyone sat eating, laughing and talking in French. They liked the trams, with their odd-sounding horns, and had discovered 'a very old lady style of pension' but they were looking for a big space, with bedrooms and a studio.[3] They must have described it all for Gwen, as well. We can only imagine the battle with Papa, but three days later Ida was telling Ada, 'Gwen John is coming – hurrah.'[4]

She was to travel over on the boat, using her third-class train ticket: 'the third class deck is most charming and when we came full of peasants – lovely people,'[5] wrote Ida, encouragingly. She and Gwen Salmond were already checking out the studios and had ascertained that the fees at Julien's and Whistler's Académie Carmen were double those at Delecleuse or Colarossi, but Gwen Salmond was still determined to go to Julien's as she wanted to work with Benjamin Constan. They were still apartment hunting and had found some lovely, unfurnished places, completely bare but for their mirrors, with all the tantalising emptiness they needed to improvise and experiment. They were even thinking they might take somewhere unfurnished, if Ada could bring them some blankets: they could get chairs, bedsteads and mattresses in Paris and eat out except for breakfast so they would not need very much furniture. 'This side of the river is *delightful*,' Ida wrote home to Ada: they had discovered the Left Bank. They were furiously sketching people wherever they went, and were keeping a close eye on the Paris fashions, which they were looking forward to studying more closely when the season started in October. Things were going to get better and better: 'We are *so* glad Gwen is coming – it makes all the difference – a complete trio.'[6]

As soon as Gwen arrived, she joined in the search for an apartment, encountering fierce concierges keen to establish their moral credentials. They now found a huge place, with three good rooms overlooking a market, but there was an embargo on male visitors: 'Les *dames* – oui – mais les monsieurs? Non! *Jamais!*' One of the Gwens assured the concierge they were 'comme il faut', but she said she had to ask these things because 'the English are so very free'. It had a very clean-looking WC, Ida reported to Ada, but of the old type you had to throw water down, not one of the new ones, with a 'regular arrangement that you pull a plug and water comes'. It was 900 francs, but between them they could just about manage it; they would have to take it for at least three months, but it was convenient for both Julien's and the Louvre. They worked out their finances, allocating funds for 'Déj & dinner in cafés, bkfast at home, trams, lodging, furniture, washing' and Ida decided, after doing the sums, that they could afford it. The address they finally moved to was 12 rue Froidevaux (they nicknamed it 'Cold Veal Street'), a wide, leafy avenue with a feeling of ancient, quintessentially Parisian beauty, and tall apartments overlooking the cemetery. After a while, Ida decided that 'vaux' did not, after all, mean 'veal', but the nickname stuck.[7]

Once they had all settled in, Ida and Gwen Salmond decided to go to Boulogne, leaving Gwen John in charge. They returned stealthily in the middle of the night, creeping in quietly so as not to wake her . . . but not quietly enough. The concierges let them in by pressing a button in their room, seemingly without waking up, and they crept upstairs. They could not find any matches, so they had to creep into Gwen's room. For a while, she slept on while Gwen Salmond searched, then they heard 'a loud O! and again O! . . . She had been listening for some minutes in fear, thinking she heard someone, and at last could not control her Os! A queer reception for a burglar!'[8] Somehow this, like the 'oh dear!' that had seemed to sum her up at the Slade, beautifully conjures her up. They sat through the night eating ham and drinking warm milk, Gwen Salmond and Ida recounting stories about their trip and finding out what Gwen had been doing while they were gone. It seemed she had already acquired more friends, including a beautiful Alsacian girl called Marthe, who sat for them, helped Ida hem her skirt and generally did whatever they needed. By the end of September, Ida had been twice to Whistler's school, and everyone was excitedly awaiting the appearance of Whistler himself. By now their housekeeping had improved, and the larder had a 'strangely stocked appearance'. One of the Gwens had impressed their new friends with an English cake; they like it very much, Ida told Ada, and 'think the marmalade very drole'.[9]

They were already painting: the Gwens painted Ida, and all three (including Gwen herself) painted Gwen John. They found a book of fashion plates for Ada, who was making French costumes for the theatre, for one franc, sixty centimes, as well as a book called *Une Siècle des Modes*.[10] Gwen did some copies of the fashion plates, which she worked up into a painting. Her *Interior with Figures*[11] shows two girls, modelled by Gwen Salmond and Ida, one in Whistlerian white, holding an open book, the other in flounces and a shawl. Open on a table beside them is a larger format book or journal, possibly *Une Siècle des Modes*. The painting is an appealing mixture of sophistication and naivety. Compared with Gwen's later self-portraits the faces and forms are crude, but the tonal registers show ambition, and the detail of the room is considered and relatively well achieved. She was probably inspired, not only by the fashion plates but by Whistler's *Symphony in White*.[12] Whistler had promised a ball in his studio, and Ida had decided she would have a dress made up for it, in cream muslin: perhaps this is the one she was wearing to pose for Gwen's painting.[13]

By this time, Whistler himself had appeared. Gwen Salmond found him 'very beautiful and just right' and helped Gwen John with money so that she could go to his classes. (Ida had already made her decision, and enrolled with Laurent.) They all loved Whistler, finding him exacting and inspiring; an alluring mixture of flamboyance and incisiveness. Ida had heard there was a blasphemous letter about him in one of the English papers and she wrote telling Ada to ignore it: it was 'very stupid and unkind'[14] – she did not even need to read it to rise to his defence. His female students adored him. The Symbolist poet Arthur Symons was to meet him at a dinner party in London, the following year:

> I never saw anyone so feverishly alive as this little, old man, with his bright, withered cheeks, . . . his darting eyes, under their prickly bushes of eyebrow, his fantastically creased black and white curls of hair, his bitter and subtle mouth, and, above all, his exquisite hands, never at rest . . . In what he said . . . there was neither vanity nor humility . . . he said it all like one possessed of a conviction, and as if he were stating that conviction with his first ardour . . . No man made more enemies, or deserved better friends.[15]

Unlike Tonks, Whistler hated the idea of art as a moral force or the artist as a social reformer. He believed, with Pater (and Symons) that art should aspire to the condition of music and that painting was essentially poetic and about the art of selection: '– as the musician gathers his notes, and forms his chords, until he brings forth from the chaos glorious harmony'.[16] Augustus also admired him and when he came to see Ida and the Gwens in Paris (where he spent much of his time looking at works by Rembrandt, Leonardo and Velázquez) they all went together to see Whistler in his studio, and found him at work on an immense self-portrait disappearing into a gloomy ground.[17] Augustus also ran into him one day in the Louvre, and asked what he thought of Gwen's work: did he not think she had a fine sense of character? 'Character? What's that?' Whistler famously retorted. 'It's *tone* that matters. Your sister has a fine sense of *tone*.'[18] (His remark seemed to establish for ever the general tenor of critical reaction to her work. But Augustus was right, she already was and would always be a unique and subtle painter of character.)

Whistler was at the end of an illustrious and controversial career. It was twenty-one years since Ruskin had publicly humiliated him, attacking him for charging good money for 'flinging a pot of paint in the public's face'. Cross-examined about *Nocturne in Blue and Silver*, he had had to explain in court that he was not simply trying to make an exact copy of Battersea Bridge; the whole notion of representation in art was a matter for the viewer, not just the artist. 'To some persons it may represent all that I intended; to others it may represent nothing,' he defended himself. By the time matters moved to the question of why his portrait of Mr Irving had been presented as an arrangement in black, the judge had warmed to the theme, and elicited laughter in the courtroom by remarking, 'It is the picture, and not Mr Irving, that is the arrangement.'[19] Whistler had always been better understood in Paris, where his work was compared with that of Puvis de Chavannes and the Symbolists, and where Rodin was a great admirer and supporter.[20] When he opened the Académie Carmen in 1898, he was only five years from his death, and his students thought of him as a brilliant eccentric, an exacting teacher and an endearing old man. After Tonks, he can hardly have been intimidating, despite his insistence on orderliness. He kept strict rules, banning mixed life classes and insisting on rigorous attention to the palette.[21] He taught his students to mix colours and tonal arrangements on the palette before making the first mark, and Gwen learned from him the rudiments and principles of Impressionist and Post-Impressionist painting.

Gwen had found her niche in Paris. She loved Whistler's teaching, she loved the city and she had no intention of going home. She wrote to Tenby to tell Papa; he decided to visit her and was duly entertained in the autumn of 1898 in the rue Froidevaux. By this time, the girls' fashion-plate research and Marthe's needlework had come together, and Gwen received her father wearing a dress she had designed herself, modelled on one she had copied from a painting by Manet (*A Bar at the Folies Bergère?*). Edwin, fresh from Tenby, was scandalised and said she looked like a prostitute. This kind of talk was unacceptable and Gwen decided she would survive without her father's help. She went on studying at the Académie Carmen – probably still helped by Gwen Salmond and already modelling, now, to supplement her keep – until the end of the year, when she and Ida went back to London.[22] That year in Paris, they reinvented themselves, and they did it imaginatively, joyfully and conscientiously. They discovered they could use the local library, and went regularly on alternate Tuesdays to change their books. They read *King Lear* and *King John* over breakfast.[23] It was now that Gwen really began to explore the possibilities of using herself as a model for self-portraits (probably because it was the most convenient and the cheapest way of getting a sitter). The apartment became more bohemian, and messier. Though they had accumulated very little in the way of furniture, the wall was already half-covered with drawings and they were gradually filling the gaps. Ida described the apartment for their Slade friend Michel Salaman, brother of Louise (the Carroty Salamander): 'so untidy – so unfurnished – . . . Gwen John is sitting before a mirror carefully posing herself. She has been at it for half an hour. It is for an "interior." We all go suddenly daft with lovely pictures we can see or imagine, and want to do . . . as a whole it is a most promising time . . .'[24]

4

The Waif of Pimlico

I walked on anemones and primroses . . . it is a good day to paint – but I think of people.[1]

Gwen John and Ida went back to London early in 1899, leaving Gwen Salmond in Paris.[2] Ida returned to her family in Wigmore Street and Gwen took a basement beneath the dressmakers and decorators of Howland Street, off Tottenham Court Road. It was this which consolidated her reputation with Augustus for favouring basements and underground cellars: she here installed herself, according to him, 'in a kind of dungeon . . . into which no ray of sunlight could ever penetrate'.[3] He worried about her: to him, the place seemed damp and ill-lit, but Gwen was delighted with it, it was hers, and it was in London: it meant that she would not have to go back to Tenby. Nevertheless, in the spring of 1900 when he was invited to stay at Peveril Tower, a boarding house in Swanage, newly opened by Mrs Everett (she of the working men's boots and widow's weeds), Augustus thought Gwen should go too. Dorset was as good as Pembrokeshire, offering the same wild, open landscapes and complete freedom. But she craved female company, and wrote from there to Louise Salaman to ask her to join them. When Louise did not reply, she transferred the invitation to her brother, Michel. She asked him if he was doing any good work, and told him she had done nothing: she had been exploring the coastline.

Yesterday I came to an old wood – I walked on anemones and primroses . . . I bathe in a natural bath – three miles away, the rocks

> are treacherous there, and the sea unfathomable. My bath is so deep I cannot dive to the bottom, and I can swim in it – but there is no delicious danger about it, so yesterday I sat on the edge of the rock to see what would happen – and a great wave came and rolled me over and over – which was humiliating and *very* painful & then it washed me out to sea – that was terrifying – but I was washed up again. Today the sky is low, everything is gray & covered in mist – it is a good day to paint – but I think of people.

She thought specifically of him, she told him, though he should not take any notice of this unless he wanted to, in which case he should tell Louise to come, as the holidays were nearly over.[4]

The delicious danger, the walks through anemones and primroses, would happen again. This Gwen who wanted to hurl herself into deep waters and abandon herself to the mercy of the elements was also the painter who knew each sky and watched it for opportunities to work; but she also needed people. She was young, and full of life and hope, with great sensual capacity. Too much, in fact, for Michel Salaman. The invitation was resisted, the holidays came to an end and the Johns returned to London. At this time, brother and sister still saw a lot of each other: they still shared a circle of close friends. The Augustus Gwen quietly went about with was a reckless, flamboyant creature who went pub crawling, got drunk, befriended prostitutes and stayed out all night. When he did come home, it was often without his key. He also seemed to have rather a poor memory for the rent. Landladies who were not terrified by him were simply irritated by not being paid. October 1899 found him back in 'comfortless quarters' himself – the old, ratty lodgings at 21 Fitzroy Street – until his friend Will Rothenstein, unnerved by its extreme discomfort, offered to lend them both his own house, 1 Pembroke Cottages in Kensington.[5]

They moved there together, quickly transforming it into the kind of disorderly environment they both favoured. Augustus used it only spasmodically, preferring to sleep in his studio, but he nevertheless managed to impose his own domestic style. When Will Rothenstein came back to his house, he found it empty and cold. 'In front of a cold grate choked with cinders lay a collection of muddy boots . . .'[6] Late that evening, Augustus returned, through a window. 'There were none I loved more than Augustus and Gwen John,' Rothenstein admitted, 'but they could scarcely be called "comfortable" friends.' Augustus soon moved again, taking up new lodgings in 61 Albany Street with a Miss Simpson, who presently made her feelings clear by marrying a bank clerk and inviting Augustus to her wedding, whereupon Gwen found lodgings at 122 Gower Street. But not for long. Next, Augustus was off to France with Michel Salaman, having now fallen for a Viennese aristocrat who wore patent leather shoes and open-work stockings and who had promised to meet him in France. 'It would be nice if Gwen could come too and good for her too me thinks,' he suggested to Michel.[7] They headed for Le-Puy-en-Velay, a medieval village in the Auvergne where Michel had taken rooms in a house called Cité Titand. The hills, 'Rembrandtesque, Titianesque, Giorgionesque', grew out from volcanic rocks, and they could bathe in the waters of Borne: it all made Augustus feel 'quite Hellenic!' he told Ursula Tyrwhitt.

Michel, alarmed by the prospect of Gwen's unchaperoned arrival, had the bright idea of also inviting Ambrose McEvoy. His letter of invitation and the cheque he enclosed (to cover McEvoy's rail fare? to make quite sure he came?) seem to have arrived rather the worse for wear, the letter 'a mere wreck covered with gaping wounds from which the cheque hung', but the idea went down exceptionally well: 'How can I thank you? Words seem so crude and inexpressive at such moments as these. Oh I cannot but believe that telepathy or some such power is telling you my feelings in a way that words never can. Such exuberance of spirits I have never known and I can say with Nietzsche I could not believe in a God who did not dance. Thank Gus for his letter which came yesterday. I have told Gwen and I think she can come on Wed.'[8] When 'the waif of Pimlico', as Augustus called her, arrived with McEvoy, 'the Shelley of British painting' (they must have cut quite a contrast) it was all too much for Michel Salaman, who beat a hasty retreat to England. Things could not have been more tense. The Viennese aristocrat had failed to appear, so Augustus had to be taken about by Gwen and McEvoy, who proceeded to 'explain the beauties and show me new and ever more surprising spots'.[9] During this month in Le Puy – September 1899 – their relationship reached a crossroads. Gwen and Augustus were both thwarted in love that summer, but it was Gwen, unexpectedly betrayed by McEvoy, who spent her time in tears. McEvoy appeared to be suffering too, but he just went silent and drank himself into oblivion, while Gwen cried inconsolably. She may have hoped, now, that their relationship could be consolidated but McEvoy had already been quietly seeing someone else, a girl called Mary Edwards. Two months after the unhappy holiday in Le Puy he announced his engagement to her, surprising everyone, perhaps even himself.[10]

On New Year's Day 1901, with McEvoy and Benjamin Evans, Gwen 'aided and abetted' the marriage of Augustus and Ida at St Pancras Register Office, in 'a wonderful fog which lent an air of mystery unexpectedly romantic'.[11] The Nettleship parents, now that the relationship was official, gave it their blessing and came to the party, together with Gwen Salmond, Wilson Steer, Tonks, Michel and Louise Salaman, and Albert Rutherston. Augustus disappeared for a while, but came back dressed in a checked suit in time for the charades, after which he and Ida disappeared for their honeymoon, which they spent back in Swanage at Augusta Everett's Peveril Tower. Gwen's relationship with McEvoy seems to have taken a while to play itself out, despite his engagement. During the summer of 1901 they shared an address – 39 Southampton Street. McEvoy and Mary Edwards did not immediately marry, and when Gwen moved out of Southampton Street, she lived for a while at the McEvoy family home in Bayswater.[12]

Clearly she did not want to go back to Tenby. She and Augustus had both begun to exhibit at the New English Art Club (NEAC), the arts society which had been established in 1886 as a reaction to the academic approach of the Royal Academy. By now it had become the natural exhibiting outlet for Slade graduates. Will Rothenstein, Orpen and Conder were all on the panel of judges and by 1900, Tonks had joined the jury. Gwen exhibited paintings there in 1900 and 1901. In the spring of 1900 she showed *Self-Portrait*, the sophisticated version of the early self-portrait, in her brown blouse with leg-of-mutton sleeves, a huge bow at her neck, which she had begun in Tenby. In the spring of 1901 she showed *Portrait of the Artist's Sister Winifred*, her picture of Winifred in serious mood, an open book on the table in front of her, hurriedly pulling on her gloves.[13]

When Augustus and Ida came back from their honeymoon they briefly set up home in a flat in Fitzroy Street, but in February 1901 Albert Rutherston mentioned to Augustus that there was a temporary post at the art school affiliated to University College in Liverpool, available in the absence of a teacher who had gone to fight in the Boer War. Augustus and Ida moved to Liverpool, where he marvelled at the tenements and thought the docks 'wondrous'. He also made friends who would become very close,

Harold Challoner Dowdall and his wife Mary (nicknamed 'the Rani'), a shocking aristocrat who dressed like a gypsy, and he began a lifelong interest in the life and literature of Romanies, to which he was introduced by the university librarian John Sampson. By the summer, Ida was pregnant, and longing for Gwen. Winifred visited in the autumn and sat in Augustus's studio with Ida, the two of them making baby clothes. On 6 January 1902 the baby, David, was born, 'a wonderful mixture of Nettleship-John' who looked like his Aunt Gwen.[14]

Gwen finally arrived on the steamer from New Quay, to take her turn with the pram-pushing, causing a stir by pausing for rests in doorways. She arrived full of emotion and ideas about painting, sounding very much as if she had just emerged from a sustained spell of work. Nevertheless, she lost no time in involving herself with the baby. Another opportunity arose to try to interest Michel Salaman, who had taken the trouble to find them a nice vase, Ida said. Gwen offered to take over the writing of the thank-you letter. She obviously also needed to tell someone how she felt, since things were not easy for her at this time. They had a studio photograph taken of the family group – Augustus, Ida with David in her arms and Gwen, standing to attention at the side, looking both dutifully included in and profoundly excluded from the ancient iconography of mother, father and child.[15] She somehow reveals in it – in her carriage, her expression, her whole demeanour – that she is assisting at the scene, rather than integrated within it.

She had been very busy with the baby, she told Michel, or she would have written before to thank him for his trouble over the vase. 'I am so glad you got it so cheap too.' He had resisted all her advances, and she now told him, 'I cannot understand what you say about yourself but it does not change what I said & I feel at ease with you & I should like you to read at will all my thoughts & feelings. I can trust you as much as Ida and Winnie with all my thoughts and feelings and secrets. You say this does not matter to you. I know but still don't be bored and whatever you do don't *laugh!!* . . .'[16] He of course had the virtue of understanding what was involved in the process of painting. Ida, too, knew this, of course, but for the time being she was otherwise distracted. Gwen does not appear to have shown it, but she must have felt frustrated not to be able to talk to her about her new work. In fact she had almost certainly been finishing perhaps the most significant painting of her early career, *Self-Portrait in a Red Blouse*.[17] She explored in it her own head and shoulders and showed herself plain, straight as a ramrod, staring straight at the viewer. It is a masterpiece of restraint, with undeniable boldness in the vivid red of the blouse, to which she drew attention in the title. Unusually for her, she signed it, then gave or possibly sold it to her old Slade professor, Frederick Brown. In his own self-portrait it is hanging on the wall behind him.[18] If this is the picture she had been working on, it would have required endless, meticulous concentration. But for all the satisfaction finishing it had given her, she told Michel, she might as well not have done it; in all the time it had taken her to do, it could not have given her more than a few seconds' pleasure.

She was being honest about this. She would always find painting in oils physically strenuous, and later likened it to doing the housework; it would eventually be her works on paper, in watercolour and gouache, which she would enjoy as she did them. But she must have felt very lonely, emerging from a sustained spell of intense concentration only to find that everybody was preoccupied with the new baby. She had been working and thinking with great precision, and wanted to continue at this level of intensity: it all had to go somewhere; she put it in her letter to Michel. She had things she needed to say, she told him, and 'To me the writing of a letter is a very important event! I try to say what I mean exactly it is the only chance I have for in talking shyness and timidity distort the very meaning of my words in other people's ears' (the Pembrokeshire intonation is audible here, as is the Welsh way of turning a phrase). It was why, she told him, she was 'such a waif. I said nothing you can deny so you have no reason to think I have a wrong idea of you. I don't pretend to know anybody well. People are like shadows to me and I am like a shadow.'[19] Ida would never be her friend in quite the same way again, she could not talk about painting with her any more; she was still hurt by the McEvoy experience. She was abashed, energetic, lonely, with nowhere except her work into which she could channel her considerable sensual energy.

There had also been another serious disappointment. She had sent *Interior with Figures* and possibly other pictures (perhaps even *Self-Portrait in a Red Blouse*) to the NEAC for the autumn exhibition of 1902.[20] *Interior with Figures* had been accepted and catalogued, but unaccountably none of her paintings had been hung. Augustus intervened the following spring, so the hard-headed Orpen told Conder; he 'demanded to know why after accepting Miss Gwendolen John's pictures – they had not hung them. But alas this question was out of order . . .'[21] It may well have been Orpen who blocked her. He told Albert Rutherston she had 'sent a very weak and bad picture to the New English'.[22] She sent nothing the following year, proudly telling Ursula that she knew she could now paint better than she used to and so was glad not to have to think anymore about the NEAC. She was clearly hurt, but she was not altogether daunted. 'I shall never do anything for an exhibition again,' she told her, 'but when the exhibitions come round send anything I happen to have.'[23] But she would not exhibit at the NEAC again until 1908, after which she showed things there every year until 1911, when she found another major outlet for her work. (She would eventually show *Self-Portrait in a Red Blouse* there, with three other paintings, in 1925.) In spring 1903, Gwen and Augustus exhibited together at the Carfax Gallery in a joint show which originally comprised forty-eight pictures, of which three were Gwen's; she later withdrew one. When he saw them at the side of his, Augustus told Rothenstein that 'Gwen has the honours or should have – for alas our smug critics don't appear to have noticed the presence in the Gallery of two rare blossoms from the most delicate of trees.' He thought her work was as 'charged with feeling' as his was empty of it.[24]

At the end of July 1902, Augustus and Ida had left Liverpool and gone back to Fitzroy Street, where in the adjacent street, Howland Street, Gwen was almost certainly now back in her basement 'dungeon'. The following March, the Johns' second son, Caspar, was born. Also living in Fitzroy Street, in a basement flat, was an extraordinarily beautiful woman. Dorelia McNeill was mysterious and beguiling, with an unusually serene sensuality. She was a junior secretary who had a job copying legal documents in the office of a solicitor in Basinghall Street. One of seven children – the daughter of a mercantile clerk and a dairy farmer – she had learned to type and got herself a job, aged sixteen, working for the editor of the *Idler*. But she always felt her destiny was with artists. She was going to evening classes at the Westminster School of Art, where she mixed with the artists and was invited to their parties. At one of these she met Gwen, who found her fascinating and immediately befriended her, then she met Augustus. By the summer of 1903, he was in love with her and she was modelling for him. He drew her endlessly, in long skirts with high waistlines and tight bodices, like the costumes of the peasant women of Connemara, making gorgeous, lyrical drawings in red chalk, pencil, pen and ink. He elongated her neck and drew her in fluid, sensual lines. Every drawing emanated mystery and sensuousness. It is easy to see, looking at them, how she captivated everyone. She was quietly expressive, graceful; she exuded peace. Everyone adored her: Augustus, Ida, Gwen. She seems to have melted in among them like something elemental. More and more frequently, she was to be found in the John household in Fitzroy Street; gradually everyone began to notice. Albert Rutherston dined with them that August and found them – Augustus, Ida, about a dozen canaries and Dorelia – 'all well', but 'John must have a secret agreement with that lady and Mrs. J. – but not a word to anyone of this – it is only my notion and a mad one at that.'[25] Not such a mad one: Tonks had noticed it, too. As for Gwen, he told Michel Salaman, 'I have never seen her so well or so gay. She was fat in the face and merry to a degree.'[26] She had found a new friend.

5

The Road to Rome

. . . like Hell or Heaven . . .[1]

Dorelia was unorthodox, adventurous, and endlessly patient: just the person to share the reckless side of Gwen. She was now at the disposal of Gwen's fertile imagination, and Gwen clearly adored (and bossed) her. She was inscrutable – different from Gwen – yet she could easily understand her. She now became part of Gwen's artistic plan. In a world in which women were still chaperoned and débutantes still 'came out', Dorelia represented the bohemian alternative. She was the perfect muse, a delicious and dependable confidante; a much-needed untroublesome companion. Here was someone who meant – temporarily, at least – the end to loneliness.

Gwen had Dorelia to herself for a while during the summer of 1903 as Augustus, overwhelmed by his own tangle of emotions, had hit the open road. He headed off to Westcot, in Berkshire, where he took refuge with McEvoy's brother Charles, resolving never again to exchange 'the horizons that one can never reach' for 'four mournful walls and a suffocating roof'.[2] He had already told Ida how he felt about Dorelia, and left to her the impossible decision as to what to do. The situation was complicated by Ida's affection for Dorelia. She knew that the only way to save her marriage was to go along with the idea of a *ménage à trois*, but Dorelia made her feel ugly and despairing. Later, she would come to feel that Dorelia was Augustus's natural wife; she, Ida, his logical mistress.[3] But she was hemmed in by children. For the time being, Dorelia became a frequent visitor to the flat in Fitzroy Street, where Augustus would draw and paint her dressed up in bright petticoats, white stockings and black boots. To some extent, as Michael Holroyd has remarked, she was his creation.[4] Will Rothenstein told his brother Albert that 'John . . . doesn't seem to be pulling himself together as he should have done.' In June 1903, Ida took herself off to Tenby with the children for a month; when she came back, things were just as she had left them. They all began to feel that the only solution was to move into a large house in the country somewhere and live all jumbled together, 'women, children, animals, friends, family, servants and, more intermittently, Augustus himself'.[5]

When Gwen announced her plan, in the midst of all this, to walk to Rome with Dorelia, even Augustus thought they were mad. But the idea had a certain logic: while they were gone, the John household would remove itself to the country; by the time they came back, Fate would have played the next hand. Perhaps somewhat surprisingly, Dorelia agreed: the nature of the project must have appealed to her and now must have seemed as good a time as any to distance herself temporarily from Augustus. Gwen master-minded the project: they would take a steamer from the Thames to Bordeaux and walk, for the first lap of the journey, from there to Toulouse. Augustus, still sceptical, thought they should pack a pistol. But Gwen would not listen – 'she never did'.[6] They set off that August, 'carrying a minimum of belongings and a great deal of painting equipment',[7] and soon sent news that they had arrived in Bordeaux. 'What a success,' wrote Ida, incredulously from Matching Green, the Johns' new house in Essex.[8] Winifred sent instructions to Bordeaux to write and let her know how they were getting on, and recommended the book she was reading, *The Law of Psychic Phenomena*, by T.J. Hudson.[9]

They began the long walk up the River Garonne, Ida writing wistfully, 'I . . . long to be with you . . . To sleep out in the middle of a river & have a great roaring wave at 3 in the morning – Really it must be gorgeous.'[10] Gwen sent home evocative accounts of their journey, lyrical descriptions of the evening light along the west coast of rural France; incidents involving the locals and bizarre, nocturnal adventures. In the villages, they drew the locals for a few centimes. At Meilhan they met a sculptor who examined her drawings, and told her her lines were too choppy.[11] They walked from village to village or hitched lifts in carts; sometimes it was a long way from one to the next and they would arrive in the dark and drink beer and lemonade with the locals while they waited to be given dinner. They would sit in the dusk, admiring the evening light, the lovely trees and ancient houses. Sometimes the locals were rowdy, or the innkeepers unwelcoming. The woman in one place said she had no rooms, which they knew was a lie so they walked up and down outside her inn practising their singing, which they did in some of the villages to make a bit of money. After this demonstration of their talent, they tried again, but with no success. The villagers obviously thought them 'mauvais sujets', said Gwen, and dinner had been two francs: daylight robbery. They slept under the stars, in the shadow of a 'terrible looking thing which made a strange noise now and then . . . with black phantoms sitting in it', which turned out to be a piece of farming equipment. Other nights, they slept under haystacks and awoke to an astonished audience: farmers, gendarmes, stray animals all gathered to have a look at the two beautiful English girls, sleeping under a pile of portfolios.[12]

They lived on bread, grapes and beer, and spent their time fending off strange men who tried to take them on detours. Gwen's stories of their journey are quite exceptionally realised: they are portentous, eerie, with a sustained mood of beauty in strangeness. Perhaps her conversations with Winifred had fed into her perceptions, and she and Dorelia were light-headed with their limited diet and with sleeplessness. Figures appear and disappear in the vivid vignettes; human presences are evoked like wraiths or shadows. The daytime stories have the same quality – they 'came to a bridge and a flock of sheep and an old man' – like a pastoral painting. They were about to cross the bridge, but the old man told them not to. Instead, he took them down a side path and made them walk along a road with him. They tried to walk faster than the sheep, to shake him off, but whenever the sheep got left behind he said something that made them all come running up. It was very dark and they could not see his face; he didn't seem to speak much French, only the local patois; they were getting very tired, but they dared not stop. At last they came to his house, and he tried to make them go in. When they would not, they shook hands and found he had two deformed fingers and a missing little finger and realised they had already met him, and drawn him, in the half-light at the inn. But it was all a bit eerie, 'it gave us rather a horrid sensation'.[13]

The village of Réole, on the hillside, surprised them with its beauty.[14] The villagers were kind and found them a stable to sleep in, where a young artist came to look at them, and gave them his address 'so that we can be models if we like in Paris'. It may have been this moment, in a stable in Réole, which was indirectly to change the course of Gwen's life for ever. Was it anything to do with Dorelia's interest in the young man, that they decided to change course at Toulouse, abandon the idea of Rome and head for Paris instead? It is possible that this is what happened and that the artist they met in the stable was Leonard Broucke, a Belgian painter who was to send everyone – Gwen, Dorelia, Augustus, Ida – into turmoil. However, for the time being, they continued their walk, stopping next at Agen and then making for Toulouse. Back in London, Augustus and Orpen were starting a school, the Chelsea Art School, and Augustus was trying to persuade them to come back and be painted, '– with your knees towards Spain – if you like'. He could not really believe they were growing fat on a diet of onions and he was worried for their safety. He was also worried about Gwen's work, reminding her that the closing day for the NEAC was 9 November. He hoped she would do a good picture of Dorelia, with all the genius of Guienne and Languedoc, 'as wild as your travels and as unprecedented'.[15]

By December, they still showed no sign of returning. 'When are you . . .? You know the rest of that sentence,' wrote Ida to Gwen, who had sent presents for Christmas: a cake, and a little lamb for Caspar. Even David was missing her.[16] Dorelia wanted to know if Augustus could come and visit them in Toulouse, which was all very well, he told her, 'But there's the question d'enfants.'[17] They were painting intensively. Gwen was doing five portraits an hour, she wrote home to Ida '– why not fifty?' came the reply. 'I suppose Dorelia does an eye in 2 hours, like Gwen Salmond . . .' and, in a moment of sudden premonition: 'Is Dorelia much admired? I can't believe you tell me everything, it is all so golden . . .'[18] They settled in Toulouse for the rest of the winter, finding lodgings and succumbing after all, said Gwen, to the bourgeois life of rooms. While life lay in suspension for the next few months, before it dramatically changed, Gwen painted Dorelia in their lamplit rooms, producing some of the most hauntingly evocative portraits of her early career.

The quality of the light, the beauty of the west coast of France, with its remote, crumbly villages; singing in the dusk, sleeping in the moonlight, and the haunting atmosphere which seemed to throw up strangers like revenants all contributed to the mood they had arrived in. Now, painting in the lamplight in Toulouse, they still had a feeling of strangeness. They were reading as well as painting. Gwen's luggage probably already contained the exercise book in which she kept careful records of the painters of the past, with their dates of birth and death; names of their tutors and other details, all in carefully ruled columns.[19] (Perhaps she had begun it at the Slade.) She copied passages from Hogarth's *Analysis of Beauty*, extracts from Burke's *The Sublime and the Beautiful*; Walker's *Locomotive System*. She copied detailed pages on colour, light, draughtsmanship and portraiture, making a note of Sir Joshua Reynolds's dictum: 'Art in its perception is not ostentatious; it lies hid, and works its effects, itself unseen.' All her life she would study the technicalities of her profession; she would always be interested in artists' writings as well as their paintings.

She now painted Dorelia as *The Student*[20] in her grey dress, lingering in the lamplight with her books. She also painted her, arms folded, in her black dress, an oddly enormous pink bow on her shoulder, in a portrait in which she was already beginning subtly to challenge the conventions of posing. Dorelia is not standing but walking, as if she is passing through space, almost like one of Gwen's village visitants or the woman in the poem by Rainer Maria Rilke: 'And that departing woman / how can she be made into metaphor? / Her soft ribbon flutters, livelier / than this infatuated line . . .'[21] She nevertheless stares straight at the viewer, with the candour of Gwen's earlier self-portraits.

As she painted Dorelia she was beginning to establish some of the hallmarks of her early style. When *Dorelia by Lamplight, at Toulouse*[22] was exhibited in 1926 at the Chenil Gallery, the critics would readily detect all the qualities of an interiorist. (Chamot wrote about this painting in *Country Life*, comparing it with Whistler's portraits but also seeing in it – and in *Dorelia in a Black Dress* – similarities with Degas and Vuillard, 'the great "interiorist"'. He remarked that he thought *Dorelia by Lamplight, at Toulouse* the subtlest of Gwen's four paintings of Dorelia, because she had achieved in it a difficult fusion of technical accomplishment – the problems of conveying artificial light – with the creation of mood: all the peacefulness of 'a modest room at nightfall, animated by the quiet but pulsing vitality of the beautiful girl'.[23] John Rothenstein, discussing the same painting in *Modern English Painters*, saw it as an example of Gwen's lack of sentimentality; of her 'serenely detached, almost impersonal' vision.)[24] She saw Dorelia both tenderly and obliquely and depicted her as innocent, fluid, fragile; with all the serenity but none of the self-possessiveness that Augustus would later bring out in her. When Gwen painted her they were alone together in a strange town, having humped their painting materials miles on foot along the open road. She was still, moreover, experimenting with her medium. She found a virginal quality in Dorelia, but the figure is, at the same time, not entirely unknowing. She seduces with a quality of strangeness; in her portraits of her Gwen managed to reconcile a hint of primitive distortion with a dark power reminiscent of the portraits of the Old Masters.

They had by this time reconciled themselves to the reality that not all roads lead to Rome: 'it seems further away than it did in England'. But she was missing Ursula. 'You would like this place,' she told her, 'it is very artistic – the country round is wonderful especially now the trees are all colours . . . I cannot tell you how wonderful it is when the sun goes down, the last two evenings have had a red sun – lurid I think is the word, the scene is sublime then, it looks like Hell or Heaven.'[25] It was an essentially classical vision of Paradise and the Inferno. Her frame of reference was already broad, and intense. She already understood the search for transcendence, she had been working intensively, and had a sense of the sublime. She was looking for something ancient and everlasting: in the search she exercised her spiritual premonition, and her eye for strangeness was still evident in her stories as well as in her painting. She was so immersed in her work that she could not stop seeing people as subjects, and 'mauvais sujets' haunted her anecdotes. They were renting their room from 'a tiny little old woman dressed in black with a black handkerchief over her head, she is wicked . . . there is something very strange about her face, I cannot look at her much, she frightens me so . . .' They were usually out when she came to collect their rent, so she haunted their nights. Gwen dreamed of a ghost and woke up terrified, 'there was such a strange feeling in the room'. The door was wide open even though she had shut it when she went to bed and it could not be opened without being unlatched. 'I said to Dorelia "Look at the door" she said she had seen a figure like the little old woman's standing by the door a few minutes before – she was frightened too because there was such a horrid sensation in the air – neither of us could think of the little old woman without nearly dying of fright, and of course we heard some strange noises and a dog in the house barked suddenly.' Gwen decided the woman must have been thinking so hard about them and the rent that she had willed herself there.[26]

Perhaps the spiritual life had its limitations. As the spring of 1904 approached, Toulouse was finally beginning to pall. Sometimes she longed to be back in London, seeing Ursula and going to exhibitions with her.[27] Painting was hard work, and now that they were settled in one place it seemed to be all there was to do, since there were limits to what you could do, unchaperoned and with hardly any money, in the middle of turn-of-the-century Toulouse. 'I do nothing but paint,' she told Ursula, 'but you know how slowly that gets on – a week is nothing one thinks one can do so much in a week.' She realised that if she could do a square inch she was pleased with, she ought to be happy, and to produce something beautiful in a year would be wonderful, but she kept thinking of the Old Masters, and even the 'modern men', and trying to aspire to their standards made her hurry, which never helped. She thought about going back to London – the thought of joining 'Orpen and Gussy's school' was quite appealing – but she had no desire to go by herself, and Ursula was not going to be in London for the time being. This life, just Gwen and Dorelia alone together in Toulouse, was 'rather hard – but I have discovered a few little things about painting (which of course I ought to have known before)'.[28] She did not say which things, but she was learning how to paint in artificial light, experimenting with light sources, exploring new ways of portraying the figure in space; and it was typical of her that what she thought noteworthy were not her achievements but the setting of new challenges; the small, diligent steps forward. Even when life became more tempestuous, that diligent tenacity, and her quiet seriousness, would endure. She had been doing drawings as well as paintings of Dorelia, in black charcoal and red chalk, with lyrical, fluid, suggestive lines. Back in London, Augustus, predictably, still could not get Dorelia out of his mind. For several weeks now he had been 'dying to inspect her fat'. He was trying to get things organised in London but there were no good models; he felt neglected. It was almost as if he sensed possible movement afoot. Nothing had arrived from Gwen for the NEAC. What was going on?[29]

'What a surprise to hear from you in Paris,' he suddenly wrote, in the spring of 1904. 'I suppose you willed yourself there'.[30] Had she sent her paintings to the NEAC? He was still the proprietorial brother, anxious for her safety and concerned for her painting. As for her modelling, which he also took seriously, 'I trust you are careful to pose only to good young artists.' The School, he reported, was all a bit dull. What was happening in Paris? Was she seeing any Géricaults or Courbets? He liked the Primitives but otherwise was scathing about what was new – 'they all seem to be aesthetic symbolical Vorticists without any real grip of life about their nose'.[31] The divide between London and Paris gapes before our eyes; from the Parisian perspective, Tonks and Steer seem a long way away. After her months in Montparnasse, and Whistler's teaching, Gwen's painting in Toulouse had already begun to move in new directions. London, with its insistence on looking backwards, was in the past for her. In retrospect, it was to seem as if the walk to Toulouse had been an uncanny, necessary preparation for all that was to come. In the spring of 1904, everything was about to change. Augustus, still anxious about Gwen's commercial prospects, sent her the names of people he thought she should be contacting: a dealer called Meier-Graefe, Cottet, 'a dear man' and Fritz Tharlow, a friend of Conder's. 'And why not call on Rodin he loves English young ladies.'[32]

They headed for Montparnasse, where they took rooms in the Hôtel Mont Blanc, a cheap lodging house at 19 Boulevard Edgar Quinet, not far from the rue Froidevaux. They moved in there with a fierce and (to everyone except them) frightening female tortoiseshell cat whom they named Edgar Quinet. Any prospect of their return now seemed very slim. 'Dora mustn't grow any prettier or she will burst,' wrote Ida from Matching Green. 'Are you both quite altered? How many years is it since you went away?'[33] But by May, Dorelia seemed to have disappeared. She said she was going to visit her family, but not even Gwen seems to have known where she really was. 'Did you over-drive her?' asked Ida, 'I know you are a beauty once you start.'[34] When they finally tracked her down, she was in Bruges. While Gwen was settling in Montparnasse and beginning to look for modelling work, she had run off to Belgium with Leonard Broucke.[35] Was this the artist who had appeared to them, almost as if in a vision, in a stable in Réole? Life seemed to hang in the balance for everyone while they waited to see what would happen to Dorelia.

Once Augustus realised what Dorelia was up to, he decided he must at all costs have her back. He knew that Gwen would be his strongest ally, and she was only too willing to help him. They both wanted Dodo back. Ida, who could not contemplate losing Augustus, realised that where Dorelia went, Augustus would follow, and with dreadful paradoxical insight she saw that to keep her husband she would probably need to collude in the winning back of Dorelia. The one thing nobody seems to have taken seriously was the idea of Dorelia, happily married to a stranger . . . except that the mere thought of it, at some deep, collective level, clearly instilled panic in everybody. Gwen quickly ascertained that if Dorelia returned she would be accepted by Ida, then wrote to Dorelia in vehemently persuasive mode. 'Dorelia, something has happened which takes my breath away so beautiful it is. Ida wants you to go to Gussy – not only wants but desires it passionately. She has written to him and to me. She says "she is ours and she knows it – by God I will haunt her till she comes back."' Augustus's love for Dorelia, she told her, was more noble than she realised. She was 'necessary for his devellopment' [*sic*] and Ida's, and he was necessary for hers. The greatest crime was surely that of taking away someone's happiness; this was no ordinary love, but a great, transcendent one. (It was what she wanted for herself, of course, though she may only dimly have realised as much; at this stage she imagined it as something collective, an extension of life at the Slade with Dorelia, now, thrown in.) She urged her to be 'brave and unselfish'. She was sorry for Leonard, she said, but he had had his happiness. It was a highly Romantic ideal, and she believed in it utterly. 'Do not think these are my thoughts only – they are my instincts and inspired by whatever we have in us divine.' She sent instructions for Dorelia to come back by the next train and advised her not to tell Leonard she was going; Gwen would be there to meet her at the Gare du Nord.[36]

Dorelia simply showed Leonard Gwen's letter, and he replied with heartbreaking plangency. Did she really think happiness was 'a thing you take like a café after dinner', that you enjoy a few times and get tired of? People like him did not fall in love often, and he had no intention of letting Dorelia slip away. He begged her to 'compare now my fate with this of John [and] his family perhaps you will see where it is heavier'. She was wrong to force the hand of Fate; she had said there was no greater crime than trying to ruin someone else's happiness, but there was one greater crime: that was 'to do things which are against the rules of nature'.[37] He generously invited Gwen to write and tell him her thoughts; she ignored this, and appealed again to Dorelia, urging her to realise she was 'bound to those with whom you are in sympathy by laws much stronger than the most apparent ones'. People were not just animal and social beings, there was the spiritual life, and Dorelia's spiritual place was with Augustus. Any man who – as Leonard did – declared that he could not live without a woman ought to be left – by every woman – to live and work alone. She was ruthless and determined. When Dorelia finally replied, she said she thought Gwen must have been writing in an 'ecstasy'. What would be more honourable, she asked Gwen: to complete a man's development or to develop a man wholly? This is a rare glimpse into the way Dorelia thought. Perhaps her patience and serenity were less to do with bohemian *laissez-faire* and more to do with Victorian devotion and fidelity than they had seemed. However, Gwen was quick to perceive her advantage. She had *not* written in an ecstasy, she said, she had not been in one for ages. Our work in the world was to fulfil our destiny and only when we did so were we of use to anyone. Gussie and Ida, she insisted, were 'more parts of you than Leonard is', and always would be; she urged Dorelia to act from her 'truest self'. To 'wholly develop a man' was nonsense. The only way anybody could develop anybody was by '*being yourself: That is what you have to think of, Dorelia.*'[38]

When Dorelia finally gave in, she did so with no explanation. In late July 1904 she sent Gwen a postcard simply asking, 'How is the cat?'[39] Leonard appeared, distraught, on Gwen's doorstep, but by then the deed was done. She left to Dorelia the business of writing him 'a nice letter – he will get very ill otherwise I think'.[40] From the Johns' house in Matching Green, Dorelia sent her some Romany verses and offered to make her a skirt.[41] Gwen sent her two pieces of cotton to indicate the size, one to measure the width of her waist, the other the length from her waist to her ankles.[42] She asked Dorelia to send her earrings or, if she could not find them, some plain gold hoops, like Gussie's. Life was becoming exciting in Paris, and she clearly assumed Dorelia would one day be back. But Dorelia now sent some news Gwen was quite unprepared for. 'No I did not know you are making a petit how could I?'[43] A baby, as far as Gwen was concerned, had never been the plan. She seems to have taken it for granted that once Dorelia was back, life could go on more or less as it had before. When they continued on to Rome, she told her, they would take it in turns to carry the baby on their backs in a shawl.

'Matching Green seems a grave now, but I live in hopes of a resurrection,' wrote Ida, dreadfully, that autumn.[44] She envied Gwen her life in Paris: 'Fancy sitting for Rodin. It seems so wonderful.'[45] One day during that spring, at roughly the same time as Dorelia had fled to Belgium with her painter, Gwen had taken the yellow tram or walked from the rue Edgar Quinet the few streets to the rue de l'Université, knocked at the door of the Dépôt des Marbres, and been admitted into Rodin's studio.

6

Rodin

he who sees the flower, must see the sun[1]

The sixth *arrondissement*, where Gwen lodged in the Hôtel Mont Blanc, was busy, grimy and smelly. It housed the military hospital, the maternity hospital and the *Asile de nuit*, the night shelter or doss house. The Hôtel Mont Blanc had cheap, furnished rooms and Gwen managed to live there for more than two years on the low wages she earned from modelling.[2] The whole *quartier* smelt of iodoform and *pommes frites*; Rilke, in Paris from August 1902 to spring 1903, thought it also smelt of fear. Electric trams sped, clattering through the street. Sometimes a cry would float from a window, out across the summer air, to be trammelled and drowned out by the trolley-buses. The shopkeepers all seemed to have cats and dogs. The dogs barked in the mornings; a rooster crowed. Or there was silence. Rilke described these silences as tangible, like the tension of the silence during a great fire . . . the flames shooting up soundlessly, everyone standing still, waiting for the terrifying crash . . . the world seemed to hang in suspension. The city yielded up many different faces: a woman fallen into herself, her face in her hands, at the corner of the rue Notre-Dame-des-Champs. Ladies of a certain persuasion were driven round in little carriages, behind frosted glass. Curtains were pulled back by maids and servants; in the evenings the gas lamps were lit.[3] Cart-horses stamped and steamed on street corners. Gwen sat in cafés and drew endless numbers of measured drawings, in close-up, of this detail of early twentieth-century street life.[4] Sometimes she would be joined by one of the 'mauvais sujets' who seemed to be drawn to her everywhere she went, in the city as well as the country. They pestered and jostled her one day as she sat on a bench, drawing one of the horse's ears. When she drew the drivers, said one of the 'mauvais sujets', she should give them asses' ears.[5]

Montparnasse, the bohemian quarter, had many little bars, junk shops, and shops selling artists' materials. The light, especially in the evenings, had a pearly-grey quality, making a bright green or red carriage on the Pont Neuf luminous; the booksellers on the quays sat with their stalls wide open on yellow books with violet-brown bindings. Artists set up their easels in the streets. You could hardly look at the façade of Notre Dame without the risk of being run over by one of the many vehicles rumbling across the open square. You could hire an open horse cab, with its hood folded back, for two francs an hour.[6] The area was full of artists' studios. Once she had settled herself in the Hôtel Mont Blanc, Gwen began the business of calling at the concierge's lodge in all the nearby buildings. She found the concierges very helpful once she explained that she was a model looking for work. They would tell her whether there were any studios in the building and which of the artists were in, to save her wasting her time. Then she would go up and knock randomly on doors. 'Who's there?' 'A model.' Sometimes silence would follow.[7] It was easier to pose for women. The men tended to be rude, devious, or assume that what was on offer was cheap sex. One day she saw four: the first was cross about being interrupted in his work and sent her away. The second asked her to undress, and when she refused, saying she would pose for a head, he told her he would like her to live with him and share his ideas. In the end she had to make a run for it. The third wanted her address; the fourth was a landscape artist who, as she turned to leave, put his hand on her breast to see if she was *dévéloppée*. She could not see why he needed to know that, to paint landscapes.[8]

She used to take the yellow tram or walk from the leafy Boulevard Edgar Quinet, opposite the cemetery flanked by tall trees, down the little streets of the sixth *arrondissement*, along the rue Montparnasse and beyond, past the Luxembourg Gardens and down the rue d'Assas, where Constance Lloyd, who had been at the Slade, now lived,[9] into the seventh and sometimes as far as the rue Notre-Dame-des-Champs where Nuala O'Donel, an Irish sculptress who was one of Rodin's studio assistants[10] lived with her friend the actress Suzanne Horden.[11] One client tended to pass her on to another. She soon built up a circle of lady clients: Hilda Flodin, the

Finnish sculptress, another of Rodin's assistants,[12] the German lady painter, Miss Gerhardie; the 'man-woman' Ottilie Roederstein, a Swiss painter; the two Miss Browns, Anna and Ida; Isobel Bowser, who was the sister-in-law of the Symbolist poet, Arthur Symons, as well as Constance Lloyd and Grilda Boughton-Leigh ('the Leer') and Miss Hart, who had been a pupil of Augustus's in Liverpool. All were entertaining, all were exasperating; all were, in their different ways, eccentric. Gwen privately thought most of their problems could be put down to their celibacy, but you had to be careful with these ladies, they were practised observers and listeners. Miss Hart provided her with updates on the activities of the 'hommes de Finlande' on the other side of her studio wall:

> One of them said to the girl, 'Do you want to sleep with us?' And the girl said, 'What, both of you?' and he said, 'Yes,' and she said, 'what, all three of us?' (Miss Hart says they've only got one single bed and that's all.) One of them said, 'How much?' and the girl said, 'Five francs,' and the Finlandais said, 'Five francs!!!' She hates them even more now.[13]

When Dorelia announced that she was going back to Augustus, Gwen borrowed Constance Lloyd's apartment in the rue d'Assas for a few weeks while Constance was temporarily in England. She wrote to Dorelia from there, hoping for news. 'You keep your movements & impressions enveloped in mystery – why?'[14] She was painting, she told Ursula, better now than she had before; it was such a help not to have to think about the NEAC, or to worry about getting a painting done in time.[15] She was happy in the rue d'Assas, where the apartments were tall and imposing, rather grand: 'the trees are so beautiful down the streets occasionally lit up by a lamp,' she told Dorelia.[16] Sometimes she slept in the Luxembourg Gardens, 'in a little copse of trees'.[17] In the daytime, she would take Edgar Quinet down there with her and let her loose. Quinet, light-headed with sudden freedom, would whirl round in circles, frantically race up trees and disappear, sometimes to be found, after much lamenting and searching, under a strange bed in a strange apartment.[18] At the end of the day Gwen would walk in the gardens or go and sit by the river to watch the boats, lit up, coming and going under the bridge. They were delicate colours and she thought the whole river scene looked like a Japanese drawing. Sometimes she attracted a crowd: people would gather round and stare at her, asking,

'What's she looking at, what's she doing, why is she there? . . . She's all alone in Paris! Poor girl!'[19]

At the end of the long rue de l'Université, close to the Champ de Mars, in a corner so deserted and monastic that you might almost be in the provinces, was the Dépôt des Marbres. The courtyard, overgrown with grass, was frosted with vast great blocks of marble. A dozen workshops lined one side, occupied by sculptors working. Two of these were used by Rodin: here he would be found hewing vast blocks, or sculpting the tiny figurines he made at top speed to take a break from an ongoing work and exercise his eye and hands. Moving constantly around him as he worked were several nude models. He watched them as they moved, like Greek gymnasts, establishing a familiarity with the human body, and with muscles in movement.[20] When Gwen arrived there towards the beginning of 1904, she knocked at a workshop door where she found one of Rodin's assistants, the sculptress Hilda Flodin, who took her into Rodin's studio.[21]

When she offered herself as a model he must have asked her to undress, and she probably showed him a few poses in the company of the other models who roamed or rested in the studio. She was desperately nervous but he was kind, and when she took off her clothes to pose he made sure she was warm, and told her she had an admirable body. Presumably, he hired her straight away. She told no one about this first meeting with the *maître*, but he must have been interested in getting to know her, and probably wanted to show off his English connections, which he was very proud of. Perhaps he mentioned some English reviews of his work, because on 2 September she sent him a postcard asking him to bring some English articles. She signed it, 'Votre modèle, Mary Gwendolen John'.[22] He would always call her 'Marie'. She was petite and shy, and she reminded him of his younger sister Maria, a devout and gentle girl, devoted to her brother, who had died of smallpox in her twenties. (Perhaps, too, he found the name Gwen difficult to pronounce, it is a hard name for the French tongue and he had practically no spoken English.) Occasionally, he would call her 'ma petite soeur'.[23] She was thirty-six years his junior. He was sixty-three, and seductive, brilliant; renowned. She called him her *maître*. Perhaps he kept forgetting to bring the English articles, despite her reminders, because a few weeks later she sent him another postcard, to remind him.[24]

She loved modelling for him. She took it seriously – it was her job – and she was supple, and prepared to attempt complicated, erotic poses. They must have talked about Whistler's work, and his teaching; he took an interest in her drawings and asked her to bring them for him to see. They talked about literature and he lent her books. The poet Rainer Maria Rilke, who had been captivated by Rodin when he came to Paris in August 1902 to write a book about him,[25] would later describe in *Die Aufzeichnungen des Malte Laurids Brigge*,[26] the Paris he found squalid, dirty and alienating. The world Rodin had created in the rue de l'Université was a haven of peace and beauty which contrasted starkly with the world outside. There, Rilke immersed himself, feeding, he said, 'on the glowing vitality of your beautiful works', dealing with Rodin's correspondence and polishing his manuscripts. One of Rodin's other secretaries, Louis Gillet, would comment that Rodin wrote as he drew, his writing was 'poetry itself' and his notes and sketches had 'the charm of a Firdausi floral carpet'.[27] Rodin soon began to give Gwen extracts to copy out and translations to work on for him. She became, like Rilke, a kind of scribe, working at the poetic and philosophical source of Rodin's ideas; accessing this divine vision and relaying it back to him.

Some of Gwen's extracts are enfolded in sheets of paper, marked, by one secretary or another, 'Copies for Mary John': she presumably copied them out for him, he read and commented on them; then he passed them back to her. Perhaps she told him she wanted him to keep them. She must have felt, as she did this work, that she had entered an inner sanctum, a world in which her own interior life would develop and flourish – as, indeed, Rodin obviously intended it to. What with posing, drawing and translating, she was soon telling Ursula, she was getting quite thin.[28] He talked to her about his work, and how he wanted to make organic forms from nature; she told him about the walk with Dorelia along the River Garonne, and their plans to go to Rome. He may have thought Dorelia was quite likely to fetch up again one day, the baby strapped to her back in a shawl, and suggest that they continue their journey. One day when Gwen arrived at his studio he was not there. He usually took the train every day from his house, the Villa des Brillants, in Meudon, arriving at the rue de l'Université at two o'clock, but today there was no sign of him, so she wrote him a letter, in French, the first of many: '*Cher Monsieur*, I don't know what to do this afternoon, because you are not here. I want to come here at least one day a week for ever, just as you said, until I'm an old lady, by which time I'll be an artist, but if you told me you didn't need me any more I couldn't bear it. I'm worried about annoying you when you see me on Saturday because I'm not particularly amusing. G.M. John.'[29]

He must have offered her reassurances, because she now became flirtatious, suggestive; daring. Emboldened by his recent attentions, she wrote to him urging him, 'Think of me when you're working with all your beautiful, educated women.' She told him she thought his work too beautiful for words. She too loved Nature as he did. He took his inspiration from the Greeks:[30] she said she had loved Greek sculpture long before she met him.[31] She was so happy about this, it meant they could really be close to each other. She wanted him to know that she would not be happy, if she ever did get to Rome, if he was not there. She was not interested in going anywhere, now, if he was not going to be there. She began to fantasise about going to Rome one day, but with him instead of Dorelia. When the time comes, she told him, don't make any objections. He would not be cold at night the way she and Dorelia had been, she would keep them warm. Didn't he know how soft and gentle the air was, and cool at night? – they had noticed it yesterday, when they stood at the gate together and saw that the sky was so beautiful, covered in stars. He surely could not imagine how lovely it was to have supper at the side of the river as the sun went down. She would wear a red dress, and they would keep the key with them instead of giving it to the concierge, so that when they came back – if they ever came back – they would find everything just as they had left it.[32]

He would see, she promised him, how organised she was, after all; he would not have to worry about the practical arrangements for the journey, she would do all that, so that he would be completely free to observe the beauty of Nature. She was happy all the time now, she told him. In the past, people she had met had always wanted her to change, which was why she had eventually turned her back on them. But he had said he wanted her just as she was. Ironically, this marks the beginning of the transformation of the bohemian, disorderly Gwen – Augustus's unorthodox, undomesticated sister – into the Gwen Rodin recreated, the orderly, tranquil, harmonious and devoted woman, *recueillie* as a woman in a painting by Puvis de Chavannes[33] (the artist most revered by Rodin)[34] who would wait patiently, in impeccable rooms. She was crying for joy, she told him; and she promised she would do her best to improve herself for him. If this letter was written before their love affair began, he had certainly already begun to be suggestive with her. It is possible that the seduction took a while –

perhaps even several months – to play itself out, while he established the basis of his work with her as a model. She said she realised he would have to finish his work on the Muse before they went away together, but she would be happy to wait.[35] By the end of 1904 or the beginning of 1905 she was telling Ursula that she was posing for him 'nearly every day now – he has begun a statue'.[36]

Eighteen months before, in the summer of 1903, while Gwen and Dorelia were still in London hatching their plan to walk to Rome, Rodin, too, had been in London. Whistler had died on 17 July 1903, and in November Rodin succeeded him as President of the Société Internationale de Londres. The Committee – which included George Wyndham and the Conservative MP Ernest Beckett (Lord Grimthorpe) – had approached him to design a monument to Whistler and he had named his price: 50,000 francs. A site was selected, the Chelsea Embankment, near Whistler's former house, and the committee suggested a 'Winged Victory symbolizing Whistler's triumph . . . of Art over the Enemies', but this was not really Rodin's style. He seems to have considered the idea: he made a drawing showing a Victory holding a garlanded medallion with a head in profile and jotted on it, 'génie de Whistler'. But he would soon develop another idea. He regarded the commission as a great honour, and took very seriously his place in English cultural life. The English had been patronising him substantially at this time, he had received commissions to sculpt busts of Ernest Beckett (a rich and powerful client, as he was heir to a banking fortune and the Great Northern Railway) and of his beautiful lover, Eve Fairfax, whose bust he had taken several months to complete after she left Paris, saying he needed time so that her 'beauty and character might work upon my soul'. When he eventually completed it, he thought it a 'masterpiece'. At Beckett's home in 1902 he had met Mary Hunter, one of London's famous hostesses, who set about adding him to her social circle. He had an enormous regard for British aristocratic life: it provided him with a new insight into the pomp and ceremony with which life might be lived, and he had attended the presidential banquet held in his honour in a fur-lined coat with astrakhan collar, white silk scarf and top hat. Beneath the coat he wore a frock coat decorated with the rosette of a Commander of the Legion of Honour; he had brought his foreign orders, just in case he was asked to appear at court.[37]

When he returned to Paris, he began work on the monument. Gwen's appearance may have enabled him to evolve the sculpture which he now began to work on, the Muse to Whistler. This was an over-life-size figure of enormous power, which forced the model to hold a difficult, complicated pose, one leg raised, head bowed, her lower torso draped with cloth; she also had to hold a medallion or, in another variant, a box.[38] When Gwen arrived in his studio and told him she was British and had been a student of Whistler, she must have seemed perfect for the piece, given her unusual combination of delicacy and strength, suppleness and balance; her Memling-style fragility and her indomitability. She now began to pose twice a day, in the afternoon for Rodin and in the mornings for the lady artists, most of whom seemed to be connected, directly or indirectly, with Rodin.

For Rodin, the model's work was an integral part of a highly complex process of transformation. He worked, he said, directly from nature, and from his own primal responses to the figure. 'A woman undressing – what a glorious sight!' he wrote in *Les Cathédrales de France* –

> it is like the sun breaking through the clouds. The first sight of that body – the general impression – comes as a blow, a shock. Momentarily taken aback, the eye darts off again like an arrow. The whole of nature resides in every model, and the eye capable of seeing can discover it there and follow it so far! Above all, it can see what the majority are incapable of seeing: unknown depths and the very substance of life – beyond elegance, beyond grace . . . But all this transcends words . . .'[39]

He had a favourite 'type', which he thought common to modern Italians and ancient models of Phidias, whose special characteristics included the equal width of shoulders and hips.[40] Gwen, with her slender hips, conformed to this type. But the main thing for Rodin was to capture movement. He believed that when a good sculptor fashioned a torso, he was describing not only the muscles but 'the life which animates them – more than the life, the force that fashioned them'.[41]

Large numbers of women artists in Paris employed female life models. Lady painters posed for each other to save money (when Gwen sat for Miss Brown she was paid 55 francs for the whole portrait.)[42] Constance Lloyd posed nude for Gwen;[43] Gwen posed nude for Flodin and both Gwen and Flodin posed nude for Rodin, but Rodin's society lady friends and admirers would never have dreamed of life modelling for him; those who did pose for busts would stop at drapery pulled down to reveal the shoulders and a touch of cleavage. When Gwen posed for Miss Hart, she posed nude to the waist, suspecting that Miss Hart would have liked to sculpt her nude, but was too embarrassed to ask.[44] She distinguished herself from Rodin's other admirers by being a professional working model, for whom conditions in Rodin's studio were reputed to be among the best in Paris.[45] But he was utterly demanding.

Rodin used his models to explore and expose female sexuality and the female form.[46] He made drawings after his sculptures, and for these he demanded blatantly erotic poses, which sometimes involved women masturbating or caressing one another. He looked at women and saw something 'utterly primeval, the way people were in prehistoric times . . . Look at those slim legs, look at those clever feet. With these she could have climbed and lived in trees.'[47] Made very rapidly, without taking his eye off the model, the drawings have summarily handled volumes and sketchy outlines. They enabled him, he said, to understand and explore 'feminine sexuality, its movements and impulses . . . because therein woman is psychologically revealed'.[48] These drawings were considered shocking – they are blatantly erotic. But they were not kept under wraps. In October 1907 he was to show more than 300 at the Bernheim Jeune Gallery in Paris; some had already been published, in *Les Dessins d'Auguste Rodin* (in the *Album Fenaille*), as early as 1897. In a special issue of *La Plume* devoted to Rodin's work, Arthur Symons wrote about them. The principle of Rodin's work, he said, was 'sex, sex . . . bodies violently agitated either by the memory of, or the waiting for, sexual pleasure . . . [The model] turns on herself in a hundred attitudes, but always on the central pivot of her sex which accentuates itself with a fantastic and terrifying monotony, like an obsession.'[49] There are more than 7,000 of these drawings in the Musée Rodin – he must have done them constantly, they were clearly an important aspect of his work, and represented an intense and focused kind of looking. The models lay splayed back on their shoulders or with their legs spread wide. Rodin's biographer, Ruth Butler, shrewdly notes in passing that if a female sculptor – say, Camille Claudel – had asked her male models to pose like this, 'she would have found herself confined to a lunatic asylum years earlier'. Rodin was 'the first sculptor to want to make women's sexuality important'.[50] Rilke realised this, too. Writing about *The Gates of*

Hell, he remarked that Rodin's woman is 'no longer the forced or unwilling animal. Like man, she is awake and filled with longing, it is as though the two made common cause to find their souls.'[51]

It is impossible to know exactly when Gwen's affair with him began, whether before she wrote to him with her vision of their escape to Rome, or just afterwards. She was journeying towards him, as she wrote those words, and she found him. She must have seemed irresistible, given her integrity and imagination, her energy and restraint. One afternoon as she posed for the Whistler Muse, naked to the waist, with one knee raised high and head bowed, he kissed her. She felt, she later told him, like the woman in the poem she had learned at school, by Sir Thomas More: 'Je sent courir sur mes lèvres des enivrements mystérieux' (I can feel, rushing across my lips, sensations of mystery and intoxication).[52] She had not really understood that poem in her schooldays; now she understood it utterly. He began to make love to her after their *séances*, and he made her so happy that her heart felt like music playing, she said, sometimes loudly, sometimes softly, like the waves of the sea – sometimes big waves, sometimes small – but relentlessly, unceasingly.[53]

This was romance. He would make love to her in the studio in secret, and soon he began to visit her in her room in the rue Edgar Quinet. He found it a bit squalid, commenting on the 'saleté' and encouraging her to impose some order on it, as well as on herself.[54] She was pleased, one morning when he arrived, that the only 'saleté' was a bone that Edgar Quinet was devouring on the bed. Rodin waited while she took it out to the kitchen, and did not seem to mind; apart from this slight hitch, he evidently found everything spotless.[55] From now on, her rooms would be devised as perfect, flawless, expectant spaces: harmonious, peaceful, uncluttered, in preparation for his arrival. He made her life feel precious, exciting; he energised her. 'I was so happy today!' she wrote to him. 'All my days are so delicious when I pose in the mornings and it's sunny and I know you're coming later.' She thought she must be 'the happiest woman in the world'.[56] She told him, disingenuously, that she would rather see him every day for a quarter of an hour than three times a week for longer, she needed him every day. She was not happy about going to bed without having kissed him.[57] From the outset, she was voracious, demanding. Rodin, at sixty-three, was easily tired. He soon began to tell her that she gave him headaches, he must save the best of his energy for his work. Well then, she said, it would suit him better, too, if they were to meet every day, just for a little while. She also needed to work well, and to be 'bien pourtante' [*sic*] (looking good) when she posed for him.[58]

He fired her imagination, making her tender, romantic, outrageously and irrepressibly passionate; he heightened her visual awareness. The world suddenly felt intensely sensual. She was happy not only when she was with him, but for the whole evening afterwards, and the next morning as she did her housework.[59] She just wanted to be his wife.[60] She thought about him all the time; she told him she would rather be alone than with other people, because then she could think about him without being interrupted.[61] Sometimes if she posed until the end of the afternoon she walked to the station with him,[62] where he would catch the train to Meudon. She went out to Meudon herself once, where she found his house and caught a glimpse of him in his garden.[63] She wrote him gorgeous, romantic love letters, painstakingly composed in careful French. She said she had been wanting to ask him for a long time to meet her at the white gate of his garden one night by moonlight, but she realised his wife would probably want to know why he was out so late, so they had better wait until spring. She wanted him to see her in the moonlight, because then he would truly appreciate her beauty. Augustus had once said she looked better by moonlight.[64] She wanted to see Rodin by all lights, she said she had never seen him in full sunlight, only once by the light of the setting sun when they went to the station together. She told him she meant to live in exactly the way he wanted her to now, because if things did not work out between them she would be ill, she could sense it.[65] She loved him, she told him, not only with her senses, but with her heart and soul. He was 'all that is beautiful and romantic in my life'.[66] Everything connected with him was exciting, especially the garden in front of his studio, where she waited for him every afternoon, lingering between the sculptures and the trees. She was sure now that the greatest happiness was 'the sympathy of two hearts'.[67]

Almost straight away, she wanted to stop working. All she wanted was to be his model. She rushed off to the dressmaker to have new dresses made; she shopped for stockings, gloves and hats at the Bon Marché.[68] He gave her books, and she spent her evenings happily reading them. Rodin was a great reader, he read Baudelaire, Verlaine, Mallarmé, Shakespeare, Dante.[69] She read voraciously, wanting to understand the whole framework of his mind. His favourite novel was Richardson's *Pamela*, the fancifully clever epistolary novel in which 'Mr. B' – with highly romantic, unorthodox unpredictability – marries his serving girl: romances had happy endings, then. He gave her his own copy of *Pamela* and she proudly displayed the volumes on the shelves in her room.[70] Then he gave her *Clarissa*, which she was more disappointed by, reprimanding him that surely he had not forgotten how unhappy Clarissa Harlowe's story was.[71] He urged her to draw, since he could see that she was a gifted artist and sensed the possible danger of her undivided attention, asking her to bring him her drawings. She drew Edgar Quinet for him, in charcoal, red chalk, and pencil and wash – animated drawings, in the style of Rodin's.[72] But she wanted him to know how deeply she felt that all the things she possessed were his gifts: she was happy in her domestic space, now that it revolved, in her mind and heart, around him, but she would give it all up – her books, her drawings, even Edgar Quinet – for him, if she could not have both.[73]

The drawings she posed for were their babies, she told him. She said she knew that people in general liked to have children – something she had never understood. Artists and poets were more 'féconds' in their souls than in their bodies. She felt like them when Rodin touched her, and his touch lingered in her memory all night. She felt they were married with an 'amitié' far stronger than those who had human children; their children – their works of art – were more beautiful, and immortal. She thought it odd that anyone would want to have children rather than make works of art. Monuments and temples were erected to the memory of great artists, honouring their work, but nobody erected monuments and temples to people for having children. She wanted nothing more than to be in the presence of the man capable of creating such beauty. She thought that with her, he would discover that the beauty of the soul was an aspect of physical beauty. If he could be sure of that, he would see it everywhere, and no one would ever be able to criticise him in the way people sometimes had in the past, because his work would become more and more undeniably beautiful.[74] She copied out a quotation from Balzac for him: 'Tout génie suppose une vue morale. Cette vue peut s'appliquer à quellque [*sic*] specialité; *mais qui voit la fleur, doit voir le soleil*': 'all genius implies a moral view, applicable to any discipline, *but he who sees the flower, must see the sun*.'[75]

'Oh, mon tendre amant!'[76] her letters to him now typically began. She had no desire to be an artist any more, all she wanted to do was to pose, if this great love and passion were to be the reward. She had been ambitious in the past, it was true she had hoped to be a great artist. She had wanted her place in the sun, she told him, but all that was over now. She was in love. She did not want fame or recognition any more, her place in the sun was with him.[77] She wanted to pose for him, look after him; and find a language in which she could express all this so that he fully understood it. She told him she was like a mountain flower, growing free. He did not appear to understand what she was saying, so she wrote to him explaining that she had discovered in herself, through her love for him, something beautiful. She did not just want it put in a window box like a pot of flowers on her sill so that she could watch it die, she wanted it to be something wild and eternal. She wanted him to share all her thoughts, even the most secret and the most crazy, to give him all her love, without reservation: 'à lui un coeur sans réserve, à lui une affection infinie'.[78]

She particularly loved the times when he came to her room. Once he came, miraculously, when she should already have left for work; after that she was reluctant to go out in case he came, and missed her.[79] The idea of going to work was becoming irritating; she found herself doing unnecessary things, to delay going out. She would wash her face again, for example . . . and sometimes it paid off, there was a footstep on the stair, a knock on the door. She played little, irresistible tricks: she called out, 'Wait!' several times and went on scrubbing her face, even though she knew it was him, wanting to delay, deliciously, the moment when she could see him. Then she was cross with herself for making him wait a single moment. When she did go out to pose, it was to knowing looks and a barrage of questions. One day, Flodin gave her a cigarette, and lit it from her own: very daring and modern. She said, 'do you know what that means? It means I'm going to kiss your favourite lover.' Then she said, 'I'm not really asking you, I'm sure he doesn't want kisses from me.'[80]

Gwen said she thought it was highly unlikely Rodin would be asking for kisses from Flodin, who said that little did Gwen know, some women knew how to get what they wanted. 'Oh *mon Maître*,' Gwen pleaded with Rodin, 'don't ask her! Oh *mon Maître chéri* you are the whole world to me, *promise* me that if you love anybody else you won't tell me, or if you kiss anybody else I'll *never* know about it.'[81] The whole situation was tantalising. She asked Flodin to pose nude for her. Flodin said no, but Gwen thought she just wanted to be asked again: 'we're like that, women, aren't we, *mon*

Maître'.[82] She thought Flodin probably considered it beneath her dignity to pose nude for her, even though she made Gwen show her some of the poses Rodin had taught her. She told him all this, promising him some 'extraordinary poses', as good as the classical ones, because she was supple. She practised them, and found it 'completely natural' when she did them on her own in her room.[83] Flodin said she had certainly changed a lot since she met Rodin, she seemed to like talking about things she had never seemed to think about before. But then she said she thought women should not love too much, it was dangerous and she feared for her. It was Flodin, Gwen indignantly pointed out, who liked drawing erotic poses and thinking about Rodin as she drew.[84] All Gwen really wanted, she told Rodin, was to be a match for all the other women who crossed his path.[85]

One morning, she slept until half-past ten. Next time, she joked, we'll have to be a bit colder with each other. She arrived at Rodin's studio tired and pale, and he sat her down in front of the fire.[86] His attentions when they were alone were intoxicating, but other people were a dreadful impediment to the progress of their liaison. When there were others at the studio and he had to talk to them, she would tremble with nerves.[87] At least he found her translations comprehensible, but she was still worried about her progress in French, convinced that she could never be articulate and brilliant, like the women he did busts of, who appeared brightly at his Saturday *soirées*. She relied on him for her education and had no way of finding things out unless he told her about them, she said.[88] She worried, too, about her letters, which she was anxious did not amount to much. Sometimes she would re-read them in despair, and find to her distress and exasperation that they did not really seem to express anything like the things she had been trying to say.[89] She told him she had been reading Euripides, and trying to write a critique. By comparison with other histories and dramas she had read, she thought Euripides showed less hypocrisy and more courage. 'He makes his characters say everything they feel and nothing they ought to say just to give a good opinion of themselves. He opens up his whole heart to us and even the heroes cry and give personal reasons for the things they do.'[90] She admired him because his work suggested that 'one must accept life in all its entirety, that everything is good in life, just as you do, *mon Maître*'. Rodin's all-embracing view of life, and the essentially amoral way in which he reasoned as an artist, chimed with Gwen's unfailing integrity. She wanted to behave as he did, and as she had advised Dorelia to behave when she counselled abandoning Leonard in favour of Augustus. But Rodin had been practising this way of life for many years and was essentially in control of it, whereas for Gwen it was only just beginning to open up before her. She wanted to hurl herself headlong into it; so the extent to which Rodin was diverted by professional and social considerations was dismaying. She was determined to live up to it all, to be everything to him; but she knew her limitations in the art of conversation, and though she was irrepressibly passionate, she was socially very shy.

There was also, of course, Rose Beuret, Rodin's companion for the last forty years, the woman who had come to Paris from Champagne to work as a seamstress in the Gobelins district in 1864, and met Rodin when he was working on the decorative sculpture for the Théâtre des Gobelins.[91] She had been his first model: the delicate, early sculpture, *Mignon* (1865–8) is Rodin's bust of Rose.[92] She had seen him through the major transitions of his working life, from his early rejections to his eventual success, and she had borne him a son, though Rodin showed little interest in him, and refused to let him take his surname.[93] People who visited the Villa des Brillants were baffled by Rose, taking her sometimes for his housekeeper.[94] He would never leave her, she was the stable point of his world: she took care of his maquettes whenever he was away and maintained his home. She remained silent, loyal through all his affairs. Gwen would never usurp Rose, and she never intended to try. She went to his house one evening to see if she could see him and instead caught a glimpse of Rose in the garden. She told Rodin she thought Rose obviously had great dignity, a quality nobody else, with the exception of Rodin, ever seems to have detected in her.[95] Gwen wanted more and more of his time, his attention; she wanted a place in his life. If only she could be sure that they would always see each other and make love often, that, she told him, would be a happy life.[96] She wanted what she had always envisaged: complete sexual and spiritual integrity, in defiance of any social convention. But integral to that vision, for her, was monogamous devotion. She did not see Rose as a threat, but other people – the life represented by the studio, the *soirées*, the travelling – were. She knew she inhabited only a small part of Rodin's life, and she was determined to extend the boundaries of her influence. She wanted to be vital, all-consuming, to him as he was to her.

He realised the depth of her feelings, and was touched by her. But the more anxious she became, the more passionately she would beseech him to assure her of his love, and because he cared about her, he was determined to make sure she stayed sane. He sent her brief notes: '*Petite amie*, be strong, eat properly, and remember that I am your friend, very tired, unfortunately, but I do read your letters, which are very touching, and I do love you.'[97] She continued to tempt him, and he was to go on coming to her room until the year before he died. He was her lover, the man who had transformed her; she was fully alive only with him. Whatever he needed she would try to do, but it was galling to be told that she could love him best by looking after herself properly and staying away from him.

She wrote to him regularly between 1904 and at least 1912 (they were still corresponding, though less regularly, in 1916, the year before he died). In these early years (from 1904 to 1906 or 1907), he read all her love letters and told her she wrote beautifully, but he soon began to say that he did not see why she had to go on writing about the same things.[98] She interpreted this as a criticism of her writing and told him writing did not come naturally to her, she would have to practise it. Because she always wrote to him in French, she had to search for words, which never seemed to her to express her thoughts exactly. She wanted her letters to be works of art, as finely wrought as her drawings and good enough to please a great artist. She told him she wanted to pay homage in her letters to something glorious and brilliant, something she thought was essentially male – a charisma, a radiance – which naturally and necessarily put women in the shade.[99] He said if she wanted to write well, she should simply write truthfully about her own experience. That, she said, was what was so difficult.[100]

So he devised a way, quite early on in their liaison, of getting her to write more anecdotally. He suggested she should write her letters to an imaginary female correspondent, 'Julie', and tell her about everyday incidents and events, just as she would to any female friend. She imagined her as another version of her sister Winifred: Julie also lived in Canada and knew about Rodin.[101] Gwen wrote to Julie every day, sometimes copying out her letter again the next day. They were stylish compositions and she polished them to make sure they were always well expressed, regaling Julie with long, amusing, anecdotal stories, beautifully observed and narrated with an acute, shrewd ear. They reveal a wonderful gift for storytelling, and they also show up the contrasts in Gwen's life at this time. With Rodin she was intense, passionate: leading a highly charged inner life. At the same time, as she fell more and more deeply in love with him, she was dealing daily with the eccentric lady painters and maintaining a colourful and chronically dramatic domestic life. She described for him in detail the personalities and habits of the lady painters and their ongoing dramas; her own peculiar domestic scenarios; and all the other hazards of life in early twentieth-century Montparnasse. 'Un incident sur moi,' she might begin . . . and a detailed story would follow, like the story of the baby bird who flew in one day, heading straight for her open wardrobe and attaching itself to a skirt hanging there. Edgar Quinet struggled and clawed at Gwen as she tried to restrain her from attacking the little bird; meanwhile, it flew round the room in a panic, its mother calling from outside the window, 'Pi— pi—': she captures the minutiae of the drama, ventriloquising all the voices, including the mother bird's.[102]

She was on first-name terms with almost none of her clients except the ones she had known at the Slade, Grilda Boughton-Leigh and Constance Lloyd (who, she told Rodin, had *nine* sisters, all above the age of twenty-three, none of whom had ever had a lover).[103] But Miss Gerhardie and Miss Roederstein, Miss Bowser, Miss Hart and Miss O'Donel all dramatically populated her stories. Miss Gerhardie, a German painter, took her with her friends to the Gaieté Montparnasse, where they saw fat women with enormous breasts displaying bare arms and shoulders and dancing in extraordinary ways, a spectacle Gwen found intriguing, and erotic.[104] Miss Gerhardie said you needed a 'bit of temperament' to paint and followed her own advice, stamping her foot and working herself up into a lather as she painted until Gwen mentioned that she had heard Monsieur Rodin say that patience was the essential thing, whereupon she noticeably calmed down.[105] Ottilie Roederstein, who wore men's clothes and a watch and chain (Gwen privately suspected she was a 'new woman')[106] tried to get away without paying Gwen for her sessions, then turned up one day with a 'hidious little bronze' [*sic*] which she tried to pass off as a genuine Rodin.[107]

But it was Nuala O'Donel who was most fatally besotted with Rodin. She lived with her friend, the actress Suzanne Horden, in a splendid marbled studio with a raised dining room and a shimmering array of liqueur bottles in silver cases. She would receive Gwen on a 'grand divan', dressed in a grey velvet tea gown trimmed with grey fur, and hold forth on her two favourite subjects: her illustrious ancestry, and how poor she was.[108] Privately Gwen wanted to know how she reconciled her poverty with her grand surroundings; even her friend the actress used to run out of patience with the 'grand sujet' of her ancestry. (Eventually Suzanne told her that we all have the same ancestors, Adam and Eve.)[109] She was exhausting and exasperating, and in 1911 (when Gwen seems to have lost touch with her) she gassed herself, (wrongly) convinced that Rodin thought she had no talent and had stopped caring about her.[110] But Gwen did her best with her. She posed regularly for her and took her to the ophthalmologist's when she had eye disease;[111] she also asked Rodin (who was on the judging committee) if he could see his way to influencing the Salon to accept O'Donel's work that season.[112] For the next two or three years, Gwen was plagued with these women and their dramas. They all wanted to know about Rodin, dropping subtle hints, as the nature of his liaison with her became more apparent, about their own real or imagined *affaires* with him. She had to say that she had met him for the first time in Flodin's studio, because she thought if she told them she had gone to seek work with him on her own initiative, they would think she was a *coquotte*.[113]

Rodin (aka 'Julie') was entertained not only with stories of the lady painters, but also with scenes of domestic life. Since she was clearly intimate with him by the time she found a room of her own in the spring of 1906, he must have visited her in the Hôtel Mont Blanc, and some of the letters to Julie must have been written from there. It seems to have been inhabited by some strange, seedy characters. She began to wonder what to tell them if they asked her what she did: the concierge and her husband saw her one day coming out of her room with Flodin, and asked her if Flodin was a painter. When Gwen said she was a sculptress, the husband began to pull faces and shriek, 'She sees men and women naked! I bet she's seen a naked man, hasn't she!' Gwen said nothing, and his wife told him to shut up, they were not to pay any attention; he was only joking, men were all the same. Gwen assumed the people in the hostel must think she was an artist because they had seen her painting and drawing, but she was worried that they would misinterpret this.[114] She saw strange forms on the staircase. Edgar Quinet would suddenly begin howling and a very pale, cruel-looking man with a sneering face appeared in her room in the middle of the night: the place was clearly not entirely safe.[115]

There was another peculiar incident: a 20-franc piece disappeared from her purse, and she had already lost some of her things, including a little mirror, which Rodin had given her. She suspected the *coquotte* in the next room, and after finding out from the concierges where she was, interrupted the *coquotte*'s evening with her friends in a local restaurant, hauled her outside and marched her to the police station. The *coquotte* protested all the way down the street that it must have been the people upstairs, but she broke when she saw the red lamp of the police station ahead. She confessed, and it ended in tears for both of them, the *coquotte*, all dressed up in white silk and pearls, meekly following Gwen back to her room and handing over the 20 francs. She would hear her in the next room entertaining men who arrived in the small hours, she told Rodin – and Gwen had believed her when she said she was pining for her lost love.[116]

In September of 1905, Ida, Augustus, and Dorelia all came to Paris. That spring Dorelia had had her baby Pyramus, alone in a caravan on Dartmoor.[117] In the autumn, the lease came up on the house in Matching Green, and Ida and Dorelia decided that if there was to be change, they might as well go to Paris. In September, the entire John *ménage*, including Augustus, arrived in the two rooms Ida had taken for them at the Hôtel St-Pierre, in the rue de l'Ecole-de-Médecine.[118] So everyone was in Paris again, including, this time, four children (David, Caspar, Robin and Dorelia's baby, Pyramus). When they visited Gwen they found that she, too, was looking for an unfurnished room. 'Rodin suggested my leaving my room this afternoon and taking an unfurnished one – wasn't it kind of him?' she had confided to Ursula, though she did not tell any of the Johns.[119] She was thrilled by the prospect; it must have felt as if he wanted to involve himself in her life. He knew nothing, she told Ursula – disingenuously – about her room in the Hôtel Mont Blanc, he just thought 'it would be nicer to be "chez moi" & he is going to pay the 3 months rent', a plan which would obviously suit Gwen, and would also probably make his visits easier. (He continued to send her gifts of money for her rent until shortly before his death, in 1917.) He wanted to furnish it as well, she told Ursula, but she was not sure she would allow that. She was, commented Ida, 'always the same strange reserved creature':[120] little did she know.

Augustus surely suspected more: he had told her to be sure to let him know when Monsieur Rodin tired of her,[121] but apart from that he appears to have said nothing. Gwen entertained them all in her room, where she fed them on eggs, spinach and *charcuterie*,[122] and Dorelia made her a black velvet coat, for which Gwen paid her a hundred francs. This was much admired by Constance Lloyd, who wanted to paint her in it.[123] Edgar

Quinet was not very popular – Gwen's little cat was '*horrid*', Ida complained.[124] (She was not the only one who thought so. The cat had sprung a vicious attack on one of the lady painters, hurling herself at her the minute she arrived, shinnying up her dress and making for her eyes with her claws out, but Gwen was sure she had nothing against anyone personally, it was just 'une affaire de nerfs'.[125] Dorelia, serene as ever, suggested that Gwen should perhaps try singing to her. She copied out the words of 'Ben Bolt' for her, but Quinet was unimpressed.[126] When she had finished the coat, Dorelia began on a cream skirt, which Gwen decided on because she really wanted a checked silk one, but the checked silk was too expensive.[127] (Eventually she did have a checked one: she did a drawing of herself – *The Artist in her Room in Paris* – seated, bathed in light, wearing it.[128] Or perhaps she gave herself one by doing the drawing. Despite having the family in Paris, however, she spent Christmas Day on her own. Flodin invited her, but she preferred to read alone in her room, since it was easier that way to think uninterruptedly about Rodin. Her days of celebration, she told him, were the ones she spent with him.[129]

She thought all the time about everything he did, remembered everything he said to her; she went on thinking about the first moment he had spoken to her. His words, the way he looked at her, everything they had ever done together, were all engraved on her heart, she assured him.[130] He spent six days in January 1906 in Chartres with Rose and Rilke,[131] so she tried to do some new drawings for him while he was away. She had not done much, she told him when she wrote to him, but her room was tidy. A week seemed so long. Flodin was not well, so she was posing for a different lady in the afternoons, and she had been drawing Edgar Quinet. 'She is very amusing, my little cat,' she told him. She knew all her little ways by now, and though she had 'a very independent and headstrong character' Gwen felt sorry for her sometimes, she told Rodin; she tried to understand so many things with her 'little, troubled soul', but mostly she seemed to understand Gwen.[132] Edgar Quinet hardly ever obeyed her, but that was because she was contrary. If the concierge or any of the neighbours talked to Gwen in a loud voice, she got very cross, but that was because she thought they were scolding her.[133]

When Rodin came back, he suggested that if she did some more drawings he could try to sell them for her. At first she said that if he did she would buy a new dress, in pale blue or white, to wear for him.[134] But when she thought about it, she changed her mind: 'I am not an artist, I'm your model, and I want to stay being your model for ever. Because I'm happy.'[135] There was some satisfaction, though, in his thinking her a 'bel artiste'.[136] She took seriously his desire to deepen and broaden her knowledge, and tried to tell herself that if she painted and drew with him in mind, her work could have a higher purpose. But at the same time, she still wanted to stop where she had found happiness and to be accepted at her most fulfilled. She did not need money, she assured him, and if she did, she could do more modelling. 'I don't want to change my life in any way,' she told him. 'I'm afraid to.' There was a danger of overreaching this happiness. She worried that she would compromise it by not being able to concentrate fully on it; he worried that she would stagnate.

By February 1906, Rodin was getting ready to go to London again; he would leave on the 20th and stay there until 9 March. She was afraid he would forget about her. All this coming and going was making her very nervous, she told Flodin, who said this was nonsense, she had plenty of moral fibre. It was love which gave her that strength, Gwen told Rodin.[137] She had found a tranquillity and a gentleness within herself, which seemed to permeate all her thoughts. While he was gone she would sit at her table to the sounds of the *coquotte* entertaining her lover in the next room,[138] and write to him by lamplight.[139]

7

La Chambre sur la Cour (7 rue St Placide)

its lovely pale, clean furniture, clean curtains, its pink floor . . .[1]

Some time towards the end of 1905 or beginning of 1906 Gwen found her new room, and early in the spring of 1906 she moved into number 7 rue St Placide, a short, busy street in the sixth *arrondissement*, not far from the rue Edgar Quinet, with the Bon Marché – the busy, popular department store with its glamorous, ornate roofs and its enormous selection of mass-produced goods – tantalisingly at the end of the street.[2] She went there often to buy ribbons, dresses and dress material, stockings, gloves, decorations for her hats.[3] Sometimes Nuala O'Donel came with her, and pointed out things she thought were 'good forme'.[4] She was an extravagant shopper: with her, Gwen spent 15 francs (the equivalent of five mornings' posing) on a velvet shawl.[5] She wore one of her new dresses to pose for Flodin, who said she looked very *coquette*, she must be in love, dressed like that; before she met Monsieur Rodin she had been 'affreusement négligée'.[6]

Her room in the rue St Placide had lovely wallpaper and a pink floor, and there was a courtyard for Edgar Quinet to play in.[7] The concierge fitted a plank to serve as a windowsill, so that she could have small pots of ferns and flowers.[8] She loved coming home to her pretty room after posing, to her portraits of Rodin on the chimney breast and her own drawings on the walls; her books, the pale furniture and curtains and the pink parterre.[9] She kept it spotless and soon Rodin came to visit. He kept trying to persuade her to be calm, tranquil; to go for walks, eat, not neglect her drawing.[10] Even before the trees came into leaf there were beautiful flowers in the streets, and her new room was lovely for painting in, she told Dorelia, who now sometimes came to sit for her.[11] 'It's so beautiful here,' she wrote to Rodin, 'when I've finished eating and everything's clean and tidy, a little fire in the grate, a few flowers on the mantelpiece, and my little cat watching me from the bed . . . Every night I read the books you have given me, the wisdom of the philosophers is so far, so far from me!'[12] Yet no matter how happy she was, he still made her feel inadequate. She said she wished her 'ésprit' was like a garden of flowers, but in fact it was more like a little bit of waste ground where a wild flower came up once in a while – if that.[13]

She went on studying from the extracts she copied from works of religion and philosophy, occasionally marking them 'pas comprit' ('don't understand'),[14] then Rodin would undoubtedly discuss them with her. Flodin lent her the works of the religious thinker, Faber; from Rodin she borrowed the works of Schopenhauer, William James and Oscar Wilde. She still wanted to be more worthy of her lover; she was sure that if only she could be with him all the time, she could be the way he wanted her to be. She did not detect any improvement in herself, she admitted: there seemed to be no difference, except that her feelings for him just grew stronger. It was amazing, she would not have thought it possible. The problem was the amount of time she had to spend without him. It was when she had not seen him for several days that her faults began to show, since then, 'The jealous thoughts rise up in my heart, and the unreasonable desires.'[15] But in her room, writing to him, she was happy with anticipation. 'I can still promise you,' she told him, 'that one day you'll have a woman you can be proud of – a woman without caprices or *méchanceté* – if you can just be patient with me.'[16] He was her whole world, her *joie de vivre*: 'think of me if you have a moment on your own sometimes,' she urged him. She thought of him every moment of the day, and 'when night falls I see you in my dreams'.[17]

He sent notes to her in the rue St Placide, which made her rapturously happy ('Heureuse, heureuse moi! J'ai reçu ce soir une lettre adorable de mon Maître!').[18] But the new room, far from giving her something to divert her, seemed to have the opposite effect, making her even more determined to reinvent herself for him. She began to get feverish with wanting him; sometimes she would stay in bed all day, determined to be completely better, and beautiful for him, by the time she saw him again.[19] She liked to lie in bed in the mornings and look at her room, with the engraving he had given her on the wall at the side of the bed, because she thought it looked perfect from the bed.[20] She loved tidying it, and watering her ferns on the windowsill when the houses were dark and there were long shadows in her room. She so wanted to be by his side all the time, she told him. She wished he could be there when it got dark, then she could light a candle, and perhaps he would put his arm round her. She would not talk, and he would probably think her stupid, but she would be so happy.[21] But all this waiting and anticipation were exhausting. She would lie awake thinking about him, then sleep late in the mornings, eating at the little restaurant in the rue St Placide at odd times of the day at weekends.[22]

'Courage,' he kept telling her: 'eat well, and know that I am your friend, alas very tired, who reads your letters (which are very touching) and who loves you.'[23] He lent her *Medée* (*Medea*), about a woman who killed her children and the woman her husband had left her for. It made her think that perhaps all women (and men) were capable of causing tragedy. She told him that if anyone tried to separate her from him she would kill herself, not someone else.[24] She had a dream about him: they were in the country together and he was making coloured drawings of the trees and she was sitting beside him. To their right there were mountains and a river, to their left, the trees. '*Mon maître*,' she appealed to him, 'what world is this world of dreams?' Whatever it was, she liked it more than the country of doubt and fear they were actually in.[25]

It hurt her that he wanted to hide their liaison from everyone, even from his friends. She was sure nobody would say anything to his wife. But it gradually began to dawn on her that this was not the problem: it was that he did not think her sufficiently distinguished to be seen with him in public. She began to wonder whether he knew that she had been admired by other men, and told him that others had seemed to find her beautiful: perhaps that would make him proud of her. After all, everyone must know they were made for each other, surely their faces gave them away. She hoped he would not abandon her just for the sake of convention and discretion. She made it clear to him that she would not be happy either if his wife found out. But at least since she was his model, he had an excuse to see her often.[26] One day, she told 'Julie', she was sure she would manage to please him. She would go on trying to entertain him in writing, and her letters would soon become so clear, so clear . . . one day, he would understand everything she was trying to say to him.[27]

By now, both Winifred and Ursula knew about Rodin; so too, almost certainly, did Rilke who was back in Paris. He had been living with Rodin and Rose since September 1905, in a small pavilion of his own in the grounds of the Villa des Brillants (he was to stay there until May 1906 when, ironically, they temporarily fell out because Rodin discovered that Rilke had been writing to some of his friends), so in the spring of 1906, when Gwen moved into the rue St Placide, he was very involved with Rodin and with his day-to-day affairs.[28] Since he first met Rodin in September 1902 when, inspired by his work, he had come to Paris from Germany to write a book about him,[29] his respect for him had been limitless, and Rodin's work, he told him, had become 'the example for my life and my art'; he wanted to learn from him not only how to work, but how to live.[30] He had been intermittently in Paris since then, and undoubtedly knew about the liaison with Gwen since occasionally, as Rodin's secretary, he replied to her letters on his behalf. He may not have talked to her specifically about Rodin but they talked as friends, and her view of love – which was essentially romantic – was consistent with his theories of romantic love. In 1903 he had been writing to Franz Xaver Kappus, a young poet who had sent his first poems to him for his comments, and during 1903 and 1904, when Gwen first started coming to Rodin's studio, he wrote nine letters which were later collected and published (together with a later one) as *Letters to a Young Poet*. They show the cast of his mind at the time, and reveal his thinking about the complexities of being a creator and the exigences of making works of art. He recommended Rodin to Kappus (along with the 'great, great writer' Jacobsen) as the greatest artist of his time, 'who has not his equal among all artists living today'.[31]

He may now have counselled Gwen, as he had recently counselled Kappus, to ignore the pressures of the outside world and 'go into yourself'. 'Search for the reason that bids you to write,' he had written to Kappus in February 1903:

> find out whether it is spreading out its roots in the deepest places of your heart, acknowledge to yourself whether you would have to die if it were denied you to write. This above all – ask yourself in the stillest hour of your night: *must* I write? Delve into yourself for a deep answer. And if this should be affirmative . . . build your life according to this necessity; your life even into its most indifferent and slightest hour must be a sign of this urge and a testimony to it. Then draw near to

Nature. Then try, like some first human being, to say what you see and experience and love and lose.[32]

For Rilke, as for Rodin, the vision of creation and the artist's search for knowledge were essentially sexual. Physical pleasure was like seeing or taste, 'a great unending experience . . . a rallying towards exalted moments'. All beauty was 'a quiet enduring form of love and longing': 'O that man might take this secret, out of which the world is full even to its littlest things, more humbly to himself and bear it, endure it, more seriously and feel how terribly difficult it is, instead of taking it lightly.'[33] It was Rilke who witnessed the process of Gwen's awakening with Rodin; he was the one who, for a while, from autumn 1905 onwards saw her every day. He respected what was happening to her, and befriended her. He also understood the difficulty, and the importance, of solitude. As he had told Kappus, 'only the individual who is solitary is like a thing placed under profound laws'.[34] But he also understood the kind of love that longs to fling itself into the abyss, the desire of the young to 'scatter themselves, just as they are, in all their untidiness, disorder, confusion . . . And then what? What is life to do to this heap of half-battered existence which they call their communion and which they would gladly call their happiness?'[35] Like Rodin, he recommended composure, the attempt to be more collected, more *recueillie*; the process of 'saving and gathering' oneself so as to love more deeply.[36] 'We *are* solitary,' he had written to Kappus in August 1904,[37] we may delude ourselves that we are not, but it would surely be better to find a way of living with this knowledge, the better and more fully to know ourselves. This is a profoundly romantic vision, taking account of the artist's need to see communion as a complex act of self-awareness and recognising the particular quality and intensity of solitude required to make a work of art. But it ignores the nature of female romantic passion, the desire to be subject *to* the all-encompassing male. Perhaps not all women feel this, but Gwen certainly did. When she said she was utterly happy sitting for Rodin and would rather model for his works than make her own, she meant it. Her struggle to paint, counterpointed with this deep knowledge that she had found fulfilment as a woman without needing to extend her ambitions as an artist, required a strength which must have felt superhuman. Perhaps, moreover, elements of her own artistic practice were germinating at the same time. It was a difficult and strenuous network of demands to maintain, particularly in the shadow of a man with the impact and charisma of Rodin.

For a while – for several months during 1905 and 1906 – she stopped painting. When she started again, it was her new room that drew her back into her art. 'My room is lovely,' she wrote to him – 'if you knew how I loved it you'd think I perhaps exaggerate its beauty. But I'm going to do some drawings or paintings to show you what I think is so pretty about it. I'm going to do some in the mirror of my wardrobe – with me as the figure, occupied somehow with something . . . like the Dutch paintings in subject.'[38] She now began some poignant, haunting self-portraits, the first of many she would do, of female figures in Parisian rooms. She began working consistently on one, and started another which she put aside, but which she would take up again and complete later: paintings of herself in the subdued afternoon or early evening light of her room in the rue St Placide: *La Chambre sur la Cour*,[39] in which the figure sits sewing at the window, and *A Lady Reading*, of a standing figure holding a book, which she finished a year or two later (after she moved away from the rue St Placide).[40] The female figure – recognisably Gwen – takes her personality from the quality of the space and atmosphere of the room she had lovingly constructed to accommodate Rodin; the pictures show the lady waiting serenely, in a Dutch-inspired interior, juxtaposed with objects – Rodin's portrait and her own drawings on the walls, a billowing curtain; her desk, bookshelves, her wicker chair – which together compose the space in which she waits.

These subtly, softly lit forms were painted in a spirit of determination and hope: the female Romantic artist longs, not for death – the final transcendence – but, expectantly, for life. The poise, concentration and delicacy were nevertheless charged with energy, the figures contained but alert. *La Chambre sur la Cour* is absolutely suggestive of serenity and harmony, conveying a quality of inwardness which Gwen was to develop as one of the main characteristics of her portraiture. The idea of painting a corner of the room may also have been one she discussed with Rilke, since he had already shared his thoughts on this, too, with 'the young poet', Kappus. Only by living wholly, by excluding nothing, he had told him, will we ever be fully alive in relation to another:

For if we think of this existence of the individual as a larger or smaller

> room, it appears evident that most people learn to know only a corner of their room, a place by the window, a strip of floor on which they walk up and down. Thus they have a certain security. And yet that dangerous insecurity is so much more human which drives the prisoners in Poe's stories to feel out the shapes of their horrible dungeons and not be strangers to the unspeakable terror of their abode.[41]

In Gwen's later work, particularly in her portraiture, she would gradually tone down the surrounding detail in her portraits, distorting the figure, muting and obscuring the ground. But for the time being, she concentrated on establishing the corner of the room. 'We, however, are not prisoners,' Rilke had continued. 'No traps or snares are set about us, and there is nothing which should intimidate or worry us.'[42]

Gwen struggled with herself as she began work on these paintings, and she fought for a long time. '*Everything* interests me more than painting,' she would still be telling Ursula, a year or two later.[43] When she told Rodin, 'I get far more pleasure now out of writing to you than I do from drawing',[44] she was being quite straightforward. What she wanted was for the room to become reality. It was meant to be a starting point, not a substitute, for the life she wanted them to have together and she wanted him in it all the time. At first, she refused to paint in it. She made it as orderly and desirable a space as she could, but she wanted to make love, not paint pictures, and she spared him none of her frustrations.[45] She was endlessly impatient for his visits: 'come yourself *mon Maître* to my room, I will be your little Marie and ask nothing of you except un embrasse and I'll be so happy, happier than you can possibly imagine'.[46] She loved him totally, and in her terms unselfishly; she would never try to disturb his work, or interfere in his *affaires*.[47] But she struggled continually with the immense self-control required by this arrangement, at the same time complying with and resisting the need to keep her feelings under control. She knew that they were creative, powerful, and integral to the search for spiritual fulfilment which, ironically, he wanted her to commit herself to in his absence. In the evenings she would sit writing to him in the dusk, reluctant to light the lamp because the lamplight seemed to interrupt her thoughts: 'Mon Maître I want to talk to you about happiness . . .'[48]

Life in the rue St Placide now began to take on a rhythm. She posed in the mornings for one of the lady artists, drew in the afternoons, and when it got too dark to draw she went for a walk, then did more drawing after dinner.[49] On sunny spring afternoons she walked by the Seine to take advantage of the sunshine, working again in the evenings by lamplight.[50] Whenever he called for her, she would go and pose for Rodin. It was still painful to leave him after the sessions. Sometimes, she would double back and look through the windows of his studio, though it was difficult to see him in the gloaming. But she had a new incentive to work, since she was trying to produce something he would be pleased with. He had brought her alive, she told him: 'I was a little solitaire, no-one helped me or awoke me before I met you.'[51]

The move to the rue St Placide, moreover, had given her more confidence with other people. Despite a stupid concierge, who never scolded her little boy when he taunted Edgar Quinet, the people in the apartment building seemed very pleasant. But she thought this was probably because she had more confidence with Rodin and so had become more likeable herself.[52] Rodin had said that the important things in a love affair were the things they did when they were alone together. But Gwen disagreed: though those times were delightful, they did not last. 'What gives me a joy which stays with me more or less are the thoughts or sentiments or half-thoughts in my heart, which come from making love with you.' The most gratifying thought of all was that he understood her, and that he understood and accepted her love.

As for the idea of loving another man, she simply could not imagine it: he would have to have Rodin's body, Rodin's face, Rodin's eyes; Rodin's way of looking at her.[53] She knew she sometimes seemed stupid when she was with him but that was because desire made her shy. But all her ideas were focused on this great love. 'Maybe if I loved you less I'd have more "idées variées",' she told him, but what would be the virtue of that?[54] He wanted her to spread her wings more, but she told him that all she could do was listen to her heart, and it always said the same things. If only they could be together more, she was sure she could become more *noble*. She could do anything, if only she could be sure of him. She thought she was living as he wanted her to, but she did feel fragile when she was alone. He made her so sad when he implied that she was not sufficiently amusing for him: 'I want so, so much to be a *grande dame instruite*.'[55]

She said she hoped he would never be angry if she arrived at his studio and found other people there.[56] But she must understand, he told her, the importance of discretion: he had some enemies, and his share of *chagrins*: she was not to exacerbate these.[57] That was understandable, she reassured him, every truly good man had enemies. He was very ill in March 1906, with a dreadful attack of the *grippe*, but she interpreted his absences as neglect.[58] She assured him of her discretion, but insisted that it was the precariousness of the situation which made her desperate to be near him. 'I envy the poets,' she told him, 'they can always keep the things they love, through the beauty of their language.'[59] He wanted to be assured of her goodwill and moderation.[60] She would acquire these things with his help, she told him. As for the difference in their ages, she could not see that that made any difference, really, except that he was a great artist, and she was going to make sure she was worthy of being his model. The more he pushed her, the more she dug her heels in.

It was frustrating, not to be able to talk about Rodin. She missed Winnie, and wished she could be with her in Paris.[61] There were people she could talk to about him – Flodin, Miss O'Donel; perhaps Constance Lloyd – but she had to refer to him as her *Maître* and an artist, not as her lover. She tried to explain to him that women did not like talking about their lovers except to very intimate friends; that was why she missed her sister. He was making it difficult for her to make friends. She could be more friendly with Flodin and Miss O'Donel if it was not for him – she genuinely liked them, and they knew this – but she could see that they were both very jealous women.[62] Flodin now began to confide her secret lesbian desires. She was not to tell Rodin, she said: of course I'll tell him, replied Gwen (and she did).[63] Occasionally, she would find him in Flodin's studio: she was struck, the first time she saw him there, by how handsome he looked when she came upon him unexpectedly.[64]

One day, she arrived home to find a note from Flodin telling her to come quickly to her studio, she might find her *maître* there. When she arrived, full of nerves, he wanted to make love with her in front of Flodin. Afterwards, he asked the two women to pose together, probably for an erotic drawing or series of erotic drawings.[65] She found the whole experience, including the posing with Flodin, very erotic and tantalising, and Flodin made sure it continued after Rodin had left. It was not the same as being with him, she later told him, but it was 'quelquechose'.[66] It is unlikely that this became a regular event, much more likely that the whole thing was choreographed with a particular set of drawings in mind. But it caused her more problems with poor Miss O'Donel, who must have found out from Flodin what she was being left out of and now became increasingly difficult and odd. Gwen had thought Miss O'Donel would be pleased when she discovered that Gwen and Rodin were lovers, Gwen innocently told Rodin, but instead she now decided Gwen was wicked. She was just jealous, said Rodin. Surely not, said Gwen, she didn't have the looks to be jealous.[67] But eventually she became so jealous and peculiar that Gwen had to stop posing for her.[68]

Rodin now asked if she had enough money. He knew she had, she told him. She could earn more by posing more often if she wanted to, but she wanted some time to herself, to think about him.[69] She went to see Flodin again, this time to help her pack to go to Finland. She went off in a blaze of poetic sentiment, saying how beautiful Gwen and Rodin had been together, showering Gwen with kisses and wishing she could take her with her. She would be delighted to go to Finland if only Rodin could go too, said Gwen.[70] She had a strange, futuristic dream. She climbed to the top of the Eiffel Tower with Rodin, and when they got there they found themselves surrounded by water. They took off their clothes and bathed in the sea, and were very happy. But after a while a man shouted, 'La machine va descender' and they had to get dressed again.[71]

Both Ursula and Winifred went on encouraging her to keep painting. Ursula was very delicate, never overstepping the mark by offering unwanted advice. Winnie was more directive. She advised her to eat more raisins and drink lemonade (without sugar). She was eager to hear all about the new room: was it 'high up or low down? I have to have a sunny room.'[72] On the subject of Rodin, she was silent for the time being, though she would later urge Gwen not to get 'soft' on him.[73] For now, she thought Gwen could try a little harder with her writing: 'Your spelling is rather bad, you will always use s instead of c. dancing. concert.' More importantly, 'Tell me what pictures you have in your mind's eye. I wish you wouldn't give it up.' Would she like to go to Canada, to visit Winnie and her new beau? The beau wanted to meet Gwen, though he did not much want to meet Papa. She was getting a piano.[74] But neither the piano nor the beau was sufficiently tempting for Gwen to leave Rodin.

That summer, in the middle of the night, Edgar Quinet produced a *petit*. In fact, Quinet had three kittens but Gwen drowned the first two. She did it very quickly, wrapping them in paper and drowning them before they could make their first cries. (There cannot have been room for four cats in one room, and the concierges would certainly not have appreciated a menagerie; Gwen evidently took the unsentimental, countrywoman's line, despite her love for Edgar Quinet.) Then she worried that there would not be a third kitten, because he came such a long time after the first two. Finally, he arrived, covered in a sort of transparent skin, Gwen told 'Julie', and the cat could not get him out, so Gwen cut him out with scissors. When the kittens were being born the cat howled so loudly that Gwen was afraid she would wake the neighbours. She shut the window, heated up some water and talked to the cat all the time to reassure her as she gnawed gently at her hand.[75]

The birth of the kitten did not seem to distract Edgar Quinet from her affection for Gwen, which she found touching.[76] But then one day when she was taking her for a ride in the train, the cat leapt out of the window and got lost. Rodin had said she should not really take her into the country but it was such a pleasure to see her outside in the fresh air, she was so happy: 'elle rayonne de bonheur,' she told 'Julie'.[77] Gwen was distraught. She did not think, she told Rodin, she could ever be pretty and happy for him again, now that Quinet was lost. It was a major disaster. Rodin wrote a note appealing for the cat's return; everyone in the building at 7 rue St Placide was alerted.[78] She was missing for eleven days. While Gwen was searching, the John family moved to rooms in the rue Dareau with all the children and were living rather like gypsies. This was not, however, sufficiently wild for Augustus, who had discovered St Honorine in Brittany, where he found a band of real Piedmontese gypsies assembled in about a hundred vans. He was drawing them in charcoal, and sent word that the others should join him.[79] They all duly did so, and Dorelia's second child, Romilly, was born there. There were 'cliffs full of arches & covered with pale green seaweed', Dorelia sent word to Gwen, from which Augustus was diving headlong into the waves; wouldn't Gwen like to join them? In June, while Rodin was in Oxford, she did so. Quinet had been found, and needed a break since she was still thin and nervous from her ordeal. Gwen, Quinet and Tigre, the new kitten (a present for Dorelia) arrived, and stayed for five days. Gwen bathed every day at Port-en-Bessin and told Augustus that Rodin had said she was a 'bel artiste'. She was back in Paris in time for his return.

Rodin was still intermittently working on Whistler's Muse, and from time to time he would send for Gwen so that he could continue with the work. He also, during 1906, completed his busts of Howard de Walden, Berthelot, Noialles, Leygues, Goloubeff, and George Bernard Shaw.[80] Occasionally, while he was working on Shaw, Gwen would peep in and see how the work was going.[81] When he was tired, he kept a low profile and she had only found out that he was working with Shaw by reading the newspapers. She was upset, because having heard nothing from him for a while she had assumed he was resting.[82] Often when she arrived at his studio, he would be surrounded by people. Sometimes when this happened, she would run after him when he left.[83] When it was clear that they were not going to have an opportunity to be alone together, he might squeeze her hand as he passed her: it was better than nothing. Her appeals to him grew more plangent. 'Will you come soon? Or ask me to come to you? It doesn't feel natural to me to go for so long without caresses from the man I love! the days are hard . . .'[84] She was trying to be patient, but as the days went by she felt real despair. When she could bear it no longer, he would reappear: floods of happiness, but then the old fear, that he would leave her alone for just as long before the next time.[85]

One day, she took a tram as far as Vanves and looked for his house again. She could not find it this time – the Villa des Brillants is tucked away at the top of a hill in Meudon, off the beaten track – and she found herself instead on a big road with fields on either side. It was a cloudy, windy day. She seemed to be in the country, there were *paysans* making fires, and strange, delicious scents hung on the air. She ended up in a small village, with houses grouped round a green, and a lake with ducks and geese. Everything was quiet and peaceful; the sun still hid behind the clouds. It began to get dark, so she retraced her steps and found a road that took her to Issy, where a woman helped her to find the tram.[86] These pilgrimages could be disturbing. She talked to strangers and got lost, and once she found herself in the country, she tended to be filled with the old recklessness. Strangers always seemed to follow her, and she sometimes scared herself before she managed to fend them off.[87] She was becoming overwrought, and sometimes she was too exhausted to hold a pose. She had to rest every quarter of an hour one day, posing for the 'Dame Allemande', who did not take kindly to this.[88] Rodin kept saying she should find more wealthy painters to pose for but she was reluctant to seek them out in case she did not like the work. Anyway, perhaps they would be like Miss O'Donel.[89]

Gwen now began reprimanding Rodin. She had burned herself. He told her she was mad; she told him that if he was determined to make her so unhappy, what did he expect?[90] He had promised to get her a copy of Shakespeare's plays: well, she was not waiting any longer, she would buy it herself. She was sick of being treated like an eyesore in his studio, she did not want to be called 'Mademoiselle' by him again. All this was making her iller by the hour: didn't he care at all?[91] But then she would rally. When spring came, she would get herself a white dress and come to Meudon, perhaps with Miss O'Donel. She would go to his garden and see him there with his dogs, and all his lovely things . . .[92] 'Everything you say about moderation is true,' she told him; he must instruct her in the art of it.[93]

By the end of the year Ida, Dorelia and all their children were still in Paris. They had seen Rodin's head of Gwen in the Salon, and came to visit her in the rue St Placide, where they met Constance Lloyd ('nice and ugly and awkward', according to Ida) and Miss Hart, who had visibly 'attached herself uncomfortably to Gwen'.[94] Christmas 1906 was spent with Ida, Dorelia, Augustus, all the children and Wyndham Lewis, who came to visit.[95] Everybody got wonderful presents, the boys had exciting train sets and they ate turkey and Christmas pudding.

Gwen had another dream: she and Rodin were alone together in a boat in the sea. All they could see was the sea around them. It was a desultory dream: she was at sea with him, and her fantasy of a romantic elopement now seemed elusive. In the dream, they seemed to be stranded together in an elemental region. Undaunted, she told him she thought this spelled out the reality of their liaison. He was alone because he was so wise and such a great artist, and they were at sea together because she loved him.[96] Perhaps the dream had something to do with the ancient poem she copied out for him, 'Le Temps', in which the sea is a metaphor for time itself.

> Impénétrable Mer, Ocean de Temps
> Des Années sont tes vagues! et tes noirs eaux
> Sont soumatre parle sol des larmes humains!
> Soi oude sans grève qui dans tes flux et flots
>
> (Impenetrable sea, ocean of time
> The years are your waves! and your dark waters
> Are all our tears
> The ebb and flow of all eternity.)[97]

Her interpretation of her dream was not a particularly inspired or inspiring one, but it expressed what she felt; its poetry was in its unflinching integrity.

8

Ida

some land of miraculous caves . . .[1]

For a year or so after she moved into the rue St Placide in 1906, Gwen worked quietly, trying to incorporate into her painting and into her spiritual studies Rodin's lessons of harmony, restraint and self-control, in a complicated search for self-knowledge and inner peace. She copied out Carlyle's maxim: 'Silence is the element in which great things are formed',[2] and she wrote Rodin a short, fourteen-page novel, thinly disguising it, when she sent it to 'Julie', as a fragment of manuscript she had found in the forest. She wrote it in the style of an eighteenth-century epistolary novel, a series of letters from the female narrator to her sister, in which she tells the story of her love affair with an artist. They have been conducting their liaison in his studio, where they are interrupted by the concierge. When he leaves the studio, the artist asks the narrator to walk a little way with him ('Vous m'accompagner un peu Mademoiselle?')[3] – the story clearly echoes that of Gwen and Rodin, who thought it very kind, and beautifully done. Her style was very natural, he told her, and the story reminded him of *Pamela*.[4]

When the summer came she knew he would be less likely to visit. He would not come if it was very hot as he said her room in the rue St Placide was too humid. She was still dreaming vividly and told Julie she had dreamt he was with her in her room, but they were interrupted before they could make love, by Julie herself, who had magically come back from Canada with a stranger, who told Rodin she had something very important to tell him, and he must go with her. Gwen asked him to come back afterwards, but he said no. She tried to get dressed quickly to follow them but struggled with her blouse, and by the time she got out into the road, half-dressed, they had disappeared. She ran to his studio but the concierge said he had just left for Meudon. She woke up in despair, and lay for hours listening to the rain and trying to recover from the dream.[5] Rodin did not seem to want them to be alone together any more.[6] She kept begging him to stop saying this: 'please, please don't say we can't be alone together again,' she wrote to him. How were they supposed to go on being lovers, if they were never alone together? She was acutely aware that he liked to be surrounded by sophisticated women, but she wished he could love her for herself, rather than trying to convince her that compared with them she had talent. She did not want to be loved, she told him, just for her small shred of talent. He walked down to the rue de Rennes with her one evening and bought her some pink paper flowers.[7] But he kept telling her she was too demanding, immodest and wild, like a little animal. Even this, however, did not succeed in beating her down. 'Je suis quelquechose,' she told him.[8] By spring 1907 he was advising her to try to find a new room, somewhere cooler, with more sunlight, telling her to give notice when she paid the rent and ask Miss O'Donel to help her find somewhere.[9] She now began the difficult task of finding a room that was neither impossibly expensive nor uncomfortably small.

She told the concierge she wanted to give notice when she went down to pay the rent. He was none too pleased, since he said notice had to be given at 'demi-terme', not before, whereupon she began to have second thoughts, since it was unlikely she would ever find a room she liked as much, with such pretty wallpaper (depicted in *La Chambre sur la Cour*, it was decorative and tasteful, with a faint stripe and a criss-cross design, very much of the period). Also, she would surely never find another room with a courtyard for Edgar Quinet to run about in, and concierges tended not to like having cats in the house, despite Edgar Quinet's evident exceptional intelligence. She liked the rue St Placide, which was a pretty street. And Rodin was wrong, her room was not humid; it was quite close to the river, and she liked its shape. If she got Miss O'Donel to help her, she was bound to choose a room a long way from the river which was ugly and square.[10]

Gwen gave notice definitively at 'demi-terme', the concierge and his wife grumbling as she signed the papers that they could not understand why she was leaving. She said she had told them months ago that she needed more air and some sunshine, but the concierge said, 'there's no sunlight anywhere in Paris at this time of year'. In fact the sun shone on the rue St Placide every morning, but there was not a ray of sunshine in the courtyard at number 7; her flowers always either stayed alive past their best or died too soon because of it. She tried to cheer them up by telling them she had not found another room yet, and if she was unhappy when she did, she would come back.[11] But the concierge was still peeved, and kept interrupting her as she tried to draw, knocking on her door and shouting in a loud voice, 'Open the door!' 'Why?' 'To show someone your room!' Then he would bring people in and stay a deliberately long time, ridiculously pointing out each item of furniture. 'Look, you can put your wardrobe with the mirror *there*, and *there* is a nice big space to put your bed, and at the side there you can put your bedside table, *like that*, and then you see you can put a work table *there*, and your dressing table just here . . .' He would go over to the window, open both the shutters and shout, 'And you'll have *plenty* of fresh air!' When he said, 'and you've plenty of sunlight!' she could bear it no longer, and called out, 'No, there's no sunlight, that's not true!' but he pretended he had not heard. His wife seemed to be equally obsessed with the wardrobe, bringing in people and shouting, 'There's a nice wardrobe over there with a mirror!' – 'As if I'd leave my wardrobe in the room!' Gwen grumbled to 'Julie'.[12]

By the summer of 1907, everyone seemed to be on the move again. Augustus had now found a studio off the Boulevard St Germain, in the Cour de Rohan, rue de Jardinet. By the time he moved into it in March 1907, Ida – now heavily pregnant with her fifth child – had sublet the studio in the rue Dareau, and Dorelia had moved with Pyramus and Romilly into 48 rue de Château. Everybody was still at reasonably close quarters, but still nobody knew about Rodin. The Johns had their own problems. Dorelia seemed to have found serene independence but Ida, exhausted sometimes to the point of despair with child-rearing and constant pregnancy, now had Alick Schepeler, Augustus's latest inscrutable discovery, to contend with.[13] Gwen decided to visit Nuala O'Donel, which turned out to be a mistake. Why hadn't Gwen been to see her before, she wanted to know, hadn't she got her postcard? Gwen said she had not realised a postcard amounted to a formal invitation, she was oblivious of such conventions. 'I suppose you think you're a complete original . . .?' sneered Miss O'Donel. '. . . because you're a model? You're not the only model I know, there are perhaps two hundred in Paris, do you think you're any different from them?'[14] This did not seem to be the moment to ask for her help to look for a room.

Finally, in spring 1907, Gwen found an attic room not far from the river, just round the corner from the rue St Placide. It was an apartment which looked out on to a pretty, light courtyard with a tree, at number 87 rue du Cherche-Midi, the eighteenth-century 'Hotel de Montmorency'. It was a much grander street than the rue St Placide, with a better reputation and a more substantial history; the painter Ernest Hébert had lived next door at number 85 during the nineteenth century. The rooms were large, with a wide, traditional staircase spiralling through the centre of the building. There were five floors including the sloping attic rooms which comprised the *quatrième étage*, where Gwen's room was. Her view out on to the courtyard was leafy and peaceful. Her room was on the left at the top of the stairs. 'Frappy fort' [*sic*], she wrote to Rodin on her first day there, 'd'être entendu à travers ma vestibule!' ('Knock hard, so that I can hear you across my hall!')[15] She had been moving all evening, from seven until 10.30, dealing with two gigantic, drunken removal men who arrived an hour late and fought her throughout the complicated fiasco of getting all her things on and off their horse and cart, up the stairs and into her new room. The famous wardrobe became a bone of contention all over again, this time because the men swore they would not be able to get it up the stairs, and when they got it up to the fourth floor, that they would not be able to get it through the door. The concierge and all the other tenants assembled to watch the display, the concierge helping by holding on to the rope and shouting a lot.

They broke off in the middle to go to the *charbonnière* for a drink (the coalseller's, which in those days always had a bar) for which they demanded 50 centimes, and they kept trying to load Gwen's paintings and her hats on to their cart, even though she had insisted she would carry those herself. They kept falling over the furniture, each one saying the other didn't know what he was doing because he was drunk. All the neighbours pitched in. At one point, she told Rodin, she saw what looked like a man with four legs in her bedroom, helping the removal man to lift the bed while he also steadied the wardrobe. A bald man from downstairs – a bit of a 'dandy', Gwen thought – busily translated everything into English, giving her a running commentary of advice on how to deal with removal men. Two ladies came and put lamps on the staircase. But the best moment was when the 'dandy', after arguing with the men for half an hour when they demanded their money, bargained the whole job down to 21 francs for her. As they became more and more furious, he stayed calm and kept saying, 'je vous demande infiniment pardon'.

She was very touched by the experience, and by the kindness of everyone in getting involved in her move. She felt sure English people would not have done so, they would have opened their doors to have a look and said to themselves, 'Oh, a girl moving house – how boring – nothing to do with us!' She asked Rodin whether she ought to pay calls to thank the neighbours, telling him she did not really want to encourage the idea that she expected to have a lot of time on her hands to stand around gossiping, but she was very touched by their display of solidarity. Later on, she went out again and found a restaurant in the rue du Cherche-Midi, where she ordered lamb with green beans and a glass of wine, pocketing the lamb for Edgar Quinet, who was waiting for her on the stairs at the rue St Placide. After another glass of wine, she went to collect her and take her to her new home at 87 rue du Cherche-Midi.

Gwen was very proud of her new room. It was a beautiful space, with slanting light, and it became the subject of some of her most serene, most harmonious paintings. It was much fresher than her room in the rue St Placide, and she woke early in the mornings, feeling the air on her face. Sometimes she was ready to get up by six o'clock.[16] One morning she woke up at four, and lay and watched the room getting light. It was curious to see it in the half-light, it looked like a different room, mysterious and beautiful. Every day she did more to it, to make it tidy and attractive, it was such a pleasure to look at. She liked sitting at the open window and looking out across the courtyard at the tree. In the evenings when it got dark she could look up at the changing sky and almost believe she was in the country. She was to draw and paint it empty with her wicker chair, bathed in light, as the central focus; or with herself as subject, alert, attentive. She waited expectantly for Rodin to visit, imagining him at home in Meudon, looking at the sky and the countryside as the sun came up, perhaps remarking that the weather seemed to be getting chiller now.

To 'Julie' she wrote, 'Ma chambre est bien fraiche et ombragée les matins maintenant' (My room is beautifully fresh and shady in the mornings now). Walking down the rue du Cherche-Midi one day, she had glanced up at a neighbouring apartment, where she noticed through an open window a room gently shaded, with softly graded light, which looked wonderfully soft and cool. One day the door to this apartment was open, so she went in and asked the owner how she shaded the room. There was a simple blind at the window; she took the details of it, and found an identical blind for her own room.[17] She did a restrained drawing in wash and Chinese white of a woman dressing, with the blind at the window.[18] She is stooped so that the viewer is looking at her back, the lower torso is draped and she bends for a moment to attend to a catch or fold in her skirt or dress; the blind is raised, the window is open and the light bathes her form as she stands just slightly to the side of the light source. It has the same haunting qualities as *A Corner of the Artist's Room in Paris*, a graceful nostalgia reminiscent of *Interior with Figures*, and also the intimacy of a painting by Sickert or Gore. The drawing is gently witty, celebrating typical Parisian features: the panelling, the huge key in the door. The figure subtly suggests the voluptuousness of Manet, or the nerved-up agility of early Picasso; light washes the ceiling, the floor, the door. The room does not look like Gwen's room in the rue du Cherche-Midi. If it is, the drawing is of a different corner from the one in the painting she later did of it, but the blind is very much a feature, training the eye towards the window which frames the light source. The model, judging from the form of the head and neck and tumbling hair, and the stance of the figure, was probably either Grilda Boughton-Leigh or her sister Chloe.

Grilda came to see Gwen at number 87 rue du Cherche-Midi and reported back to Chloe how pretty and tidy it was. Chloe now came to pose, alert but slightly dishevelled, for a new portrait. She sat in a crumpled, grey checked dress, her hair down, her hair ribbon and pendant slightly askew. The figure is caught almost in mid-movement and the pose seems glimpsed, like a moment caught by the camera. It has something of the delicate intimacy of *The Student*, the portrait of Dorelia which Gwen had painted in Toulouse. Chloe gives the impression that the artist has just caught her in the frame, as she is about to raise her left hand or to say something; or as if she has just stopped talking. Gwen did not yet know her well (at this stage, she was still 'Miss Leigh') but her openness, and Gwen's sympathy with her subject, are evident. Though their relationship was still quite formal, the portrait has a quality of intimate informality; it is a subjective interpretation of her sitter, suggesting unpretentiousness and gentleness and hinting at reciprocal warmth. Somehow, through her candid attention to surfaces – the crinkled dress, the hair, the texture of the skin – Gwen has succeeded in conveying the exact tenor of the sitter's inner life, and Chloe is attentive, alert, preoccupied, ever so slightly *distraite*, with the potential to be both nervily and deeply engaged. She was interested in Gwen's work, and they discussed it together. Over the years, they would become close friends. Gwen told her she had begun to work on another painting, and when Chloe went back to London they wrote to each other, Chloe referring to the new painting as the 'chef d'oeuvre inconnu'.[19]

In the spring of 1907 Gwen started going to classes again, at Colarossi's school.[20] The portrait of Chloe shows the effects of new thinking about the function of portraiture, as well as the infiltration of new technical ideas, and it is consistent with the French school of subjectivism which, with its attention to surface, aimed at capturing through a rapid glimpse the inner life of the sitter and at the same time the nature of the artist's subjective response to the figure. One of the portrait's striking features is that the space Chloe sits in functions more effectively as ground (simply a way of highlighting the form and tones of the figure) than, in the more representational sense, as an 'actual' room. The room as a space to situate the figure now extends out beyond a corner or slice into a more infinite space, the larger space Rilke had described as the natural setting for Poe's characters, who were exposing themselves to a more risky but more profound style of self-knowledge than those content with knowing only a corner of themselves.[21] The ground is more or less abstract, and the single framed drawing which hangs to the left of the figure, just above her head, is a comment on perspective rather than a representational indication of her lifestyle. (The perspective and proportions of this portrait were obviously crucial; after she had finished it, Gwen later added a strip of wood, three-quarters of an inch high, along the foot of the picture, enabling her to paint in the whole of the hands, which in the original version were cropped for no apparent reason.)[22]

Chloe recognised that Gwen was doing important new work; she said she thought she should really be going to classes at the Sorbonne. She knew Gwen was posing for Rodin and she was anxious that his head of her would turn out well, but if she knew any more than that, she never gossiped or pried. She was a diffident, affectionate, scrupulous friend, and very practical. She was making Gwen a grey jacket; she said she hoped she was not seeing more of Miss O'Donel than could be helped, she was so bad tempered.[23] After she and Grilda went back to England, Chloe and Gwen corresponded regularly; from time to time she would come back to Paris for a while, and Gwen would soon paint a new, even more experimental portrait of her.

Gwen seemed, despite her anxieties about Rodin, to be getting back to work again. Life had been complex and fraught, but she loved the rue du Cherche-Midi, and expected to be happy there. But that spring there was a terrible tragedy which shocked and disorientated everyone. During the first week of March 1907, Ida walked round to the nearby Hôpital de la Maternité in the Boulevard du Port-Royal, to have her fifth child. Her baby was delivered but there were complications: she had puerperal fever and peritonitis. On the evening of 10 March she was operated on but she could not seem to surface from her delirium. Her mother had come to Paris and paid £60 for the very best possible treatment; thereafter, she told Ida's sisters, she paid 16 shillings a day for her room. It was thought that Ida had an abscess, and she had to be moved from the maternity hospital to a *maison de santé*. Ada Nettleship busied herself running around after doctors. The baby was doing well, but she hoped he would turn out to be worth all this trouble. After the operation, Ida seemed better than everyone had expected, but she was still weak, and 'being very unreasonable and wants all sorts of things that are not good for her'. Ada told Ursula and Ethel that they were not to come over unless she wired, there was nothing to do but wait. She did not want Ida to realise how ill she was: 'it all depends on her not giving way'.[24] The family were all hoping for the best, and Ida had so much natural vitality that they hoped she would pull though. However, by 13 March they were just waiting for the end, and Ida was no longer fully conscious.

On the night of 12 March, Augustus scrawled a brief, distraught note to his close confidants at the time, Rai and Meg Sampson, 'Ida is most seriously ill after an operation. Excuse more just now.' On 14 March, he wrote again. 'Ida has gone to some land of miraculous caves where the air is pure and light enough for her to breathe in peace.'[25]

9

The Artist's Room (87 rue du Cherche-Midi)

I think that is a beautiful idea, that we dig out the precious things hidden in us when we paint – and quite true.[1]

Ida died in her thirtieth year, on 14 March, at the Maison des Soeurs. 'It was all very peaceful at the end,' Ada told her daughter Ursula. 'She left off suffering and smiled but she never knew she was going to die. I could not tell her just to distress her – The nurses folded her hands with a bunch of violets Gus had brought her and put a crucifix and candles by her side.'[2] They decided on a cremation because of the difficulty of tending a grave in France and because Ada thought it was what Ida would have preferred. The nuns offered what comfort they could: 'One of the nuns was so nice to me – she said "C'était sa destinée" – and we must believe it was the right thing for her.'[3] Augustus, released from the dreadful anxiety of waiting for the worst, was drunk for several days, and seemed, to the uninitiated, elated. His close friends knew better, and his sister, of course, knew best. Gwen spent the next few days at his studio at the Cour de Rohan, looking after him. It was not only that she understood how to be amidst dreadful, incommunicable feelings, she was also the one who had been close to Ida: 'She was one of those who *knew* da,' [*sic*] Augustus said, and knew that she was 'the most utterly truthful soul in the world'.[4]

Gwen may not have been at the crematorium of Père Lachaise the following Saturday for Ida's cremation, since almost no one was there, not even Augustus. He hated formal displays of sentiment and had reacted to Ida's death with confused demonstrations of strange exhilaration, refusing people's offers to come over from England, including that of William Rothenstein, who never forgave himself for not ignoring him. One person who did defy Augustus was Gwen's old beau, Ambrose McEvoy; he 'had the delicacy to keep drunk all the time and was perfectly charming'. Henry Lamb, who had taken Ida to a music hall the night before she went into hospital, attended the cremation. When the coffin and body were consumed and the skeleton drawn out on a slab through the open doors of the furnace, they saw Ida's bone structure, recognisably intact; with one tap of the attendant's crowbar, it crumbled into dust.[5] If Gwen was spared this final glimpse, she may have been at the informal memorial held later in Lamb's rooms after the ashes had been taken round in a box to Augustus.

Ida's death certainly cast its shadow over her life at this time. Ursula Tyrwhitt acknowledged it first. She had not really been in touch with Gwen for more than two years. Now that she finally found time to do so, she was full of sadness and regret. She apologised profusely for not having written for such a long time; now it was all so sad and she could not stop thinking about Gwen and Augustus. Rodin sent an immediate telegram. Gwen's first reaction was disappointment, since it meant he was around after all; because he had not been in touch she had been assuming he was abroad. She told him she had hardly slept since she heard the dreadful news, and his portrait had been her only consolation. She urged him to rest well for their next meeting, in ten day's time, since she needed him now more than ever. The feelings which accompany bereavement are lingering and strange. Light and shade both seem more distinct, flowers may seem harder and brighter, open windows may be slightly haunting; flesh feels oddly fragile, then weirdly substantial. Loneliness takes on an invasive quality; life becomes more vivid, and more draining. During the long months of 1907, Gwen found it difficult to work, though she tried to focus her mind by learning extracts of philosophy. When she posed for Miss Bowser she read extracts during the breaks, and while she was posing she talked to her about them and tried to learn them by heart. She wrote them out, sometimes, for Rodin.[6]

Ursula came to Paris, and was there for several months. She decided she wanted to learn sculpture and spent the summer months working in Rodin's studio. She made a terracotta head of Gwen; when Rodin saw it he said, simply, 'Continuez.'[7] With Ursula nearby, Gwen managed to work, posing for Ursula, Isobel Bowser or Constance Lloyd, but she rarely managed more than one session a day as she was quickly drained and at times despairing.[8]

The *Self-Portrait*[9] she made at this time, a simple pencil and wash sketch on paper, showed her with her hair down, unadorned, disarmed, preoccupied. All her sophistication and passion seem to have been stripped away, and she looks far younger than her thirty-one years. Edgar Quinet was an essential distraction: Gwen sketched her in many closely observed drawings in pencil and wash, showing her asleep or awake, curled up or sitting attentively. Her little *chatte*, now as ever, was vital to her.

But then Edgar Quinet suddenly disappeared. She seems to have gone missing twice that year, once in July and again in August, when Gwen took her for a walk in the forest at St Cloud and she sprang off into the bushes.[10] The forest was a favourite haunt of theirs, Gwen had made a cave among the bushes inside the big plantation of trees, where she used to sit and draw, and she now went there every afternoon, but there was no sign of Edgar Quinet.[11] After a while, she decided she should be there at night, too. She did not camp out there as the place was a popular venue for *mauvais sujets*, but stayed at a cheap hotel at 3 rue Royale, in St Cloud. Even in the hotel, which cannot have been particularly salubrious, she kept being bothered at dinner by men who hung around trying to make conversation in *double entendres* about her losing her cat.[12] She travelled into Paris every morning to pose for Constance Lloyd.[13] After a while, she stopped eating in restaurants and brought food into the plantation, where she dined in her cave, sheltered by a climbing plant and surrounded with shawls, her overcoat and her writing things. She felt like Robinson Crusoe, she told 'Julie'.[14] It seems to have been quite a well organised episode, despite the fact that she spent long afternoons creeping around in the bushes. She made leaflets and had them printed, giving a description of Quinet and offering a reward for her return – even for the return of her body – which she distributed in all the cafés in St Cloud. When her hair got tangled and dirty she went to the hairdresser and had it properly washed. Strangers with gleams in their eyes would tell her they had found her cat but it was a scorched corpse, or an attempt to entice her into the bushes. A man with a pack of dogs warned her not to go into the garden of a strange, tall lady who dressed like Napoleon; a policeman warned her against the man with the pack of dogs.[15] Miss O'Donel warned her she could 'catch a tumour' – she knew two young women who had both had tumours, she said. This was the final straw in the ongoing dispute with Miss O'Donel, and Gwen now decided, she told Rodin, that she was 'une méchante femme et lunetique aussi!' [*sic*][16]

She was beginning to think Quinet must be dead.[17] She was collecting stories from the locals about what might have happened to her cat – she had died of *ennui*; died of *chagrin*; been eaten by undesirables; fallen into a pit; gone back to Paris; been crushed by a train; was living in the bushes; had fallen down a drain.[18] Eventually, as the nights were beginning to draw in, Gwen decided she had better return to the rue du Cherche-Midi as she did not want Rodin thinking she had not been taking care of herself.[19] When it seemed unlikely that Edgar Quinet would ever come back, she wrote her a poem, 'Au Chat', which she gave to Rodin. It is successful, in its own terms, with simple, sensitive, unobtrusive rhymes and an archaic, essentially French rhythm, like a French nursery rhyme:

Au Chat

Oh mon petit chat
Sauvage dans le bois
As tu donc oublié
Ta vie d'autrefois

Peut-être que tu es
Fâché avec moi
Mais j'ai tâché de comprendre
Tout ton petit coeur

Je me sentais jamais
Ton supèrieure
Petit âme mystèrieuse
Dans le corps du chat

J'ai eu tant de chagrin
De ne pas te voir
Que j'ai pensée de m'en aller
Dans le pays de morts

Mais je serais ici
Si tu reviens un jour
Car j'ai été comfortée
Par le dieu d'Amour

Gwen was still mourning Edgar Quinet the following spring, when Ursula suggested bringing her a new kitten. No, she said, she did not want to get attached to 'a little beast' again, it was too dreadful when she lost her. 'I think I should put all that energy of loving into my drawings, don't you?'[20]

By the autumn of 1907, she was beginning to acknowledge the fact that Rodin's interest in her had waned. She still saw him sometimes, but she told him that seeing him no longer made her happy. He seemed to think of nothing but his business matters. She still posed for him but he never seemed to want to spend any time with her after the sessions. For the first time she began to think that if she could, she would find another lover. But she did not see the point of having an affair with one man while she was still in love with another. She began to get fractious and angry. She told 'Julie' she was not going to write to him or pose for him for a week, since what was the point in earning money if she was so miserable: what for? What was the point in having nice clothes if he paid no attention to them?[21] It was probably her fault, she was not 'spirituelle' enough to interest him, he obviously would rather talk to other people. He no longer seemed to notice if she was not well, and rarely appeared to be listening when she spoke to him. She asked him for some poems to read and translate, and he forgot, and gave them to somebody else. She was sick at heart, she told him. He still found her seductive, but it was not 'tout l'amour'. She was thoroughly miserable, and she wanted him to know it.[22]

She swung between fury and yearning. She vented her pent-up frustration, anger and grief on him. She sometimes thought she might as well be dead, she told him, since she would never be of any real use to him, she was intellectually inferior and now she was too exhausted with sadness and longing even to pose properly. Once, she threatened him: she meant to die. This tolled a warning bell. He sent an immediate telegram. 'Pardonnez moi mon intention est bonne affectueusement lettre suit Rodin.'[23] ('Forgive me, I meant well, affectionately, letter follows . . .') In his letter, which arrived six days later, he told her she was making a desperate mistake. She must recognise, with all her advantages, that she could be happy if only she could keep calm. She needed tranquillity, especially if she was to pursue an intellectual life. It was her lack of self-discipline which was making her ill. If she could not pose regularly without exhausting herself with these emotional outbursts, she would never be of any use to him. Take my advice, he told her, 'je vous aime, et je vous désire heureuse' (I do love you, and I want you to be happy).[24]

But she was not to be fobbed off. She replied in a stylish frenzy of colloquial anger. It was all very well to send telegrams like that, but he seemed to be trying his best to make her realise he did *not* love her. He passed her in the street without acknowledging her, he neglected her, and then he expected her to be well and happy to pose for him. Did he really think that if he stopped treating her like this she would suddenly start being rebellious and disobedient?[25] These flare-ups must have saved her sanity. Gradually, she would soften and come back round, going to the café on the corner near his studio to write him a contrite letter, or taking the train to Meudon, hoping to catch a glimpse of him in his garden. She was kept going, now that their meetings seemed to be becoming increasingly rare, by his letters. They were almost never more than brief notes arranging their next rendezvous, but they meant everything to her. The drawing she did of herself holding one of his notes, *Autoportrait à la Lettre*,[26] shows her blissfully clasping it, her eyes shining, mouth slightly open; utterly receptive and joyful. A letter from him meant the continuation of life as she envisaged it, herself centred in a harmonious, expectant space, with Rodin as its essential source of energy and inspiration. However brief and sporadic his letters, his sending them meant that she was still in his head and heart.

She swung between expressions of bliss and pleading, and outbursts of unhappiness in which she accused him of criticising her too much and told him he obviously did not love her any more. It seemed to be getting more and more difficult to get him to herself. She was still posing, but he did not seem to want to make love to her afterwards. He was always saying he was tired, but 'you didn't *seem* tired,' she told him. He went on counselling her, over and over, to be tranquil, focused, *recueillie*; to study, read and draw. But that was not what *he* appeared to need, nor was it what the other women he knew seemed to be like. 'You make me feel that if I "criais fort" and wore bright colours and travelled all over the world you'd think more highly of me, *mon Maître*,' she wrote, angrily.[27] He always seemed to be in company. That summer, in June 1907, he had been in Oxford, at the ceremony for his reception into the University, an accolade of which he was inordinately proud.[28] It meant he had forgotten Gwen's birthday, on the 22nd. She told him she felt bitter about this, but he went straight on from Oxford to stay with friends in Chelsea. Then in the second half of July he was off again, to

Bois-le-Houx, Dompierre, Coutances and Le Mans, in the company of an American woman with a fake title, Claire, duchesse de Choiseul. If anyone knew how to wear bright colours and *crier fort*, it was the Duchesse.

Gwen was still writing to him every day, and keeping her new room spotless, in anticipation of his visits. But she was nevertheless spasmodically managing to paint, and the *chef d'oeuvre inconnu* was nearly finished. She called it *A Corner of the Artist's Room in Paris*,[29] a poised, muted interior in which she captures the essence of the atmosphere of her attic room in the rue du Cherche-Midi, with its sloping ceilings and light falling softly across the eaves. She painted two versions, both of which highlight her empty wicker chair. In both variants, the chair is draped with a discarded jacket or dress, but in one she added a rolled umbrella balanced against the chair leg. The room is a suggestive, subdued interior space, in which the quality of absence is tangible, even tactile. The empty room, with its evidence of the artist just arrived or departed or even just out of view, and the still point of the wicker chair, shown *contre-jour* against the light source of the window, draw the eye to the slanting diagonals of the eaves and the room itself becomes the subject.

There may be a subtle suggestion of narrative linking the two variants. In the version with the rolled umbrella the window is closed and there is a small pot of tightly clustered flowers on the artist's desk; in the other version the window is open and there is an open book on the desk, in place of the flowers. In the second variant, perhaps activity, continuity, a quiet momentum; the momentary dishevelment of everyday living have all now been resumed. This room is the space the artist goes from and returns to, which can conjure up expectation as well as loss, absence and the anticipation of return. The chair, the desk with the open book, the open window all open the room up wide, capturing a quality of strangeness, and the room is suffused with spiritual tension (a quality which is more or less lost in reproduction). In both versions, Gwen fused the conventional devices of the suggestively placed objects and single light source, with a more off-beat, shadowy quality which hints that the real subject of the painting is in the shadows, rather than in full light. The tonal orchestration of yellow ochres, blues and greys creates an overall effect of restraint and stillness.

Gwen was unaware that she was making any kind of experiment when she painted these pictures and it is ironic that they are among the most well known of her works, since they are uncharacteristic in that she apparently attempted to break no new ground. She was unsatisfied with both versions and did not even consider trying to either exhibit or sell them.[30] It is possible that she began them with Ida in mind. She was not particularly pleased with the results, but with the combined, solicitous encouragement of Rodin, Ursula, Chloe, and intermittently Augustus, she went on painting as well as drawing, working through feelings of tiredness, frustration, bereavement, as well as the ongoing strain of feeling that Rodin was slipping out of her grasp. When she managed to concentrate, she miraculously found a depth of concentration which from now on would be increased rather than diminished. Her friends supported her, both through their intuition and kindness and because they understood the nature of the process. The knowledge that Ursula was also painting, and the exchange of ideas between them, were especially sustaining.

Christmas 1907 was a solitary time. On Christmas Eve she gave the concierge's wife ten francs: she was very pleased by this as she seemed not to have expected anything, and could not stop thanking Gwen. A letter came from Winnie, with a little parcel containing a ribbon and a necklace, which was strange, since a necklace was what Gwen had thought of for her. Isobel Bowser gave her a pair of beautiful gloves, which Gwen thought very generous, especially since she had not known her all that long.[31] On Christmas Day she went to the service at Notre-Dame, partly because she thought she might see Rodin, but he was not there. Then she stayed in all day, thinking he might look in. It was a Wednesday, a Miss O'Donel day, but she had given her the day off for Christmas. On Boxing Day she went to pose for Miss Bowser.[32]

In the spring of 1908, Ursula came back to Paris. She lit things up, as she always did, energising Gwen and being amusing with the neighbours: 'Sometimes I think of you talking to Mr. Cott, & that amuses me so much, it makes me laugh to myself no matter how miserable I have felt the moment before,' Gwen told her afterwards.[33] They went shopping, buying clothes and fabric for dressmaking from the Bon Marché, and they investigated the galleries. They talked about getting a flat together so that they could share a model or take it in turns to sit for each other. Ursula saw the portrait of Chloe and the interior, *La Chambre sur la Cour*, and persuaded Gwen to send them to the NEAC. She was apprehensive and excited, spurred on by Ursula's telling her that if she could sell her own paintings, she would be able to come back to Paris. Gwen now focused wholeheartedly on the business of getting her paintings over to London. She sent one off, unprotected by glass, then worried desperately until she heard it had arrived safely. 'Is it last Saturday?' she asked Ursula, 'I mean the sending in day? I hope our pictures will hang together!! I feel so lonely in the New English!'[34] She was excited, now, by the idea of selling a painting. The thought of having money for clothes was one incentive; she had been back to the shops to order some dress material Ursula wanted. (Rodin still gave her money for her rent, but not enough for clothes, as he thought that would spoil her.) She was anxious to be reassured that Ursula's picture had been sent off. She had been hoping she might have had time to do two, like Ursula, but she realised she would have had to have something in mind, or even half done if she was going to send in another one now. 'One ought to have pictures always ready & for that it is necessary, to me at least, to disappear for a few years!' Ursula must have persuaded her that both the portrait of Chloe and *La Chambre sur la Cour* were more than ready, because she eventually sent both. She did not care whether or not hers were accepted, she said – sensitive still, probably, about the NEAC's last rebuff – though 'of course it would be a pleasure if they were hung well to hear from you how they looked there'.[35]

In May 1908 news came from Mr Winter, at the NEAC: all the paintings had been accepted, and he had sold the portrait of Chloe for £15. Gwen had asked him for 15 guineas, but he was 'incorrigible – he *loves* lowering prices'. This was nevertheless good news; in the same post a letter arrived from William Rothenstein, who had judged the paintings and now sent Gwen, she told Ursula, 'praise that took my breath away'.[36] Ursula, by this time, was back in London. '*Do* go as soon as you can to the N.E.,' Gwen urged her, 'it would be as good as my going, to hear where everything is hung & how they look.' Life went eccentrically on in Paris. She was still posing for Miss Ludlow and for Miss Bowser (who was very kind-hearted and had given her a frying-pan, a saucepan and a devil knife for her kitchen), but she had had a set-to with the 'man-woman' Ottilie Roederstein, who had engaged her, then put her off for two weeks. Just as she was going to bed one night, Ottilie had arrived with a huge bunch of flowers and five francs, to 'démonage' her. She also brought 'a hidious [*sic*] little bronze, saying it might be by Rodin and asking me to show it to him and get his opinion'. Rodin said, rather splendidly, that 'he would tell her his opinion of it when she had payed [*sic*] me five francs a *séance* for 2 weeks!'[37]

She had had more 'scenes' with him, she confided to Ursula, but he was always 'adorable at the end'. She said she thought these episodes were necessary to him, but wished they did not make her so ill. 'I have been very stupid in never scolding him enough, I see now I should have done so much more – there is no one else but me to do it everybody spoils him. I scold him therefore now, but what I say runs off him like water off a duck's back.' When she reprimanded him, he always came back 'like a poor little punished child', which made her very remorseful; she had said some dreadful things. 'I said "if you met a dying dog you would still be too 'bosculé [*sic*] par le monde' pour faire attention." Do you think that was very bad? He is always saying he is too "bosculé par le monde."' (Gwen's spelling of 'bousculé' – harried, mithered). She desperately wanted uncomplicated intimacy: 'I adore him and so it is dreadful to be angry with him – I see that it must be so, though.'[38]

The difficulty was that just when she was completely distraught with waiting, he would reappear. She pleaded with him to stop telling her off for not working: she could take his criticism when he was actually there, but his absences, coupled with his unjust accusations that she was neglecting her work, drove her wild. 'I suppose you let your dogs and all your other animals die of hunger while you're bothered by *le monde*,' she told him, indignantly.[39] If he placated her with love-making, she would weaken. Then when she felt distraught again, she began to wonder whether it wouldn't be better just to be a lady painter, painting away all day, with no love. But he kept on coming. The worst times were when he called unexpectedly and she was not there. Why did he do that? Whenever it happened, it felt like 'un nouveau cruauté'.[40] She always regretted showing her anger. 'I try to quarrel with you but it makes me too unhappy,' she told him. 'I'm going to leave quarrelling to other women, who seem to be stronger than I am. Other women always seem to be quarrelling with their lovers, but perhaps I'm just not strong enough. One day of argument is too much for me. You are all the happiness in my life, so I ought to be able to put up with a few little *chagrins*!'[41]

She still adored him, and still found the experience of working with him captivating. 'I should like to be able to tell you things Rodin says,' she confided to Ursula. She could not remember his exact words, but he was '*in love* with Nature and by such virtues as patience and humility he has got to understand her'. When someone was in love, she reasoned, there were really no such virtues as patience and humility because being in love meant everything. 'But if one did not say Rodin is in love with Nature one might say he works with humility and patience.' Most people who thought they were 'following' Rodin simply tried to imitate the appearances of his work, taking short cuts without understanding anything of his philosophy. If you were really influenced by him, he made you strong, it was the same as being 'influenced by Nature, by Life'. He never criticised, or said 'think of the Old Masters' or anything they said in schools. Instead, 'if we wanted to do an arm, for instance, we should try to do a portrait of it. Not to think of any theories or maxims. Observe the grace of life, make it without timidity – not be preoccupied by the details but not leave gaps either.'[42]

Early in 1908, a rumour that Rodin was going to show the Whistler Muse in the Salon had begun to circulate. The Monument Committee of the International Society of Sculptors, Painters and Gravers got wind of it, and insisted that they wished to see a photograph. Funds had been raised and they required some proof that the work was actually under way. Rodin, in a letter to them, described the monument as a Muse who would hold, or have near her, a medallion portrait of Whistler. When the photograph came, 'it showed an over-life-size figure of enormous power with the left leg raised high and the knee pivoting to the left in a compelling and awkward pose . . .' The muse, an 'uneasy' figure, gave 'a powerful impression of [Gwen] John's striking oval face pressing forward on a long columnar neck'. The Committee was dismayed, but the press was full of praise, especially for the figure's back: Louis Vauxcelles described it in *Gil Blas* as 'sublime, Rembrandtesque', and Lucien Cantal wrote in the *Action Française*, 'In the back of this *Muse* one perceives trembling flesh that has a modern beauty equivalent to the most beautiful art of antiquity.' J.L. Blanche, in the *Grande Revue*, also singled out the back as 'one of the most astonishing things I have seen in a long time'.[43] But despite available funds, enthusiastic patrons and the perfect model, the Muse never seemed to be finished, since Rodin was forever *bousculé par le monde*. He was also becoming very fatigued and somewhat depressed, though he seems to have hidden this from Gwen. He even told one of his close friends and confidantes, Helene de Nostitz-Wallwitz Hindenburg, that he felt increasingly 'consumed by the idea that he had not yet found a real personal life'.[44]

The girls in the Jardin du Luxembourg walked with their lovers in the warm summer evenings. Gwen watched them and told herself not to be sad, she would be seeing hers soon. Ursula envied her her freedom. By now in her late thirties, she was still living with her parents, and finding her financial dependence on her father increasingly inhibiting.[45] But 'one can be more free and independent in the mind and heart sometimes when one is tied practically,' Gwen reassured her. She had read somewhere that the girls in harems were actually 'more wonderful and advanced than any women'. She herself was tied to the effort of trying to be self-contained: 'Il faut vivre la vie intérieure, et très indépendante,' she promised Rodin[46] – I must learn to live an interior life, and to be independent. Most of the time, she reminded him, and herself, she succeeded. Then the old, fiery Gwen would re-emerge: 'Vous me traty [*sic*] comme un enfant' (you treat me like a child). Sometimes she felt he treated her like another man; he seemed to have no regard for her feelings as a woman. She told him he had not understood her character. More ominously, 'Vous mentez toujours': you're always lying.[47]

Rodin, meanwhile, continued to confide in Helene de Nostitz-Wallwitz Hindenburg, granddaughter of the German Ambassador to Paris and daughter of a Prussian general, whom he had met in 1900, through her mother Sophie. They had a villa on the Tuscan coast where Rodin had visited them in autumn 1901, since when he had maintained a personal and candid correspondence with Helene, 'the most gracious and beautiful woman in all of Germany', and thirty-eight years his junior.[48] He wrote to her regularly, confiding his deep sense of loneliness, his shock, on realising that he was growing old; his thoughts about the function of the artist's muse. 'God is too great to send us direct inspiration,' he told Helene, 'he takes precautions relative to our weakness and sends us earthly angels . . . For an artist, a soft woman is his most powerful dispatch, she is holy, she rises up in our hearts, in our genius, and in our force, she is a divine sower who sows love in our hearts in order that we can put it back a hundred times into our work.'[49] It is possible that when he wrote these words, Gwen had recently entered his life. (She met him in late 1903 or early 1904.) Clearly, it was intended as a compliment to Helene, but he was also thinking more broadly. Rodin's declaration is the traditional, archetypal, essentially Christian statement about the function of the Muse which has informed the work of great artists from Botticelli through Michelangelo, to the Pre-Raphaelites and beyond. It goes some way towards explaining the way women entered Rodin's art, but it also draws attention to the difficulty of *being* the Muse. It was probably essentially how he saw Gwen, and her volatility, her profound sense of independence and her need to love actively rather than passively, meant that her vision of love, even though she needed to submit to him, was fatally incompatible with his.

In her romantic imagination and in her need to be adored, Gwen was the perfect Muse for him, but she needed to access and control her own muse, a problem which historically has been insoluble for the woman artist. Gwen longed to be Rodin's angel, but she also yearned to play a more secular, material role in his life. In May 1906, at about the time when she was moving into the rue St Placide, he had told Helene, 'there is something wrong with me, I don't know how to get on with happiness': 'Life is a mosaic of black stones.'[50] His darkest moments were like 'the flower of the seeds that I have planted . . . *La volupté* is too important in our time, and it is called *la douleur*. It is true that suffering with the person you love is a kind of voluptuousness, as Francesca da Rimni, the saint of love, has told us. Do you want more details? I feel that my life is over, I have conceived of a tower that is too tall in proportion to my force . . . *mon amie intéllectuelle*'.[51]

His overwhelming sense was that his powers were failing. In January 1908, Rilke had written a new study of his sculpture and sent it to him together with a book of poems.[52] By March Rodin was writing to invite him to move back into his old room in the Villa des Brillants[53] and throughout the year he sent him invitations to dine with him in Paris and Meudon. He badly wanted to be surrounded by people who understood him. But Gwen was too demanding, and he respected her needs as an artist. He wanted the material things taken care of while he protected his increasingly fragile artistic powers, and never perceived Gwen as the kind of woman who could have shed her own artistic life and taken on the organisation of his – which had expanded into proportions she surely could not have imagined. The tragedy is that she genuinely wished (despite doubtless having no idea what would have been involved) to do this. But she was not worldly in the way he needed, and it was Helene he addressed as *mon amie intéllectuelle*. Gwen had a different quality: a more ancient style of intelligence, an 'intellectual' wisdom of a different order. She reasoned through her senses and her instinct, and her spiritual understanding was consistent with the romantic, melancholy side of her nature.

Rodin sensed this, and tried to respect her and encourage her to be herself. But he failed to respect her equally instinctive, ardent exuberance. He realised, of course, how much he meant to her, and this touched him. But he was always busy, always *pris*. (In Rodin's enormous archive in the Musée Rodin there are only three mentions of Gwen, two notes to Rodin from secretaries reminding him of appointments with her, and a reference to her in a couple of letters from one of Rodin's models, who was soon to model for Gwen, a somewhat wild, 'bohemian' girl, also known to Augustus, called Fenella Lovell.) In December 1908 he wrote to Gwen telling her that he was old, he needed to be left alone to live the life of ideas. He was like a cracked vase which, if it was touched, would fall to pieces.[54] While he travelled, returning each time to Meudon and Rose, Gwen painted some of the canvases we have come to know her by, evocative depictions of her attic room, lit, expectant, empty, suggestive of loved presences, difficult absences. Ursula sent her the stories of Edgar Allan Poe, an inspired choice, which tided her over a Saturday night and the whole of Sunday. She 'read all the livelong day, and the night before, and afterwards entered refreshed into a new phase of life, very mysterious, which still savours of him'.[55]

In July 1908, good news came from England. Winter had sold *La Chambre sur la Cour* for £30, though he did not tell Gwen who the purchaser was. (She did not find out until 1926, when William Rothenstein revealed that Frances Cornford, née Darwin – Gwen's 'one rival' – had bought it.)[56] Ursula was missing her, and was trying to persuade her to go to London. The idea of going to London was a lovely dream, Gwen said, she wished she could, if only for a few days, but the problem with England was the climate. Tenby, for example, was too mild, though at a place four miles from Tenby 'the air is very bracing. But Tenby is shut in by an island etc. (Do you think I am turning into a guide book?)'[57] She was obviously in good spirits, cheered by the sale of the second painting. She wrote to tell Winifred the good news, and also that Rilke was back in Paris. 'I am *so* glad you have sold two pictures, that is *lovely*, one can be so calm and happy,' came the reply. Gwen must have told her that Rilke was a distraction, because she joked that luckily there were 'no poets or any kind of foreigners' there to disturb her peace, Gwen should just keep working, then they would surely leave her alone.

She sent Gwen a photograph of herself and Aunt Rose, imperious and straight as a rod, with Winifred, soft at her side with her pale eyes, as gentle as she is in Gwen's drawings, without a hint of the intrepid effervescence that comes across in her writing.[58] She said she thought she herself resembled their elder brother Thornton, 'Monarch of all he surveys and happy . . . to have all his possessions in a small compass and floating.' She wondered, in passing, whether it might not be a good idea for Gwen to visit him, 'and draw boats from all points of view?' She warned her, 'Don't be soft on the subject of R. Be firm and sacrifice all to work. I am going to. I don't want ever to "fall in love" again.' She signed off with an idea which would turn out to be a crucial contribution to Gwen's work. She said she wished Gwen would draw the small girls she had mentioned, in their felt hats and dresses.[59] When she did, she produced pencil and wash drawings which brilliantly capture the restrained movement and vulnerable concentration of little girls, a subject which was to yield, over the coming years, some of her most affecting and dynamic works on paper.

Gwen had been drawing herself nude in the mirror, in watercolour mixed with Chinese white, but she was still exhausted in the aftermath of Ida's death, and from worrying about Rodin: 'I have no energy & so hardly do anything,' she told Ursula.[60] Rilke lent her a book, *The Love Letters of a Portuguese Nun*,[61] which she agreed with him were very beautiful, written with a lovely simplicity, 'like a bird singing'.[62] They were ostensibly written anonymously in 1669. More than a hundred years later, the nun was identified as Mariana Alcoforado (1640–1723), a Portuguese gentlewoman cloistered in the Franciscan convent of Beja. More recent scholarship identified the actual author as Gabriel de Lavergne, vicomte de Guilleragues. The letters chart not only the unhappy love of the nun for the French officer who loved and abandoned her, but also the progress of her mind, as yearning and despair give way to an increasing sense of honour, self-regard, self-discipline, and finally, outrage. If this was the model Rilke hoped to offer Gwen, she missed (or ignored) the point. *The Love Letters of a Portuguese Nun* may have been a gentle, covert warning, since Rilke must have known about the most recent events in Rodin's life. Perhaps he told her, or perhaps Rodin did. By 8 November she was writing in despair to Ursula, 'The worst of it is I don't know when I can begin to live again – oh it is not the want of money – in case you may think it is that.' Ursula, as ever, counselled her to try to work and not care: she would try to, she promised.[63] But things were going to be very difficult now.

That summer, Rodin had begun work on a bust of the American

'Duchess' Claire de Choiseul.[64] Gwen undoubtedly did not know this, but Claire had been known to Rodin since 1904, when her husband had contacted him hoping to sell him a bust of the seventeenth-century sculptor, Antoine Coysevox. He visited them at Boix-le-Houx in September 1907 (the month in which Gwen had sent him her desperate telegram), and found Claire fast, loud, and a bit too fond of her drink, but he also found her oddly compelling. By 1 July 1908, she and Rodin were constantly in each other's company. Claire's husband left her, and wrote to Rose Beuret to say that he presumed she would similarly be arranging a separation from Rodin.[65]

At first, Gwen thought the bust of the 'Duchesse' would take Rodin ten days. She told him she realised he might prefer her not to come to his studio while the Duchesse was posing. It gave her nightmares, she had a recurring dream that he was surrounded by people and she could not get near him. When the ten days were up, she went to his studio but was reduced to tears: seeing him was all too much. She had another terrible dream: that he was only a few steps away from her house and she saw him go in, but when she tried to run after him she could not move her feet. She was burning up with desire, trying to control it by reading and studying, but this was an exhaustingly unsuccessful strategy. She went to the station and waited for hours every day, hoping to see him get off the train, but she was terrified of running into 'votre Amie Américaine'.[66] Why didn't he come to see her? Everybody seemed to have a piece of him, except her. The Duchesse had taken a shine to him, and seemed without warning to have made her presence felt not only as his new lover, but as his constant companion and business manager. Just thinking about this woman 'm'a mit en fièvre', Gwen indignantly told Rodin. But it was too late, he was hooked.[67]

Rodin tried putting her in the way of other artists, but it was too impossibly humiliating. 'Why did you make me take my clothes off for that man?' she asked him, in despair. She felt like going off, hitting the road again.[68] When she realised what had happened she felt like a ghost, or dumb, like the birds. She tried to occupy herself with sewing; she went to the baths, cleaned her room, and told herself he would be pleased with her if he knew she was getting on with her life. But she was beside herself. When he finally turned up at the rue du Cherche-Midi she was out, which felt like the final cruelty. Why had he done that? She asked him, furiously, did he really think he could come to her room again, just as before? Did he think he still had a right to her, just because he felt like it? Had he thought about what his new friend would say if she knew? If only she knew![69] In her notebooks for 1909 she recorded her intense pain, and the gruelling need for stamina, courage and determination. What had happened was unbearable, but she somehow had to find a way of thinking about it which would not drive her mad. Being *recueillie* now meant being enormously strong. 'Give a survey of your mind from to time – of its rhythm and currant [*sic*] . . . Look at every position from a spiritual point of view', she instructed herself, 'your whole life has been wrong.'[70] Ursula sustained her. 'Your letters always give me a certain pleasure which I never find in anything else except in painting,' Gwen told her, in February 1909. 'You belong to a part of my heart & mind – the same part where my love of art is – which is undisturbed by the events and difficulties of life.'[71]

An acquaintance of theirs, Lily, had advised her to concentrate on her two aims: did she mean the cat, for one, she asked Ursula? She busied herself trying to find dress material, which she wanted to take her time over. There was a full moon, so she decided to stay out all night. When she heard the neighbourhood cats making love, she ran to see if Edgar Quinet was one of them. Eventually, she managed the superhuman feat of channelling her fury and anguish into her work.

In the spring of 1909 she began a new, ravishing portrait in oils. Rodin was painting the young Fenella Lovell, who had also crossed paths with Augustus. Gwen met her at tea with some other lady painters, where she was sitting on the floor telling fortunes, with cards and the lines of their hands. She looked like a little 'romencheil' (romanichelle – gypsy), Gwen told Rodin, and all the ladies thought she was wonderful. She told Gwen's fortune, though Gwen would not tell Rodin what she had said.[72] He liked the idea of her making friends with Fenella – he probably thought she would be a useful distraction – and suggested they go for a walk together in the country. They took the train to Malakoff and walked in the woods at Clamart, near Meudon, which were as lovely as Rodin had promised. There were a lot of people around, all of whom noticed Fenella looking like a gypsy, with bohemian sandals and no stockings, so they were followed and pestered by men, which irritated Gwen and pleased Fenella. They dined in a little restaurant at Clamart, where everyone stared and talked about them.[73] She had her own opinions about Fenella, Gwen told Rodin, but as Fenella was his model she would keep them to herself.[74] Privately, she thought Fenella sulky and infuriating, and confided as much to Ursula. But she now began to paint her, beginning on the first of two portraits, either a gorgeous nude draped at the lower torso, or the variant, in a demure white dress.

For the next year or so, Fenella posed grumpily, driving Gwen to distraction. She worked furiously, hating every minute, but infiltrating into this work all the recently acquired technical knowledge she had brought to her portrait of Chloe, concentrating again on the opaque, abstract ground, the muted tonalities, the slight elongation of the limbs; the preoccupation in the face. In the nude variant, *Nude Girl*,[75] she made the back of Fenella's chair just visible; in the clothed version, *Girl with Bare Shoulders*,[76] she reduced the suggestion of the chair to a shadow. In both versions, the elongated neck, the sloping shoulders, the emaciated arms, the hollows in the face all contribute to the powerful sense of the personality of the figure. She worked intermittently for more than a year on them. Many years later (in 1946, after Gwen's death) Wyndham Lewis saw them, immediately recognising in them an astonishing spiritual depth. He thought the figure seemed 'painfully galvanized by something underneath which we are not shown – or drawing herself up into the air by some pestiferous *vase*'. In the clothed figure, he saw 'a woman strained up, as it were, in painful religious vigour'. In the nude Fenella, he found the same quality of spiritual anguish and concentration. 'Indeed, these two pictures, like the *Maja vestida* and the *Maja desnuda*, are the Woman clothed and unclothed. But with the one here it is a revulsion from her nakedness – an Eve after the Fall.'[77]

One day when Gwen came in from posing, the concierge asked her to go and see her in her lodge, as she and her husband wanted to talk to her. The husband seemed nervous and ill, and told her the doctor had ordered him to move into a less stuffy room, so would she be prepared to exchange her room for theirs? Gwen knew theirs was a claustrophobic room on the ground floor, with no air or sunlight and dark as a cave, so she said she was very sorry, but she needed air, too, whereupon they said that though they liked her very much and had found her a good tenant and very kind, they would regrettably have to ask her to leave by the following July. Trying not to show them how upset she was, she said that in that case she would naturally leave. By the next morning, she had resigned herself to looking for another room.[78] She wrote to Rodin about it, telling him that she had done a new drawing, but had no confidence that it was any good. It was difficult to get her room warm enough to draw in, and she kept having to stop because of the cold. It was midwinter, and already beginning to snow.

Portrait of Mrs Atkinson, c.1897-8

Self-portrait, c.1900

Dorelia in a Black Dress, 1903-4

A Corner of the Artist's Room in Paris, 1907-9

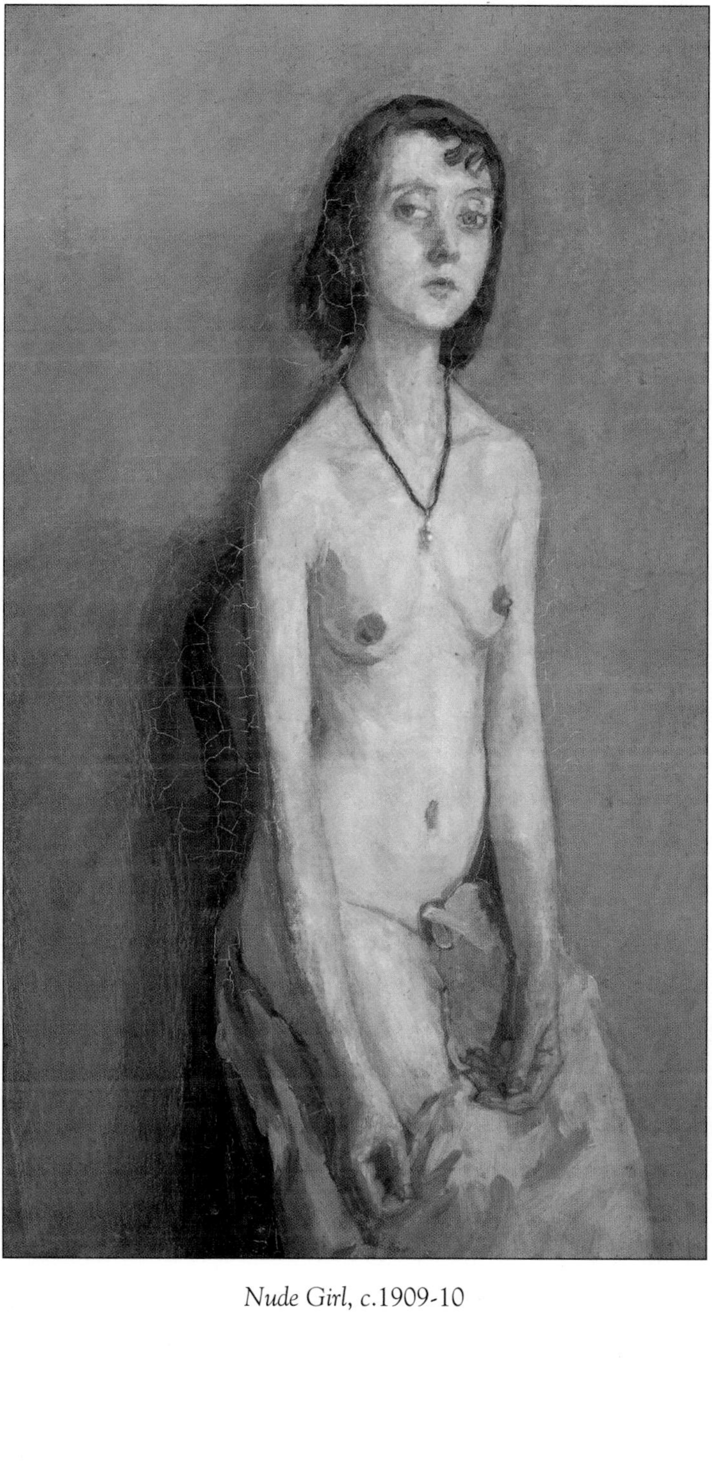

Nude Girl, c.1909-10

A Lady Reading, c.1910-11

Mère Poussepin Seated at a Table, mid-1910s

Girl Holding a Rose, c.late 1910s to early 1920s

10

Osez! osez!

. . . to be sure and certain for ever of some ideas of painting . . .[1]

The move to number 6 rue de l'Ouest never felt particularly successful. The room was square, and the wallpaper was not very pretty.[2] Gwen was never entirely happy there. She felt displaced, and by now was in despair over Rodin. He was still telling her she should try to live for happiness and harmony rather than for isolated moments of intense pleasure, but she wanted everything. She began to develop an abscess under a tooth, which made her feverish, and she longed for some country air. She often took the train to St Cloud or Meudon and walked, but all she really wanted was to be with him. 'Oh what inquietude,' she wrote in her notebook: 'realisation of an eternal adieu, & perhaps the advisability of it.'[3] 'Do not criticize R,' she told herself, and 'don't expect anything more from love, but know that you *can* get everything. Love the difficulties.' The effort to be collected and serene was now a matter of courage. 'Osez! osez!' she instructed herself. 'Osez être dans l'harmonie.' She tried to remember that 'A beautiful life is one led, perhaps, in the shadow, but ordered, regular, harmonious.' But the passions of men meant that they could get away with forgetting this and just seize life as it passed at random.[4]

The search for harmony was anything but an expression of quiet, modest serenity. In actuality it was a daily, gruelling battle to subdue her most deeply felt desires, her passion, her physicality. The delicacy Gwen achieved in her work, with its aura of quiet, almost mystical serenity, had to be arrived at through immense efforts of will and herculean battles with emotional, sexual and psychic demons. She was grappling with profound feelings of inner turmoil, but there were also new external reasons for her distress. In the autumn of 1909 Rodin had found a new studio space in the beautiful Hôtel Biron, which only served to put him more firmly and more demandingly at the centre of a world Gwen had no place in. By this time the Duchesse seemed horribly indispensable. When Gwen wrote to Ursula protesting that she no longer felt she knew how to live, she had surely found out for certain about the role of Claire de Choiseul.

The Hôtel Biron – ironically, given the heartache it was to represent for Gwen – had been discovered by Rainer Maria Rilke and his wife, the painter Clara Westhoff. Clara had discovered the beautiful, rundown building, at the corner of the rue de Varenne, within view of the gold dome of the Invalides, a few streets from the rue du Cherche-Midi. An eighteenth-century mansion, later a convent confiscated in 1904 by the state, it was now rented by artists. Matisse had a teaching studio there and Isadora Duncan had a long gallery against the garden wall. Clara Rilke rented her room on the main floor in May 1909, and when she went back to Germany in August, Rilke took over her space. He wrote to Rodin, telling him about the idyllic garden which had impressed the young poet Jean Cocteau, who also rented a room there: 'It was hard to imagine that Paris lived, walked, rode, and worked around such a pool of silence,' he said (it still feels like that today). Rodin came to see Rilke on 2 September, and in October he rented four rooms on the ground floor. He moved in furniture, brought over sculptures from his Dépôt des Marbres and overnight became the hotel's most illustrious tenant.

The Duchesse was in her element, and though neither she nor Rodin ever actually lived there, was soon referring to it as 'our enchanted abode'.[5] Rodin now seemed to be fully serviced by women: Helene was still his spiritual confidante; the Duchesse ran his business affairs and indulged his sentimental streak, Rose was still home, and Gwen would continue, agonisingly sporadically, to be his lover for another eight years, until the year before his death. When he scrawled his new address – 77, rue de Varenne – on the back of an envelope for her, however, he must have known that this was the beginning of a big change in his life. From now on, the Duchesse effectively helped to wean him away from the difficult struggle for spiritual integrity. She took over his practical arrangements, got his work sold in America and organised his social life. What she provided, and very restful it must have been, too, was diversion. By keeping Rodin amused, she allowed him the silly youthfulness of old age; by giving him this licence, she also – by very virtue of the fact that she understood nothing about it – freed up the ailing part of his psyche with which he still needed to dedicate himself to his work.

During the day, he continued to work with his models, sometimes still with Gwen. In the evenings he had found new transports of delight – a wonderful new toy. Rilke described it:

> He now has a gramophone. The Marquise winds it up and the thing wheezes round. I was apprehensive when I found myself invited to hear it. But it was marvellous; they have bought records of some old Gregorian chants which nobody likes and which, apart from the dealer, nobody possesses but the Pope. But when a castrato's voice intoned a requiem of the 13th or 14th century, wailing forth like the wind from a crack in the world, then you forgot all the fatuity of the instrument, all the stupid mechanical noises.

Rodin himself, while all this was going on, was apparently 'quite quiet, quite closed, as though facing a great storm. He could hardly breathe with listening and only snatched a little air when the force of the voice abated for a few bars.' Watching them with their gramophone, Rilke began to see the point of the 'Marquise': she could 'lead Rodin slowly down from the great heights beside some merry watercourse. Perhaps Rodin really does need this now, some one to climb down with him, carefully and a little childishly, from the high peaks he was always straying among. Formerly he used to remain up there, and God knows how or where and in what pitchy blackness he finally made his way back again.'[6]

The famous phonograph ran to music hall waltzes. His guests were invited to listen to them and his secretary Marcelle Martin was asked to wind it up as Rodin lay listening to church music, hand in hand with the Duchesse. When they progressed to folk dances from the Auvergne, Claire would drape herself in a black shawl and dance across the room. She had some competition when Isadora Duncan arrived and danced for Rodin. More and more guests were invited as his friends adjusted to this unexpected change in his emotional fortune. Monet sent 'hommages' to the Duchesse; she and Rodin lunched, dined, travelled together. Friends now needed a note to get past the Hôtel Biron's concierge, and that included Gwen, who was still posing for the Whistler Muse. Claire was increasingly irritated by the spectacle of Gwen, shadowing Rodin like a wraith. When Gwen arrived at the Hôtel Biron, the door would be opened by the Duchesse (radiating spite, it seemed to Gwen). While Gwen was dressing one day after her session, Claire, who was now there every day, gave her a banana and some sweets and said she knew some Americans who would give her work, if work was what she needed.[7]

Back in her room, she was safe and in control, surrounded by her drawings and the photographs of Rodin which he had given her. She made some drawings of his head, probably from the photographs.[8] She wished, she told him, she could be in her room whenever she was not with him, since she was truly at ease there. He would caress her as she posed for him, and he was still prepared to accept and read her letters, despite the Duchesse's attempts to put a stop to this. She was finishing *Oreste* (*Orestis*), Gwen told him in one letter, and was touched by the discussions between the sick Oreste and his friend about whether to live or die. She was on the edge, but she was still absolutely determined. She was less embarrassed than she had been, she said, about bringing letters for him, since she had read in a book that great men had always received letters from the woman they loved: even Seneca, 'tout philosophe qu'il était', was suffused with pleasure when he received letters from Lucile. Even men of the Church – the Augustines, the Jeromes – wrote to and received letters from women. When you read these names, she appealed to him, don't forget mine.[9] She was sure he would rather be quietly at home with her. She was inspired by what she had read in Euripides: 'Heureux l'homme dont la vie s'écoule à l'abri des orages, ignorée et sans gloire! Mais ceux qui vivent dans les honneurs me paraissent moins dignes d'envie.' (Happy is the man whose whole life unfurls in the shade of the storms, anonymous and without fame! Those who live in the limelight seem to me to be far less worthy of envy.')[10]

'What thought opens the door to the interior world?'[11] she asked herself, in her notebook. It is unlikely she knew much of what was happening in Rodin's world; she hardly ever knew about his trips abroad until he wrote to tell her where he was; we can assume she knew nothing of the evenings with the gramophone. All she knew was that *le monde* had claimed him, and that he was surrounded by more socially adept, more articulate women than herself, whose 'intelligence' presented an immovable wall. It was Ursula who kept her going: she wrote to her urging her just to paint, not to worry about exhibitions or sending paintings in time for NEAC deadlines. Gwen's notebooks now began to reflect a new effort to realise creative resources within herself, rather than needing them to be constantly reflected by Rodin, and this coincided with new experimentation in what she called her drawing – that is, her work in watercolour or gouache, as opposed to oils. She told Ursula she thought that 'if the greatest misfortune happened to me, I could go on living not unhappily because of some ideas but perhaps that is saying too much'.[12] She had been working hard. She felt there was very little to show for it, but with Ursula's encouragement, she kept going.

Despite the complications in his own life, Rodin still took an interest in Gwen's work. He brought some Japanese drawings to show her, and they made a big impact, moving her towards further new discoveries, not only in her drawings but also, ultimately, in her painting. Rodin sometimes used a process of tracing which she now began to take ideas from, and the two ideas – the Japanese drawings and tracing – fed into the experiments she was already making. She had already begun five new drawings. She described them to Ursula:

> I first draw the thing then trace it on to a clean piece of paper by holding it against the window. Then decide absolutely on the tones, then try and make them in colour and put them on flat. Then the thing is finished. I have finished one, it was rather bad because of the difficulty of getting the exact tones in colour and the hesitation, and not knowing enough about water-colour. I want my drawings, if they are drawings, to be definite and clean like Japanese drawings. But they have not succeeded yet. I think, even if I don't do a good one the work of deciding on the exact tones and colour and seeing so many pictures as I see each drawing as a picture [*sic*] – and the practice of putting things down with decision ought to help me when I do a painting in oils – in fact I think all is there – except the modelling of flesh perhaps.[13]

She was now drawing simpler, more expressive self-portraits, in which she is strong, determined, and sometimes subtly seductive. Some of them implied a covert invitation to Rodin to come and rescue her from her solitude. In two of them, especially – *Head of a Young Woman*[14] and *Woman Leaning on her Hand*[15] – the collusion between thin, scribbled pencil marks and broad, approximate washes is vividly reminiscent of the style of Rodin's erotic drawings. Both heads suggest proud, blissful serenity. *Woman Leaning on her Hand*, particularly, implies post-coital lassitude and contentment. She told Rodin she was only drawing to prove to him that she was not being lazy, she had done them using a mirror and they had been difficult to do. But they were successful: candid, uncluttered, discreetly erotic; unfussily alive. She had moved a long way from her earlier self-portraits. The faces showed a deeper emotional register, the earlier, slight element of defensiveness or expectation of confrontation had gone, and the figures now seemed more usually to be looking inward than outward, in suggestion of deeper engagement. After practising her new methods for a while, she went back to work on Fenella's portrait – or perhaps began on the second of the variants – working with this new directness.

The painting of Fenella was obviously done in a state of high tension. Gwen disliked her intensely, and told Ursula how glad she would be when it was finished: 'it is a great strain doing Fenella. It is a pretty little face but she is *dreadful*.'[16] At first it seemed to be going quite quickly. In September she told Ursula, 'I think it will be good & principally because I have not thought about it being seen by anybody.'[17] She knew both paintings were good, but when she thought about sending them to the NEAC it began to occur to her that there was no reason why anybody would want to buy a portrait of Fenella Lovell, let alone two: 'It was rather foolish of me to begin it but I meant to do others at the same time.'[18] She wanted to send both paintings, because if she could sell them she could pay Fenella off and never see her again. (The following spring, Fenella was going around lying about her financial arrangement with Gwen, telling people she had paid her nothing when in fact Gwen had advanced her money as promised.[19] By May 1910, Gwen would still be working on the paintings.)

The winter of 1909 was very trying. Her tooth was bothering her and was beginning to make her feel ill again. She had not been eating properly. She still spent whole days waiting for Rodin and sometimes at the end of the day she would go and sit in the Luxembourg Gardens until they closed. She was still posing all week, for the usual ladies; if she had a free afternoon she would wait at the station for Rodin. All she wanted, she told Rodin, was to be happy, 'comme tout le monde et la nature'.[20] She was still reluctant to go out if there was any chance at all that Rodin might arrive unexpectedly.[21] Her clients, particularly Miss Brown, had begun to notice that she was not looking well. She was sleeping badly, and had begun to feel that if she did not soon get to the country she would not be able to work at all. Miss Brown and Miss Ludlow had a house at Monneville and asked her if she would like to go and stay with them there for a few days; she wrote to Rodin to tell him she had decided to go, but when she came back, would he please give her 'un peu d'amour?' She was miserable about going, because she could not be sure he would be there for her when she came back. She felt very unstable, not wanting to move from the spot in case she missed him, but desperately in need of fresh air and a break.

She decided to go to Monneville, persuaded by Isobel Bowser, who said that Gwen seemed so unwell that she was not posing properly. (Privately Gwen thought the problem with the painting had more to do with Miss Bowser's failing than with her own: she told Rodin she thought she could do a better job herself, and began work on a new self-portrait in oils, though she does not appear to have pursued this.)[22] She told Rodin she was going and asked him not to come to the rue de l'Ouest while she was away; she would probably stay for about two weeks. Three days later she wrote from Monneville to say she was ready to go home. It was pleasant there and Miss Brown and Miss Ludlow were being very kind, but she had not a moment to herself to think about him except during the night, because when she was not posing she helped them with the housework, and she was doing her best to be amenable because they were so kind to her. After dinner was the best time, when one of them read aloud while the other two sewed.[23] They persuaded her to stay until the weekend, and she wrote to tell Rodin she would be catching the train on Sunday night: she would expect him on Monday morning. She had waited so long, she could hardly bear to wait until then, all she could think about was that soon she would be back in her room in Paris, and he would be there.

She arrived back from Monneville to find that he had been to the rue de l'Ouest that morning. She went straight to the little café at the corner of the rue de Varenne and wrote to him there. She had missed the train, it had not been her fault; but she was back now. By the following Saturday, he still had not materialised. She had counted on at least seeing him on Saturday evening, but he was at the Hôtel Biron. This was absolute abjection: if she had known she would miss seeing him she would have stayed in Monneville another week. Now, all the good the place had done her was undone; she felt ill again and she knew it irritated him when she was below par. She had been happy in the winter countryside and was beginning to feel better, but now it was all ruined. By Tuesday morning, she was writing to tell him he was cruel to leave her like this. Although she had not been well, she was better now than she had been three months ago, and tomorrow she would have to go out and look for work again. She went out every day at 12.30, so if he wanted to come in the afternoons, he would need to let her know in advance.[24]

Isobel Bowser was still worried about her. She knew about Rodin, as Gwen had taken her to meet him at the Hôtel Biron.[25] She now gave up her time to go shopping with Gwen to choose clothes, and invited her to have coffee with her, listening patiently while she talked about him.[26] Inadvertently or otherwise, Isobel may have had quite a profound impact on Gwen's later years. She took her to Meudon one afternoon after posing to visit a friend of hers, a painter who lived alone with a child. She lived in Meudon, she told Gwen, because it was cheaper than Paris. Her house was at the top of a steep slope, near the Observatoire in the grounds of the old château, where you could look down and see the whole of Paris, and the Eiffel Tower in the distance. Gwen also worked out where Rodin's house was, though it seemed a long way off.[27] It was perhaps at this point that she began to hatch a plan; certainly Miss Bowser now remarked that she thought Gwen was beginning to look a bit better.

In spring 1910, she was still working on the portraits of Fenella. 'It is not my work that troubles me so much,' she wrote to Ursula, 'but that little creature Fenella. You cannot imagine, or perhaps you can, what a bore she is . . .' She thought she was a fake: 'Oh it is impossible to describe her. She has no character or rather she has a horrid character.'[28] After the sessions, the two of them went for a walk in the Luxembourg Gardens, Fenella as usual dressed like a gypsy and grumbling about some man she was in love with, who was not in love with her, getting all angry and indignant, Gwen told Rodin, as if she assumed she had a right to be loved.[29] But all this was an incentive to work faster. While she was painting Fenella, she still posed every day as she needed the money. She had stopped posing for Isobel Bowser for a while, as Rodin had introduced her to a Monsieur Jacques, who was making a statue of her. He was not unpleasant to pose for, even though she thought his statue did not look like her. He was very respectful and never touched her, but the work was exacting and fatiguing, and when she got home she was usually so tired that she threw herself on the bed and lay there for a long time in the dark until she had to get up because she was hungry. Then she would eat whatever was in the cupboard, and read while she ate. What she really wanted was to pose regularly for Rodin, but days now went by without his sending for her. The statue of the Whistler Muse still had no arms, but he seemed in no hurry for her to pose for them. Hadn't his assistant Guioché marked them out yet? she asked him.[30] In the end she decided that if she could not pose for Rodin she would rather pose for Isobel Bowser and she went back to her, because the work for Monsieur Jacques was so exhausting.[31]

Gwen was still considering sharing an apartment with Ursula. She realised it would be a long time before she could expect to earn money from a painting, so she planned to put some money aside to pay for it.[32] She was beginning to feel that it was a good thing she had to sell her work, since it would be all too easy otherwise to become over-sensitive about it, so she wrote to the secretary of the NEAC, promising to have a painting ready to send within the next few weeks. What she really needed, since the move to the rue de l'Ouest, was studio space, so she borrowed Chloe's apartment for a few weeks, while she was in London, but then Chloe came back and let the apartment before Gwen's picture was finished, which threw her.[33] She was still not happy living and painting at 6 rue de l'Ouest, and Ursula, concerned, suggested she should move again. It was 'sweet of you to think about my room – & the wall –' Gwen told her. 'I cannot move though, till I have more settled money, which I think will probably never be, as it is very difficult to get a cheap room, & there are reasons which make this quite possible to live in' – it was quiet, the concierge was pleasant; the neighbours never disturbed her.[34]

Ursula seemed faint-hearted about her own work, so Gwen took her in hand. She should not let herself be discouraged, she insisted; her paintings would always mean a great deal as they had such distinctive personality. She would surely improve technically if only she could concentrate her thoughts a little on the 'rules and problems' of painting.[35] 'I don't know if you could do in a very short time better work than you have,' she told her, 'but in a long time you would, & in the meantime – do as good I think & without so much *chance* in the doing of it, & *no* depression.'[36] She told Ursula she had been making some new discoveries about form, and if she was doing figure painting, there were some she could share with her. Ursula should not let herself become emotionally preoccupied, then she would be more focused. Gwen felt that something new was happening in her own work, and she wanted to 'fix something' in it.

> When I say fix something I mean be sure and certain for ever of some ideas of painting that have half shown themselves in the last two days, that sounds as if I am working hard and am very interested in painting doesn't it? But don't be deceived, everything interests me more than painting I am frightened at my coldness towards painting which gets worse and worse.

This is, surely, the feeling which always accompanies the effort of experimentation and technical innovation: anything, anything to avoid taking these new, unspeakably demanding steps. But Gwen was committed to her new discoveries, and determined to earn some money, and perhaps go to London. Soon, she was assuring Ursula that she still felt 'cold' towards 'Fenella, and vague things and people', but not towards her painting. She could not imagine, she said, why her vision would ever have any value in the world, she was so much less of an artist than Ursula, 'and yet I know it will – . . . because I am patient & recueillie in some degree'.[37]

It occurred to her that it might be possible to send drawings to the NEAC, since in her estimation her drawings were at least as valuable as her paintings. She was not sure what she could reasonably ask for them, she told Ursula, but 'I like them, so I think I should ask a good deal.'[38] She wanted to send some new ones, including one of the heads of herself, and some less recent ones, probably of Edgar Quinet. But she was not at all convinced that the NEAC's judging panel would share her view of them. It also occurred to her that communication might prove difficult, as she was anxious not to disclose her address. Her private life was sacrosanct, and she had to be protected from the possibility of uninvited guests in case of a visit from Rodin.

In the midst of all this, Edwin John arrived, expecting to be escorted around Paris by his daughter, but Gwen found him tiring and suspected his motives. She was sure he was only there to boast to relatives and friends that he had been with his daughter in Paris, 'and for that I have to be tired out & unable to paint for days. And he never helps me to live materially –

or cares how I live.' His presence, of course, brought back all the frustrations of family life. 'I don't think we go to Heaven in families any more,' she wrote exasperatedly to Ursula, 'but one by one.'[39] It was all intensely irritating; she was preoccupied by the new discoveries she was making and just wanted to get on. 'I have been thinking of painting a good deal lately,' she told Ursula. 'I think I shall do something good soon if I am left to myself & not absolutely destroyed.'[40]

Working under this strain, Gwen produced her two striking portraits of Fenella – *Nude Girl* and *Girl with Bare Shoulders* – and fixed something new in her painting, finding a unique way into the inner life of her subject. In these paintings she moved towards a kind of Expressionism worthy of comparison with some of the work of Picasso's Rose and Blue periods. Picasso himself had arrived in Paris in 1903, the same year as Gwen, and was experimenting with elongated forms, hollows and monochromatic colour, taking his subjects from the low life of artists in Montparnasse. In 1903–4 he painted *The Actor*, the large, vivid painting which seems to straddle his Rose and Blue periods; in 1909 he painted the intense, Expressionist *La Estera*. Gwen must surely have seen his work in the avant-garde galleries, though she never expressed any strong views on it. She was to meet him, in passing, in 1921 and the man himself made no particular impression on her.[41] But the Fenella paintings, and another in two variants, *A Woman Sewing* (perhaps begun at Monneville)[42] – definitely owe something to him, perhaps most strikingly in their debt to the Old Masters, in their use of exaggerated lines and in the way shadows and hollows suggest interiority. In *A Woman Sewing* as well as in the Fenella portraits, the hollows of the face reverberate with the directions of the figure, evoking an inner emptiness which seems to draw the eye inwards – an impression highlighted by the experimental use of yellow to depict lamplight. (Cecily Langdale has compared this painting with Picasso's *The Frugal Repast* and his *Woman with a Crow*.)[43] In a sense, Fenella was absolutely of her time and place. Slightly sickly, living frugally among the artists in Montparnasse, she conjures up not only a timeless spirituality but also a mood very much of the moment. There is a raw, direct sexuality in the depiction of her, similar to the hunger Picasso was describing, and subtly evocative of deprivation and depravity.

When Chloe came back to Paris in September 1910, Gwen began another portrait of her – possibly as a way of retaining the space she had become used to working in. Again, the work had to be done fast. Chloe would only be in Paris for three weeks, and expected her portrait to be finished in that time,[44] which put Gwen under pressure, but she was determined to get everything done so that she had something to send to the NEAC. It was very frustrating to have to work so fast, when she knew that 'everything that I do has to grow slowly'.[45] But in fact, as with the paintings of Fenella, she moved something into play which seems to have benefited from the need to establish forms and directions quickly. The portrait of Chloe[46] was also gently Expressionist, with elongated lines and an emphasis on the hollows of the hands and face. She did this portrait, too, with a restricted palette, distorting the figure with enlarged, bony hands, sloping shoulders, a slanting neck. The discreet use of red in the hands and face to highlight the bones (much more delicate on the canvas than it seems in reproduction) animates the figure, so that the clothed torso seems startlingly juxtaposed with flesh and bone. The rose-flesh of the exquisitely drawn mouth suggests a naked integrity. The amber colour of the pendant at her neck is shadowed in the hands, with their fine skin and long bones.

With nothing in the background, not even a hint of chairback – just the merest suggestion of a curtain to the left of the picture, echoing the folds of her dress – the figure seems to be floating, suspended in space, an impression highlighted by the reflection of the blue, grey and green tones of the ground under and around the figure's eyes. Looking askance at the viewer as if shielding something, she seems to suggest an animated, equally suspended inner life. There is collusion between painter and subject, not voyeurism. Gwen was quite clear about the new technical departure she was making, and sure that this painting was very different from the early portrait of Chloe, with its meticulous fragility.[47] The new portrait was more sombre, with its large hands, broadened and elongated haunches and high colour in the face. The result is, as in the portraits of Fenella, ever so slightly decadent. This was not quite what Gwen wanted to achieve, and despite the huge technical advances she was making she was never happy with the picture, always feeling it had been rushed.

Gwen was moving into a period of intense experimentation, and this could be nerve-racking. She tried to train her mind to be *recueillie*, focused. 'Do not be depressed by the idea of falling short – you can go some distance,' she copied into her notebooks, from the writings of 'S.J.'[48] In the summer of 1910, she was beginning to make abbreviated notes to herself about 'J.C.' –

Jesus Christ – and to study more seriously Catholic texts and tracts. During the next three years she would begin to make contact with the nuns at the Convent of the Soeurs de Charité Dominicaines de la Présentation de la Sainte Vièrge de Tours at Meudon. She also copied out extracts from 'Le Feu', meditations on the theme of finding interior strength and harmony which claimed that the education of the spirit and the search for spiritual peace and strength integrated 'beauté' and 'harmonie', and recommended a continual search for 'la perfection'. The human spirit was fugitive, decadent, and needed to be disciplined into strength, calm and courage. These teachings now became closely bound in with the vision she consistently attempted to realise in her work.

She went on demanding of herself intense self-discipline and concentration, and the self-control she imposed during these years was substantial and inflexible. 'Decide on subject, before sleeping, for the unconscious mind,' she wrote in her notebook.[49] A link between the Catholic philosophy of selflessness and her experimental approach to her portraiture was gradually being established. On the next page she wrote, 'Ask God to help you. Keep his comandement. Think of the circumstances of peoples lives, their degree of develloppment, etc.' [*sic*][50] She was profoundly questioning her own spiritual state. On her birthday, she asked herself, 'serai-je plus pres [*sic*] ou plus loin?' (am I getting closer, or farther away?)[51] The rules of self-discipline continued to apply, and they included the monumental effort to prioritise her painting over Rodin: 'Spend little time on letters, etc.'[52] He was still intermittently working on the Whistler Muse, and from time to time he would turn up in the rue de l'Ouest. She kept every note he sent her, however perfunctory (8 January 1910: 'please come next Tuesday a little before midday,' 2 February: 'come tomorrow to the rue de Varenne, and don't forget your letter to get you past the concierge.' 10 April: 'stay well. I have been ill and also away.') He was still paying her rent, as he had been, throughout all three of her moves, for the past five years. ('Come on Monday to the rue de Varenne, I've also got your rent for April.') On 3 May, he left a calling card; on 8 June he called and found her out again; on 10 June, he asked her to go to the rue de Varenne at about four o'clock. On 19 July, he sent for her to come to see him the next day; she also went to his studio to pose on 7 and 14 August, and again on 13 September.[53] It was impossible simply to put him out of her mind.

Rodin continued to try to find her new clients. In December, he wrote asking her to come to the rue de Varenne as he wanted to introduce her to his friend Monsieur Soudbinine, who wanted her to pose for him. (She did follow this up, but when she got to his studio the concierge directed her to his apartment, where she found him at home with his wife, all muffled up in a chair. On another chair sat the dog, also muffled up. Monsieur Soudbinine said they were both ill, he thought he had an abscess and could not imagine what he was going to do with himself, now that he was unable to paint. Never mind, said Gwen, at least you can think. He seemed to find this hilarious.)[54] Rodin kept on pleading tiredness, insisting that she must have courage, he was weary and old; she was asking too much of him. But it was not as if she played no part in his life; the reassurances kept coming: 'I love your little devoted heart'; 'Be patient, and stop getting so angry. Je vous embrasse.'[55] Gwen was still in anguish when she could not see him, and made sure he realised it. When she was desperate, she would go to the Hôtel Biron and wait for him in the street, but the Duchesse now usually intervened and protected him. He kept on asking her to come to the rue de l'Université or the rue de Varenne, however, despite the constant presence of the Duchesse. When the Duchesse intercepted Gwen's letters, he told Gwen to write to him at the rue de l'Université. Although at one level he had withdrawn from her, they were still nevertheless consistently in touch.

In the afternoons sometimes she would go to the Grands Magasins du Louvre – the shops at the Louvre – and write to friends on the headed notepaper supplied in the tearooms there, or to the Taverne de la Brasserie Dumesnil Frères, in the Boulevard Montparnasse, to keep warm because her room was so cold in the afternoons. (It had to be heated with a coal fire in a stove that didn't work very well, which was a lot of work, and she put all the effort of keeping it warm into the mornings in case Rodin arrived.) A band played in the Taverne de la Brasserie, and there were 'a lot of startling ladies amongst the men' (think Picasso's *La Estera*) but Gwen was left alone because she spread her books and notepaper all over the table, 'so they think me only a mad Anglaise'. But 'I don't want *anybody* to come to my room in the mornings,' she told Ursula; 'it would be tragic at some times, so I always make a rule to tell people.'[56]

As she went on making new technical discoveries, her drawings and watercolours became increasingly important to her. In addition to the self-portraits she did in 1910, she also did two somewhat uncanny drawings of

Ophelia. She was reading *Hamlet*,[57] and her Ophelia was largely done from her imagination, but she may have based it loosely on Grilda or Chloe, since the head and features of the figure in *Ophelia: Portrait Imaginé*[58] look very like those in the portrait of Chloe which she was also still working on. (Eighteen years later, in 1928, she would give it to her neighbour, Véra Oumançoff, by which time she had added flower sprigs to Ophelia's hair and inscribed it on the back, 'Ophelia. Portrait imaginé. Avril [erased] Sept 3. 28.' She also added an 'explanation. Ophelia was in love with Hamlet but he wasn't really bothered so she went off and drowned herself in the river, singing' – an account of Ophelia's plight surely unrivalled in its succinctness; and pure Gwen.) The figure is *distraite*, but not disturbing; whimsical, rather, even slightly fey. She did another drawing in a similar style, also oddly out of character. This one was called *Étude pour 'les Suppliantes'* and the model for this, too, could have been Grilda or Chloe; in fact it is very similar to some of the drawings which relate to the portrait of Chloe. What is remarkable is that on exhibition that year at the 'Exposition des femmes peintres et sculpteurs' was a work by Camille Claudel, the mistress with whom Rodin had had an intense love affair during the 1890s. The sculpture being exhibited was Claudel's *La Suppliante*, the sculpture she had been working on when her affair with Rodin came to an end: it shows her imploring, humiliated, naked, on her knees.[59]

The story of Rodin's love affair with Camille Claudel was well known. He had met her while she was a student and fallen madly in love with her, and she with him. Their affair was torrid and destructive: he called her 'ma féroce amie' (my savage/wild friend) and wrote to her of madness, torture, agony; of her 'terrible force': she had been 'the part of heaven that came into my life'.[60] She had been intensely jealous of the other women in his life, and infuriated by the presence of Rose Beuret; Rodin was worn down by the conflict and the affair ended when he moved to the first house he shared with Rose in Meudon.[61] In 1910 when Gwen did her drawings of *Ophelia* and *La Suppliante* Camille Claudel was still exhibiting but she was in a state of gradual disintegration, and in 1913 she would be discovered in her apartment, surrounded by broken sculptures, and removed to an asylum. Perhaps Camille's sculpture caught Gwen's eye and she was drawn by the subject matter to make a sketch of it. Rodin may have had a version of it in his studio. It is also possible that Chloe or Grilda sat for Camille as well as for Gwen: if so, the subject does not appear to have been mentioned. But at some level, Camille and Gwen now gravitated weirdly towards each other for a moment, as if to establish some fleeting testimony of connection. Perhaps Gwen had known about her all along and, for once in her life, wanted to punish Rodin.

In May 1910, she finished the two portraits of Fenella and sent them off to the NEAC. Only one was catalogued (in 1911 as *A Portrait*, which suggests it was probably the clothed version) but by the end of 1910, Gwen was writing to Ursula to tell her that her elder brother Thornton was in London and would be bringing it back to Paris for her. She felt silly for having sent it, she thought it looked dreadful and needed more work, which she would do when she could find the time. The fate of the second portrait, *Nude Girl*, is somewhat more mysterious. It was acquired by an anonymous member of the Contemporary Art Society, who presented it to the Society the following year, in 1911. Gwen made no further reference to it, at least not specifically. But there now began an interest in her work which made a significant change in her working life. Augustus knew, through Ursula, how worried Gwen was about money. He was selling paintings to an American lawyer and patron of the arts, John Quinn, a great friend of Yeats, who had introduced him to Maud Gonne, Ezra Pound, T.S. Eliot, James Joyce and other writers. Quinn knew Satie and Apollinaire. He was hugely active in promoting and supporting writers, and was also a close friend of Henri-Pierre Roché, the dealer who would later write *Les Deux Anglaises sur le continent* and *Jules et Jim*. Quinn also collected modern art, and wanted to build a substantial collection of contemporary European paintings. He knew Paris and was familiar with the Parisian art world, patronising Brancusi, Derain, Picasso, and later such painters as De Segonzac, Rouault, Rousseau and Marie Laurencin. He was anxious to extend his collection, particularly of work originating in France, and Augustus had mentioned Gwen's work to him. He had already unsuccessfully expressed an interest in the works she had exhibited at the NEAC in 1908, the early portrait of Chloe in a grey checked dress, and *La Chambre sur la Cour*. He now became more forthright. By 18 August 1910, Gwen had received from him a promise of 500 francs, and Augustus already had £10 as a commission fee.[62] Augustus was having one of Gwen's paintings (presumably *Nude Girl*) photographed. Quinn had already expressed an interest in buying a subsequent painting, so she may have told him that she was at work on a second portrait of Chloe. The following day, on 19 August, she wrote to him again to tell him she had now received his letter reassuring her that he did not mind waiting.

Two years later Quinn was still waiting for his picture. In November 1910 Gwen wrote innocently to Ursula, 'Has anything interesting happened in the NE? Are you exhibiting? What do you think of me *not* exhibiting? I am so glad, but I should like to have the American's picture done.'[63] Augustus had (in 1904) been elected as one of the original members of the Society of Twelve, a group of British draughtsmen, etchers, wood-engravers and lithographers whose secretary, Muirhead Bone, was organising its exhibitions at Obachs in New Bond Street in London. Gwen had promised him *Woman Sewing* but somehow had not got round to sending that either. He too had written a polite letter reassuring her that she need not hurry, but the date he had named was now long past. By now, she was posing every day and had stopped painting altogether; everything seemed to have caved in on her. 'I got so tired over Miss Leigh's portrait, they kept me at it too long and were always hurrying me,' she told Ursula. 'At last I could not go on any longer and I stopped and refused to send it to the NE. They are offended and hurt I don't know why.' A month later, she was writing to thank Ursula for her letter about the NEAC. 'I am so sorry I had to get that picture sold. I feel very much ashamed.'[64] Augustus had sent her the £10 as an advance, since Ursula had told him Gwen was short of money. It had been kind of him, she told Ursula, but she did not want it to happen again. 'I don't want him to know,' she wrote, then crossed that out: she did not want him to send her money again.

Since she was working on a picture for 'the American' and had not yet finished her picture of Chloe, since the two Fenella portraits were the only paintings she sent to London that summer and since the clothed portrait came back to her with Thornton; since Augustus had photographed a painting with Quinn in mind, having even already organised a financial transaction, we can only assume that *Nude Girl* had been intended for Quinn, but was somehow in the interim snapped up by somebody (Ursula? Chloe? Rothenstein? Augustus, even, for reasons best known to himself?) and re-routed to the Contemporary Art Society. Whatever happened, Gwen appears to have been paid for it, but the details had to be kept dark because of the risk of embarrassing not only Quinn but Augustus. The following January, John Quinn was still waiting, gamely assuring her not to worry 'a particle in regard to my picture. Take your time with it. Whenever it is ready, at your own time . . . let me know . . .'[65] He would finally get his picture – a completely new work, *Girl Reading at the Window*[66] – nearly two years later.

Ursula was still hoping to come back to Paris. The plan was still to paint and sit for each other, but Ursula initially only wanted to come for two weeks and Gwen was not sure, especially given her struggle to paint Chloe in three weeks, whether she could do anything in that time. She would not now be able to stay with Ursula, she said, cryptically, and probably would not be able to be there in the mornings. If they worked in the afternoons they could sit and paint on alternate days, which would give them each about six days to do a portrait . . . it was beginning to seem less likely.[67] Anyway, Gwen now had other plans.

In February of 1910 Rodin's studio at the rue de l'Université had been flooded, but there was no serious damage to the Whistler Muse. It was uninjured, he had asked the newspapers to reassure their readers, since it had been executed in plaster of Paris except for a portion of drapery at the base which was made of fuller's earth, which would have to be redone, but only about sixteen inches of drapery had been affected because the statue was about eight feet high, and erected on a sixteen-inch pedestal. The water had risen to within a few inches of the knee, but the damage was not major. It was impossible to say when the work would be finished. 'I have not abandoned it, you see, only I am hard to satisfy,' he told reporters. On 15 November, it was his seventieth birthday. The newspapers reported it the following day: 'numerous students and friends of the master gathered to mark the event, and to offer up their deep and respectful admiration'. He was photographed in his studio, working on a small maquette of the Whistler Muse.[68] Gwen, in the interim, had been hatching plans of her own; she now took decisive action.

11

29 rue Terre Neuve

Your life can still be a work of art . . .[1]

'Now I am going to tell you my little joy,' Gwen had written to Ursula towards the end of 1910. 'I have taken a little flat in Meudon!'[2] It was to be a source of great pleasure to her for many years. The flat was the top storey of 29 rue Terre Neuve, an old house near the forest, at the top of a steep, crooked little street leading down from the Terrasse of the Observatoire to the elaborately decorated station at Meudon-val-Fleury, down past the local shops – the baker, the butcher – and the church. It offered her not only proximity to Rodin (the Villa des Brillants was about twenty minutes' walk away), but access to country air, trees, flowers, in dense woodland. The Observatoire had been built on the site of the château, which burned down in 1871. In its place was a grassed Terrasse, with an avenue of trees, high up where the air was fresh, with a spectacular view to one side.

The village of Meudon, just six and a half miles outside Paris, is built on the steep hillside stretching from Clamart, down through the woods as far as the *arrondissement* of Versailles and the department of Seine-et-Oise. You can look down from the hillside to where the Seine runs as far as Paris. From the Terrasse – just at the top of the rue Terre Neuve, a minute's walk from Gwen's apartment – you can see the whole of Paris, with a clear view of the Eiffel Tower. From now on she would follow Rodin's pattern of living in rural surroundings and travelling in most days by train from the station at Meudon-val-Fleury or from Bas-Meudon along the Seine by river steamer. Just beyond the Terrasse, further up the hillside, is a winding lane into the forest of Meudon, a densely wooded forest of tall trees with several lakes, where people used to go in their charabancs for summer outings, picnics and tea parties. A photograph taken in 1910 shows the crossroads of the lake of the Fonceaux, one of the prettiest spots in the forest. A tea booth has been set up with tables, and the visitors, in long skirts and huge hats, are taking tea, evidently in holiday mood: the forest was somewhere to take the air and have your photograph taken. Regarded as one of the most important 'massif' forests to the west of Paris and covering more than 1,200 hectares, it has vast areas of unspoilt woodland. Half consists of chestnut trees; the rest is rich with oaks, beeches, wild cherry trees, ash, silver birches, maples, hornbeams, limes, false acacias and conifers. The birdsong is lively, and noticeable in all the winding, leafy streets of Meudon. But the greatest advantage of the forest was that it was so near to Gwen's apartment: two or three minutes' walk up the hill past the Terrasse, and she could be deep in the woods.

In spring the forest paths were covered with bluebells and anemones. In olden times, Druid cults had been practised there. It was a natural habitat for Gwen, reminiscent in some ways of the leafy, wooded lanes of Pembrokeshire; particularly ravishing in the summer, and with a spectacular quality of stillness and complete silence, except for the sound of the birds. Coincidentally – though Gwen may not have known this – the name Meudon (*Meodum*) is Celtic – it means mountain of sand. If she went down through the village in the opposite direction, turning away from the Observatory then down the steep lanes along the rue Jacqueminot past the Gare Meudon-Montparnasse (one of Meudon's four railway stations) she could walk to the 'quartier Bas-Meudon', which stretches right down to the Seine. There you could dine by the river at La Grotte, le Martin-Pêcheur or la Pêche Miraculeuse, famous restaurants frequented by visitors and artists who wanted to sample the local fried fish which was their speciality.[3] These restaurants were very expensive – too expensive to become local haunts for Gwen – but she liked the look of them, and told Ursula she would like to try them when she came to stay.[4]

The atmosphere of Meudon was – still is – a peculiar mixture of the devout and the whimsical. There was a convent, with an orphanage attached, and the orphan children worshipped at the local church, which was the source of social contact, and determined the mores of the community. The children would arrive with the Sisters from the convent and sit towards the front of the church in their pinafores and hats, observed by Gwen, who now came to sit in her black cape drawing them from the back. Saint Martin and Saint Blaise is a light, spacious, uncluttered church, with stained glass windows and paintings, depicting stages of the story of the Crucifixion. She enjoyed seeing the little girls all huddled together at the front of the congregation, and she now began to make carefully observed sketches of the worshippers, particularly of women and children, the nuns and the orphans bent over their prayer books, wriggling in their seats or bending to exchange a furtive, whispered comment or two during Mass.[5]

But the character of Meudon had other determining features: the Observatoire, the forest, the Orangerie. Also on the site of the new château – more quirkily – was the Établissement aérostatique, an aerostatic school. The Établissement aérostatique had been founded in 1877 by Captain Charles Renard around the lake of the Chalais. He had achieved there, in 1884, the first closed circuit flight in the world in a balloon, on board the *La France*. His flight had captured the popular imagination: *Le Pèlerin* for 20 January 1884 reported that Captain Renard's hot-air balloon navigated its route high above the nests of the forest of Meudon. The balloon was now kept in its hangar, a local site of great interest, called 'Le Hangar Y'. This appealed to Gwen's sense of humour: she was to immortalise the hangar, in her own way, some years later.

She told Ursula she would be taking the top floor of 29 rue Terre Neuve in January. She was renting it from the Joly family for 45 francs every three months, and the original idea was that Chloe or Grilda would take it for some months, presumably while she spent time in Paris. She had not been sleeping well in Paris, and she needed country air. She planned to keep her apartment in the rue de l'Ouest as a studio. When Ursula came to stay she could have 'a lovely room with the sun coming in nearly every morning and no street noise'.[6] There were three rooms as well as 'a little kitchen and heaps of cupboards and a grenier and one gets into the Gare Montparnasse in half an hour'. The rooms were sparse, with no carpets, and she kept them like that. She had very little furniture and no bathroom, but it suited her, and she could paint in it. (She bathed at the public baths, in a *double salle* where she went regularly on Sunday afternoons.) After the war she gave up the rue de l'Ouest altogether, and painted in the rue Terre Neuve.

It was a life, in some respects, like Rodin's. The Villa des Brillants, built in Louis XII style, was nevertheless relatively modern and in Rilke's view very ugly: was built of stone and red brick right at the top of the hillside overlooking the Seine valley. There, Rodin indulged his delight in the countryside and his passion for nature, surrounded by animals, including a monkey, dogs, swans and pigeons, and taken care of by Rose, who ran their country domain, appearing from time to time to wait at table if visitors arrived, but never forming part of the assembled company. Sometimes Rodin's guests were not even introduced to her, and assumed she was his housekeeper. For the most part, this was his escape from the pressures of secretaries, technicians, unwanted visitors and being *bousculé par le monde*. In the grounds of the Villa des Brillants was the pavillion d'Alma, part-museum, part-workshop, where he kept his sculptures and maquettes. It was here that Rodin developed the sketches and plans for all his works, and where occasionally his subjects would pose for him. He worked in Meudon all morning and caught the train in time to be at the Hôtel Biron, where his model usually awaited him, by two o'clock. He normally went from the station at Meudon-val-Fleury, down beyond the foot of the rue Terre Neuve, rather than the station closer to the Villa des Brillants, Meudon-Montparnasse, because although it was a quarter of an hour away it was more or less on the flat. He did this walk on foot until he got too old to manage it, then he used to be picked up from the station in his horse and cart, pulled by the 'placide Rataplan': occasionally, he would give Gwen a lift in it. Sometimes he took the passenger boat from Bas-Meudon along the Seine.

Now it was easier to go to Rodin's house, and try to catch a glimpse of him. Sometimes, Gwen would linger at the gate to the garden at the back, and occasionally she would see him come out in the evenings with his dogs, to watch the dusk.[7] But there were to be no delicious, illicit encounters at the Villa des Brillants. Rose presided there, and was there all the time; it was where Rodin went to relax and escape. But even if Gwen did not see him any more frequently than before, living in Meudon meant she was nearer to him at night, and since he came and went with reliable regularity, she knew where he was. When he left Paris to go home, he would still be nearby. They now shared a world. It was as close as she could get to him, and indisputably it made her happier.

'Don't be afraid of falling into mediocrity – you would never,' she resolved, at the beginning of 1911.[8] She was clearly delighted with

Meudon, and working hard, but still felt that to some extent she was groping in the dark. She confided some of her anxieties to Winnie: 'don't be conquered by your nerves and body,' came the reply, 'just send them about their business and you will find they will be obedient to you.' She was to tell Winnie all about it. 'Aunt R reminds me of you,' she warned: 'sometimes she says she can't write unless she has a cup of tea, or an ice cream and when she has had those she finds some other excuse, she is governed by her body – *such a mistake*.' Aunt Rose had asked Winnie to tell Gwen she was trying to get her a book she thought she would like, *How to be Magnetic*. So just remember, 'To be magnetic one must be calm – a nervous person is *not* magnetic, so relax and relax until it comes easy, that is the way to conquer nerves. *Do Do Do*.'[9]

Gwen headed her notebook entry for 2 February 'R', which may mean she was quoting Rodin. 'Live largely and deeply. Do not be afraid. You can do some good because you will it. Be humble and modest. Don't be a poor little worldly frightened thing!' Her 'Rule for life' that month was 'Don't expect anything more from love . . . Love the difficulties . . .'[10] She told herself to 'keep down the animal nature', but it was an anguishing struggle. A brief encounter with Rodin at the concierge's lodge preceded two days of anguish.

Although the move to Meudon did nothing to bring Rodin more closely or more frequently into her life, it did serve to extend the range of her vision. She made new friends among the neighbours and the congregation of the church, and she now gradually increased the pictorial vocabulary of her drawings. The notebooks she drew in were small enough to fit in a pocket: sometimes minuscule, pocket-diary size, often with cheap, flimsy paper. The sketches she made in the church had to be done quickly, before the little girls moved, so she developed a new method of making rough, rapid marks *in situ* to broadly establish the forms; she would then go home and elaborate on the drawings later. She worked rapidly in soft pencil or charcoal, making initial drawings from a few quick, rough marks and working them up later in a mixture of pencil and watercolour or gouache. A lightness, and a strong sense of movement, now characterised her drawings.

Meudon also gave her a new community. Her domestic life included neighbours, and friends with whom she shared none of the intensity of her friendship with Ursula, but they were loyal, affectionate and she saw them often. Her special friends were the Joly sisters, daughters of her landlord, the elderly Monsieur and Madame Gervais, whom she visited regularly as they grew old and ailing, and Angeline Lhuisset, a gentle, sickly girl who spent a lot of time in Dieppe and later in Lailly. When Angeline was away from Meudon she and Gwen corresponded regularly, and it is quite possible that Gwen used her as the model for 'the convalescent', who was to appear during the next few years in a number of paintings of a girl in a wicker chair, often wearing a distinctive, plain blue dress.[11] In one sense, Meudon was a retreat into privacy; in another sense, it socialised her.

The desire to work more freely and intuitively, finding new subjects in her new surroundings, coexisted with Gwen's other new obligation, to John Quinn in New York. She had begun work on a new painting with Quinn in mind. She had been to see an exhibition of Dutch paintings, which included some fine Rembrandts, and she wrote to him about it that August. Her painting for him was still not done, she told him: 'I have been unable to paint for months this year or it would have been done before.' But the exhibition of Dutch paintings had fired her imagination. She may also have been looking at work by the German Renaissance painter, Dürer. She drew directly on Dürer's work in the picture she was now working on: a tiny oil painting in dark colours, damasks, dark browns and almost-blacks, of a girl holding an open book.[12] Light falls gently from behind the figure, irradiating her face, and across a swathe of checked curtain at a hidden window. Behind her is a writing table: a book, a pencil and her open notebook are visible on it, and on the far wall are Gwen's drawings of cats, and a less distinct drawing, which could be one of Rodin's. The girl's forehead also gently catches the light, giving her a slightly heavenly impression; the face suggests piety: Gwen told Ursula that she had consciously modelled the head on one of Dürer's.[13] It is slightly reminiscent in mood of her earlier portraits of Dorelia, but the treatment of the figure is far more concentrated, and the overriding mood is one of dynamic movement. The figure is radiant, expectant; poised almost as if for flight, or a dancer's leap. The pious impression is fused with something powerfully charged.

As she worked, she wrote from time to time politely and informatively to Quinn, assuring him that the painting she planned to send him would presently be finished. She sent him friendly, chatty letters, keeping him in touch with events in Paris: Henri Rousseau had died, and his work was being exhibited at the Indépendantes and she was full of admiration, telling Quinn that 'at 50 years old he felt he must paint and so he painted not knowing at all how to paint. The pictures are very remarkable works as you can imagine, they are works of art.'[14] Quinn himself was a confirmed Modernist, he told her, 'a man of my own day and time', rather than 'travelling over the beaten path' of the work of earlier generations. 'I think there is a lot of rot written about many of the old masters,' he added, fatally. 'The most of them ought to be called "Old fakirs" instead of "Old Masters." A bad picture doesn't become a good picture merely by growing old.'[15] (As a statement of his position, it clearly did not inspire any particular confidence: it must have confirmed Gwen's fears about the reliability of his judgement, but at the same time, she did not hold it against him.)

It was Ursula's opinion she really respected, however. She now wanted her advice on the new painting, *A Lady Reading*, and very much wanted her to come to Paris: 'If you possibly can Ursula do come soon!'[16] She had nearly finished the painting, it would be done in two or three days now, so then they could paint each other, as they kept meaning to, or go off on a trip to explore the old cathedrals. She did not want to run the risk, she said, of influences or opinions which would throw her off course: 'When one sees a few people only as I do it is almost as dissapating [*sic*] to the mind as living always with people as one impression does not chase out another at once but the old one lasts too long.'[17] 'You are working for those you love,' she told herself on 27 September 1911, 'being *recueillie* will be your strength.'[18] From the works of Youimoto Yashi she noted that, 'Dépasser le but n'est pas l'atteindre': to overreach your goal is not the same as attaining it.[19]

When Ursula still seemed unable to come to Meudon, in late September or early October Gwen sent the painting to her in London where, perhaps recognising its unusual intensity, she passed it on for a second opinion, meanwhile writing to Gwen with her own reactions to it. She assumed it was a self-portrait and said she thought it was a bit 'artistic', particularly the head. She also assumed the figure was supposed to be sitting on the table, which horrified Gwen. At first, she was puzzled by the fact that Ursula thought it too 'artistic' – surely they used to think that was a good word? But on reflection, she could see what she meant. 'You are so right about the head. I tried to make it look like a vierge of Dürer, it was a very silly thing to do. I did it because I didn't want to have my own face there.'[20] She now began another version for Quinn: *Girl Reading at the Window*,[21] which was similar in composition but done in different colours, and with a different head. This time, she used her own face, with the distinctive black bow tied round her head which she usually wore in those days.[22]

Ursula, in London, showed the first of the two paintings, *A Lady Reading*, to a gentleman whose name she did not disclose, even to Gwen: the business of gathering opinions in London still had to be done surreptitiously while Quinn was still waiting patiently in New York for paintings he might never get. When it came, the response delighted Gwen. The man had compared her to Dostoevsky. 'Tourgeneff used to make me see pictures when I read him,' she told Ursula, 'but I should like better to be like Dostoevsky!!'[23] She was now wondering whether to send 'Mr. Quinn's picture', together with some drawings, to the NEAC, since she was reluctant to send drawings by themselves, and she was still worrying about Quinn's judgement. She wanted Ursula's opinion because 'I should never have known what it appeared like to people if it was sent at once to Mr. Quinn, who doesn't know anything about painting.' She was longing for Ursula to come and spend some time in Meudon, and assured her that if she did she would be able to work entirely undisturbed; she had lately read somewhere that 'Anything very good, the greatest people who think are of the opinion, must be done "dans l'austere silence".' They would only see each other at breakfast and supper, as she would be going into Paris to work. If Ursula came soon, she could work for nearly a whole month, and have time to submit to the winter NEAC. It was now mid-September and the summer was practically over, but she still hoped she might manage a visit before it got cold. She was loving Meudon, and had spent the last few days clearing the place up and resting. She loved the feeling of being in the country, especially in the autumn evenings: 'last evening I walked in the forest,' she told her, 'in the dark & rain, it was lovely walking through the fallen leaves I picked up a bundle of wood for my fire there was much wind too'.[24]

'Write when all is known!!' she urged Ursula – she was counting on her advice as to whether to send the second painting to London as well as the first. In fact, the two paintings are completely different in atmosphere and mood. By comparison with *A Lady Reading*, the second painting – *Girl Reading at the Window* – is stilted, wooden, bland. It has none of the Rembrandtesque qualities of *A Lady Reading*. The change of colour scheme, from dark reds and rich browns to yellow ochres and pale blues, has effected a complete transformation of mood. *Girl Reading at the Window* seems to have lost all the purity and focus of its predecessor, and it has lost, too, the atmosphere of contained joy and radiance; all the sense of concentrated expectation which gives *A Lady Reading* its dynamic, its whole point. However, the movement away from representation is clearer in *Girl Reading at the Window*, and Gwen may even have felt, particularly in the light of Ursula's apparent objection to the 'artistic' style of *A Lady Reading*, that the second painting was more consistent with the direction she had begun to move in. Certainly, when she had finished it she was pleased with it, and thought it expressed her mood. Ursula must have advised her to send it to the NEAC because it was shown there, and attracted several press notices. In November Gwen wrote to tell Quinn she had sent it, and that it had been praised. 'I don't know what it means,' she modestly told him, 'but I suppose it means something. However, I have heard from several artists who can really judge it that it has given them pleasure to see it, and I know it expresses something of what I felt, so I am glad to send it to you.'[25]

That November she 'tired herself in shops and streets' during the day, and in the evenings concentrated on her studies, continually making new resolves ('Controle your emotions. They are infidelities to God. be glad at every opportunity to control your mind and body . . . Keep a calme exterior . . . Always be making an effort . . .' [*sic*][26] She was living in a community in which she was now far more visible than she had been in Montparnasse. The congregation of the church were her neighbours, and they all met in the butcher's, the baker's, out walking, as well as in church. She was also dealing with the religious community of the convent, and did not always find the nuns easy. But she was nevertheless considering becoming a Catholic. 'I read to stop myself thinking,' she had written, earlier in the year. She had copied into her notebook an unidentified religious extract which offered a definition of the soul. Distinguishable from sensibility, with which women were apt to confuse it, the soul should be thought of as the 'interior eye' which fixes on God and infinity. If you close this interior eye, she had noted, you close the eye of the soul.[27] From this time on, her paintings and drawings began to take on a religious significance.

Living alone was difficult: it made it hard to meet people because the contrast between domestic space and society was so marked. But when she went to church and studied her Catholic teachings, she could discover the freedom of finding an authority for her thoughts: 'God will tell me what to say.'[28] 'He will also tell me what people to talk to . . . and how to arrange my life. I saw what a difficulty there is in following the simplest rule by myself.' She enjoyed the singing at Mass, and began to think about joy and kindness, and to see these things as 'of the same nature as the ecstasy of the saints'. What Meudon offered was a delicate sense of community. The Catholic teachings were comforting – a way of enabling her to feel that the self-discipline she practised was justified, and applicable to community as well as in isolation. Sometimes she felt as if she would like to escape: to 'go and live somewhere where I meet nobody I know till I am so strong that people and things would not effect [*sic*] me beyond reason'.[29]

She learned religious meditation, and the lessons of the saints. She noted down Carlyle's remark, that the important things are formulated in a condition of silence.[30] 'Be simple,' she told herself, in her notebook for December; 'expect nothing from circumstances.' On 21 December 1911 she noted, simply, 'romance all day'. She would try to remember that to pay attention is creative; in future she would look at 'everything, every thought, attentively'.[31] She could always go on loving Rodin, she decided, it was just that she must realise that she could expect nothing from the relationship. She saw herself, straightforwardly, as 'a young woman, with a longing and a hope to be good, not caring for the opinion of anyone, not afraid of obscurity or contempt',[32] despite support from Quinn, who was one of the major New York dealers, acceptance by the NEAC and a number of encouraging press notices. Her new home in the rue Terre Neuve had not really brought Rodin any closer, but on the other hand she had not lost him. She would continue to love him, and to work, study and struggle for self-knowledge. Her notebooks constitute an ongoing artistic struggle in their own right; the evidence of a consistent, concerted and imaginative striving for artistic integrity: 'Your life can still be a work of art,' she reminded herself.[33]

12

The 'Nun'

. . . this desire for a more interior life.[1]

'Do you still see little Marie?' wrote Fenella Lovell to Rodin, on 20 February 1912. 'Is she well?' She was in Menton but she hoped to be in Paris in April. Rodin had contacted her and she was writing to thank him 'with all her heart'. Her nerves and lungs were bad; she had heard nothing from Augustus since last July, but the last two letters she had had from him had made her 'heureuse! heureuse!' She sent regards to the Duchesse, and offered to sing for Rodin when she came to Paris.[2]

In March, Augustus remarked to his friend Meg Sampson that she would be clever if she succeeded in inducing Gwen to leave France. 'I wish she would take a change.'[3] But by now nobody really believed they would succeed in enticing her away, though clearly everybody worried about her. Gwen's notebook for 3 March shows her making ten 'Rules to Keep the World Away', among them, 'Do not listen to people (more than is necessary)'; 'Do not look at people (ditto)'; 'Have as little intercourse with people as possible'; 'When you have to come into contact with people, talk as little as possible'; . . . 'Do not look in shop windows.'[4] She was still hoping Ursula would come to stay. She had been to the Futurist exhibition and wanted to go again with her. 'There are some painters who call themselves "Futuristes" exhibiting now,' she wrote to her on 7 March. 'I should like to go and see them . . . They are very amusing, and have great talent I think. I don't know whether it is Art . . . The school of Matisse is far, far behind them and most academic and conventional beside them.'[5] When Ursula did not materialise, she went again to Dieppe for a few days, and to Bossnet, where she spent her time gathering flowers. On 9 April she resolved, in her notebook, 'Be alone. Do not search for sympathy where it is not to be found. Do not care for the opinion of people – or work for it in any way.'[6] She was working for her own sake, and needed solitude to enable her to make new discoveries and explore new directions.

At about this time she began regular visits to the Mother Superior of the Convent, who counselled putting thoughts of the past away from her, and encouraged her in her Catholic instruction. In her notebooks, she addressed her tendency towards disobedience and recorded her strenuous efforts at self-discipline. Surely she had 'fallen so much' because she had failed to make 'definite resolutions'. 'Oh that I could forget everything in my past life which hurts me! (which is a prevention to my becoming a child of God.)'[7] The cultivation of the idea of herself as an obedient child now began, an aspect of her inner life which may be best understood as an interpretation of one of the tenets of the Catholic faith: we all begin as innocent children, blessed by God, until knowledge of the world corrupts us. Religious obedience is about struggling to retrieve and re-establish the state of innocence with which children are blessed, so that we attain a state of grace and become, again, children of God.

The mystery of Rodin's failure to complete the Muse had hit the press again; England was still waiting for the tribute to Whistler in which so much had been invested. The *Manchester Guardian* sent reporters to Paris and ran a story on 9 April, 'A Visit to Rodin': 'Whistler's bust? No, it's not finished . . . it *will* be done – in time. I cannot fix a date . . . I must work when I feel I *can*.' He kept having to turn to other things. 'But England shall have the bust.' He had been very proud to be awarded a Ph.D. from Oxford University at the same time as General Booth. The reporter had heard that *le maître* was arrogant and difficult, but he found only 'a simple-mannered, warm-hearted old gentleman', so much so that he confessed his own secret ambition to make a great work of art. 'No, no! that would not make you happy,' replied Rodin, 'for you would still doubt. One always doubts, always!' They seem to have parted the best of friends, and when the piece came out, Rodin appeared in it as a kind of honorary Yorkshireman. If he had been richer, he might have been a great painter, but he turned to sculpture after studying the statues at the Louvre because he could afford only 'rough paper and charcoal': 'Canvas and colour were too expensive for the lad.'[8]

Posing for the Muse was becoming more difficult, since the Duchesse now made her presence increasingly strongly felt. She was a fascinating talker, and had recently made a great hit when she accompanied Rodin to Rome, with her repertoire of stories about the Pope and cardinals. She was humorous, some said 'Balzacian'; the consensus was that she was very bright, if a bit common. Certainly, she knew how to keep the show on the road.[9] But the sight of Gwen hovering outside the Hôtel Biron waiting for Rodin, or knocking at the door asking to give him her letters, infuriated her. Gwen tried to circumvent her by waiting for Rodin at the station, but while she waited at Montparnasse he invariably left from Invalides. She felt 'sick at heart' with it all. She told him she knew perfectly well that he was worried about her being seen by his 'amie' but there was no need to worry, she would make sure Claire did not see her again. But how could he have so totally forgotten her? It was 'cette femme' who had caused this, she was wicked and stupid. 'What a life you have given me!' she protested. Why was he doing this to her? He had always known the depths of her feelings; what had she done to deserve this loneliness?[10]

The Duchesse undoubtedly played her part in Gwen's need, at this time, to cultivate solitude. The world cannot have felt a very accommodating place, given the state of things at the Hôtel Biron. Be calm, Rodin told her again and again, beauty is to be found in harmony, not in this disturbance. One week she went to the Hôtel Biron six times and each time the concierge told her that he was away. She refused to believe this, and eventually he came out and spoke a few words to her; but the Duchesse now pitched in and was trying to put a stop to any contact. She was trying, Gwen told him, to establish harmony in her life, but she needed love. He was asking her to be harmonious, then stopping her from having what she needed to achieve it. Writing to him helped, but what was she to do if even her letters began to be refused? He had talked of the needs of the heart and spirit, but she needed him to fulfil those needs. Ever since he moved to the rue de Varenne she had been unhappy. She still longed for him, her room was still fresh and pretty, she was still always prepared for him. When they told her he was away she believed them, but she could not stop waiting for him in the street. Why was he pulling away from her, surely he knew she was obedient and discreet? She was posing for two hours a day, she told him, and keeping her room clean, and sometimes she sewed, but mostly she just waited for him and prayed. It was a 'grande tristesse', and it made everything she tried to do feel hard. After a while, she would begin to feel better and suggest posing for the Muse again, but if he replied through one of his secretaries, she told him, her heart would freeze with anguish. She was going mad alone in her room; finally she took herself off to Monneville, where she felt calmer and stronger, and bought some new clothes. When she came back, she told him, she would be waiting at the Gare des Invalides to show him her new things. 'Oh *mon Maître!* . . . when it comes to me, please don't listen to that jealous woman!'[11]

Rodin still came intermittently to the rue de l'Ouest, but he was becoming increasingly fragile, and his failing health made him very vulnerable. Among those who could see that his health was failing were opportunists who were prepared to take advantage of this, and without really realising it he had become rather worn down by the Duchesse. It was an odd year for him, with an incident which left him disillusioned and jaded. At the end of May, the Ballets Russes returned to Paris for Nijinsky's fifth Parisian season, and Nijinsky danced *L'Après-Midi d'un Faune*. Rodin publicly praised Nijinsky's highly controversial, seductive performance, and in so doing unwittingly set himself up as an Aunt Sally to Nijinsky's fiercest and most powerful critics. The editor of *Le Figaro* attacked Rodin in the press, drawing attention to the fact that this was the man who displayed his brutal and immodest drawings on the walls of the Hôtel Biron, once the chapel of the Sacré Coeur. His reputation was temporarily undermined by this, even though eventually he turned it to his advantage. In the end, the episode meant a new round of publicity for him, and the Ministry received a flood of letters recommending a Musée Rodin.[12] Asked, years later, for her views on the Russian Ballet, Gwen was to say that she had once seen it but had found it impossible to watch, it was too powerful.[13]

But that was not all that happened that summer. The Duchesse was finally dispatched, on 13 June, over a row about a box of drawings which had mysteriously disappeared. Rodin's then secretary, Marcelle Martin, was the chief suspect. She appealed to the Duchesse, and in the process discovered that it was the Duchesse herself who had placed her under suspicion. Rodin's friends now pitched in and began to issue him with stern warnings about the wisdom of continuing the liaison. By the autumn, it was all over. The *New York Times* for 16 September ran a front-page article headed 'Rodin and Duchesse Quarrel', reporting that the split was welcome. She 'had exercized too great influence over her master . . . and generally monopolized the sculptor's affairs'. Rilke was unequivocal. 'The awful Mme de Ch . . . is no longer there . . .' He wished the cause of her removal could have been something more profound, and that Rodin could have derived greater pleasure from her departure.[14]

Everyone seemed to feel by now that Gwen should be watched to make sure she did not retreat altogether. No one said so, but those close to her may have worried about the virtue of the Catholic conversion. She must also have seemed less accessible since she had moved out of Paris. Everyone tried to make her take a holiday. Isobel Bowser was in Pont l'Abbé with the painter Ruth Manson and her daughter Rosamund, and Ruth wrote urging Gwen to join them; Grilda and Chloe went off to Margate for the sea air, and asked her to go with them. Gwen's elder brother Thornton began to write to her regularly from British Columbia, where he was prospecting for gold, regaling her with his adventures. He was in a part of the country where the mountains went straight up and the rapids straight down. 'The upper one is Surprise and the lower one Death. I think they are not so bad as they are named and I think I will call one Sure-As-Hell and the other Ennui.' He told Gwen he was in touch with Aunt Rose and Winifred.[15]

In July, Fenella contacted Rodin again. She had happened to be near his house and had seen a lot of cars coming out of his gate, so she knew he was there. She wanted to see him but did not dare go near, there were too many people. But she had a proposal. If the statue he had begun with Mary John was still not finished, would he like her, Fenella, to model for it? She thought she had more or less the same physique as Gwen's, though she was slightly smaller, and not as beautiful. But Augustus had said she had a very good body, and Epstein had said she was beautiful; so had other artists. Of course, if he wanted to finish it with Gwen he was not to give Fenella another thought, she would not want to deprive Gwen of work – not for anything! But she could do with a little help . . . Rodin gallantly sent her 20 francs and the matter seemed to be closed.[16]

Earlier that year, in April, the *Titanic* had gone down. Gwen had read reports in the newspapers and cried: here was a much larger tragedy than any sadness of her own.[17] With the *Titanic* sank a manuscript by Joseph Conrad and a number of valuable paintings. In August, Gwen wrote to Quinn to say that she had left the sending of *Girl Reading at the Window* to Augustus to arrange, and had been expecting to hear for months that Quinn had received it. 'I think my picture is now at the bottom of the sea with the "Titanic." I am hoping to hear from you that it is not so.' By now, she was dissatisfied with what she had achieved. 'It is not as I want to paint like [*sic*], and I now know a little more what I want to do.'[18] She had been doing gouache drawings for a long time, though she had also begun several paintings. 'The drawings must be done,' she told him, 'because I feel so much inclined to do them, and I learn from my pictures in doing them. The subjects keep on presenting themselves to be done,' but she hoped she would soon finish the last of them, then she would be able to finish a painting. She hoped he did not mind her being so 'unbusiness-like', and assured him his next painting would be 'none the worse for coming later'.[19]

Quinn replied that no, he had not yet received the painting from the Chenil Gallery in London, but in the course of writing the letter he remembered that he had not, after all, sent instructions for it to be shipped from there, so it could not be with the *Titanic*. In fact it was in a lot with sixteen studies by Augustus, a painting by 'a young Hebrew named Mark Gertler', three studies by Innes, a couple of paintings by Spencer Gore, and others. Knewstub at the Gallery had sent a photograph of it, which Quinn had shown James Huneker, the art critic. He had been enthusiastic, and Quinn would not think of doing anything, he said, but keeping it. 'It is the way for a conscientious artist to be dissatisfied with what has been done. That shows that the artist has developed the critical spirit, and without the spirit of self-criticism there is no progress in art.'[20] Gwen said that when it arrived, he was to let her know if he liked it since 'I cannot judge my own work well.'[21]

Quinn came to Paris that autumn hoping to meet her and see more of her work, but she missed him by just four days, which she regretted. She had been to the country, she told him – she may simply have been lying low in Meudon while Quinn searched for her in Paris; or she may have gone briefly to Dieppe, where Angeline was spending the summer. Quinn now offered her another commission, an opportunity for which she was grateful, though she felt somewhat rueful about having kept him waiting so long for the first one. But if he had not paid her an advance, she assured him, she could not imagine when she would have finished it. If he did want another she felt it should stand its trial with him when he saw it, or at least a photograph of it, as she did not want to appear to be taking advantage of his generosity. In principle, she was delighted by his offer to buy another but she did not feel able to accept more than he had paid for *Girl Reading at the Window* – £30. Fifty pounds, which he was offering for the next painting, seemed to her too much. He – diplomatic in his turn (and possibly prompted by Augustus?) – told her he was the proud possessor of a Puvis de Chavannes, which of course impressed her. She told Quinn (echoing Rodin) that she thought Puvis de Chavannes 'surely the greatest painter of the century'.[22] He also suggested that she should go and see the dealer James Durand-Ruel's collection of pictures, which included some Renoirs. She decided to go with Ursula when she came, since Ursula was 'as much charmed by Renoir' as she was herself.

Quinn's main concern was that she should send him another picture, so he replied that he was delighted by her promise to send him her next one, 'not in place of the one which I already have, but in addition to it'. She was to put her own price on it, and take her time over it. He suggested that when she next went to Durand-Ruel's, she might introduce herself and he would show her his best things, and perhaps even the paintings at his apartment. He was a gentleman, a great friend of Puvis de Chavannes, who with Degas had been best man at Durand-Ruel's wedding. But don't go at weekends, Quinn warned her, it was very unpleasant as there were 'all sorts of Germans and foreigners and Swedes there then'. In November *Girl Reading at the Window* finally arrived in New York and Quinn's response to it, Gwen told him, 'quite warmed my heart'. On 17 November she wrote thanking him for his kind offer to buy all her pictures and send money regularly. 'I cannot decide on my answer now but will in a few weeks. It would be very good for me to have money regularly and so be able to have models but I am not sure at this moment whether my pictures will be good.' She would send some photographs and perhaps he would like one enough to want the picture. But she thought perhaps he might find a 'genre' picture more interesting.[23] She was obviously already beginning to think about, perhaps even to work on, the painting she would begin in earnest the following year, encouraged by the local priest, a portrait of the Foundress of the Convent at Meudon. This portrait, based on a prayer card (based in its turn on a contemporary oil painting), was to go through six or seven variants and it would take her seven years.

Clearly, Quinn's offer to advance her regular sums of money on account would be a practical solution to the problem of making regular sales of her work, and it would mean that Gwen worked consistently on her paintings as well as her drawings. But she must have realised that it would also put pressure on her. She began to worry all the time that her paintings would not be finished and she became increasingly perfectionist. She also, more discreetly, worried about Quinn's taste. She wanted her work to be good, and was anxious that he was no judge of her achievements. He – perhaps sensing this – tried to reassure her by seeking second opinions from New York artists, critics and dealers, who gave him the seal of approval. Moreover, he genuinely admired and took pleasure in Gwen's work. What he paid her was never astronomical, but she might not have made more elsewhere, and might well have done less painting without Quinn's support. Her drawings were her real focus of experimentation, and it was with watercolour and gouache that she derived more emotional satisfaction from her work, partly because in these media she could explore the subjects which presented themselves in her new environment – the foliage and flowers she picked in the forest and hedgerows, the little girls of the orphanage, and other members of the congregation. But it was the paintings in oils that Quinn wanted, and he favoured her portraiture, so she took models from her neighbourhood, including the 'convalescent', possibly Angeline, whom she painted many times, and continued to work on her portraiture. She began to transpose into her paintings the technical discoveries she was making and the lessons she was learning in her drawing.

While she embarked on her portrait of the Foundress, she continued to sketch in watercolour and gouache. Her most responsive subjects were the members of the congregation of the church at Meudon. They were subjects suited to Gwen's talent, and to her new practice of making quick marks, elaborating them more carefully later and then quickening them again with washes, in the style of Rodin's drawings. While the avant-garde of the Paris art world moved towards abstraction, Gwen was perfecting her own method. She made conventional drawings in the style of the Old Masters, but with abbreviated lines, determining the directions and establishing a sense of movement with the use of watercolour or gouache washes.[24] The quick, subjectively observed impression was thus arrived at through a kind of abbreviated draughtsmanship to give a sense of something glimpsed. Unlike her portraits in oils, the subjects of her drawings were usually unwitting; certainly they were seldom posed. Her paintings, in contrast, were deliberate, reflective; pensive and spiritually aware.

Quinn now began to receive drawings of little girls praying, seen from the back – the orphans from the *Orphelinat St Joseph* – and some delightful back views of women in the congregation, muffled in their coats and hats. Gwen had captured tight gaggles of girls, kneeling, sitting, or wriggling in their pews; solitary figures, their heads bent in prayer or meditation; or one little face, suddenly turning round, caught in a distracted moment. The poignant, restrained energy of little girls trying to concentrate makes these drawings moving. She did them in delicate tones of pink, green and ochre on a restricted palette and the drawings she based them on still survive, in her cheap, pocket-sized notebooks, some of them consisting of little more than one or two quick, rough marks. The reproductions of these drawings hardly convey their extreme sweetness, delicacy and wit. The subjects were dear to her heart, and there is an inevitability about them. They had to be done; as she had said to Quinn, they 'kept presenting themselves'.

When Ursula did finally pass briefly through Paris it was not for a long stay and she missed saying goodbye. She left lovely presents with the concierge – a rose tree, a tie, a basket and a Chinese plate. But her visit made a huge difference. Gwen confided in her about how difficult she now found it, not only to paint but to sleep: she was kept awake, these days, by a persistent headache and sense of unease. Augustus was anxious about her, and wanted her to go and visit him, but she had no desire to leave Meudon. Ursula, as ever, was understanding and supportive. She knew, Gwen told her, that she did appear at some level to be retreating, but Ursula understood that this was increasingly necessary for the work. 'You have given me so much encouragement Ursula you seem to agree with my decision to live as much as I can in a way that I have collectedness of thoughts. Gus worries me so much, and others, about it and sometimes I think I ought to go and stay with him.'[25] But she needed to be alone to work. She was absorbed in her new drawings, and now had the added impetus of needing to produce new things for Quinn. 'As to whether I have anything worth expressing that is apart from the question. I may never have anything to express, except this desire for a more interior life. I am sure you are right in what you say about artistic people and artists. Some people inspire one too and interest one who are neither artists nor artistic. Their sensibility comes from the soul I think and the sensibility of others except the best of them, comes from the nerves.'[26] She noted down, from the works of Henri Sugo: 'Vous devez demeurer en vous même et vous faire une vie intérieure, si vous ne voulez pas vous égarer comme le font ceux qui n'observe pas leur règle.'[27]

She continued to make notes in her notebook about her Catholic teachings. 'Don't be afraid,' she told herself, on 8 September, 'and don't think about what others think of you. You don't yet feel "indépendant des hommes" . . . ? Pray! If you pray, all will be well.'[28] On 17 October she reminded herself, 'Unless you have the will to be great you will fall into mediocrity', but it was a disinterested ambition for greater artistic achievement rather than for public acknowledgement or success. She also chastised herself. 'Too much vanity. Too much care for material things. Too much sensual reverie . . .': 'You have put yourself away from God; disobeyed God. You have been undoing the work of the past; . . . putting aside God's gifts . . . God, your lover, is waiting for you. Make the step that will bring you nearer to being a saint . . . Every moment is holy. Do not soil the moments.'[29] This is an aspect of Catholic teaching. Its power for her and the impression it made on her were undoubtedly partly because it was new to her, she took it as seriously as she had always taken her spiritual study. In addition, to some extent it channelled a physical need, and brought her work as an artist into connection with a justification for self-denial. We can having nothing but respect for the enormous demands of this struggle and the tremendous effort to believe that in presenting and directing her work through the medium of this demanding spiritual journey, she would confer on it a yet deeper resonance and value.

Winifred, Ursula and increasingly Chloe understood the importance for her work of this effort to be *recueillie*, and in their different ways, both her brothers sympathised with and supported her. She had sent Thornton some 'gorgeous' books that summer, including one by Dostoevsky and an elaborate French dictionary. He rewarded her with more stories and a gift. His cabin was 'the envy of all who have seen it – only 2 so far' and he had been washing the gravel for gold. 'I am sending you a "color" wrapped in a leaf – open it carefully.'[30]

By January 1913, Gwen had made her decision about the arrangement John Quinn was proposing. She wrote to thank him for his cheque. 'I must tell you I am glad of the money. I can now go along without worries until I have done some things.' She agreed to accept an advance in part payment for the next picture, and when she was sure she could send him two or three pictures by the end of the year she would let him know. She was planning to send one small picture and had begun a number of others but had nothing ready to send yet; she could only promise that she would try to send as soon as possible the one she was trying to finish: 'The name *A Woman in a Red Shawl* price £30.'[31] Quinn was already planning to exhibit it, together with *Girl Reading at the Window*, in the 1913 International Exhibition of

Modern Art or 'Armory Show', a historic event behind which Quinn was a moving force. Organised by the Association of American Painters and Sculptors, of which he was an honorary member, the show opened in New York at the 69th Regiment Armory in February 1913, and subsequently travelled to Chicago and Boston. It was a huge exhibition, including more than 1,300 works by 300 artists, and was viewed by 75,000 people in New York alone.[32] It is unlikely that Gwen had any idea of the scale of the event, but she told Quinn she was pleased to have an opportunity to show her work, though she warned him that she would have to keep the new picture until two weeks prior to the exhibition to make sure it was dry, as pictures were always touched. If this meant it was too late for the exhibition, he could keep it for the next one, but she felt confident that it would arrive on time.[33] He was still hoping she might send two, he reminded her. This prompted the arrival, on 25 January, of a cable. 'One. Gwen John.'[34]

Quinn replied gallantly, assuring her that if the painting did not arrive in time for the opening of the exhibition he could send it a week or ten days late, and if she was sending it through Durand-Ruel she should tell them to hurry it, or to send it specially without waiting for a regular case.[35] In February, Gwen was back in touch, ashamed to admit that the picture had not yet been sent. She had found things she wanted to alter in the face, so she did it again thinking it would take her another three days, but it was still not finished. She was still working on it and on another she had been doing in tandem, but she realised it would now be too late to include it in the exhibition. She would send both in a few days, and if he was now not willing to buy them, would he consider keeping them for the next exhibition?[36] Eleven days later she wrote again, thanking him for troubling to send *Girl Reading at the Window* to the exhibition, and reassuring him that she did not mind missing the current exhibition with the new painting as it meant she would have two or three paintings and some drawings for the next. Did he think it was 'better to have several things at a time, to give an impression of one's work'? By June, *A Woman in a Red Shawl* had still not arrived. Gwen had not been well, she told Quinn, and so had been away for a while to get stronger but she was now back at work and would send something soon. She had finished *A Woman in a Red Shawl* but did not like it, so was at work on another. 'Please do not send any money again in advance,' she now guiltily begged him. 'I am so ashamed of not keeping my word.'[37] In July, she sent assurances that she was now working regularly. 'I must never say I will have a picture done soon again and perhaps I ought never to take a commande [commission] again. I am working regularly now . . .'[38] She was grateful for all his assurances about money, and realised it was not the usual procedure to pay for pictures so far in advance.[39]

It was quite all right about not managing to send it for the exhibition, Quinn assured her. It had been a great success, the *Craftsman* had reviewed it and he was sending her a copy. He was pleased by her mention of 'two and some drawings', and urged her to take them to Durand-Ruel, who would forward them. Quinn's forwarding agents (Marzloff & Co.) would make the customs declarations and have them packed in strong wooden cases so that they would not be broken in transit. He wanted to have some good old, carved frames for them, and told her that if she could find suitable ones, she was to let him know the cost and he would pay for them.[40]

Still, no painting materialised. Quinn never did get *A Woman in a Red Shawl*, though he had hopefully included it in the catalogue for the Armory Show. It is quite possible that Gwen went on working on it, abandoning it and starting again on four different canvases, but that she never felt sufficiently satisfied with it to send it to Quinn. She did paint four variants of a painting of a young woman in a red shawl (though they have been (speculatively) dated late 1910s or early 1920s). But she apparently abandoned work on them.[41]

By now she was fully preoccupied, no doubt encouraged by the priest, with the painting of *Mère Poussepin*, which was proving excessively difficult. It was to be the first of several similar paintings, since the nuns now decided they would like one for each room in the Convent (had the priest seen the four variants of *A Woman in a Red Shawl*?)[42] and it set a precedent for Gwen's habit of making several variants of the same subject. She chafed against this commission from the start, wanting to do other things but feeling an obligation to the nuns, who slowly began to drive her to distraction with their impatience, since they could not understand why it should take so long to produce a painting. Though she usually referred to her 'Nun' in the singular, she worked on all the versions concurrently, tiring herself out over this for the next seven years.

It was a hugely exacting commission, particularly since she undertook it at the same time as her conversion, in 1913. The finished paintings would have to be approved by the priest, and Gwen clearly regarded it as a test of her commitment to the Convent, and perhaps also the faith. The Convent refused to lend her a nun's habit, so she bought some cloth and had one made, having to have it altered and remade twice before it was right.[43] The priest pressurised her for it and the 'Nun' continued to exasperate her. (Eventually though she produced at least six portraits of Mère Poussepin, all close variants; three are closer than the others to the portrait on the prayer card.)

It is not clear whether Gwen knew that the Duchesse had by this time made her departure. There is no evidence that she knew, but in February of 1913 Rilke came back to Paris and Gwen contacted him to ask him whether his wife, Clara, would give her some modelling work. If she and Rilke actually met during the spring of 1913 it seems likely, though not certain, that he would have told her. What we do know is that there was some kind of misunderstanding between them that year. He had sent her a letter in which he offered her congratulations, but which she misinterpreted, reading unintentional irony into his praise. When he re-read his own letter, he could not see what he could possibly have said to hurt her. He felt sure that had he said it in person she would have taken it in the way it was intended. Neither letter has survived, so we do not know what she had told him, but he assured her that truly, he was delighted with her news and had meant to congratulate her. What possible reason could he have for wanting to harm her and, even worse, by a pleasantry in bad taste and 'du mauvais coeur'? He felt like a chemist being accused of having given someone a dangerous poison when he had meant to dispense medicine; he had meant to give her 'du sucre pur, innocent et vrai. Je vous l'assure.'[44] But despite her offering him all the appropriate reassurances, this does seem to have driven a wedge between them, something she later felt very rueful about.

In April 1913 she went to visit Ruth Manson in Pont-l'Abbé. She loved Brittany and worked happily there. When she returned in May, Rodin came to see her in the rue de l'Ouest, but she felt sad and ill after his visit. She sensed a *faiblesse* in them both, which seemed to brush against her own mortality: 'perhaps, *mon Maître chéri*,' she wrote to him afterwards, 'it was your coming to my room to make love to me that has made me feel as if I am dying.'[45] Something was fading between them. She continued to work, through the long, hot summer of 1913, on the *Mère Poussepin*. 'Every hour of recueillement and prayer devellops [*sic*] your soul,' she noted in her notebook, that August. But 'I have a headache and long for the sea.'[46] She could obviously be sure now of Quinn's commitment. All she had to do was finish the 'Nun'.

13

War

> When the war is over, I think I'll try to earn some money and buy a little house, and try to arrive at some kind of permanence and truth . . .[1]

'I saw your picture and drawings at Chenil's and admired them very much,' Augustus wrote from Alderney Manor in Dorset (where he now lived) at the beginning of 1914. 'Thank you for letting me know about them. Quinn will be very glad to have them, I know. He has often asked me if he had a chance of getting more of your work. I hope you'll send some more over before long – Besides Quinn there are plenty of others who want to have your things.'[2] Gwen had sent *Study of a Woman*,[3] her second portrait of Chloe which she had done most of, and been dissatisfied with, in three hectic weeks in the summer of 1909, together with some of her pencil and wash drawings of little girls and young women.

She still had not finished anything new – at least, nothing she was satisfied with. She had not been well, and as usual had started too many things. But she was aiming to have two to send to Quinn by the end of March. The seven 'Nuns' had clearly been taking their toll. Chloe was not the only one who thought the nuns were capitalising on Gwen's goodwill. She later felt strongly enough to say so: 'Do you still like your "Mere Superieure" so much but I hope she is not still wanting you to go on painting for them. If you have given them one, I think they ought to be satisfied.'[4] Everybody became rather confused about the 'Nun' and why it was taking so long. 'What a pity you cannot finish the picture of the nun!' sympathised Grilda. 'I don't wonder it is impossible if she doesn't pose for it herself – but I don't quite understand about it.'[5] She urged Gwen, that August, to take a break with them. A change might mean she could do a beautiful picture in a week.

But instead, the difficulties of painting the 'Nun' six or seven times had quite the opposite effect on Gwen's working methods: she seemed to slow down, from now on, rather than speeding up. She now began another series of variants, eight similar paintings of a seated girl in a blue dress, all virtually identical in style and composition. In seven variants, the sitter's dress is decorated with white spots, in the eighth, it is plain blue. The stool the model sits on is more visible in some of the variants than in others, but the model holds more or less the same pose, hands clasped, in all of them. There are differences in the ground itself: in six of the paintings, the background is a plain wall, in the seventh, the wall is horizontally divided and part of the floor is visible; in the eighth, a rectangular shape, presumably a window, can be seen. But none of these differences vitally alters the composition. The main experimentation seems to have been tonal.

The model Gwen used for this painting could well have been Angeline Lhuisset. Their friendship was close and caring. She appears to have been an unchallenging and restful sitter, and it must have been refreshing and galvanising to paint from life after all the interminable copying from a prayer card. The minor differences between variants in the blue dress series would have been occasioned by the sittings, as the model made infinitesimal changes to the pose; and the physicality of working from flesh rather than a photographic image must have felt very demanding, but the 'Nun' had clearly introduced new ideas about how to make different descriptions of the same form. In a sense, the *Girl/Woman in a Blue Dress* series was Gwen's secular version of the 'Nun'. She worked intermittently for the next two years or so on this series. In 1924, discussing the version she was to send to Quinn, she told him that she could account for five: one in the Salon des Tuileries; the one she was sending him, and three more she had turned up in her attic: two in a spotted dress, one in which the dress was unspotted. Cecily Langdale has commented that 'she rather disingenuously added: 'When I do a lot they are all studies for the last, which I send you."'[6] But perhaps in retrospect, when she came to select one for Quinn, this felt true.

The experiment of making tiny compositional changes and producing contrastingly radical effects in mood in a series of similar variants is one that began, now, to dominate her painting habits. It is not an uncommon method, applied to the practice of drawing, but it is less common a procedure in oil painting, simply because one oil painting takes much longer to execute. Also, the changes of mood effected by differences in the modelling of figures against grounds may often only be judged at a distance and over time. The subtle changes she made as she drafted one, then another, variant may have enabled her to make technical discoveries about the relationship between figure and ground which, achieved painstakingly in painting, could now be transposed into her drawings: the painting began to inform the drawing, now, as well as the other way round. Similar little girls in church – at prayer, seated, standing, huddled together, poignantly alone – convey strong, atmospheric worlds of their own. In her watercolour and gouache drawings, tiny variations in posture and in the placing of figures in relation to objects – chairs, windows, books – enabled new experiments in the creation of personality. Furthermore, as Gwen herself commented, the works gained momentum and depth when seen together. The process of painting one figure several times exercised her observation very sharply; and she could not ignore the newly discovered facility to *see* in possible variants and to pursue new opportunities, from the outset, for discerning in a single picture multiple relationships between forms. The watercolour and gouache drawings she did at this time have, seen together, something of the spirit of early twentieth-century French cartoon-style sketches. Her drawings of little girls also resemble Bonnard's drawings of children.

It is not clear whether she reworked her portrait of Chloe at all during this time (probably not) but Quinn finally received this as his second painting. *Study of a Woman* arrived on 31 August, together with two beautiful drawings of girls in church and a painting by Ruth Manson, *Effet de Neige*, a snow-covered landscape which he politely thought 'a charmingly conceived work'.[7] Neither Gwen nor Miss Manson took it for granted that he would necessarily want the pictures and they were waiting for his reactions, Gwen assured him. He was tactful about Ruth Manson's picture and presently sent a cheque for the required amount; he was also happy with Gwen's drawings, but it was the portrait of Chloe he was most thrilled by: he pronounced it 'finer than anything of that kind that Whistler ever did'. He showed the works to his friends, the painters Walter Pach and George Of, and both had fallen in love with them – especially with the two drawings. 'All I can do,' he assured her, 'is to admire and appreciate them and tell how much I like both your drawings and your paintings, and how glad I am to have them.'[8]

There were, by now, other serious matters to be considered. 'I wonder if you are going to remain in Paris during the war,' Augustus wanted to know. He had been hoping she would not, as he was anxious that she would find life very hard. It was not too late to come back. He had looked up train times and wrote to let her know that there were still two running from Paris to London via Boulogne, at 9.55 a.m. and 10.20 p.m. He warned her that food would be very expensive in Paris and that it would be difficult or even impossible to send money over. 'Let me know what you decide and if I can help in any way.'[9] Clearly, it was a very important decision and she realised he was concerned. 'Your letter gave me great pleasure and still does,' she told him. 'Thank you for it, dear love.'[10] He had told her things she had not known, 'and put it clearly'. There were white blanks in the newspapers, so she knew that the censor was already at work. By October the French mood was one of deep sadness, even of mourning. The French had never shown any excitement or enthusiasm about this war, their memories of horror were too recent for that. The war, by the late autumn of 1914, had already cost them too much. They were 'wonderfully philosophic', she told Augustus, and she was energetic in her admiration: 'defeat would be worse for them than for the others however it would mean extinction of the race almost. It will be a step in civilization to put a check on this brute force!'[11]

She was writing to him outside a café, where everyone was looking up at a 'Taube' – though she was unable to tell a Taube from an aeroplane so she could not be sure. 'The Taubes have been dropping lots of bombs and there have been a good many victims the day before yesterday. They hit children generally.' Gwen had made herself useful interpreting for the soldiers at the Gare de Montparnasse. The officers often lost their luggage and wasted no time either in searching for it or in attempting to master the language: 'they take what they want in the shops they say "souvenir" & put things in their pockets. The French are ravi at that.' All the English seemed like boys; the first thing the officers did on arriving in Paris was to go to the 'Madeleine': 'they go in twos and ones, they walk well & have a good physique. The French are ahuri [*sic*] before the Highlanders and no wonder!' Augustus had said he would like to come to Paris – had she seen Veber's war drawings and lithographs? They were too expensive for her, Gwen told him, 'I must give my extra money to the needful now.'[12]

She had decided to stay. In early September she wrote to Ursula that 'every day after seeing the gare Montparnasse crammed & luggage & cattle trains loaded with frightened people I felt more and more disinclined to go. I suppose I am rather contrary.'[13] By early September the Germans had retreated slightly from Paris. She had seen the name Tyrwhitt in the newspapers and realised that one of Ursula's family had joined up. 'You are quite right to be proud – we cannot pity the enemy any longer they are such brutes and vandals.'[14] She drew a diagram for Ursula of the Paris fortifications: there were '3 ceintures des forts without counting the fortifications you see Paris is well defended'. She was painting a portrait of an old woman in a blue dress, knitting – a picture which does not seem to have survived. Perhaps she gave it to the old lady.[15]

The war was heartbreaking, she wrote to Quinn, and 'the horrors don't seem to end'. She had thought at first of leaving Paris, 'but when the danger got nearer I found I wouldn't. If the mayor at Meudon had made all the people go I should have come to stay in my room at Paris, which I keep on.' She was going every day to the rue de l'Ouest to work on her paintings. A lot of people had left Meudon, out of fear. Ruth Manson was one: she thought it safer to return to England with her child. The memory of the German invasion of 1870 made everyone fearful. But Meudon offered a compelling vantage point from the grounds of the Observatoire – 'it is very high there and we can see all Paris. We saw the aeroplanes when the enemy dropped a few bombs there those afternoons.' Paris itself seemed eerily quiet. A lot of the shops had closed, and there was less traffic. 'One sees a crowd round a wounded [person] now and then, and bodies of soldiers marching. Those are all the differences.'[16] Quinn had several friends in Paris, among them Maud Gonne, who was living in Passy with her son Seaghan. She and Gwen were to meet the following year, and it was through Maud Gonne that she would finally become aware of the seriousness and horror of events. For the time being, she told Quinn, she was not going to think about it too much. When she did think about it, she was philosophical. It was freedom at a dreadful cost, but it had brought out 'so much bravery and endurance . . .'[17]

Everybody worried about her, of course. But she was making herself useful interpreting for the soldiers,[18] which Augustus was pleased by, probably because this meant she was not spending long hours on her own. He told her he thought the best political commentary was in the *New Age*, and offered to send it to her regularly. The British soldiers all seemed like 'boys not to say babes'; thousands of Canadians were landing, and there were still territorials to be drawn on. 'It seems impossible to work consistently through all this. Will the world be very different afterwards?'[19] She had also asked Ursula to send news, since, as she had told Augustus, the French papers said very little and the censor's blank spaces, left for fear of frightening the public, did little to inspire confidence. The wounded were now being brought to Meudon. One had just died. The placing of the wounded was organised by the priest, and he had said that Gwen's help might be needed to talk to the English and confess the Catholics. 'I don't know how I could help him but I said I should be delighted of course,' she told Ursula. 'I speak to the English soldiers when I see them. They are so pleased to be spoken to and I find them so charming they all have something young in their faces like boys of 14, even the old ones.'[20]

Ursula sent *The Times*, from which it was possible to deduce a little of what the English were feeling. Gwen and the priest read it together, and it made her realise that 'England had become quite a foreign country to me.' It was very cold, and she wished she had Ursula to talk to. Ruth had now taken lodgings, on her way to England. She was glad to be alone again, but she missed Ursula: 'I feel very nervous tonight, perhaps it is because of the wind and readying of the Merchant ships sunk in the Channel by submarines, and I feel as if the war is not going quite well. How dreadful that the Channel is not safe now! But perhaps it is safe on the lines that the passenger steamers come by?' She asked her to please write, she would not feel safe until she heard from her again: she sensed that although it had not been mentioned in the press, there was a possibility of an invasion.[21] Ursula had seen Belgian refugees arriving at Charing Cross, carrying 'pathetic little bundles done up in handkerchiefs' and telling terrible stories of hardship and cruelty; she would not tell Gwen any, she must have read them in the newspapers: they were true.[22] The sight of the refugees made it difficult not to fear the worst, but surely it would soon be over, those in a position to know had predicted three to six months. Thornton, in British Columbia, had for a long time been oblivious of events. He had had no news of the war at all until mid-August, when he had gone to Vancouver and been shocked at what he heard. He now knew that the Germans had failed in their efforts to take the Channel ports, and wrote to say that they could surely assume that France would soon be rid of them.

Thornton had obviously been very unwell, with a foot injury and a hernia; he had taken laudanum for it and had a 'dazzling vision', with 'wonderful light and colour, intense blue sky . . . and then I felt myself forcibly coming back to my body.'[23] Gwen copied out extracts from her spiritual texts and sent them to him. She also sent some to Rodin. In the New Year he had written to tell her he was slightly unwell in the Villa des Brillants – she was not to look for him on the train. Then he wrote from Châtelet to say that he would love it if she would write to him there to tell him her news and let him know if she had been doing her drawings. The extracts she had sent were beautiful; he was overcome by her sweet thought.[24] He was very frightened by the war: he was afraid for the safety of his work, and never convinced it would be a short war. Those around him were surprised and disheartened by his lack of faith in the French generals and his refusal to be confident of a French victory. In August, the Prime Minister's wife, Madame Viviani announced that she wished to establish a children's centre in the garden of the Hôtel Biron, with a field hospital in the chapel. He replied that though he was obviously willing to participate in the war effort, he was very nervous, and hoped she would not be offended by his intense desire to protect his sculpture.[25] All work on the Whistler Muse had been suspended, because of the war.

On 24 August a million Germans marched through the northern provinces towards Paris. A week later the French army was placing charges under the Seine and Marne bridges. Everyone was reminded of 1870. The generals told politicians to leave Paris; the Germans distributed leaflets: 'There is nothing you can do but surrender.' The German army had launched its attack via Belgium while the French generals focused on the business of freeing Alsace, so in the first days of the war the two armies did not meet head on. But by the third week in August, the entire frontier on both fronts, Flanders and Alsace, was a long line of battles and France began experiencing a series of defeats. The French believed the Germans capable of anything, even of destroying the great monuments of Paris. Rodin was terrified of danger and expecting, in his confusion, to be given instructions by the Minister as to whether to go or stay. He felt that as France's 'only great artist', who had given all his works to the state, it was the business of the state to protect him.[26] Gwen still waited for him every day. She had bought some clothes and was anxious for him to see her in them. When she did occasionally see him at the Hôtel Biron, it was all the more disappointing to have to come home without him. She was trying to throw herself into her drawings, though even now she still could not really see why he should think better of her for doing a few drawings. She would rather be helping him in his studio or modelling, but he refused to let her make herself useful. He was probably reluctant to engage her in anything even vaguely ongoing, being so unsure about whether he would go or stay.

Early on the morning of 4 September, she had a message from one of his workers, Eugène Guioché, who told her that Rodin had something for her. She made her way to the Villa des Brillants, and as she turned into the avenue of the villa she found a man behind the grille taking care of a horse, who said that Rodin had left the country. She told him he would surely be back by the end of the day, because he had asked to see her. She began to start back for Paris, but felt so despondent that she sat down and rested in the road. Suddenly, a horse and cart packed high with luggage came hurtling towards her, flying past her down the avenue. She knew it was Rodin, so she took the train into Paris and went to the Hôtel Biron, where the concierge told her he had gone to London. But surely he would be back soon? The concierge was in a state of high anxiety, 'afraid the Germans would come and eat us'. So back she went to Meudon, which seemed to take for ever because the train kept stopping. Eventually, she found Guioché, from whom she discovered that Rodin, who at the time was desperately worried about money as well as everything else, had left a 100-franc note for her. (When she wrote to thank him, she reassured him that she was grateful but she had enough money for a siege.) Guioché could not tell her where Rodin was or when he intended to return. Madame Guioché told her how frightened she was that a bomb might drop on their house, which Gwen thought highly amusing. She told her she thought it unlikely the enemy would want to drop a bomb on such a little house; they were probably far more interested in the great monuments of Paris.[27]

Rodin was, in fact, on his way to London with Rose and his friend and secretary Judith Cladel. He went on to visit various friends in England, including Mary Hunter at her country house in Epping Forest, and Gwen wrote to him there, urging him to love his enemies; he replied thanking her for this admirable advice. The following March he went to Rome, where the Pope sat for him, at Rodin's request. (He regarded this as his war effort, and ran his affairs in Paris from a distance for four months while he waited to be granted his audience with the Pope.) It was not a successful encounter: on the third sitting, he asked the Holy Father to change the pose and the Pope refused, which ended the sittings. Gwen wrote to him in Rome and he told her he was comforted by her letters.

She was still insisting that France was a safer place to be than England, despite everyone's fears to the contrary. Like Maud Gonne, who according to Quinn 'just sets her teeth and refuses to look at the ruins',[28] she focused on the courage and bravery of the French. Quinn insisted he could not agree, and asked her to tell him if she needed money. Edwin John, in Tenby, began to worry about his daughter. 'I hope you are quite all right Gwen? . . . I am myself very well now – having at last got rid of the cough that clung to me so persistently after the Influenza . . . What a splendid reception the French nation gave to our King and Queen! It was very glorious and I am sure the visit will strengthen the entente cordiale between the two countries – are you not? Will send a photo of self in a few days.' (He did.)[29] She asked Chloe and Grilda to come to Meudon, but Chloe was working as a nurse on night duty looking after the convalescent wounded, many of whom had lost a leg, an arm or an eye. She and Grilda asked Gwen to visit them, but Gwen was determined to stay put. She wanted Chloe's opinion of her early portrait of her, still on display at the Chenil Galleries. She was worried about the frame, as Quinn had wanted to change it but she overruled him. She liked its smallness, and it toned with the picture. The frame had temporarily been removed, Chloe reported back, and being critical was not really her forte. One effect of the war on Gwen was that it made her less solitary. She went more often to the cafés and bars, and wrote to Augustus from the Rotonde, where she had struck up conversation with a 'Gypsy'. He wished he was there, came the reply, 'with you and a couple of grogs Americains to neutralize the cold'. What gypsy was it – anything to do with Fenella Lovell? He told her to look out for Modigliani, who used to frequent the Rotonde, and Beatrice Hastings, who wrote in the *New Age* under the pseudonym Alice Maning. He would try to 'dash over to France' soon. 'Don't let yourself get frozen dearest. Take exercises.'[30]

In the New Year of 1915, Quinn sent an advance to cover another painting. He was pleased to know that Gwen would be sending a picture and some drawings soon. The war was heartbreaking and horrible. He sang the praises of France, brave, free from 'hysterical appeals to God' and 'spy mania', courageous in air raids; altogether different from England. Artists were having a hard time in New York, he reported, though Walter Pach had been abroad for the Carroll Gallery and brought back works by Matisse, Picasso, Dufy, Derain, Duchamp-Villon, Renoir, Gleizes, De Segonzac and others. The prevailing aesthetic climate, which New York was importing from France, was of Impressionism moving through into abstraction. The Picassos he favoured were those of the Blue period, which he thought 'magnificent things'. Several artists were at the Front and some were wounded. There was constant speculation about Russia's part in the war. One theory was that while Russia had the men, she lacked ammunition and the powder, artillery, equipment and railway facilities. Germany had the ammunition and material for powder and explosives to last six or seven years, and had been accumulating it for seven or eight years. In England's place, Quinn said, he would be stoning the Germans out. Having failed to smash France in September it seemed less likely that Germany would conquer her now. He encouraged Gwen to keep painting. He hoped she was not 'nervous about aeroplanes or anything of that sort'.[31]

The 'Nun' was still not finished, but Gwen was trying to work on her every day. She was also now working on an 'Interior'[32] which she was doing for Quinn, and which now went into four variants: a corner in close-up of a room in 29 rue Terre Neuve, showing a small round table, viewed against part of a mantelpiece, with a pot of pencils at the end, in the background. The slicing of table and mantelpiece and consequent illusion of a cropped frame is essentially Impressionist, giving the feeling that the scene is being glimpsed intimately. On the table are Gwen's teapot, cup and saucer and jug, with a slightly crumpled, just-read newspaper; beside it is a stool on which the absent figure has left a closed book. This is domestic life in Meudon, probably done in the mornings just after breakfast, when Gwen habitually drank tea. It is a scene of ordinary domesticity, an intimate glimpse of a life in process, as evocatively suggestive of her presence as, for example, Virginia Woolf's description of Jacob's empty room in *Jacob's Room* (her novel about the war) is of his. Gwen discarded at least one version; two of the ones she kept are called *The Teapot* and *The Brown Teapot*. She was pleased with them, and thought she might give one to Isobel Bowser.

She had also begun work on another painting, the standing figure of a little girl[33] – almost certainly a Meudon neighbour, possibly one of the Joly children. It is more abstract, more a study of forms than *The Brown Teapot*. The child clasps a piece of cloth, the crumpled form of which is repeated in the bow in her hair, and again in the indistinct, cluttered forms on the table at her side. The atmosphere is one of intimacy, of things seen in close-up; the figure, though formally posed, is cropped just above the knee and the tension between formality and abstraction is discreetly expressionist, suggestive of a form about to burst its bounds or exceed its frame. The elongation of the figure and breadth of the hips both contribute to the suggestion of childhood on the brink of adulthood. The gently toning pinks and blues and the dry, impasto brush marks imply a closeness of paint and flesh; the light source, to the right of the painting, and uncluttered by objects, focuses a figure in the process of being brought strongly into relief. In the face there is the straightforwardness of innocence and the strength of barely hinted experience. While Gwen painted on, the news of slaughter began slowly to filter through. Those with inside information now knew that at every advance of a kilometre there were 3,000 dead. The Germans were so strongly placed that it meant death to dislodge them. They seemed fearless: they came on over their own dead and shot down thousands. 'France is giving all, the new generation as well as the old one are being wiped out, the maimed left will not be able to bring forth a strong generation in short France is ruined already,' Gwen wrote to Ursula in the spring of 1915.[34]

Her source was still Maud Gonne, still lodging in Passy, in the rue de l'Annonciation. Quinn had continued to write to both women encouraging them to meet, and finally, on 23 April, Gwen went to Passy to tea. The two women liked each other very much. Gwen thought Maud Gonne 'very beautiful and charming',[35] and Maud Gonne admired Gwen's 'quiet and sincere way of looking at things'.[36] It made her think that Gwen's work, which she had not yet seen, would be intense and original. She showed her some of her own drawings. Her son Seaghan, who was doing his lessons in another room, came in to meet her. They talked about the war, and Maud Gonne's account of it, Gwen told Quinn, 'frightened and chilled me for several days'. She only hoped she believed things to be worse than they really were.[37]

In fact, Maud Gonne's ear was characteristically close to the ground. She was working as a nurse and she knew the wounded were being brought home in trains during the night so that they would not be seen; everything was being done to prevent knowledge filtering through, to stop people from panicking. Quinn was sending her money, since the French economy allowed scant funds to keep their military hospitals going. Marcel Duchamp, still in his twenties, had been rejected for military service and had fetched up in New York, where he had impressed Quinn. Of his brothers, Duchamp-Villon the sculptor and Jacques Villon, the Cubist painter, one was at the Front and the other was acting as a surgeon in a hospital near Paris. But paintings were still crossing the Atlantic, and Odilon Redon, Derain, De Segonzac, Chaband, Gleizes and Picasso had all exhibited in New York the previous year, he told Gwen. He was interested to know whether she was familiar with the work of Dufy or Rouault. She may have discovered Rouault's work as a result of Quinn's enquiry. He was to become the painter she most admired: she was fascinated by his experimentalism, his stark contrasts and his strangeness. Later she would experiment in her drawings with a similar use of black line and way of sketching forms.

There were air raids in England. Ursula sent news of them and said she was trying to paint, but without much success. Arthur Rothenstein had tried to enlist, but was refused. She seldom saw anyone from the old Slade days, just occasionally McEvoy, Wilson Steer and Orpen. The 'best' paintings in the National Gallery had been put in the cellars, and the Elgin Marbles were safely stowed beneath the British Museum. The wounded were arriving every day in Oxford and Ursula had been requisitioned to teach them French (presumably in preparation for their return to the Front). She had been to London and seen some of the damage: the Lyceum Theatre had had a full house when a bomb dropped close by; apparently the show went on, though Ursula thought this may have been apocryphal. Still, the newspapers reported very little, even about the raids, and no one on either side of the Channel had any real idea of what was actually going on. Ursula thought people would be more indignant than frightened if the truth began to get out. 'One poor woman my sister met whose house was next to the one that had been destroyed – 6 children 2 women and all in it said "I call this open Anarchy" shaking her fist at the sky.'[38]

Gwen sent nothing to the NEAC in the autumn of 1915 – the 'Nun' was still in crisis, and the packer in Paris advised sending nothing until the danger at sea was over, though she had now completed both *Interior* and *La*

Petite Modèle. She had hoped Quinn would be able to come over that summer and see her work as she still found it difficult to judge things herself, but she realised that if he crossed the Atlantic now he would probably be risking his life. She was hoping things would have calmed down before the winter. For now, she assured him, she enjoyed hearing from him and valued his friendship: 'it is something my art has brought me unexpectedly'.[39] In her extracts for the spring of 1915, she had noted down from her religious teachings some reflections on peace: 'is peace not simply the radiance which reveals spiritual beauty? And is spiritual beauty not simply the harmony of all our strength, marshalled by the soul, gathered in unity by the goodness permeated by divine strength?'[40] Towards the end of the year, Winifred wrote in joyful French with exciting news. 'J'ai une petite fille! . . .' – 'I have a daughter! She was born on Saturday 6th November and she is *perfect* – with a little round face. She has dark hair and blue eyes, and tiny hands with very long fingers . . . she is very beautiful and we are very well.' The baby sent kisses to her Aunt Gwen.[41]

In February 1916, Gwen finally sent Quinn the *Interior* (with brown teapot) and – somewhat confusingly – *Seated Woman in Blue Dress* (which she referred to and he catalogued as *La Petite Modèle*, the title of the painting Gwen had promised him) together with nine gouaches. (He did eventually get *La Petite Modèle*.) He cabled back £20 for all nine gouaches and offered her £30 for *Seated Woman in Blue Dress* and £25 for *Interior*. On reflection, he decided that £3 per gouache would be fairer, whereupon Gwen decided she should ask only £17 for *Interior* and £2 each for the gouaches. After some toing and froing they compromised on £20 for *Interior* and Quinn overruled her on the gouaches. 'There is an old maxim in the law,' said Quinn, 'that a man should not be a judge in his own case. I am not quite certain however whether in overruling you I am judging in my case or in your case.'[42] He hoped she would do two more oils for him. 'The nuns'(or rather, her paintings of them) were responsible for her long delay in sending work, she said, not the war, though Pottier, the packager, had told her he knew that some collections which had been sent by sea had been lost: thankfully, none of his. Insurance on shipping had gone up during the last two days and she had had an involved discussion with Pottier about getting a *certificate d'artiste*, which he initially said would cost 15 francs. When she began to look in her purse to see if she had 15 francs, his conscience pricked and he advised declaring the value as below 500 francs, so that there would only be 6 francs to pay. He then had a better idea: he would charge the 6 francs to Mr Quinn's account. They agreed that Quinn would be happiest with this plan.[43]

Gwen had also embarked on another project. She now sent Quinn a portfolio of six drawings of heads done from photographs which she wanted him to try to sell for her. She asked him to recommend a shop in New York which she could send them to: it was, she said, 'an idea of Monsieur le Curé!'[44] Quinn, who was clearly unexcited by them, said he thought they were 'quite interesting', but their saleability depended on what price she had in mind. She should cable him a price – say, a hundred and fifty francs for six? – and let him know how many more portfolios she could supply.[45] These were Gwen's drawings of generals: she drew General Mangin, General Carodna, Vice-Admiral Sir Archibald Moore and others, from newspaper photographs, a military variation on the idea of reproducing the image of Mère Poussepin from a prayer card, and the Curé obviously thought they would be regarded with equal veneration. Quinn, after some hedging, dispatched them to the Ferargil Gallery in New York, but he clearly regarded them as an insignificant diversion. In fact, they are exquisitely and imaginatively done: at first glance, conventional drawings of men in uniform which highlight the military bearing of the figures; on closer inspection they are witty, vivacious, full of character, and in some cases almost caricatures. General Mangin has a wittily elongated neck, exaggeratedly broad torso and large, expressive hands; General Sarrailh has staring eyes; he looks upwards as if suddenly taken unawares, the whites of his eyes emphasised. Gwen obviously enjoyed doing them and once she had started, could not seem to stop.[46]

At the end of February, Quinn was still waiting for his paintings, but this time she had actually sent them. 'I am dreadfully afraid my work is sunk as you have not received it,' she wrote to him in mid-March. She asked him about the drawings from photographs. She had not initially named a price, she said, because she wanted to see what the shop offered, but she thought 150 francs a very good price. She was quite impatient to sell them: 'If you find you have not the time please send me a card with the name of a shop, and I will send a portfolio on approval and say the price is *150 frs* and that I could let them have *10 sets in a month's time*.' She hoped he would come to France soon, but she warned him that 'Paris is sad.' The wounded were beginning to filter through. 'It is dreadful to see the maimed in the streets it is still more heart-rending to see a body of the blind (but it is a rare sight). A man goes before and cries Faîtes place! Faîtes place! and the poor men follow holding on to one another.'[47]

By May, Quinn had done a bit of surreptitious reconnoitring. He wanted to pay more for the *Interior* and for the drawings of children in church, but he was now suggesting £5 for the portfolio of drawings from photographs. Gwen was inflexible (perhaps she had consulted the Curé). She said she really could not take £5 for them, she would rather take nothing at all. A month later, she wrote again: 'I allow you to overrule me for the drawings. Not for the other things.' She had now sent off five more albums of similar drawings from photographs and clearly suspected he had not really appreciated them: 'look into one,' she instructed him, these new ones were better than the last portfolio. She had now done seven more albums, as it was quicker to do them all at the same time than to keep coming back to them. She had also finished a new painting, but she proposed, again, to do several before choosing one to send him.[48] Instead, by July he had another five sets of six drawings.

In September she went to Finistère for a few weeks, possibly on her own (she stayed with a Mlle Stepham in the rue de la Caleri, Loctudy.) She sent her address to Quinn in case he wanted to get in touch with her about the drawings of generals and a month later, back in Meudon, she was still asking him about them. She was remarkably persistent; perhaps the Curé, having had the idea in the first place, was reluctant to let it go. It was Ursula who finally diverted her from this project, telling her she should not be doing 'such stuff'.[49] Gwen reluctantly agreed: she thought they were valid works of art, but the trouble was that after the first one, the project had become rather mechanical.[50]

During the summer, she finished another painting. She was now referring again to a little 'blue' painting (not to be confused with the variants of *Girl/Woman in a Blue Dress*), possibly *Girl in Blue*,[51] in which the sitter resembles 'la petite modèle', a year on – her hair is different but her features are similar. In *Girl in Blue*, Gwen took even further the experimentation with elongated and broadened forms: the large haunches and hands are emphasised by the way the figure is placed in the corner of the room, with walls widening out each side of her in the background. This portrait extends the experiment Gwen had begun in her second portrait of Chloe. She now made several portraits of the little girl who posed for *La Petite Modèle*, and eventually she sent Quinn two further, similar portraits (*Portrait of a Girl, with Hands Clasped* and *Girl in Rose*[52]), though he would not get them for at least another six years.

Gwen was happy that summer, recording in her notebook 'moments of sweetness, of harmony, these evenings of solitude when we can pray . . . how grateful I must be for them!'[53] She joined in the neighbourhood life of Meudon, attending the priest's fête in August and lunching in restaurants,[54] and in October she went to Finistère again with Ruth Manson, encouraged by Winifred: 'I am glad you are at the sea, get strong and forget everybody in Paris.'[55] (Picture postcards were now strictly forbidden by the censor, but it is typical of Winnie that hers somehow miraculously got through.) Gwen was reading Dostoevsky's *The Idiot*, which she thought so wonderful it made her tremble.[56] In her notebook for 18 August, she copied down an extract from a young philosopher/soldier who had just been killed. 'When the war is over, I think I'll try to earn some money and buy a little house, and try to arrive at some kind of permanence and truth.'[57] She seems to have been optimistic. She decided she wanted to exhibit her work, and wrote to Ursula to ask whether she could be persuaded to exhibit with her.[58] Everybody still thought the war would be over by Christmas, but as winter approached there was no change in the situation. The winter of 1916 was exceptionally cold. Chloe sent furs and muffs. By mid-December there was frost and then deep snow, but Gwen was still painting.[59]

14

17 November 1917

I am like a butterfly comming [*sic*] out of a crysalis [*sic*] this Spring.[1]

Gwen began the New Year of 1917 by making her resolutions: she would not become too immersed in either her housework or her art, and God would be with her in both activities.[2] Her canary had died, despite expert advice from Chloe and Grilda, and God had comforted her in her agony. She was slightly unwell, with a cough and the *grippe*, which seemed to improve when Ursula sent some clothes – dresses, coat-and-skirt ensembles, hats, a little 'cache-corset', finer than the ones she could get in Paris, and a grey silk blouse and some ribbon. She was delighted: 'It is wonderful the influence upon the mind clothes have.'[3] They cheered her for more reasons than one, she told Ursula – she was presumably pleased to have new things to wear for Rodin who was back in France. It seems unlikely that she fully realised how frail he was by now, as he had been pleading illness and fatigue more or less since they met. She still expected his visits. She probably had no idea that on the bitterly cold morning of Monday, 29 January 1917, in response to firm persuasion from his friends, he and Rose were finally married at the Villa des Brillants: Judith Cladel could see how weak they both were and had managed to get a letter from Rodin's doctor, enabling them to conduct the ceremony at home.

Man and wife were then put to bed, as the villa was cold and the fuel which had been provided for the ceremony had run out. Two weeks later, Rose contracted bronchitis, which turned into pneumonia. Almost immediately, she was dead. Rodin was seventy-seven, and his life was now more or less in the hands of others. Surrounded by people who tried to keep watch over him at the Villa, he would nevertheless manage to wander off alone occasionally, getting himself to Paris and the Hôtel Biron, but he was dying of congestion of the lungs.[4]

Léonce Bénédite, Director of the Musée de Luxembourg, was concerned for the fate of the Whistler Muse: the newspapers in Paris, London and New York had been announcing its near, or actual completion for the past seven years and the International Society had been intermittently exerting pressure, to no apparent avail. They now sent a committee – which seems to have consisted of William Orpen, Derwent Wood and Augustus – to examine and report on it. With the exception of one member, who was a painter (Augustus, surely), they agreed that it was a 'poor thing, quite unworthy of Rodin and the master it was supposed to perpetuate'. According to Augustus, it was Derwent Wood who advised the Committee to retract the commission on the grounds that the statue had an uncompleted arm. On 8 May 1919, the Committee finally sent Bénédite official notice that the commission was formally retracted; in 1922 the funds amassed were returned to subscribers.[5] Augustus's view was that it would have been 'a superb and appropriate monument to the painter',[6] but it remained, in its several variants, dispersed between the pavilion of the Villa des Brillants and a shed at the Hôtel Biron until Augustus, and later the curators of the two Rodin museums, resurrected it, after the deaths of both Rodin and Gwen.

Gwen was busy working in the rue Terre Neuve, doing new gouache and watercolour drawings, and negotiating a price with Quinn for some new albums of drawings. They had decided she would take 50 francs for each album, which meant that she owed him 100 francs. He would rather take two more albums, he said, and he was not prepared to reopen negotiations on the nine drawings which she had suddenly decided she owed him a pound each for.[7] He had taken advice from Walter Kuhn, and he was sure that what they had agreed was fair. 'What you call your indecision about prices is, of course, not annoying and is a natural thing for an artist, but at the same time I think I am a very good judge of prices and I hope you will let that matter stand.'[8] He asked her to send him two or three drawings like the ones she had sent a couple of years ago (little girls in church, rather than generals). During the next few years she would develop her watercolour and gouache work to include larger and more detailed portraits. She also now began to experiment with flower pieces, increasingly abstract in conception, which strongly resemble Bonnard's paintings of flowers. She began to transpose into her notebooks in a much more detailed way than before the evidence of her thinking about tone and form. On 6 October 1917 she mapped out:

Treatments:	the blob, the end 3rd lines. dry painting
note:	in 2nd 3rd line the masses lighter.
portraits	dry painting the masses put in first but as much
cats	together as possible line & masses. the line of equal value with masses.
Dark motives	Night street. Twilight street. Night forest. Twilight forest. In church, eve.
	Sounds at night with fish boxes. Grey dress on a brune.
Rule for tones	Find *first* the tones of the principal point.[9]

Here the work on tonal relations is integrated with notes to herself about precise plans for the drawing of forms. These notes give us a sense not only that we are leaning over her shoulder and seeing exactly how her pictures were made, but also that we can appreciate the precision with which she needed to plan and make marks now that she was working in an indelible medium. They reveal the extent to which we may now almost hear her thought processes. They draw us into the poetry of her vision: 'Night street. Twilight street. Night forest. Twilight forest . . . Sounds at night with fish boxes.' She *heard* her work. This is a revelation, and tells us something about how its inimitable atmosphere and poetry were achieved.

The stillness and harmony which Gwen achieved within her work have been consistently remarked on by critics, and the degree of self-discipline required to realise these qualities was phenomenal, particularly amidst zeppelins and explosions and air raids. Quinn had bought another two albums,[10] and by April she was thinking about sending some of her new work to the NEAC, and still hoping Ursula might see her way to exhibiting with her in Paris. There were no exhibitions for the time being because of the war, but she was beginning to get a sense of achievement from the discoveries she was making: ' I think there will come a time when we will never paint for a few hours without doing something. A picture for every sitting, or a part of one. At present I, at any rate, do so many canvases to be thrown away. But this period has almost come to an end now, not quite.'[11] We should keep this in mind in relation to works such as some of the *Blue Dress* variants, or the clearly unfinished version of the *Interior* with the brown teapot. Perhaps they were quite calmly and intentionally abandoned, and stored in the attics at the rue Terre Neuve (rather than thrown away) partly because if she eventually did decide to abandon them, the canvases might be used again.

Some of Gwen's paintings bear the first marks or last traces of other paintings on the back of the canvas. The Pictures and Maps Department of the National Library of Wales holds a series of unfinished, powdery marks, made repeatedly on separate boards, which are unfinished studies for a painting of small figures making their way up or down the hilly rue Terre Neuve, a painting she did in a number of variants. By now she seems to have almost invariably used paint in the way she used words, drafting and redrafting numerous times until she had the version which she felt best expressed her idea. Even when she had a finished version, she would sometimes go on redrafting, either because she wanted to do several to arrive at the one she thought closest to the pictures originally in her mind's eye, or sometimes because she thought that several variants (like variations on a theme) could interestingly comment on one another. She could not know in advance how the variants would comment on, improve on or enhance one another. As a result, her work gained a strong, fluid sense of immediacy and an intimacy between artist and subject which she was consciously developing in her portraiture as well as in her drawings.

'There must be so much weakness in me doing so little work and never exhibiting,' she wrote to Ursula. The 'Nun' still seemed to be no nearer completion, but she strongly felt that she had arrived at a turning point. 'I have had a tiring life for some years and so I seem only now to begin to paint!' Typically, she had self-knowledge, but not complacency – 'that may account for something, but not for much perhaps'.[12] She was writing all this without even being sure that her letters would ever find their way to England. Nobody could really count on anything any more. The United States had now joined the Allies and the world would be at war for more than another year. The American allies had given France 'new courage and energy', she assured Quinn.[13] The retreat had changed things, too: she thought there was generally less of the helplessness which everybody had felt, though the newspapers had never acknowledged it. But she spoke to very few people about it, and knew that nobody really knew anything, even now. To Gwen, as to Rodin, the destruction of the castles and churches seemed particularly dreadful, and all the beautiful villages and woods: people said these last acts of violation had made the soldiers furious and when they got into Germany they would show no mercy. In the midst of all this, she found a place near the opera which she thought might be able to dispatch her pictures, since there was no *grande vitesse* or *petite vitesse* any more, though they warned her it might take two or three weeks. Determined to exhibit her work if she could, she decided that if there was an NEAC exhibition that autumn, she would send everything on by *spécial expéditeur* a month in advance to make sure it got there, and if necessary pay for it to be stored.

'I am like a butterfly comming [*sic*] out of a crysalis [*sic*] this Spring' she wrote to Ursula, with staggering indomitability.[14] The 'Nun' finally seemed to be finished, which surely accounted in large measure for the sudden release of new energy. She had been worried, too, about the safety of *Dorelia in a Black Dress*, which she had rather recklessly sent to Ursula. When she heard it had arrived safely she was 'a Maman who knows her baby has a home'. She was keeping up, through Ursula and Augustus, with what was happening in the London art world. Someone sent her a long piece on the Royal Academy, with which she was unimpressed. 'As to the "British gallery of Art",' she responded indignantly, 'all that strange plastering of canvases that I used to see, passed in procession before my mind.' It seemed nothing had changed there, and nothing ever would. 'All other human institutions have some movement, the "Royal Academy" is superior and alone.'[15] France was her spiritual home now.

Soon – possibly because she was planning to send her best things to the NEAC – she was writing to Quinn to say that she had 'come again to the difficulty of judging my canvases'. It would be a while before she could send him anything as she was still not satisfied with anything she had done. She had been thinking a lot about Maud Gonne, and hoped he would write to her on Gwen's behalf as he had promised. There was some expectation that the war would end that autumn. If it did, she hoped perhaps Quinn could come to Paris before the winter. There was a new feeling of discouragement: 'America has done [France] good in a way but there is a sort of hopelessness now.' She did not feel the French would be able to be courageous for much longer, though she was sure they would fight to the end. She wondered whether there was perhaps less endurance in the French character than in the British. It rained incessantly that summer, and everyone's spirits seemed to be low. Quinn sent her a book, which she was delighted by. 'All these days are under its charm,' she wrote, gratefully. 'It gives me more joy than has anything for a long time.'[16] But he was still waiting for a painting.

The war had a serious impact on Quinn's style of correspondence; he now made extra carbon copies of all his letters, sending another copy a week or ten days after the original by a separate boat, a practice Gwen found infuriating. He would also occasionally add notes of verification for the censor. The carbon copies bore clippings stating that they were copies; the notes to the censor informed him that this letter was actually being sent by the person named as the sender, and that it was actually intended for the person named as the recipient. He does not seem to have occasioned any undue suspicion. He was, of course, thrilled at the news that America had joined the Allies: that day had been 'one of the two greatest days in the world', 'the day of the Russian Revolution' being the other.[17] The news of Maud Gonne was not good. In November, she had let go her apartment in Passy and packed everything up; she got her passport endorsed, her tickets bought and places reserved to go with her little boy to Dublin, but the day before they were to have started she was officially informed by the British War Office that she could go to England, but not to Ireland. No reason was given.[18] She could think of nothing but her need to get back to Ireland. Her husband, Major John McBride had been executed as a rebel in Ireland in July 1916.[19] She was worried about the allocation of food for poor children in schools, which she had successfully initiated but which had been neglected in her absence.[20] She had written to Lloyd George and the Irish members of Parliament to ask for an explanation, but none seemed to be forthcoming. For the time being, she was stranded in Passy, living in a tiny attic on the seventh floor which she had rented to store her furniture in. Gwen, who had assumed she was in Normandy, had written in the New Year to say that she thought she would be better off in Paris than in Ireland, and asking Quinn to tell her she very much wanted to see her, but felt reluctant to go and see her without an invitation. She thought Maud should settle in Paris: 'I should not think she would be happy in Ireland now. I know I've got a cheek in pretending to know.'[21]

In April, still worried about her, she wrote to ask Quinn if he had passed on her message as she wanted to write but still thought she should wait to hear from her first, since Maud Gonne, by Gwen's standards, seemed very conventional.[22] Quinn duly passed this on, adding that Gwen, 'a little pathetically', felt 'she couldn't write to you again until she had heard from you, or something to that effect . . .'[23] This elicited no response. When he wrote again in June, he added a more diplomatic postscript: Gwen was still hoping to see her again…

> She apparently was very much impressed by you and seemed to like you. She wrote that you had said you would see her again and she felt that she could not call upon you again until she had heard from you. I never met her personally. I imagine she is a very shy person. She is a very fine painter indeed. I don't want to urge you to see her if you do not feel inclined to do so, and I mention what she wrote because she seemed to be sincere in her liking for you.[24]

Maud Gonne was still trying to get back to Dublin. She went to Calvados in the summer, then back to Paris, then London, where she hoped she would be able to get the ban on her return to Ireland lifted. In December she was in Chelsea, still longing to get back to Ireland. She wrote to Quinn from 265 King's Road with the news that she often saw Arthur Symons. He now seemed wonderfully well again after a nervous breakdown and had 'regained something of his old brilliance'. She had also been to see Augustus's wonderful portraits, including some lovely pictures of Dorelia in a cornfield and the mountains. She heard there that Quinn had bought Augustus's portrait of Symons. Augustus himself was now at the Front, 'in khaki', painting the soldiers. This seemed an appropriate context to mention Gwen. 'I liked his sister whom you introduced me to very much. We did not see so much of her as I would have wished, for first, she was away and then I was away. I was really very little in Paris since the war. After it I hope we shall see something of each other, for the little I saw of her, I liked greatly.'[25]

The war showed no sign of ending. Gwen was still painting, with her Meudon neighbours as subjects. She posed them sometimes with her cats, and in the late 1910s and early 1920s she did a series of variants of a girl holding a black cat (this may have been Valentine, her oldest, toothless and most terrifying cat). In one (*Girl in a Blue Apron with a Cat on Her Lap*)[26] she peers out somewhat menacingly; in similar paintings she is clasped tightly to the model; in *Young Woman Holding a Black Cat*[27] she looks perilously as if she is about to make her escape. There were more casualties of war, Gwen told Quinn. Verhausen was killed at Rouen station. She had admired his play, and was shocked to hear of his death.[28] But through all these isolated events, life went on, and Gwen went on working.

But then there was dreadful news. At 4 a.m. on the morning of 17 November, Rodin died. Ursula was the first in England to hear of it, and she wrote immediately. Gwen got her letter on 22 November and replied straight away that it had done her good to hear from her: she did not know what she was going to do. She had not seen Augustus yet, but she was expecting him.[29] On the 23rd, Thornton wrote to say that he had made enquiries about travelling to Paris and discovered that he would need to get a passport from the Foreign Office but they could be granted only in cases of urgent necessity. He would have to be photographed and it would be expensive, but he had already written asking for information on all the formalities. Was she very ill? If not, could it wait until after the war? His work was very important and he did not want to risk his job; his landlady was very good to him: she cooked and shopped for him and in return he kept her company in the evenings. He sent a present of £5 in case Gwen was in need of money as well as sick and unhappy. He assured her he was thinking about her: 'When I think of France it is the terrace at Meudon and the woods behind it.' He made the necessary arrangements to get to her as quickly as possible if it really was essential but he would also need a reference from a magistrate, doctor or banker. The war looked as if it might end 'in a draw and perhaps sooner than we think', and then of course he would visit. For now, 'I think I could manage the thing in an emergency . . .'[30]

It was Augustus who arrived, two weeks before Christmas, to comfort his sister. He took her to dinner at the Café de Versailles, next to the Gare Montparnasse, and told her all his news, which cheered her. The next day he went to see her in Meudon and took her back to Paris with him in his car. It had been good for him, Gwen afterwards thought, to be there meeting such different people: she must have introduced him to her friends and neighbours in Meudon.[31] She was grateful to him for coming, and rewarded him by finding a magazine called *Colour*, which featured two of his works. She told Ursula she thought them 'rather good. They want something which perhaps will come soon!'[32] She thought the magazine itself dreadful; it confirmed her feeling that she was done with English pictures – there were only two or three English artists she ever wanted to see again. She realised, she told Ursula, that she would be unwelcome company for a time while she did not feel 'normal' but she was beginning to recover, and had already started to paint. Temporarily at least, she recovered from the shock of Rodin's death surprisingly quickly, though it was to catch up with her later. She kept no known record at this time of her grief. But perhaps she had mourned their love, and lamented his absence, while he lived. What was removed when he died was the anguish of knowing that while she was alone and longing for his love, he was somewhere else. Augustus's visit undoubtedly contributed to the speed with which she apparently now moved from grief and shock to a new burst of energy.

In her notebook for February 1918 she began to mark something off against the days of the week – the number of meditations or prayers? On 4 February she made three marks and noted, 'Your meditation is the event of the day.' On 8 February, '111 Give up your art, everything that you have to Him.' On 10 February, '111 A part of you is Love. The rest will be done away with.' She timetabled herself: '6 to half past 7 breakfast and ménage [housework] half past 7 to 1/2 past 8 prayer.' She threw herself into her faith as a way of feeling less lonely, making rules to discipline herself into a new routine of prayer. '*Rule*: Controle [*sic*] your mind so that you can pray.' She thought of herself as God's child – 'A Child by her Mother's side' – the power of God was maternal, paternal, and enabled her to focus on the interior life.[33]

She was still living in a bombarded city. 'We have the dangers now, the avions and the canon a longue porte,' she told Ursula in March 1917. It looked at this point as though within the next two or three days there might be more certainty as to how it would all end. 'It will not be the end of course,' she shrewdly realised. She felt more anxious than ever before, since everyone knew by now what the Germans were capable of. The newspapers were now becoming more revealing: reports were that some divisions of the army had been 'hacked to pieces' rather than give in. A shell had fallen on the church and caused a lot of deaths. They were now coming every hour. One had fallen in the Avenue de Marine that morning while Gwen was shopping in the markets in the Boulevard Edgar Quinet: 'It is rather a loud noise, not very loud, not deafening but there is no mistaking it for anything else!' Several had fallen on the rue de Rennes and near the Gare de Montparnasse, though there were no reports of victims. Meudon seemed safer, being to the west of Paris, and there seemed to be no bombardments outside Paris itself, but one never knew where the next shell would fall.

Every day, Gwen moved more of her things from the rue de l'Ouest to the rue Terre Neuve, where it felt safer. She was also more protected there from the shells though they had caused some damage. There were no victims, but four unexploded shells were found. 'From my window here I see the lights of the avions and sometimes I have seen a ball of fire falling. I don't know what it is,' she told Ursula.[34] When there was an explosion, she went down into the cellars of the rue Terre Neuve, where she was forced to listen to the 'uneducated talk and nonsense' of the other inhabitants of number 29 – any company must have been trying in the circumstances, given the strain, the loss of sleep and the combined impact of everyone's fear, but it was difficult to have no one near she could talk to intellectually. Ruth Manson had now fled to Brittany with Rosamund, feeling that it would be too dangerous to stay in Paris with a child.

Despite all this, she confessed to Ursula that 'I feel as if I have been ill for a long time and am getting better.'[35] She seems to have been able to make a clear distinction between the interior life, now cleansed, to some degree, of an immense emotional strain and moving forwards into a new and clearer spiritual dimension, and the external world of events, no matter how closely they impinged. A sense of detachment and clarity now made her feel strong, even elated. Her ability to be objective was quite remarkable: 'When the Gothas [shells] come over one thinks more about them than the war,' but 'One shouldn't of course.' Perhaps what sustained her at this time was the feeling that, for the first time since she met Rodin – fourteen years previously – she could be independent and make decisions entirely for herself. Even so, she showed amazing courage. 'I can't stay when the bombardment is very bad, in my logement,' she told Ursula, 'because it sounds almost overhead. So I go to some friends, a man and his wife, a good long way off. I can't get dressed in time always before the tire de barrage commences and I feel rather frightened in the roads.' She used to take a short cut down the hill through the winding roads behind the rue Terre Neuve along the secluded rue des Clos Moreaux, with its high walls, all alone in the dark. It was as sheltered as a country road and 'so beautiful at night', she reassured Ursula, but it must have been terrifying. 'In these moonlight nights the bushes have dark shadows and look as if there were "mauvais sujets" hiding in them to spring out on me as I pass.' One night, she dreamt that she was being pursued by the Boches. 'I tried to hide under the leaves but they were never thick enough and I was always discovered.' Sometimes there were two alerts in one night and she would come home and go to bed only to have to get up again, though she would lie there until the noises got too loud to ignore. The Gothas were being aimed at Versailles and the cannon at Meudon fired at them as they passed, so the noise was deafening, even though Meudon had only one cannon. They would hear the alert sound from Paris: the cannon being fired three times, then the sirens, and then the *beloque* [*sic*] – 'a gay little tune played on something on an auto which passes through the streets of Paris. It is so loud that it is quite clear for miles.'[36]

Maud Gonne had been arrested. Ezra Pound wrote to Quinn in October telling him that she had been arrested in Ireland a few months ago and had been in prison in England ever since, but she had also been diagnosed as tubercular. One lung was partially collapsed, and she had chronic fever.[37] Knowing none of the details, Gwen passed on the news to Ursula: 'I see Maud Gonne is arrested, isn't she silly!'[38] She had always said it would be safest to stay in Paris. Quinn wrote to the House of Commons, pleading for her release. The doctors wanted her released immediately and sent to a better climate. By 7 November she was out of prison and on her way to a sanatorium. Quinn was determined that she should not go to Ireland, convinced it would be detrimental to her health: 'Should go soon possible Switzerland or Pyrenees. Complete rest open air treatment suitable climate,' he cabled Ezra Pound.[39] Thornton, now in London working at the Arsenal, had heard about the Paris raid and wrote to Gwen to tell her he was planning to leave and longing to be out of doors again. He was hoping to get work at Gravesend, in a shipwright's yard, making spars for ships. If the bombardment continued she was to go to the country, he advised, otherwise her work and her health would suffer. In April he sent her Omar Khayyám's *Rubaiyat*: he had not been able to find an illustrated edition so he sketched into it some drawings of his own. In May, Ursula sent more clothes – a blue serge coat and skirt – she thought Gwen ought to get herself tto Cassis, 'where the earth is almost red', the countryside was 'wild and curious' and the people were friendly. There was another lovely village nearby, La Citoyer, with sea and great rocks. Ursula was sending a small oil painting to the NEAC, and had been asked to lend for an exhibition a painting Gwen had given her (probably *Dorelia in a Black Dress*). She said she knew that Charles Aitken (Director of the National Gallery) was behind this; he was 'determined to filch the painting from me' but she had resisted because she and Gwen had agreed long ago that if ever Gwen had an exhibition in London, this painting should be included.[40]

It was strange that Ursula had advised her to go to the sea, Gwen told her, as she had just decided the same thing herself. Ruth and Rosamund Manson were now in Pléneuf, a tiny, beautiful old village just a few miles from the seaside resort Val-André, on the north coast of Brittany. They were staying in a pretty cottage the locals called 'Chaumine' with their friends Madame de Willman Grabowska and her daughter Elisabeth.[41] In August 1918 Gwen took the train from Montparnasse to Lamballe and went to stay with them for a while; there she made some beautiful watercolour portraits of Elisabeth and a drawing of the house. She loved the coastal wildness of Pléneuf and was very happy there. The church at Pléneuf, with its enormously tall steeple, had a shrine to Saint Thérèse of Lisieux, the young saint known as the 'little flower' who had died aged twenty-four. (Over the next few years Gwen would make hundreds of drawings of the child who was later sanctified, posing with her younger sister for a formal photograph in a photographer's studio.) The Breton coast calmed and inspired her: it is very like the Pembrokeshire coast, rugged and wild, with rough paths down to the sea and a buttery light, yellow ochre and pale, muted green, the beach flanked with the black rocks Chaucer immortalised in 'the Franklin's Tale'. Even now, Pléneuf feels secluded and unspoiled. Gwen felt immensely liberated there, organic and free, part of the elemental fusion of yellow light, salty air, craggy rocks, dancing leaves. This was the first time since she had arrived in Paris in 1903 that she was able to leave her home and really enjoy being elsewhere without worrying that she might be sacrificing opportunities to be with Rodin.

In Pléneuf that summer she was peaceful, untroubled and focused. She decided she would go back there as soon as possible in the New Year; and in one of those odd strokes of Fate through which the very thing one needs suddenly presents itself, the day before she left she took a walk along a rough track leading down to the sea, and discovered there, in its own shade beneath the trees, 'an old chateau with some wonderful rooms in it'. She made enquiries and discovered that they were very cheap; it also appeared that if she took them in the New Year she would be alone there.[42] When she arrived back in Meudon she wrote to Quinn, telling him how beautiful she had found Pléneuf, and how conducive to her work it had been. She had not been painting, but she was now doing drawings which expressed exactly what she wanted them to – much more so than the paintings she had been doing before she left Meudon for Brittany. She promised to send him six or nine drawings; he was to send back any he did not want. Arriving back in Paris had been a fraught experience. It had taken her several days to find her trunk at the Gare Montparnasse, there seemed to be thousands of people there, like a nightmare. It would have been a 'misfortune' to have lost it – something of an understatement since it contained all her drawings.[43] She asked Quinn for news of Maud Gonne. She knew nothing about conditions in prison but she did know about her political commitments. Had she been freed yet? As a political activist, 'perhaps she didn't mind being arrested?'[44] The enemy had by now accepted the proposed conditions. Surely, that must be good news.

Back in Paris, she felt that among the new drawings she had done in Brittany there were perhaps twelve or fourteen good ones. Quinn, of course, was disappointed not to be getting any new paintings.[45] He was pleased with his six drawings, though he would really have liked nine. He said if there had been nine he would happily have paid at least 600 or 800 francs, in fact he thought they were worth 800.[46] Gwen had stayed in Brittany longer than she had intended to, and done a great deal of new work. During these years following Rodin's death – from about 1919 through the early 1920s – her rate of production increased immeasurably. Cecily Langdale details forty-eight drawings from about 1919 to the early twenties, and fifty-eight paintings. Gwen did many drawings of Breton children, smartly turned out in their dresses, ribbons and hats, often patiently posed with clasped hands, reminiscent of the photograph of the eight-year-old Gwen in her smart black dress, her hands gracefully clasped. As well as Elisabeth de Willman Grabowska she sketched other local children who would wander into the garden of the château from the adjoining farm, capturing their absorption in their task as they sat for her. Some children sat several times: Marie Hamonet, Odette Litalien, daughter of a local farmer, and others who posed in the open air, sometimes on the rocks. They sat with touching concentration, and she would give them a few centimes for their trouble. She often drew them with clasped hands, a pose which probably helped a child to sit still and concentrate. Many of her most striking and best known drawings of children were done in Brittany, among them *Little Girl with a Large Hat and Straw-Coloured Hair*,[47] in which the model is dutifully muffled in smart clothes, wearing a hat with a broad ribbon, her shoulder-length straw-like hair stuck out in stiff, vertical swathes (perhaps it had been coaxed out of its plaits especially for the sitting). She did them by finishing the figure first and re-doing the background afterwards, she told Ursula.

One little boy, who appears in several drawings, must have been a very good, patient sitter, able to hold long poses. In two variants in particular (*Le Petit Garçon Sentimental* and *The Little Boy*)[48] he is strikingly similar to Picasso's *Child with Dove*. The marks have clearly been reworked within the drawing itself, and the tonal relations are subtle and careful. He has a natural simplicity, with his vulnerable wrists in slightly too large sleeves observed in firm, gentle lines; his pose, the angle of the clasped hands and the extraordinary serenity of the face capture exquisitely his vulnerable innocence. Gwen also did a rapidly sketched, two-dimensional drawing in wash on paper of *A Rag Doll*,[49] which flops lackadaisically, its arms outstretched, its dress taut across its chest, across a roughly sketched ground, where somebody may have thrown it on the floor. It – or its prototype – appears again in the lap of Elisabeth de Willman Grabowska, its head now comfortingly cradled, in the large wash portrait sometimes known as *Seated Girl* or *Girl Nursing a Doll.*[50]

Gwen now became convinced that her drawings looked much better if several were seen together. She was not sure why, but 'Perhaps on looking at one or two the details would be noticed too much or something like that.' The atmosphere of the drawings was the important thing; the exquisite tonal beauty of them seems to have absorbed the atmosphere of Pléneuf, the dappled shade of its leaves, the soft, salty light of its coastal stretches. The notation, rather than the draughtsmanship, makes them live; this was the essence of her experimentation at this time, a radical departure from her earlier insistence, schooled by Brown and Tonks, on accurate drawing. She became increasingly more subjective, and correspondingly more suggestive, moving in one sense, therefore, towards the subjective philosophy of Post-Impressionism, the mood of this work finding equivalents for innocence, vulnerability; liberty. The enemy had just proposed an Armistice but she refused to get excited about this: she thought they just wanted an opportunity to talk and play for time.

Augustus was back at the Front, working on a Canadian war picture. 'I trust you to believe,' he wrote from there, 'that my infrequent letters don't mean that I don't think of you very often. I'm so very glad Brittany did you good.' What was she doing now she was back? Still 'shoving all your belongings on a handcart from Paris to Meudon? That must be tiring!' He had wanted to go back to France. The authorities had refused permission but he was hoping to get to Paris again some time during the next year, if only for a short while. Like Gwen, he took a cautious view of recent events. 'The Allied Peace will have to be careful or Germany will be stronger than ever before long (plus German Austria) and break out again.'[51] By November, she had decided she would definitely go back to Pléneuf in the New Year, and she made arrangements to take rooms in the château. She wondered whether Quinn would like to visit her there: 'it is such a wonderful place . . . There is a wild lonely bay near the chateau and beautiful places to walk too.' For now, she reported 'a wild joy in Paris' and touching scenes in the streets.[52] The Armistice had been declared. Everything, now, was about to change. Peace had come.

15

The Château Vauclair

Do not have many little aims but the one great: – to be a child of prayer and God's artist.[1]

Now that it is over one will work better I hope.[2]

The war was over, Rodin was dead; Gwen was forty-two. When peace was declared on 11 November 1918, 'London went mad for a week,' Augustus reported to Gwen. His boys were growing, all in different schools and making plans for the future. David wanted to be an aviator, Henry hoped to be a historian. Their bees were providing lots of honey; Dorelia was well and wanted to see Gwen again. Thornton was discharged from Woolwich Arsenal. ('I suppose,' surmised Augustus, 'he will live in his boat and catch fish.') Life could now be resumed. Augustus was anxious to know whether Gwen was managing to work. By 4 January 1919 she was already back in Pléneuf, happily installed in the Château Vauclair and writing to Isobel Bowser to tell her it was a 'chez-d'oeuvre' [*sic*].[3]

Travelling to Pléneuf meant taking a train from the Gare Montparnasse to Lamballe in Brittany – a journey which today takes three hours. At Lamballe, a diligence took her the rest of the way – about six miles. Away from the centre of the village of Pléneuf there is a road which eventually leads down towards the beach: a fairly large road cuts across it; you cross this and continue on down into a rough track under the trees. Not far along, to the left, a great wrought-ironwork pair of gates, beautiful as cobwebs, protects a *manoir* – elegant and veiled by leaves. In late August or early

September when Gwen first discovered it, the two horse chestnuts would have been laden with fruit; two limes and an ash cast a shade, making the light shift from yellow to greenish gold across the path and making the grey gates of the château seem misty. The château is set back from the road, with grey shutters echoing the striped light cast by the *palmier* which rears up against the front of the house to the left of the main door. When Gwen came back in January, the house would have seemed even more ashy: shy, discreet and dignified, with its coat of arms visible above the door. There was a statue of a woman in the centre of the lawn, circled by a path and the whole view of the house had an air of fading grandeur, quintessentially French, romantic and mysterious. Gwen told Quinn she thought there was something sad about it, and that what she loved was the poetry of the place. The statue picks up the milky light from the sky and seems to wrap it lightly round so that it veils the pale blue/grey stone.

These days, you reach the house across an overgrown, brambly garden, high with nettles,trailing thorny tendrils which catch at your ankles; there is an apricot rose, leaning among the grasses. In 1919 the garden was still unbounded by the low, stone wall built later to separate the grounds of the house from those of the adjoining farm. Then, animals and people from the farm wandered over into the grounds of the château, which was probably one reason why Gwen found the local children so accessible. Then as now, the garden was something of a nature reserve, alive with butterflies and gnats in summer and with an air of abandonment in winter. Visible from the rear of the house is a turreted tower, which gives it truly the air of *château*, though it is invisible from the front of the house. Coming back round the house to the front again, still ankle deep in nettles and grasses, you pass the kitchen, at the front of the house and to the right, down in the depths of the house at basement or cellar level. In 1919 the salon must have had the same scent as now – an immediate, pungent odour of centuries of wood smoke – and a manorial air. There is a wrought-iron filigree chandelier, baronial chairs, candles on the table. The walls are yellowing-cream; at some stage in the house's history the ceiling has been lowered, so that the beams seem oddly low. The narrow hall gives on to another room, but you mount the narrow staircase from the main reception room, with its ornate baronial banister.

Upstairs and to the right there are small bedrooms: the servants' quarters with their sharply sloping ceilings. The little room inside the turreted tower, now a bathroom, was empty in 1919: one would have washed with jugs and basins, with water heated in the *sous-sol* kitchen. There are three more, slightly larger bedrooms, and the master bedroom. One of these rooms would have been Gwen's: perhaps the one lined with bookshelves, facing out to the front of the house, with a view of the front garden and the statue. The whole of the upper floor is tucked in under the eaves, and the rooms are smaller than the elegant façade of the château suggests. Outside again, the road down to the beach takes you to the grassy cliffs overlooking the sea.[4]

The light seems to change and change, from glinty green to yellow/gold, to dove grey: there is a feeling of being secreted in this ancient, unspoiled land. Here is serenity, mystery, scope for the imagination to run wild, and the freedom of somewhere undisturbed, a land of memory and renewal. In the contrasts of soft grey, yellow ochre, olive green, and the dark, Breton rocks, there is a visual magic. It communicates itself powerfully in the tonal nuances of Gwen's Breton drawings. It is reminiscent, too, of the Celtic landscapes of Haverfordwest and Broad Haven, where the leaves cast a soft, dappled yellow and green light against pale stone.

Brittany was renowned as a retreat for painters, but Pont-Aven was the popular, scenic spot preferred by artists – Sérusier, Gauguin. Gwen had been to Pont-Aven with Ruth Manson but in comparison, Pléneuf is tiny and unspectacular, a little village up on a hill, which plunges down towards the seaside resort of Val-André on one side and the bare, wild coastline on the other. There were painters living and working in this region, too, but Gwen almost certainly knew nothing of them. Pléneuf was for her own work, and solitude and spiritual renewal. 'God will form me. He will change me,' she noted to herself, that spring.[5] She worshipped Saint Thérèse in the church at Pléneuf.[6] When she wanted company she tried to persuade her friends to visit: she would have liked Chloe to share the experiences of travelling on the top of the diligence, having tea outside under the trees and sleeping in the château. It was the perfect retreat, she told her. But it sounded a long way from England, and she reconciled herself to being totally alone. It suited her utterly, and most of the time she was not lonely. She was still there in February, but by now she had learned that the château was up for sale. She dispatched this news to John Quinn in New York, together with an invitation to come and stay. She would not be staying there much longer, she told him, because of the sale. 'I am disappointed but I know it doesn't matter where we live.'[7] This was putting a brave face on it. At one level it might be true, but she had decided she longed for nothing more than to live there. She read Bertrand Russell, noting down his remarks about the relationship between creativity and integrity. 'The world that we seek is a world in which the creative spirit is alive, in which life is an adventure full of joy and hope, based rather upon the impulse to construct than upon the desire to retain what we possess or to seize what is possessed by others. Such a world is possible . . .'[8] Quinn suggested she take some photographs of the château, and offered to send her a camera.

Still she stayed on, reluctant to leave because she was afraid that even if she was ever able to come back, the château would never be the same again. As the spring wore on, at the end of each month, the owners told her she could stay another month. In April they said she would have to leave for certain at the end of May. Quinn had for some time been trying to get her to send an affidavit authenticating her paintings, a document Pottier needed now that her work was being regularly dispatched under his auspices. But she would have to go to Paris to get the relevant papers signed and she could not bring herself to leave Vauclair with the threat of the sale hanging over her. She was drawing all the time; she had space, freedom, and the peace of mind that came from feeling entirely at one with her surroundings. She loved the look and feel of the place; it corresponded absolutely with style and rhythms of her imaginative life. She was reading Saint Catherine of Sienna, Thomas Aquinas, Novalis, Saint Luke. Catherine of Sienna had written, 'Habite avec toi-même' – live fully within yourself.[9] From Ribert, she noted, 'a soul in prayer is, through the action of prayer, *recueillie* – collected – vigilant in thought and action, mistress of the self, held within God's regard'. In April, she was still wishing she could get Quinn to come over there. Replenished herself, she was sure it would refresh him. She thought, she told him, that 'when one gets tired one looses [*sic*] something which one never gets back again'.[10] The château was still not sold, and it now seemed as if she would probably be able to stay for a few more months. She really wanted to be there during the summer. It had been a particularly long, dark winter and by mid-April there had been just three sunny days, but it was still very windy and cold. She liked the idea of the camera, and told Quinn she would very much like him to send her one if he could. She was obviously keen for him to see why the place meant so much to her.[11] The Château Vauclair, like Rodin – and earlier, Dorelia – fell into the category of something Gwen knew she needed. Again, she had found it.

Now as before, she was prepared to fight with every strategy available to get what she wanted. The château really mattered, and she began on a surreptitious project to try to secure it.

She stayed there, in the end, until at least June, when the château was finally sold to a Monsieur Bourdin. She told Quinn that she planned to be back in Paris by the end of the month. (She dealt with the problem of the affidavit, which had to be settled by mid-July, by asking for an extension on the grounds that the aftermath of the war made it impossible for her to travel to Paris for the relevant documents. It worked: she got another three months.)[12] She was finally back in the rue Terre Neuve by September – perhaps earlier – and now began painting with new vigour. All she had learned by working with the children of Brittany she was able to translate into her painting, and the children of Meudon appear as sitters in her paintings of this period. The model for *La Petite Modèle* sat for several works.[13] Because Gwen never dated her paintings it is impossible to know which were begun before she went to Pléneuf and which she did after she came back, but between 1919 and the early 1920s she did over fifty paintings. It is most likely that Pléneuf enabled her to resolve and develop in her mind the discoveries she had begun to make before she went, and quite possible that when she returned to Meudon she resumed several paintings she had already begun to work on. The drawings of children had exercised her hand as well as focusing her mind.

The subjects of her paintings now appeared increasingly in the mood of collected repose so strongly realised in *Girl with Cat*, in which the figure enables her to make a compositional study rather than a conventional portrait. The sitter is drawn almost symmetrically, becoming monumental, weighty, approximate, while the face, by contrast, reflects inwardness. The foreshortening is all created by the hands, which are big enough to stop the figure looking flat; the integrity and spiritual interiority of the face is partly emphasised by the way the cat is being drawn into the figure, stressing inwardness. This contrast between the reflective, realist face and the monumental figure is entirely her own. The flesh tones in the face are soft, subtle, delicately natural, while the sculptural forms and colours of the torso and full skirt challenge traditional ideas about spatial relations and make us aware that she is modelling the figure in space in a way that recalls Cézanne, Picasso and, of course, Rodin.[14]

She did many portraits in which she experimented with this contrast, and she worked as a matter of course on several variants at a time. In some the suggestive bulk of the cat is exchanged for clasped hands, a piece of sewing or an open book; in others the figure is exposed in space, the vulnerability of the torso accentuated by a locket or coral necklace. In many, the haunches are weighty and monumental while the torso seems more vulnerable, more fragile. In all the portraits, the female sitters are reserved, collected, integral within themselves. She worked now to create atmosphere and a repertoire of moods: of meditation, reflection, inwardness. With a flagrant disregard for the laws of foreshortening her figures are elongated or bulked out, with a suggestion of heavy, massed forms. The legs of her seated women are imposingly long, the hips and haunches borrowing from the spaciousness of the ground; hands holding folds of cloth become almost, themselves, massed folds. She now also did a series of paintings of a girl reading a letter, seated in the recognisable basketwork chair (which had already appeared in *A Corner of the Artist's Room in Paris*) beside a table bearing teapot, cup and saucer, and newspaper: the model may again have been Angeline. Isobel Bowser loved this painting. She was by now seriously ill with cancer, and Gwen wanted to finish the painting and give it to her. She told Isobel's sister, Nona Watkins, that she was calling the painting *The Convalescent* as a kind of joke: Isobel had put herself in the hands of the Christian Scientists, refusing conventional medicine as she was convinced her faith would cure her. Gwen (hence her 'joke') was more sceptical about their powers.[15]

The integrity of sitter with ground gives the paintings of this period their aura of silence; if we compare this work with the early portraits of Chloe or Fenella we see that all the restlessness of the sitters has disappeared, the figures are utterly introspective. They neither face the artist out, as in the early Toulouse paintings of Dorelia, nor are they shown in a state of heightened, oblique awareness, seated slightly askance, asserting their nerved-up uniqueness the way she had depicted Fenella in *Nude Girl* and Chloe in *Chloe Boughton-Leigh*. They have moved far beyond the classical poise of *Self-Portrait in a Red Blouse* or *A Lady Reading*. The work has moved fully now in atmosphere from a classical radiance to the kind of strangeness Edgar Allan Poe thought consistent with beauty in art, and to the experimental interpretation of spatial relations being practised by Cézanne.

That September, as Gwen was settling back into Meudon, Augustus was in Normandy painting a portrait of Lloyd George. He bought a guide to

Brittany and found Pléneuf described as commanding 'l'immense panoram [*sic*] sur le Val André, la baie de St. Brieu Paimpol & l'Ile Brehat.' Couldn't they consider buying the Château Vauclair, she asked him, even now? It had occurred to her that just because it had new owners, there was no reason why *they* would not be prepared to sell it. She had proposed as much to the *notaire*. Perhaps Augustus could afford it. Of course, he rashly replied, why had she not asked him before? Châteaux were always 'deficient in sanitary contrivances', but all the same 'it would be lovely to have one . . . and it would just suit us'.[16] He would try to come and see her there before she went back to Paris; meanwhile, perhaps Dorelia could manage to get to Brittany and see the château. He was not the only person she had written to about the sale. Her father, assuming she was still in Pléneuf and discovering Augustus was in Deauville, consulted his atlas in Tenby and decided he did not see why brother and sister could not meet: Deauville did not seem to him impossibly far from Pléneuf. He now acknowledged the 'pretty picture card' Gwen had sent him, of the château. 'Is that the house you are living at? I see the name Vaux-Clair is spelled with the letter x.' (It was not, always: the spelling of the name varies.)[17] He enclosed another impressive example of his 'self-photography'. Nobody realised the urgency of the situation regarding the château. Neither Augustus nor Dorelia seemed to be about to arrive in Pléneuf, despite their good intentions; and Gwen now received a response from Maître Leclerc, the lawyer she had written to asking whether the owners would consider re-selling the property. Monsieur Bourdin would be quite willing to sell the château, he reported, if she could offer a reasonable price – say, around 50,000 francs, in cash.[18] This was clearly well beyond anybody's means; unless, suggested Augustus, John Quinn might want to buy it.

She wrote tactically to Quinn the day she got the letter from Maître Leclerc, ostensibly to say how pleased she had been to get an extension on the affidavit, but really to tell him how hard she had found it to leave 'that old chateau in Brittany, it had an atmosphere of its own of beauty and poetry'.[19] At the beginning of October, she heard that Quinn had been awarded the Legion of Honour. She wrote to congratulate him, and again broached the subject of the château. She intended to settle back into Meudon now, she told him, but it was difficult to get models because nearly all the young people worked in the factories. She could not forget the unique beauty of the Château Vauclair. 'It is not grand at all. It has a beauty of its own, rather sad. It is four or five centuries old. It has wonderful trees and the gardens are beautiful, too; of course, all grown savage now, but that gave them more charm to me.' The new owners were cattle merchants, 'and so not used to thinking of what is beautiful'. She was afraid they had bought it just because it was a château and would renovate it in ways that were not in keeping with its character. 'They were going to make more windows, but I said it wouldn't be Vauxclair then, and that seemed to impress them. They are going to paint the grille white, instead of grey which it is and which is in harmony with the house. They said it would be "très chic" white.' She thought they were actually rather afraid of living there because it was so isolated and that they would only be there for two months of the year. 'They do not really want it, I think, because they would sell it to me not dear at all, and I think I shall live there again some day.'[20] It was nice to be back in Meudon now for a time, she added diplomatically.

In fact, the return to Meudon was a disaster. Not long after she arrived, Isobel Bowser died, before Gwen had had a chance to finish the painting she had promised her. She was devastated, partly because of her 'joke', which she now felt mortified by, and partly because the disappointment over Vauclair had made her emotionally vulnerable. Moreover, she had not really yet mourned Rodin. Isobel's death was a dreadful catalyst, and the timing was unfortunate. 'Do not for God's sake, allow it to make you morbid,' warned Augustus. He told her that anyway she had 'too much sense and esprit', but this was optimistic. He did his best: he said he wished he could see her work at the Salon; she should send more of her things over to London, where a number of people longed to acquire her work. But he knew her well. 'I regret Vauclair. Fine air is the best thing in the world. I'm afraid you'll not be happy at Meudon after the loss of your friend.'[21] This was, of course, perspicacious. She had borne Rodin's loss remarkably; now perhaps something would give, particularly after the disappointments surrounding the Château Vauclair. Chloe was also on the alert. Was she sure, she wrote, that the new owners of the château would not be willing to sell? Gwen was willing to try anything. She confided to Chloe that she was thinking of going to a Jewish money-lender, but Chloe warned her that this was not such a good idea, as they tended to charge huge amounts of interest and if it was not paid they would seize the property. She was in despair; and her confessor had also disappeared while she was away in Pléneuf. Chloe advised finding another one, and said she should talk to the Mother Superior.[22]

Isobel's death was hard to bear, because it brought with it guilt – an element which had been missing from her bereavement when Rodin died. Gwen had been going to take *The Convalescent* to the clinic for Isobel while she was still alive, but she had said 'it isn't done she said why it hasn't even got a spout!'[23] She had also been waiting, before she gave her her painting, for Ruth to bring some drawings from Val-André which she wanted Isobel to have. Also, Isobel had disliked the frame on the painting, so she had intended to get that changed . . . all these little things now felt overwhelming, she could not get them out of her mind: if only she had given Isobel the pleasure of the painting before she died. She confided all this to Nona Watkins, Isobel's sister, telling her that without her to talk to it would all be unbearable. The 'little joke' went on torturing her. As if that were not enough, she had also owed Isobel money, but Nona kindly told Ruth to make sure Gwen knew that this debt was 'now annulled'.

Nona was full of solace and comfort: she just said, 'my dear, dear Gwen'. All the tension of worrying about the château now surfaced, together with this terrible shock and sadness and undoubtedly her residual grief over Rodin, in a new flood of distress which felt tactile, primal. She was desperately homesick for Pléneuf and the Château Vauclair. She told Nona how she used to go out at night and pick leaves and grasses in the hedges 'all dark and misty and when I took them home I sometimes found my hands were full of flowers'. The loss of Rodin now found oblique expression: 'Nona, you are like a sculptor who models the clay . . . almost without thinking and suddenly he finds . . . a lovely form.' The suppressed frustration and tension of having to live without love found their way into her plangent appeals for care and reassurance. 'I need you Nona. I am a beggar at your door. I know that now. I know I wrote I don't ask for your tenderness but only let me speak to you.' She felt frightened and overwhelmed; now, as before, she needed to feel that there was someone she could have uninvited and unconditional access to. 'I will not trouble you much, only when I have to,' she wrote to her in mid-November, still in the clutches of shock. Nona, in the midst of her own grief, was endlessly soothing and philosophical. Eventually she reminded Gwen that the war was only just over; there were hundreds of thousands of bereaved, everyone had terrible sadnesses to bear at this time. She would remember her wise words, Gwen told her, gratefully, and 'that there is another side to our sorrows and about friendship . . . I take it to think about and believe in like a child takes things, because it is my only nourishment, because all the other things I knew before have gone away, now, from my memory.'[24] This is, of course, one of the terrible things about bereavement, the dreadful, disorientating amnesia.

Isobel's other sister was the actress Rhoda Symons, Arthur Symons' wife. Nona now had the brilliant idea of showing them Gwen's work. She took them some of her drawings, including a drawing she had made of Isobel, and Arthur was captivated: he said 'the very living Isobel' rose up before him. He thought they had something of Augustus's 'sombre passion'; he also thought they had genius. He wanted to buy three drawings, and told Gwen how deeply moved he was by her obvious devotion to Isobel; he was quite in agreement that 'those awful Christian Science people . . . killed her'.[25] He told her he knew Augustus well, and had had a high regard for Rodin. He was planning to go to Spain for the winter, so hoped it might be possible to meet her in Paris on the way. Gwen was clearly thrilled and comforted by his letter. She responded by making him a gift of one of her loveliest Pléneuf drawings, of Elisabeth de Willman Grabowska with her doll, *L'Enfant à la Poupée*,[26] which he thought 'a miracle of strange beauty'. He had heard Gwen was not well. 'Do take all possible care of yourself,' he urged her. '*One has to live*: and with that, one's Art . . .'

There were other – at least, provisional – notes of optimism: the Salon d'Automne now announced that they had decided to make her an 'associataire'.[27] The painting of *Mère Poussepin* was finally finished after all these years. She was also sustained by her friendship with Chloe, even though she was still unable to come to Meudon. They went on exchanging novels and prayer cards, and sharing their ideas and thoughts about their conversion to the Catholic faith. But soon more stress and anxiety followed. Kiki, one of Gwen's cats, was ill and Christmas was spent, on Chloe and Grilda's instructions, looking for a suitable vet. (They sent detailed advice and special powders, and advised taking her to the surgery with a hot water bottle and a blanket in her basket.) It was a difficult and stressful end to such a promising year and 1920 would turn out to be a very odd year, with more illness and continuing strain. But the New Year would also bring significant and inspiring new friendships.

16

Jeanne

I still see you coming to meet me in your dark cloak . . .[1]

. . . perfectly poised, a great lady in a way . . .[2]

After the war, the world changed. One expressed surprise if anyone still spoke, wrote, painted in the same way now as they had before the carnage of hundreds of thousands of young men. Women had been working – as nurses, like Maud Gonne and Chloe Boughton-Leigh, in the munitions factories, or translating for the soldiers, like Gwen – and had a new sense of the outside world. The world *looked* different; the difference between private and public experience seemed less marked. Nearly a million young Englishmen had died in the war, and more than a million more were disabled and disfigured. The 1918 'Spanish' influenza epidemic reputedly killed more people across the length and breadth of Europe than had died in the war. In the wake of it, there was another invasive force at work in parts of Paris, a 'curious blood disease', which had attacked Déshanel, among others. (The rumour was that he was taking narcotics to subdue the symptoms.)[3] Rilke wrote about the changed world: 'Into everyone's breast, suddenly no longer one's own, leapt a heart like a meteor, an iron heart from an iron universe.'[4] For Gwen, the immediate retreat to Pléneuf had been perfect. Sequestered there, she could work with the children in the garden and walk by the sea in peace. The return to Paris had not been easy; in her imagination, she had not really let go of the Château Vauclair.

After Isobel's death it was Constance she turned to: Augustus's prediction that she would now be susceptible to another bout of mourning had been wise. She was very fragile again; desperately trying to work, and tormented by the old yearning. Being ill, and working at a high pitch to continue the experiments she had begun to make in Pléneuf, had nerved her up into intermittent fever. In early January she steeled herself to face the Gare Montparnasse and the train, and somehow got herself to the Boulevard Henri IV and Constance's high flat with its view of the Seine. She felt very ill, and even a short visit brought back all the old feelings of desperation and dependency. She had been working hard despite not being well, and she was exhausted with grief. Constance's sympathy and care meant that all the old needs came flooding back. For a while, Gwen transferred her feelings of yearning and fragility on to Constance, at the same time trying to channel them into the familiar, hard-won self-knowledge and self-discipline. Everything felt like a herculean physical effort again, but 'It is in the effort [that] one's value lies, perhaps.' She drafted a number of letters to Constance which she probably never sent, searching within herself for some kind of equilibrium: 'Try and see another's outlook, & Possess your soul . . . question. Is my life more courageous, more harmonious, more spiritual?' The way forward was to 'Be God's child. Make the effort to-day.'

Constance became a kind of muse. Physically weakened, Gwen longed for love. 'When in love, all comes unconsciously,' she reminded herself. 'She will love you for the good she does you.' The old feelings for Rodin, and the excessively demanding constraints that went with them, were undoubtedly being called up again: 'Accept everything always.' In her confusion, she began to fantasise about Constance. 'Let her draw you to her to kiss your hand . . . Later you can kiss her more willingly with love & you can later still put your arms round her neck & kiss her, giving yourself. She may love you for your meekness.' In society, she told herself, 'be very calm and composed'. Alone with her, 'be timid & meek & yearning'. These were profound, regressive feelings: 'Sometimes be like two girls.' She wrote down her prayers: 'Oh God, who hast helped me in the past, oh help me now!' As always, the intense and tremendous struggle for self-control was tempered with the essentially Catholic struggle for piety. 'You *make* a life,' she reminded herself ' . . She will love you for your striving.'[5]

January 1920 brought a breathless communication from Rhoda Symons: 'Gwen – I'm Rhoda – I feel as if knew you – Nona and Isobel have told me so much of you – & I feel Gwen that I love you, because of your wonderful self – & because of your understanding of – & love of – Isobel.' She wanted to buy a drawing of a little boy in a Zouave jacket, but asked, could she have it for 'the same absurd sum' as Arthur had paid for his? It had, she added, obscurely, 'all that Isobel died for in it'. Gwen responded to her warmth, but candidly replied that she was unable to part with that particular drawing. Rhoda was clearly quite unoffended and said she was sorry if she had hurt her by asking. She was touched by Gwen's friendship with Isobel and wanted to talk to her about her. Like many sisters they had quarrelled, and now she could not stop thinking about her 'lying there stiff & cold & alone'.[6] The Symonses would come to Paris that summer and Gwen was to find both of them exceptionally sympathetic; she recognised their integrity and they came to mean a lot to her.

They were anxious to invite her to London, but for the time being she needed the countryside. Since coming back from Brittany she wanted to go on drawing wild flowers, ferns and grasses. She found some tiny notebooks in a sale (their *solde* stickers are still intact) and when she walked in the forest she took her notebooks with her in her pockets, looking for 'motifs' for her drawings, natural forms which she now increasingly used as starting points for more and more abstract work. She gave them titles like *Flowers and Leaves in Colour*, *Various Greens* or *Flowers in Wall – Black and White*. Or she took them home and painted them in vases, tilting the vases against the picture frame, their forms following the directions of the foliage or flowers in organic, rather than representational compositions. Her newly abbreviated lines meant that she could experiment with new ways of turning the forms inside out, so that inner and outer forms seemed to be in dialogue (as they are in Cubist art). In *Faded Dahlias in a Grey Jug*[7] the placing of the jug at a diagonal to the forefront of the picture frame means that the outer form suggests the nature of its inner space; the ground, like the ground in a Bonnard painting, seems to be wrapped in vertical sections, like the folding sections of a Japanese screen, around the vase. (Gwen must have seen Bonnard's work as it was exhibited during this time at the Bernheim Jeune Gallery in Paris. Perhaps oddly, she does not seem to have mentioned his work to anyone, but she had certainly been influenced, through Rodin, by Japanese drawings, as had Bonnard.)

Other pictures she did during the 1920s are even more lyrical: *Brown Bowl and Flowers in a Brown Vase*[8] has a rhythm achieved by pushing the brown bowl so close up to the picture frame that the outer form of the vase vies with the partially exposed interior space. By setting the brown vase of flowers back toward the ground, but then bringing the flowers forward with the use of stark white juxtaposed with green, she then tricks the eye again, lighting the far wall with violet-white. The title itself suggests an experiment with juxtaposed forms; artifice is being introduced in such a way as to highlight what Cézanne called *sensation*.[9] As for the mood of the picture, it is vibrant, enticing; it moves right away from the inwardness of the earlier Gwen John into something far more essentially dynamic. In general in her work, now, modelling began to give way to a process of putting down flat tints of colour – Gwen called it 'blobbing'.

She still took her pocket notebooks to church with her, on some pages making just one or two marks before her subject presumably moved, experimenting with making simple, suggestive forms in abbreviated lines. When she worked the drawings up in watercolour and gouache, back in the rue Terre Neuve, she would introduce into them occasional flat tints of red and orange, as in *Les Chapeaux à Brides*[10] or *Two Little Girls in Hats, in Church*,[11] making little moments of electricity or expectation in drawings which would otherwise have been essentially introspective. At times she introduces a wry humour, the kind she sometimes displayed in her comments about people. It is clearly detectable in *Profile of a Bourgeois Couple*,[12] which has very much the French cartoon-style quality. It shows a man in a railway carriage, bolt upright by the side of the smaller, formally more subdued wife, who nevertheless articulates through the assertively stark whiteness of her hat, fur lapels, stick and glove, her grim domination of the scene. Tucked in next to him and technically behind him in the picture plane, she nevertheless shines out, determining through the artifice of the radiant white details of her costume the character of domineering wife.

Gradually now Gwen would also begin to use heightened, more emphatic colour touches: at first more pinks with browns, then gradually over the next few years occasional touches of cerise, orange, lilac, turquoise or red (as in *Still Life with a Vase of Flowers and an Inkwell*,[13] with its startling use of red smudged in to highlight the distance between the painted object and the ground) to suggest atmosphere, energy and emotion. The effect was subtly authoritative. It was Rodin more than anyone else who had originally shown her what could be achieved by blurring drawn parts and outlines with colour washes; she now developed this method to work towards greater abstraction. Perhaps because she had learned her methods with a sculptor and draughtsman rather than a painter, the emphasis of her work was always on form rather than light. (Reproductions, particularly of her early paintings – *A Corner of the Artist's Room in Paris*, for example – are deceptive in this regard: on the canvas her work is strikingly matt; in her later work light is suggested by colour 'blobbing'.) But she now began gradually to move away from her old concern with tone to experiment with juxtaposed colour. In the 1930s she would go with Constance to some of André Lhote's classes, and learn there things she felt she had already worked out for herself. He taught his students to think in terms of 'passages': a 'passage' consisted of spreading '*by the side of the object* a value which is borrowed from it, light or dark'; but the essential thing in painting was what he called *transposition*, that is, the transformation from the solid, modelled object to the abstract, painted object. The process of making the transposition retained within it traces of the artist's sensation, thus, it was 'not on how much the painted object approaches the actual object but on *how nearly it departs from it* that the whole secret of art depends'.[14] Gwen had begun to learn this as soon as she came to Paris: it was how Rodin painted in watercolour. Now, in the early 1920s, she came to think of it more specifically in the theoretical terminology of moving towards abstraction. Now values were no longer strictly tonal, but symbolic: shadow could be expressed by a bluish tint, light by orange (the colour Apollinaire had called 'the beautiful fruit of light').[15]

She began to scribble tonal numbers across the drawings themselves as well as making detailed notes on composition: her notes suggest a clear sense of methods being followed, and a newly analytical approach to her drawings. Subtly discernible here are the beginnings of her later experimentation with flat, juxtaposed planes and her movement away from naturalism in her depictions of landscape. She made some deceptively simple, impressionistic drawings of the rue Terre Neuve seen from her window, experiments in perspective, with figures seen in motion from a distance. The figures, suggested by little more than an evocative smudge, are like Bonnard's figures in his early sketches of Parisian streets, or the figures in Pissarro's paintings. In *Rue Terre Neuve, Meudon*[16] the street is described in a couple of broad gouache diagonals; in a similar gouache, watercolour and pencil drawing, *Rue Terre Neuve*,[17] the house is seen in close-up, diagonally placed at the edge of the picture frame so that both the immediate space in front of the house and the line of trees on the horizon seem pressed up close; the drawing is wrapped around the space and the position of the viewer is implicitly somewhere within, rather than outside the picture. Over the next few years, Gwen would transpose some of this experimentation into her painting. She did two almost identical oil paintings of the rue Terre Neuve (one showing an old woman with a walking stick, the other a woman walking with a child).[18] They are quintessentially French: impressionistic in conception, but essentially Post-Impressionist in their evocative use of diagonals and in the smudged, cartoon-like quality of the figures.

Her work in watercolour and gouache became increasingly atmospheric. *Street at Night* (another, very different view of the rue Terre Neuve, this time by lamplight)[19] shows a man in a top hat walking up the dark slope of the road past a house with lit, yellow windows. The long fingers of shadow are done in simple verticals down the side of the house, and rapid horizontals across the road give the picture an Impressionist atmosphere, but the effects are achieved through juxtaposition rather than blurring and the windows are simple, yellow oblongs. She captures something almost haunting, a feeling of strangeness: here the obvious comparison is with Van Gogh rather than Bonnard or Cézanne.

It is impossible to know exactly when she did which drawing, or to trace with exact precision the details of how her drawing and painting practices changed. But we do know that over the next decade or so she moved steadily towards abstraction, struggling, particularly in the first two years of the 1920s, with chronic feverishness and probably an undiagnosed condition, which may have been glandular as she was intermittently delirious, chronically exhausted, the condition of her teeth was affected, and she had symptoms which may have indicated an early (or temporary) menopause.[20] It all points to a virulent attack on the immune system, possibly even the 'blood disease' that had affected Déshanel. But though Gwen was ill enough for everybody to realise there was something wrong, she refused to see a doctor. The lack of a diagnosis meant that she also feverishly carried on working, determined to continue her studies as well as the discoveries she had made by being able to work in such a focused way in Pléneuf. She now missed the sea air, and tried to compensate for it by walking in the forest. In the minuscule notebooks she used to make quick sketches in church, she also cryptically recorded her working methods:

Methods. the snowdrop in the earth
dry blob & 2nd 3rd the road
2nd 3rd dry blob the pink flower[21]

As she walked along, she would note down possible motifs, together with her thoughts about how to make them into pictures. A '2nd and 3rd dry blob' might mean that as she looked at a flower she was already thinking in terms of depth of tone: in watercolour, each superimposed one on the other, successively deepens the tone. She labelled one notebook 'Motifs', and made in it tiny sketches of a house with windows (possibly an early set of ideas for *Street at Night*), notes on colour and lists of possible subjects: 'sepia hair; water; nasturtiums; Roses; king cups; Bluebells'.[22] She also listed 'Rules': 'Rule 1 The black of the bluebells is cassels'; 'Rule 2 The subject can be copied. The lights of a subject can be done with atmosphere, & atmosphere can be done round.'

Throughout the spring of 1920, she worked at connecting elements of picture-making and mapping out ideas for pictures, sometimes just making sketchy notes or jotting down ideas for possible subjects; sometimes working out definite colour and tonal notations. The notes show her thinking about new ways of describing forms: 'the atmosphere can be done round' may suggest the opposite of what it sounds like, perhaps the kind of wrapping round she did in *Faded Dahlias in a Grey Jug*, where the ground is 'wrapped' round the form of the jug in sections. A list in a similar notebook[23] shows her thinking more generally about possible subjects: 'orpheline; toiling up roads; obscure churches; obscure people; quiet rooms; flowers and leaves'. She also wrote notes to herself about her attitude and approach: 'For this technique – for this put away worries, act quietly and shortly and decisively' – the artistic self, the inner emotional resource, still had to be endlessly primed and prepared.

In some of the notebooks many of the pages are blank, some bear no more than a mark or two; on some, she made her rapid sketches of people in church, seen from behind, in various attitudes (some of them look as though they may be singing).[24] There are lots of backs of heads and shoulders, and women in hats with characterful faces made in just a couple of quick marks. On some pages, there are just a couple of lines (her subject moved?); some are more thoroughly, though still obviously very quickly done. Some are nearly finished, recognisable as sketches for later work: the initial sketches for women in tall hats who appear again in fully worked drawings now begin to appear in the notebooks, as do the mysterious tonal numbers scrawled across the drawings. She was clearly being exposed to a number of different influences and impulses; experimenting, and more purposefully aware of and attentive to the work of other painters.

She was still making plans for Ursula to come and stay. She had discovered a small, private hotel on the far side of the Terrasse, the Villa Calypso, where she took a room for her, but still she did not materialise. On Easter Sunday, she went to see Constance again. They talked, as she had talked to Rodin, about literature; and Gwen came home with 'a big roll of English literature'. She put it on the table and sat with it and thought of Constance, she told her, and did not feel so lonely. She thanked her for her 'hospitality towards "the Convalescent"',[25] though she was still by no means well. But she obviously now felt easier – thanks to Constance, Nona and the Symonses – about Isobel. She told Nona about the experiments she was making in her work, which Nona was relieved to hear about, assuring Gwen that she still often thought about her, and wondering 'how you meet life, for you do think deeply or certainly instinctively and not many really do'.[26]

In May, Arthur Symons announced that he and Rhoda would be in Paris the following week and would like to come and see her. He sent her a book of prose and a manuscript book of poetry, which she was thrilled by, telling Quinn that it had been 'my consolation this dreadful winter'. Tucked into the manuscript of poems was a copy of 'Faces', a poem Symons had written in 1892, which now made him think of her. She was as touched by the poem as she had been by his appreciation of her work. She copied it out and sent it to Quinn, who had been doing some lateral thinking and now suggested Symons as a possible purchaser for the Château Vauclair; but Gwen said she thought that would not be practical. She thought he liked to spend a lot of time with his literary and artistic friends in London, and so would be too lonely at Vauclair. As for Rhoda, she would surely 'not stay there three days, no, not one'.[27] It was a pity Quinn had not bought it four or five months ago, since by now all sorts of new work would have been done. The new owners 'will have taken away a great deal of its beauty perhaps'. She had heard there were workmen in, putting in new windows at the front of the house. She told Quinn she had enquired four or five months ago about the possibility of buying from the new owners, when Augustus had said he might be interested in it, but that the lawyer had quoted 50,000 francs. 'Gus hadn't got the money and thought it too far away too,' but now it would be even dearer, because of the new windows and the erection of a wall between house and farm to stop people and animals coming in. It had been purchased for only 20,000 francs as there had been no other bidder. Gwen thought the new owners had simply bought it as a speculation because the value of the land was going up and in two or three years they would be able to re-sell it for four times that amount. There was not a lot of land, just a large meadow at the side with a stream running through it, but it was a lovely meadow, with 'heaps of flowers'. Again, she told him there was not much there for 'people who are not artists or poets'. It was not a grand house, but she liked its 'humble beauty' and its 'atmosphere *un peu triste*'.

It must suddenly have occurred to her that the improvements might even appeal to Quinn: electricity was being installed, she told him, and a bathroom. The two rooms on the ground floor were to be knocked into one large hall, which would be more consistent with the style of the château. The salon was beautiful and the kitchen very large. It was about eight minutes' walk from the village of Pléneuf, where you could buy everything you needed, and only about half an hour's walk to Val-André, a fashionable seaside resort with hotels, tennis courts and its own bay. The road down from the main road to Vauclair was a very bad road, she warned him, leading past some hovels, and the bay at Pléneuf was about fifteen minutes' walk from the château through beech trees, but it was 'very wonderful' and you could walk for miles along the bay when the tide was low. The station was at Lamballe, the nearest big town, about thirteen miles away, and you got to Pléneuf by taking the diligence. There were fruit trees in the garden behind the château and the house could be heated by stoves, or wood or coal fires. She had not seen the neighbours; the purchasers had told her they were savages, but she assumed they meant the people in the village of Pléneuf. 'I will tell you more about Vauclair if you want to know more,' she promised. 'They might have taken away a great deal of its beauty. Perhaps the people would not sell it now.'[28]

There was no response to this. The Château Vauclair, therefore, looked like a lost cause. But Gwen had obviously thought it worth another try. It would have been the perfect place to work, to have friends to stay; to walk by the sea. It had everything she needed, and she now craved some land of her own, a space where she could walk in her own garden, play with her cats, grow a few flowers. But 50,000 francs was ambitious by any standards, as indeed was 20,000. Nevertheless, it was a profound disappointment: she had imagined herself into place there, and now had, at some level, to deracinate. It undoubtedly contributed to the stress and nervous tension that made her ill. Nobody was able to rise to the challenge of Vauclair. Both Quinn and Augustus seemed to lose the thread; Edwin John had never got the point in the first place. His main source of grief that spring was that Augustus had again failed to be elected to the Royal Academy: 'No doubt this does not trouble him . . . Indeed, in an interview that I read in the Daily Mail lately I believe he practically asked not to be elected.'[29] He had appointed Thornton executor of his property before he left England, and had tried to persuade him not to leave. 'I said,' Thornton admitted to Gwen, 'I could return in the event of his death.'[30] There were further disappointments and frustrations. The Salon sent news that they would not after all be making Gwen an associate as they had decided not to admit foreigners.[31] The Convent had finally hung the portrait of *Mère Poussepin*, but so high that Gwen was convinced nobody could see it. (She decided to ask her confessor if he would climb on a chair and move it down.)[32] She conveyed this news to Quinn, who said that if the nuns did not really want it, perhaps they would consider selling it to him. Gwen was amused by this, and told him he would probably get it at a relatively modest price since they would doubtless be delighted to part with it for cash: 'it seems to me their real God is money'[33] – one of her not infrequent moments of cynicism, where the nuns were concerned. For a while – or at least, intermittently – her spirits seemed to have revived.

When the Symonses came to Paris in May 1920, they went to the rue Terre Neuve to see some of Gwen's new work, and then took her with them to look around Paris. She showed them her albums of watercolour drawings, which Arthur Symons was enchanted by, they created 'so many visions' for him. One of the drawings reminded him of a drawing by Degas. He was delighted to hear about her connection with Quinn, whom he regarded as 'a man of taste'.[34] His book on Baudelaire was about to be published; when he got home he sent her a photograph of one of Baudelaire's letters. They still very much wanted Gwen to go and visit them in England. They were fascinated by her, and she talked to them about her technical experiments. 'I don't think one *ever* conquers one's feelings,' Rhoda said, 'for the more one is capable of expressing the more one discover in one's self to express – & the more one discovers to express the more technique one requires to express it – so one ought to go on ever and ever making one's technique more elastic – more supple – so that one is capable of expressing the finest of subtlest shades of one's own being.'[35] It is easy to see why Gwen took her seriously. She told Quinn that Rhoda was not at all as she, Gwen had thought an actress would be, and Symons had told her Rhoda was more lovable the more you got to know her.[36] The camera he had offered to send to Pléneuf, she took the opportunity of mentioning, had never arrived; he replied straight away to say that he had already sent another.[37]

The Symonses, back in London, finally caught up with Augustus (who since 1913 had a house and studio at 28 Mallord Street in Chelsea, as well as Alderney Manor). They met him at the opera and Rhoda told him Gwen was planning to come and stay with them in Kent in September. Augustus warned Gwen that Arthur must be 'troublesome to be with' for more than five minutes and wanted to know why she was not going to see him: Rhoda had told him about her new work and he was anxious to see it.[38] The plan seemed to be quite definite: Rhoda was sending her a ticket, renting her a studio and getting someone in to cook and clean for her so that she would be completely free to work. Augustus had apparently told them she had 'no respect for material things', but Rhoda was unconvinced, she told Gwen: 'you inwardly appreciate them as much as anyone'. She also imagined that with Gwen's sense of line and colour she could probably 'dress very charmingly and make a very picturesque effort'.[39] Gwen seems to have taken all this in good part.

In July, the first of Quinn's cameras finally arrived; she now began immediately to worry about the second one. She had had no news of it, nor heard anything from Jeanne Robert Foster, Quinn's close friend, who was in Paris and promising to visit. She was by now quite excited about meeting her. 'I have never met a poetess nor any woman writer,' she told Quinn.[40] 'I am tortured by shyness with strangers but I am sure I shall like her.' When he replied, he asked if she was familiar with Marie Laurencin's work. She said she was not, but had been resolving to be a bit less shy about getting to see other people's work. Perhaps defensively, she told him, 'I like being alone. But I don't pretend to know how to live and sometimes I think everything I do is wrong.'[41]

By 2 September, there was still no sign of Mrs Foster. Gwen's visit to the

Symonses had had to be postponed, because of strikes in England. Quinn sent 3,500 francs which, she told him, 'takes my breath away'. She assured him that he must not feel he had to continue their arrangement of a stipend for another year, as her work had changed so much that it might no longer be what he wanted. She was, however, extremely grateful for the money, since she had been wanting for a long time to start painting again. Now that she had the resources she could engage a model. She knew which girl she wanted, and would now be able to take her on straight away.[42] Still, she heard nothing from Mrs Foster. Twelve days later, on the afternoon of 14 September 1920, there was an unannounced knock at the door: Mrs Foster had arrived. She had found number 29 rue Terre Neuve, 'a crooked lane that backs up against the great terrace of ancient fortifications' and, finding no concierge, made her way inside. On the stairs she found a woman, whom she asked if there was anywhere she could leave a parcel. Miss John, the woman said, was away, but the door to her apartment was open. If she liked she could go in and leave a note. Mrs Foster went on up two more flights of stairs and found 'a low ancient looking door under the eaves'. She took the precaution of knocking, and was embarrassed when Gwen herself opened the door.[43] Gwen was equally taken aback: she was unprepared, and certainly not dressed, to meet Mrs Foster.

Jeanne was thirty-five, dark-haired, stylish and beautiful, with lovely clothes and jewellery. She had been a model,[44] and she wore the latest fashion in dark, svelte dresses and low-brimmed hats, long strings of ivory beads and silver bracelets. She was working as Ford Madox Ford's associated editor on the *Transatlantic Review*,[45] and she was also a poet. Her book of poems, *Wild Apples*, had been published by Sherman, French & Co. in 1918. The *Detroit Sunday News* had compared her with Masefield and predicted that she was 'bound to take first rank among the poets of the present generation'; she had 'originality, virility and power, sentiment and thoughts beautifully expressed'. She was romantic, affectionate, energetic and mystical: in 1906, aged twenty-one, she had joined the Theosophical Society.[46] She was passionate about paintings, and eagerly networking with all the painters and sculptors of Quinn's acquaintance in Paris. That summer and the next she met Picasso, Pound, Satie, Brancusi, Matisse; and sat for a portrait by Derain. She genuinely admired Gwen's work and was anxious to secure some of it for herself, rather than see it all go to Quinn.[47] The idea was to persuade Gwen to come to New York and exhibit there, and she and Quinn also hoped Gwen might paint her portrait; but she had an open mind and her first priority was clearly to get to know her properly and if possible to befriend her. Though she and Quinn seemed very much an item, she had known him for only two years when she met Gwen. She was besotted with him, very much in love, and anxious to be all he needed and wanted. (It is unclear whether they were lovers; certainly, if they were, Quinn did not want it known.)[48] Gwen, surprised by the entrance of this beautiful, sparkling woman who was equally surprised and embarrassed to find her in, was kind and welcoming. Jeanne went up to the Terrasse and photographed the children playing while she waited for Gwen to dress, and half an hour later Gwen joined her. 'Mr Quinn said, I must treat you decently otherwise probably I shouldn't,' she said.[49] Jeanne did the right thing: she laughed, whereupon Gwen took her for a walk round the Terrasse, then back to the rue Terre Neuve, where she gave her tea and showed her her drawings.

Jeanne thought Gwen probably seemed younger than she actually was, and guessed her age at thirty-eight or forty (she was forty-four). She noticed that she also created the impression of being taller than her actual height – she seemed taller than Jeanne, though she was probably a little shorter. She thought Gwen looked a bit like a nun, with her dark hair parted in the middle and 'framing her face in an oval rim of shadow'. She described her for Quinn: her face was 'a pure oval', with a dark, not very clear complexion and narrow eyes, 'almost Chinese in shape and of a clear extraordinary blueness'. Her voice was quiet and 'wavering', though 'occasionally broken by contralto notes of a fantastic determination to live as she pleases'. She noticed her hands, 'the slightly swollen pointed graceful hands of the heaven-born artist', and that she moved swiftly but with a slight, attractive awkwardness. Jeanne thought she would never describe her as shy. 'She is perfectly poised, a great lady in a way, bitter towards the average person, determined to get her own way, proud, savagely proud, yet childish, very affectionate, wanting love, yet refusing it.'[50] She also described the house, which she said was not (as either Rhoda or perhaps Augustus had obviously suggested) a 'hovel'. She found a stone floor, with no rugs, and no furniture in the living room except a very hard couch, a tiny coal stove and battered little oil stove, a small bookcase in the wall, a bare pine table (the round one which appears in the *Interior* paintings), a 'stand' (a simple easel) and three chairs. There was one picture on the wall, a drawing of Augustus's.

Jeanne told Gwen how much she admired his work, which clearly pleased her. The hall, broken by dormer windows, was absolutely unfurnished. Jeanne peeped into another room, which looked as if it served as a kitchen, and saw some cupboards, 'but nothing else, no comforts, no heat, no bath'. The overall atmosphere was, she thought, 'monastic', rather than impoverished. 'Rhoda Symons might be shocked,' she told Quinn, but she, Jeanne, was not, 'for I am capable of doing just what Miss John has been doing', despite the fact that she was living in splendour and lunching at the Ritz. She loved the mood of the place, and appreciated the beauty of the magnificent view, with the old fortifications, the trees, the silence.

Gwen accepted an invitation to lunch, and told her she was planning to stay with the Symonses in London. She asked Jeanne about Quinn, wanting to know what his office was like, what his house was like; all about him. All this made her realise how important he had become. When she got out his letters to read some of them to Jeanne she suddenly felt tearful. She showed Jeanne her drawings, and Jeanne said she thought she saw a Chinese influence, which pleased her.[51] They also discussed Matisse, with whom Gwen was unimpressed: she thought him a snob. She told Jeanne she had met him, and that he had told her 'in a cock-a-lofty manner' that '"I squeeze the juice from the fruit" so to speak of the new art, those who come after me may have the rind and the dried pulp' – at least, that was what Jeanne relayed to Quinn.[52] Jeanne showed Gwen how to use the cameras. She had brought the second one with her, so Gwen now had two Eastman Kodaks, a 1A and a 34A. She tried to make Jeanne take one of them back, but she would not hear of it. They talked about speaking French. Jeanne was making good progress, she said, but she had needed a grammar book and a teacher; she would have found it impossible to learn by ear, as Gwen had done. 'I felt that you have given her back to the world,' she later told Quinn, melodramatically. She thought she had probably seemed strange to Gwen, 'but I loved her at once with real affection. Here is a woman brave enough to live touching spiritual reality every day of her life. All the pathetic dramatization of life has fallen away; she is real.' She generously realised that Gwen might not necessarily like her, but did not think that mattered, she thought Gwen 'very fine'.[53]

About two weeks later, on 4 October, Gwen went into Paris and met Jeanne at eleven in the morning.[54] She was unwell, and preoccupied. Jeanne had been hoping to sit for her and had been looking for a studio because Gwen wanted to paint in Paris rather than Meudon, but she could see that she was probably too ill to paint. She came in 'wildly', she told Quinn, 'half dressed, her face drawn and colorless'. She ate no lunch, just drank a little wine. Jeanne asked her about herself, and she began to tell a story she does not seem to have told anyone else, about the priest who had apparently encouraged her to paint the *Mère Poussepin*. Possibly triggered by Jeanne's beauty and romanticism, she now suddenly spiralled into sadness, remorse and despair. Encouraged by Jeanne, she began on a rambling, peculiar story: the priest had always loved her, but their relationship had been platonic, because of Rodin.[55] He had encouraged her in her work. '*He had made her an artist* not Rodin,' confided Jeanne to Quinn, interpreting with wild inaccuracy. It was he who had commissioned the seven *Mère Poussepins*, even though she had never before painted figures. (Jeanne must have misheard this: Gwen had hitherto painted mostly figures, but she had never before painted a figure from a prayer card.) He had pressurised her for seven years, trying to get her to finish them; then he had been sent by the Convent to Versailles.[56]

A desperate feeling of loneliness emerges from this exchange, exacerbated by years of relentless work and nervous strain and Gwen's deep desire, now, as in the past, for love and protection. She had told Jeanne she had not written to the priest in Versailles because she had not realised how much he needed her, and then suddenly she heard he had died. The story now became increasingly peculiar and macabre. The nuns had told her he had died of grief over the recent death of the older sister who had brought him up. She went to Versailles to draw him on his deathbed, and noticed that 'his spread [bedspread or cover] was drawn up high around his neck'. She pushed it down a little to get the lines of the neck and saw a violet bruise on one side of his neck, which she thought strange. The next day, she read in the newspaper that the priest had committed suicide by hanging or strangling himself with the window cord; he was hastily buried in holy ground while the bishop of his diocese was away. 'She blames herself for the tragedy,' Jeanne told Quinn. 'If she had seen him more, he might not have killed himself, she argues.'

Clearly feverish and very fragile, her tongue loosened and her mind distracted by the wine, Gwen asked Jeanne what she thought of the condition of souls after death and told her she had been annoyed by evil forces. She was obviously overwrought, and Jeanne was no doubt an encouraging listener. One 'very interesting fact' emerged, she told Quinn: Gwen knew 'the mysterious "country of flowers" which I have visited in dreams since childhood. She described the same luxurious masses of bloom, the strange forms, the size of the blossoms, the white star-flowers. I told her of the "flower fields" described in the Apocryphon – the "flowers of the field of Araath." (I firmly believe that the field exists and that the pure-minded and the very young may go there at will.)' All this was integrated into an apparently quite civilised day: they had gone to the Louvre, lunched at Bernard's and later had tea on the rue Royale. It was before tea, as they sat together for two hours in the gardens of the Louvre, that all this had come out. Gwen was weepy and depressed; she told Jeanne she wanted to die but did not want to commit suicide. She was clearly exhausted.

Later in the afternoon she recovered a bit and talked to Jeanne about her childhood, telling her that all the John children had learned to draw by colouring outline pictures in drawing books. She told her about Winnie, who she said was 'quite wonderful', with 'a practical instinct for life'.[57] Later still, she seems to have become depressed again. 'I have become corrupted and depraved,' she told Jeanne. 'I am eating food now and thinking that it is good. I am *lying* – that is I lie sometimes; I no longer desire to live a religious life. Had I gone to Versailles to be with my friend as I intended, I might not have been able to endure the long hours in the church. He was intensely religious: he really had faith. There,' she now challenged her, 'I like to torment people sometimes.' They walked back hand in hand to the Carleton Hotel, now talking about Arthur and Rhoda Symons and Augustus.[58]

They saw a lot of each other over the next few weeks, going to the galleries together, to the Salon to see Gwen's drawings (which were almost all sold) and then back for tea at Meudon. While Jeanne was there, Quinn wrote to Gwen to say he wanted to exhibit her work in New York at the De Zayas Gallery with Marie Laurencin's, as he now had five 'important' paintings by her. He thought their paintings would complement one another because they were the only two women artists he knew of who painted as women: 'most women artists paint like men and so they paint badly'. She was not to fear comparison as Marie's painting was more mannered than hers, and Gwen's showed her 'own individual style'. So if she had 'an oil painting or two' ready, the time was ripe. He suggested she and Jeanne might like to go and see some of Marie's work, which they would probably find at Hessel's Gallery.[59]

By 16 October, Jeanne was privately longing to be back in New York. She had heard that Walter Kuhn was in Paris, and she wrote to Quinn urging him to encourage him to make contact: 'Please remind him that there is a friend in captivity over here who wishes to hear from her friends.' She was missing Quinn. Paris in the autumn was very beautiful but 'even beauty becomes a cage for the active person. And without intellectual companionship, it is dust and ashes.'[60] Gwen, however, especially in the mood she was in that autumn, was obviously a constant source of diversion. They hunted in all the galleries for Marie Laurencin's work, but could not find any. Afterwards they went to the Salon again, and had tea in 'a little rosy tea room' which pleased Gwen. They talked over tea, and Jeanne came away with more melodramatic stores. We only have Jeanne's side of this exchange, and it sounds compromising and odd, but Gwen was obviously ill, and may have felt unglamorous and shabby beside Jeanne. Her feverishness probably addled her brain, making it hard for her to think clearly. Whatever Gwen said, Jeanne's interpretation sounds imaginative. She told Quinn that Gwen said she had been hungry for several years; she had had nails driven into the heels of her shoes to keep them from wearing out; she had 'no warm clothing of any description, that her hardships had been – inconceivable'. Apparently Augustus did not help her at all, and why all this misery? Because 'Miss John's mind is extraordinarily fluid. She flows into that which is nearest. She is more myself than I am, when I am with her.'[61] She was such a captive audience that it was probably tempting to tell her whatever she wanted to hear. Gwen could not live, she told Jeanne, where Augustus – or anyone – could come in every five minutes and advise her to paint in this way or that way (ironically, the odd remark of this kind became as apocryphal as Augustus's equally occasional remarks about her).[62]

She had not painted more large pictures, she told Jeanne, because she had not always been able to hire models but she was now able to do so thanks to her financial arrangement with Quinn. (This was probably an effort at diplomacy, since it was not strictly true.) She told her that there were three heads of her in the Musée Rodin; and a little about Rodin, though Jeanne does not appear to have pressed her on this point. They wondered together whether Quinn really might be able to get the *Mère Poussepin* away from the nuns, and Jeanne said there was an alcove in the De Zayas Gallery where it would look wonderful. Gwen told her her drawings should be grouped in a particular way, and that she did not like to see small drawings hung beside large ones. They then discussed Augustus. 'Do you know anything about my brother,' Gwen asked her, 'I mean his manner of life?' She had found out all sorts of things from Rhoda and Arthur about Gus and the things that went on in the Café Royal. They had told her about people going away together, she told Jeanne: 'I suppose that means . . . the *worst*, doesn't it.' They had also talked about things 'as if *they* enjoyed it'. She said she thought Arthur liked to be surrounded by young girls, and to give the impression that he had as good a time as Gus.[63] She found all this, she said, quite wonderful to think about (this may have been a ploy, of course, to get Jeanne off the subject of Rodin).

They then went off to an exhibition of Matisse's work. Jeanne, though she liked his 'melting flowing color,' thought his work lacked spiritual depth; Gwen found it over-intellectual. Still they could not seem to turn up anything by Marie Laurencin. They asked in three galleries but, despite her reputedly established position in Paris, no one seemed to have seen or heard of her. They did, however, know of Gwen John, and the Salon, Jeanne told Quinn, exaggeratedly, took all she could send them. They finally found some of Marie Laurencin's work at Rosenberg's Gallery, where Rosenberg waxed lyrical on the subject of Picasso; neither Gwen nor Jeanne was convinced. Jeanne thought he must have bought too many Picassos, he seemed so anxious to sell them. She liked his things, she said, but not 'the freakiest of them'; Gwen was unmoved by his work.[64] There were three Marie Laurencins, two that Quinn had already bought and another one, which Jeanne liked better, though if she were buying for herself, she told Quinn, she would buy Matisse, Dufy and Gwen John rather than Picasso, De Segonzac or Marie Laurencin.[65]

On 1 December 1920, Jeanne set sail for New York on the *Adriatic*; just over a week later, a blue flower and some photographs of Longfellow's rooms arrived.[66] It had been a dreadfully trying year for Gwen, alleviated by the dazzle of Jeanne's visit but punctuated by ill health, disappointment and worry. A plan to establish a working relationship with the painter Camille Prouvost had never materialised. They had intended to sit for each other, and Gwen wanted to do a profile drawing of her to give to Nona, but both Camille and Gwen had been ill.[67] Blackie the cat had had kittens but, Gwen told all her friends, 'they paid a very short visit to this world'.[68] The Symonses were still looking forward to her visit, and still had her interests at heart. '*Please* Gwen,' Rhoda was urging her, '*do* write Quinn about the Marie Laurencin pictures – he's been very nice – & I think you ought to write and tell him – Buck up and write a few lines there's a good soul!'[69]

In one of her little pocket notebooks, in among her sparse notes for pictures and rough sketches of people singing in church, Gwen made a list:

3 tables
1 armoire à glace
2 glaces
1 sommier
1 lit en fer
4 chaises
4 chaises en osier
1 elagère
1 rechaud à gaz
a petite table
2 petits tabourets
vaiselle
utensils de cuisine
bouteilles
chiffons
placard

What was this? – an inventory of the things she would need to make the dream of Vauclair into a reality? It is just possible.[70]

17

Recovery

Travail immédiat, même mauvais, vaut mieux que la rêverie[1]
Charles Baudelaire

Early in 1921 Gwen began to put 29 rue Terre Neuve in order. She was making a roof garden, despite the freezing weather. She had hired her a new model and begun a 'little blue picture'[2] – a portrait of a young girl seated, holding a fan of cloth or paper, very much in the style of her earlier portraits of young women seated. She gave Constance some drawings to send her sisters for Christmas, sketches of women in the congregation at Meudon. They were still friends but the deep need for intimacy seemed to have abated; perhaps it had been diluted by talking to Jeanne.[3] Arthur Symons had increased her interest in poetry. In January she copied down an extract from a review in the *Times Literary Supplement* of a new book of poems by Laurence Binyon. The gist of it was that there was nothing new under the sun; poets could only refine and diversify and continue to search for and redefine the 'always unpredictable, the never-recurring moment which is the artist's experience, the substance of his creation . . . he will always be original if he succeeds in giving the unique occasion'. Binyon was not a great but he was a 'true' poet – 'the first prerequisite of greatness'.[4] It is an essentially Modernist position, and relates not only to Gwen's abiding interest in poetry but also to her attitude towards drawing and painting. (It explains why the same subject could be painted again and again, each variant providing a subtly different occasion for the painter's eye.)

Ida Brown (one of the lady painters Gwen had modelled for in Montparnasse) was in Cassis and trying to persuade Gwen to go and stay, but she was working with absorption and unwilling to be distracted. She was still making compositional notes in her notebooks and working out tones numerically. She had begun to study the Cubist painter Gleizes's writings and may even have attended his lectures, as some of her notes now read as if she were taking notes on a lecture. She also now began to get into the habit of dating her notes – not invariably or accurately, but with more regularity than ever before, which also suggests that the note-taking was done on specific occasions. A note for March 1921 reads, 'blocking then drawing / drawing then filling in.'[5] Jeanne, too, suggested a holiday. She was grateful, Gwen said, but thought she should stay at home this summer and work quietly. If Jeanne was planning to come back to Paris, now would be a good time to do her portrait: 'I am in my work now – in the harmony or the "atmosphere" or whatever it is called. You won't find me sad now my torment went away in January.' She asked her to bring the sonnet 'with the "half forgetful smile"'. She sent Jeanne a drawing of the rue Terre Neuve and told her *Girl in Blue* would soon be ready to send to Quinn. She brought her up to date on domestic life at the rue Terre Neuve: 'Tum-tum is very very well she has a very fat black kitten you were right about Kiki he had the gall.'[6]

With her new model she was beginning to transpose the discoveries she had made in her drawings into her painting: *Girl in Blue* reflects new ways of designing and blocking a work, probably as a result of reading Gleizes. She made detailed notes on colour, form, tones, and the drawing of a figure in a portrait: 'Painting of pt. in colour by blocking & drawing in short dry lines.' *Girl in Blue* reflects all these ideas, it is blocked out in a series of repeated, almost geometric forms. The lines of the model's waist and hips repeat the lines of the wall and floor of the ground and are repeated again in the piece of cloth she holds, which also repeats the lines of her hand. The shoulders too follow the lines and proportions of the ground, rather than strictly naturalist anatomical proportions; the curved arms are given a geometric function by the structure of the window, which draws the eye away from the bulk of the figure and emphasises the blocking of the drawing rather than the curves of the woman's body. As always in Gwen's work the surprise, in geometric terms, is in the face, which is moody, atmospheric, essentially naturalistic; in all other respects the painting articulates a definite movement towards abstraction.

The numbered tones now appear in earnest. The same entry (for March 1921) continues,

> Tones after sunset. Road 3.2. roof 13 to 23.
> grass 23. black cats 3.3 white colours 22.
> drawing of heads 2.3. faces 32 & 13.[7]

She was either dividing her own colours geometrically into tones on the palette, or may have been using tubes of colour which were manufactured under numbers rather than names. Some six years later she would buy a colour wheel, and arrive at colours by moving the wheel round to bring tones into line with one another, but not yet. At this stage she was possibly making – for example – two 'blobs' of tone number three; three 'blobs' of tone number two. We cannot be sure what these numbers specified, but it is clear that she was working out infinitesimal gradations of tone in her notebooks before making her marks on the canvas.

The numbers appear in her notes as well as on the drawings themselves as she works out tonal relationships:

> faded Panseys on the sands at night.
> Tones. Sky 22 clouds 13 houses & bushes
> & grass 23 & 13 road 32 people 33.[8]

Occasionally, her notes sound more as if she is listening to someone lecture, even watching someone analyse a painting:

> April.
> Face. Chin. top cushion. Under cushion.
> Cheeks. honey pot. lower cheek. jam pot.
> lower cheek. jaw triangle.
> measurements. jaw limit to muscle line.
> Muscle line to square of chin.
> square of chin. [*sic*] Square of chin to
> muscle line muscle line to jaw limit
> jaw limit. [*sic*] jaw limit to upper cheek

upper cheek to slope. slolope [*sic*] to eyebrow,
eyebrow to hair.
Placing of mouth. Measurement from end of muscle line.[9]

It is possible here to imagine the speaker moving his wand as he describes sitter and setting, blocking out the space area by area. It is even just possible that she jotted down a couple of notes on the artist/speaker's attitude and demeanour: 'Face. eyebrows to eyes; trances de poitron [*sic*] Life to m. [*sic*] *Calm*. firm. silente.'[10] On another occasion she made a note to remember 'observation of the 4 points'; and 'lilies in pencil for eye training' – almost as if she was writing down her homework. Her subject on that occasion was to be 'pink rose on school-room table'.[11] It is impossible to know; but it does look as if, at least sometimes, she was working elsewhere than in the rue Terre Neuve.

She may then have translated this terminology and style of observation into her study of her own subjects. The same page is marked, at the foot, simply 'La Bretonne'. On the next page:

April. Face *slopes*. little basket
little apron.
Forehead. bumps, Nose. the bag.
Cheeks. cushion of crest. square of crest.

Another page reads,

April. Face. *nose* bags of step
wedge road *Forehead* fans
scoop cube.[12]

She was now studying technique in relation to the creation of atmosphere and mood. The word 'strangeness' appears again; she went on trying to determine, in the move from naturalism to abstraction, 'the strange form' within the work:

April
Method of observation. 1) The strangeness 2) Colour 3. tones. 4. per. form.

Method of execution 1) observation of the 4 points
2) mixing of colours 3) lilies in pencil for eye training
4) background 5) painting of per. forms and of background.[13]

Every last detail seemed to have gone into the notebook ('drawing, filling in'). All this was being done through the haze of more illness, she had a bad cold and debilitating cough which kept her awake all night for a month, so that she was exhausted all day.[14]

She wrote to Quinn explaining why she still had not finished *Girl in Blue*. He replied, full of sympathy, to say that he was very, very sorry, but that he did feel like scolding her for not taking his advice and consulting a 'good and wise' doctor. Typically, he had an explanation. 'A cold generally comes from toxins (poisons) in the system, and the best thing for a cold when one feels it coming on is to clean out the system by taking a couple of good doses of castor oil.' He himself did this, then relaxed in a hot bath and went to bed early; in the morning the cold was gone. 'Have you been seeing a doctor? You see, I am going to make you tell me the facts.' She had not seen a doctor, and there was no bath at 29 rue Terre Neuve.[15]

Her thrice-annual payment was due. Quinn now cabled 3,496 francs and stern advice: 'Strongly urge you to consult good doctor.' The exhibition of Marie Laurencin's and Gwen's work had still not been held, but she was not to go making herself anxious about the three paintings she still owed him, he would assume she was just steadily working on them even though the last of the three was already overdue: she had promised him they would be finished by the end of March. He still wanted as many of the 'late and best' drawings as she could send.[16] It was already too late for Mr de Zayas's deadline – he had wanted everything by mid-May – but he could probably still get something arranged for the autumn. He had got Jeanne to write to the Convent about the *Mère Poussepin*, which he was still hoping to buy.

Now, however, somebody (Gwen herself, possibly) had alerted him to the fact that she had no positive feelings at all about Marie Laurencin's work. Constance Lloyd had met her, and been unimpressed. Apparently she liked to shock, and to talk in public about her lovers and her constipation – hardly Gwen's style. Quinn now began, accordingly, to change his mind about Marie Laurencin; his new view was that her paintings were 'interesting but by no means *great*'. He still liked the way she painted as a woman rather than trying to paint like a man, but he had noticed 'a good deal of monotony in the colour and theme' and 'too much sameness of colour'. He had two of her paintings which he now found he did not care for, 'and between you and me I am going to return them to Rosenberg'. Between him and Gwen also, he meant to purchase no more of her work. He would rather have 'one good painting by Matisse than any number of paintings by her'. If he could go on collecting indefinitely, he confided to Gwen, he would buy 'in the first class' Picasso, Matisse, Derain, and 'in the second class', De Segonzac, De la Fresnaye, Dufy and others. Furthermore, size was no object. 'I would not give up the four paintings by you that I have, although two of them are comparatively small, for all the Marie Laurencins that I have or any number of her things. That is how much *more* I think of your things than I do her paintings' (although he could not resist pointing out that Marie commanded higher prices). He was clearly under pressure, and anxious to go on buying well. He told her that America was in a financial depression which amounted almost to a crash (he was counsel to a large bank with over thirty offices in different parts of the country and they were all in financial trouble). The situation would inevitably affect the Parisian dealers, who would have to bring their prices down if they wanted to go on dealing with American purchasers. Prices had dropped, and no one was buying art. He was nevertheless unfailingly solicitous, assuring Gwen that Jeanne had liked and admired her very much and 'would not have jeered at the death of the kitten'; she was quite sympathetic and 'able to understand other people's likes and moods even though she did not share them'. He was also gratified that Gwen had listened to him. She had fallen downstairs in her high heels, but she had taken heed and had rubber soles put on them at once. 'So I am glad you followed my advice in that respect even if you did not about the doctor.'[17]

In Britain, things were similarly depressed. ('We are living under the cloud of the great industrial crisis,' Edwin John lamented, dramatically, from Tenby. 'How is it going to end?')[18] But the Symonses were still making preparations for Gwen's visit at the beginning of June, and had now arranged for her to go and see them at their cottage in Wittersham in Kent, where they had taken a room for Gwen in the bungalow opposite where she would sleep, and be with them at the cottage during the day. They had seen Augustus, who was exhibiting at the Alpine Club. He said a man named Howard was planning a huge show, and wanted to include Gwen's work, but that he knew she would never send anything, Gwen would never do anything, whereupon Arthur had said, 'she's coming to stay with us anyway!'[19] Perhaps partly because she was planning to go to England for two weeks in June, she worked ceaselessly throughout May, even through the exhaustion and depression – the aftermath of the previous year's illness – which still endured throughout most of another year. She was resolutely self-disciplined; she jotted down Baudelaire's resolution that 'Travail immédiat, même mauvais, vaut mieux que la rêverie' (producing something, even if it's bad, is better than day-dreaming)[20] together with her own sketches and jottings: 'May. Dry short line. D.33 line. washes through line, leaving the line clear. line 23 tone.'[21] When she was tired, she seemed to work even harder. 'Work though suffering has another quality, not necessarily inferieur [*sic*] to work through tranquillity,' she noted. 'Your tasks must be done, not by the strength of the forced energy of the moment but by the strength which shall come from your normal and daily discipline.' She made daily resolutions. 'Rectify position and mentality several times a day'; 'Meditation every day'; 'be that inspiration'.[22] She was immersed in her work: the neighbours started worrying that they had not seen her about. (Later that summer they were to have an unexpected pleasure when she took John Quinn to meet them.)

On 1 June, she arrived in Kent. She went to a dinner in London where she saw Augustus, but otherwise she stayed quietly with the Symonses in the country, where she made a number of sketches of Arthur: gentle, brooding studies, some of them done quickly, probably without his noticing; in one he has his face in his hands, in another he is raising his hand to his cheek. They are careful, quiet depictions of a reflective man, and she clearly found him inspiring since more than ten years later she was to make further sketches from the ones she did that summer.[23] Rhoda also sat for her, though she was an infuriating sitter, she would insist on *posing*, Gwen later told Jeanne. 'Every time she sits down when I want to draw her, and every time she stands up, she poses.'[24] The conversation at dinner in London with Augustus seems to have been about Augustus's disgruntlement with Quinn. He asked Gwen whether he was buying all her pictures, now. When she said yes, he said, 'Well, that is the only good thing I've heard of him recently.' They may all have gone to the Tate to see *Nude Girl*, Gwen's portrait of Fenella, since Rhoda mentioned it when she wrote to Gwen shortly after she left. The trip must have been tiring, and it was clear to the Symonses that she was still not well. She was to see a doctor, Rhoda told her, '– *& let me know what he says?* & that you'll set to work *after*'.[25] Gwen may still have been worried about Isobel, since Nona had to reassure her all over again that whatever we do we are bound to wound someone. 'We are all dreamers Gwen' – it was all to the good to 'see strange countries in the distance' as long as we did not lose ourselves wandering there – 'so all is for the best!'[26] Perhaps Gwen had let her mind wander a bit when she was tired, and talked to them the way she had talked to Jeanne.

That August, Gwen finally met John Quinn. He had been to Dinard in Brittany, then motored through the devastated and unforgettable battlefields from Paris to Verdun.[27] He told Maud Gonne he had gone to Brittany on a business matter and for a rest by the sea, though he had not got what he went for. It would be agreeable to imagine that while he was there he made his way to nearby Pléneuf and went to have a look at the Château Vauclair: not impossible, though Jeanne had been in Dinard the previous summer with friends, and they already had connections there. But if he did surreptitiously check out the Château Vauclair he did so very discreetly, and nothing came of it. He arrived in Meudon with Henri-Pierre Roché, the dealer and writer who was a close friend of his and Jeanne's, and together they saw *Girl in Blue*, which he thought 'a beautiful jewel'.[28] Gwen also showed him her drawings. While he and Roché were looking at them, Gwen went into another room to dress to go out with them, whereupon Quinn and Roché selected seven drawings and put them aside for her to send to America through Pottier – either with the *Mère Poussepin*, said Quinn, or separately, just as she liked. He picked one of a little boy, which Gwen was especially fond of. When she came back in and saw what they had done, she was speechless with surprise: the little boy had been for Ursula and she did not see why Quinn should have it. She wrote in exasperation to Ursula, asking her to tell her if she thought she had the right to refuse to send him the drawings, since though she owed him several paintings, she did not consider their arrangement to cover her drawings. She was extremely irritated by this. 'He thinks he has the right to all, I believe. He bores me.'[29]

Quinn was quite oblivious of his effect on Gwen. He came back to Meudon with Jeanne the day before he sailed back to New York, and the three of them spent 'a beautiful Sunday' together. They lunched in the forest, spent the afternoon in Versailles and had dinner at the Pavillon Bleu, and afterwards they chauffeured Gwen back to Meudon. In fact, Quinn formed the impression that Gwen had quite got the point of him, and told Jeanne how pleased he was that she saw him as Jeanne did. He departed from Paris regretfully, leaving Jeanne to sit for Gwen. She planned to stay in the Villa Calypso, the small hotel at the far end of the Terrasse which Gwen had found for Ursula, and pose for ten days; she promised, rather ominously, to 'sit *very still*'.[30] She and Quinn were already squabbling about who would have the finished work: Jeanne wanted to make a gift of it to Quinn; Quinn wanted to give it to Jeanne.[31] The picture, of course, was not even started yet and Gwen had never done a portrait in less than a month. She explained to Jeanne that she did not work absolutely every day, and she had to do several canvases before she was satisfied with one. She would like to take her on a voyage to a strange land, said Jeanne: even better, said Gwen, would be a few more days to do the portrait.[32] The next question was where to do it: she did not really want to do it at 29 rue Terre Neuve but they could not seem to find a suitable studio in Paris. Ruth Manson, who was in the Loire Valley for the summer, had offered to lend her apartment, but that did not seem conducive either so Gwen eventually, somewhat reluctantly, decided on the rue Terre Neuve. By 12 September, Jeanne was installed in her little room on the second floor of the Villa Calypso, where she amused herself by trying to communicate with the young Italian *propriétaire* – who spoke about as much French as Jeanne did – while she waited for Gwen to come back the next day: 'one of her mysterious disappearances'.[33] Four days later, with exactly two weeks at their disposal, the sittings began.

The sittings were frustrating, entertaining and unconventional, a very different experience for Jeanne from sitting for Derain, who fussed adoringly around her and told her that as long as he thought himself a great painter, he was truly inspired.[34] With Gwen, things seemed surprisingly slow to get going. 'I have sat for Gwen John this morning,' she wrote home to Quinn.

> I have been sitting for her three days. I have posed for drawings in every corner of her studio but she has not begun to paint. I go for a while in the morning and she makes a drawing of me in the morning light. In the afternoon she makes another drawing before tea. After tea she does another one. I have not seen any of them. She is impatient if the pose grows stiff and she says she had rather not do me at all if I am going to pose. I explain that my posing is quite unconscious and ask her to teach me 'not to pose.'[35]

She had had just this trouble with Rhoda Symons, said Gwen, she had found it impossible to stand without posing. 'If you pose,' she had had to tell her, 'I'd rather not do you at all.' But once she was sitting as she wanted her she could not endure having the pose changed 'by a hair's breadth'. She took down Jeanne's hair and arranged it like her own to get the shape of her head. She got her sitting as she did, until Jeanne felt 'the absorption of her personality as I sit'. She made her take off her Egyptian necklace and two bracelets; in the middle of the sitting, Jeanne suddenly realised she was still wearing her watch and disturbed the pose to take it off.

While she sat, they talked. Gwen asked Jeanne about Augustus and Mr Quinn: did she think they had had a disagreement? She told her what he had said when she met him at dinner in London with the Symonses; Jeanne said she thought not. She thought Augustus very handsome now, said Gwen, not at all as he used to look; his hair was thinner and his beard shorter but she thought it was 'a nice look'. In the past, he had looked like Jesus Christ. Once when his hair was long and parted in the middle and he had a long beard, they had been eating out somewhere and a woman had come in with a child. 'Tell me who does the man look like?' said the woman, and the child said, 'Jesus Christ.' She had not approved of this, said Gwen, it was not very nice to go around looking like Jesus Christ if you were not like him. She thought this disagreement with Mr Quinn was all because Quinn was 'under the influence of a very bad American artist', a Mr Kuhn: 'Tell me about him.' Jeanne said Kuhn's work had improved a lot over the past two years, but that it was rather brutal and some of his drawings and paintings were obscene: not Gwen's sort of thing, she thought. She liked him, but she agreed that he had not had a particularly good influence on Quinn, though she thought Quinn had now rather outgrown him. What about Marie Laurencin, asked Gwen, did Mr Quinn like her? Jeanne said she thought he did. 'Describe her,' said Gwen. Jeanne said she was buxom, of medium height, with a strong, slightly grotesque profile, a heavy nose and mouth. She moved with 'swift darting flights', like a snake or a bird, and wore a tight, 'pinky-lavender' dress like the ones in her paintings. 'Constance Lloyd,' revealed Gwen, 'does not like her. She says that Marie came into a studio where several artists were sitting and the first remark she made was: "Je suis constipée." Constance Lloyd said that no one cared whether Marie was "constipée" or not.' She had also announced that she was going to divorce her husband: 'He cannot be my lover. Why he sees so much of me. He sees his mother very seldom; he could be his mother's lover more easily than he could be mine.' Constance had also said that Marie was 'annoyed if you did not think her the victim of *some* perversity'. There was no answer to this.

The next morning, Gwen decided she wanted to finish some canvases for the Salon or prepare canvases for other paintings, but they agreed to have lunch together as usual in the garden of the Villa Calypso. Jeanne had invited Ezra and Dorothy Pound, who had been living in Paris since March, in the afternoon, but Gwen was distracted by her canvases. At 3.30 the Pounds arrived at the lower gate of the garden. They had come up the back way, through the steep rue Jacqueminot and Pound was very tired and warm, so Jeanne ordered tea with plenty of hot water, which arrived with little cakes and a plate of delicious honey. After drinking five cups of weak tea Pound felt strong enough to make the tour round the Terrasse, but it was a misty day and they could see the Sacré Coeur and the Eiffel Tower only as shadows in the mist. They walked the full length of the Terrasse and looked at the monument to Janssen at the other end, and she pointed out for Pound the three bas-reliefs at the base of the pedestal. There was a couple embracing under the trees, and the gash of the woman's red coat impressed itself on Jeanne, it seemed to be an integral part of the day – as if there was something weirdly tense, not quite real, about the whole experience.

After their walk, they went back to the Villa Calypso, and Pound suggested she go to get her book of verse, which she had asked him to look at. He spent some time on it with her, offering detailed criticism, disapproving her 'echoes of the Victorians' and taking his scalpel to particular words. Afterwards, Jeanne and Dorothy went upstairs to rest; then Jeanne went off to the rue Terre Neuve to fetch Gwen, but she came back without her as she was still not ready to join them. Pound seems to have been a model guest. 'I like the garden,' he said: 'Was there a château here once?' Jeanne told him that Gwen said there had been a very beautiful château on the site, but that it had been burned, together with the château at St Cloud, in 1870 by the Germans. Still, Gwen did not emerge from her work.[36]

The portrait of Jeanne was not finished by the time she had to return to New York. She left Gwen promising to try to finish it when she came back the following March, saying she would not be satisfied with anything less than a portrait of her which they both really loved.[37]

That October, someone new appears to have come into Gwen's life. An entry in her notebook on 17 October seems to suggest a new appeal for love and endorsement. 'Don't abandon me,' it reads, 'I will never leave you. My lapses will not be taken into account, and my works will be a prayer for you and me. My lapses will not be taken into account but God will look into my heart and see my love and submission. You say you will be my love.' It was beginning to look as if she had found a new focus for her need to confide and trust. 'Reasons to live –' the entry continues: 'I may have the consolation of seeing him. I would be disobedient if I didn't strive. I must finish my work. He and she may be pleased to see me brave. Means to live. Don't look in the past. Tell him everything. Wait for his answers and advice.'[38] For the time being, she was otherwise silent on the subject, but she was preoccupied.

On 11 December, she told Quinn she was about to send off to Pottier 'the blue picture' and some drawings. *Girl in Blue* had been finished for a while – he had seen it in August – but she had been hoping to finish other paintings, and send them all together. However, he 'must go on excusing much this year – this year only, I think & hope'. He had written to her confiding his troubles. He had returned to his office to find a dreadful legal wrangle which had led to litigation, and he had been under terrible strain.[39] Gwen said she was sure he would always be successful in 'whatever you undertake with your whole will'. She complimented him on the Picassos he had bought, admitting that they did not do much for her, but presumably it was good for him to have them as an example of the latest phase in the painter's development.[40] Quinn, jarred by this, replied that this was not why he had bought them: works of art should be judged on their own merits, for their intrinsic beauty or appeal; if he had to choose between his Gwen Johns and his Picassos, he would 'cheerfully sacrifice the Picassos'. Gwen's painting was 'a very beautiful and sincere and fine thing'.[41]

He was very understanding about the sittings with Jeanne and said he was sure that Gwen would have done a fine portrait if they had had more time. 'I always say that a good portrait that is also a work of art is a miracle, and miracles don't happen often.' He had never been happy with any of his own portraits, even the ones Augustus had done, and neither he nor Jeanne particularly liked Derain's portrait of her. As for Marie Laurencin, he now could not stand her work and did not want any more of it. He had succeeded in enticing the *Mère Poussepin* away from the nuns, and was looking forward to its arrival. As soon as it came he planned to have it photographed and send Gwen two copies for herself, and two for the convent. He sent her her draft for 3,362 francs and 50 centimes (the equivalent of 250 American dollars) due on 15 December, and told her he had known she would like Jeanne, she was saintly in her devotion to others, 'often at the detriment of her own work and peace'.[42] Gwen wished him a peaceful Christmas, even if his work problems meant it was not really time yet for him to expect peace. 'However sometimes it comes unexpectedly, & serenity & joy, & one doesn't know why they come or where they come from.'[43]

The end of the year was cold. Jack Frost drew on the windows at the rue Terre Neuve, making white acacia leaves on the panes even when the fire was lit. Ursula sent greetings from England: she had met a Mr Lewis, but surely not Wyndham Lewis, Gwen said, as she had met him: he was 'rather a brilliant young man', she thought it unlikely he would either be painting gypsies or have red hands.[44] Edna Clarke-Hall (née Waugh, Gwen's brilliant young friend at the Slade) had found a new departure in her work and was producing *peintures-poésies*, whimsical, romantic pencil drawings with threads of poetry set in drifts across sketched forms (she would exhibit them, eliciting clamorous reviews, at the Redfern Gallery five years later).[45] Gwen was sceptical. This sudden literary blooming seemed a touch abnormal to her; 'I suppose however that no art is *normal*, but . . . Try and make her more restful!'[46] Ursula sent a print, 'a little feast of colour' which Gwen looked at over meals, instead of reading. She urged her to keep the drawings she had sent her, insisting that she was not to think of selling them, she had meant them as a gift. She thought they did look very much better in sets; she confided to Ursula that she had been disappointed when she had seen them at the Symonses', hung individually. She had her overcoat trimmed with fur, so that she could go out without getting too cold. The cock crowed every morning in Meudon, and she loved the sound as it meant 'long quiet days of work (for me or for others) and other happiness'. She felt recovered, and optimistic. 'Me I'm like a plant that was dying and nearly dead and begins to grow again. How almost unbelievable and what a joy it is to live!'[47]

18

God's Little Artist

God's little artist: – . . . a seer of strange beauties, a teller of harmonies . . .[1]

I am quite in my work now & think of nothing else . . . Every day is the same. I like this life very much.[2]

At the beginning of January 1922, the *Mère Poussepin* arrived in New York, in a cargo with the Derain portraits. Jeanne thought they were 'as horrible as ever', but that the *Mère Poussepin* was wonderful.[3] The cargo did not include *Girl in Blue* because when it was nearly finished Gwen had started something else, a nude, for which she had a new model, a dark, slightly Slavic girl with black hair and strikingly arched brows:[4] she intended to send both paintings when the new one was finished. She was working with intense concentration, focused by her conversations with the priest (either the one who had encouraged her to do the drawings of generals, or perhaps a new one), who took an interest in her work and encouraged her to think of herself as 'God's little artist'. She jotted down in her notebooks new 'rules' and 'thoughts': take strength from the sacraments, be a good Catholic; 'Don't look in the past': 'You are a seer of beauties, a teller of harmonies, a diligent worker . . . God's instrument'.[5] Possibly encouraged by Arthur Symons, she read Blake, trying to absorb his doctrine of forgiveness and the struggle to forget past selves; she studied Donne's reflections on distractions in prayer.[6] She now began to take her drawings to show the priest; she signed one of her early letters to him, 'Your very obedient servant, Mary John.' The disciplines of learning obedience to God and becoming 'God's little artist' were dangerously close to the quality of yearning she had felt for Rodin. 'Dear Father,' she wrote to the priest that spring, 'When I come to you, I must. Don't think I could do otherwise than come, nor be impatient. Little animals and birds do what they must I am like them.' (She signed this, 'Mary'.)[7]

In New York, Quinn was proudly showing off the *Mère Poussepin* to his friends Arthur Davies and Walter Pach, who thought it 'intrinsically finer' than anything Augustus had done; Jeanne was moved by its 'eloquent beauty'.[8] The exhibition was now set for 2 March, at the Sculptors' Gallery on Fifth Avenue. Things were not easy for Jeanne as both her sister and her former husband were ill and she was feeling nostalgic for Paris. She missed Gwen, and dreamt she was walking up the winding street to 29 rue Terre Neuve; she missed her 'talk, your face, the drawings, the flowers on the walls, the pitiful *chat*'.[9] She wanted to come back in the summer if she could, but it was beginning to emerge that Quinn was not well. He had bought some new paintings, a Seurat, a Picasso and a large Cézanne landscape, which Jeanne sweetly worried that he could not really afford, but his paintings were his life. If Gwen could see him, she told her, she would understand that he had 'gathered something from each beautiful thing he has seen and bought, until his sensitivity is so great, life hurts him'. Human nature, she confided, was beginning to jar on him; his paintings gave him a sense of peace. They had obviously had some distressing discussions. 'Things are the same with us,' she told Gwen, 'only now there will never be a future together. I shall go on loving him and he will never know that he does not love me, *nor that I know he does not*. He is a genius, a great man, and a blind child warped together in a physical mold of morbid sensitivity, utterly lovable but emotionally dependent.' He was fretting because Gwen did not seem to be sending him a new painting, could she see her way to sending him something soon?[10]

In March 1922 Gwen took *Girl in Blue* to Pottier's, together with seven drawings. Quinn was, predictably, delighted with *Girl in Blue* and told her he looked forward to getting another one. He described the Sculptors' Gallery for her: it was a large gallery space with artificial light, with the sculptors' studio (unconnected with the Gallery) at the back. He had organised two exhibitions, one of British and the other of French artists. The first would include work by Epstein, Gaudier-Brzeska, Wyndham

Lewis, James Dickson Innes, Augustus and Gwen John; the second, Brancusi, Duchamp-Villon, Derain, Matisse, De Segonzac, Rouault, Picasso, Braque, and five paintings by Marie Laurencin. There were also, he innocently told her, one or two things by Rodin, but he thought they looked weak by the side of the Brancusis and the Raymond Duchamp-Villons. He acknowledged that her work really belonged more naturally with the French artists, but had decided to include her with the British group because that way he could give her more space. He was showing not only her oil paintings but also a selection of watercolours and gouache drawings of little girls; Arthur B. Davies had made the selection and it had all been beautifully hung.[11]

Jeanne now drafted a brief article on Gwen for the New York market, which spectacularly contradicted her private opinion of her and did nothing to invalidate the impression Quinn had formed (without meeting her) of a shy, reclusive figure. With Marie Laurencin and Irène Lagout, the article claimed, Gwen was one of the three women artists currently most discussed in Paris. She was 'English', the sister of Augustus John and a student of the English art schools. After she came to Paris, her contact with French art and friendship with Rodin had turned her away from 'the worship of mere skill in representation' and she adapted Modernist technique 'to utilize it in a feminized charming manner entirely individual to herself'. She was

> a slow worker, who often draws and paints the same subject several times before she is satisfied to exhibit her work. Personally, she is a rather shy person, extremely modest about her painting and she prefers to lead the life of a recluse in order to have more leisure for her craft. Her hair is black and she arranges it simply in a low knot. Her face is oval, her eyes brilliant, and her figure is slim and delicately rounded. She has no theories. If she were to say anything on theory, she would say 'Be truthful be natural.'[12]

Quinn, despite ill health, was still energetically networking from New York. He was very keen for Gwen to meet De Segonzac, who he thought was underrated; he also wanted her to see 'a very important painting by Seurat called *The Circus*'.[13] He had heard from Arthur Symons, who was apparently 'in despair about money matters'. In Quinn's view, Rhoda was to blame, she was 'a woman that has a millionaire's appetite for spending money that she does not earn', and now apparently wanted to build a studio, 'the walls panelled with mirrors, no doubt'.[14] Gwen dealt with this like a professional: 'Poor Arthur and poor Rhoda too!!! I have been laughing over your criticism of Madame Rhoda. I hope you write soon to Arthur Symons he would like a letter from you better than money I'm sure.'[15]

She still had not finished the painting of the nude but she had now started working with another new model on a painting called *La Concierge*[16] – a portrait of another strikingly dark girl, younger-looking than the model for the nude, with a not dissimilar oval face and black hair in a fashionable fringe. Over the next couple of years this model would pose for at least ten paintings, all variants of *Girl in a Mulberry Dress*.[17] In all of them the colour of the dress strikes the emotional note of the painting. As in Cézanne's several variants of his portrait of his wife, the figure is in the service of the colour geometry of the painting rather than sitting for a conventional portrait; Gwen would, over the next year or two, experiment quite radically in her portraiture with the spatial relationships between figure and ground. In the most extremely experimental version, the front of the sitter's skirt is left unpainted so that it looks stripped back to the naturalistic colour of the wall and skirting board; the space immediately surrounding the figure takes its colour tones from the figure's mulberry torso. She probably did the most conventionally realised one first and – as it were – gradually stripped the painting, as she worked through its successive variants, down to its essence. In the first version, *Girl with a Blue Scarf*,[18] the colours of hair, face, scarf, jacket, belt and skirt are all blocked out distinctively; the blue scarf functions as a gestural flourish which distinguishes the model's face from the bulky torso. Its pinkish, mulberry mass against the pale pink and ivory colours of the wall suggest a rhythmical weight of flesh; the model's vibrancy and vitality are thus articulated through subtle colour contrasts, and a depiction of mass which hovers between Naturalism and abstraction.

Gwen was very pleased to hear the news of the Sculptors' Gallery show, though she thought it a pity that the *Mère Poussepin*'s name had been spelt wrongly in the catalogue. She decided she would not mention this to the Mother Superior, who undoubtedly thought of the *Mère Poussepin* as 'a means of propogande' [*sic*]. But she was at least satisfied with the painting, and told Quinn that when she had gone with Jeanne to see it at Pottier's with the other paintings Quinn had bought, she had been proud, in fact she thought it the best picture there, though she did like the Seurat. He would get the new painting soon, she promised him. 'I am quite in my work now & think of nothing else. I paint till it is dark, & the days are longer now & lighter, and then I have supper and then I read about an hour and think of my painting and then I go to bed. Every day is the same. I like this life very much.'[19]

Late spring brought lovely weather and the days were already warm enough to go for lunch in the forest. There were new green leaves on the trees even though the beeches were still red, and the bluebells and anemones were out.[20] She was making charcoal drawings of the anemones in the woods, and of Tum the cat.[21] The nude now went into several variants, and she also painted the same model clothed. 'Don't be too harsh a judge of your own work,' Quinn urged her. 'I don't mind waiting but I should prefer to have you let me be the judge of your work.' Any pictures she had ready during the next month or two were to go straight to Pottier.[22] Jeanne did not come to Meudon after all that summer. She was unwell, and taking a long rest at her mother's home in Schenectady. Quinn sent word that he was having the *Mère Poussepin* photographed to send copies to the Convent, and was worrying about Marie Laurencin, who was very ill. At first it was thought she had tuberculosis of the intestines, but they now thought it might be something worse, even malignant. Gwen went to Rosenberg's and saw some of Marie's work. She had heard nothing about Marie Laurencin's health, she told Quinn, but she thought the work at Rosenberg's was charming.[23] A few days later, the first photograph of *Mère Poussepin* arrived, framed and under glass with Mère Poussepin herself duly acknowledged and correctly spelt on the back.[24]

Gwen painted quietly throughout the summer of 1922, working on the nude and the *Concierge*, and probably by now on *Girl with a Blue Scarf*. She picked primroses, which she sketched or gave to the priest. She committed new 'thoughts' to her notebooks. 'Make your harmonies, keep your harmonies.' The effort of creation was, as ever, sustained through moments of sadness and sudden losses of energy, when she told herself, 'Turn gently towards your work. Instead of this sudden discouragement and sadness take up in your mind a leaf – a flower – a simple little form and find its form, take it into your possession as it were . . . every flower and leaf – and other things may be taken into your possession as it were. You have seen nearly everything vaguely.'[25] She was beginning to see more strongly organic connections between herself and the subjects of her still life pieces. She had always had a sympathetic rapport with her models (as when she had had Jeanne sit, and arrange her hair, as she did herself), and she was beginning to make the same essential connection with her 'motifs'. By early September, having begun and discarded many variants, she thought she had two new paintings ready to send Quinn. Then she had a completely new idea: why not just send them as she did them, and let him decide which ones he liked? – after all, his preference was a matter for him, and the ones that succeeded should surely have a quality common to them all.[26] Unsurprisingly, he thought this an excellent idea and was sure he would love them all.[27]

By the winter of 1922 she had a little *caisse* of drawings ready to send to Jeanne: sketches of a house at Meudon, a cat, and various abstract flower pieces.[28] Jeanne was delighted with them, and wanted to use the black and white drawing of flowers on a wall to illustrate her new book of poetry, *Rock Flower*,[29] which pleased Gwen. She said she was looking forward to reading the poems. Now that some time had passed since she had seen Jeanne she had had time to think about her, and thought she probably understood her better now: perhaps when they were actually together, her own personality got in the way. She processed things slowly, and was anxious that she had not taken sufficient notice of Jeanne's illness that summer. She felt sorry when she thought about it now – at least, when she thought about it 'in the ordinary sort of way' – but she also thought illness enabled a kind of thinking you could not do when you were well, 'good thoughts I mean and you are a poet'. Novalis had said that there may be a religion or philosophy of illness that should one day be written.[30] Jeanne, relieved, sent photographs of Quinn, some blue flowers and the promise of a gift: what would she like? What she most wanted, said Gwen, was for Jeanne to bring her manuscript to Paris and read her poetry aloud.

By the New Year of 1923, Quinn was still waiting for his three new paintings: the whole household at 29 rue Terre Neuve had gone down with the *grippe*. He had had further health problems of his own, he told Gwen, 'a kick-up or a flare-up and almost a break-up or a break-down', but he was still longing for his paintings. 'Do not paint out anything and do not throw anything away,' he begged. 'Just send them to me. There's sure to be something in each one of them.'[31] Gwen's resolution to send him each new painting as she did it seemed to have gone by the board. By March 1923, he was still waiting for his paintings. He would have got them a long time ago, she explained, if only she had not suddenly been discontented with them just as she was about to take them to Pottier's. But he would get them soon.[32] Augustus was in New York in May and he contacted Jeanne from 1 West 67th Street to say he had heard she had befriended Gwen; he would love to see some of Gwen's work.[33] She and Quinn went to see him, taking a copy of *Rock Flower* and some of Gwen's paintings to show him and he was delighted, especially with *Girl with Cat*. For some reason they did not take *Mère Poussepin* – perhaps because it was having its glass replaced. He was keen to see that one, he said, and he was glad the connection with Quinn had borne fruit. Quinn's having behaved decently to Gwen more than counterbalanced his lack of consideration towards him. Augustus made a fine drawing of Quinn and when the evening got late he suggested that if Jeanne cared to adjourn to his studio he would be happy to draw her, too. (She demurred, because it was midnight and he had drunk a quart of whiskey.)[34] He was very pleased to know Gwen was working so consistently, and liked the idea of her taking a holiday with Jeanne by the sea. If Jeanne could find a little house for them to stay in, he would be glad to help with it . . . 'Or perhaps now the chateau is vacant again?'[35] But the idea of the château had now long been a thing of the past.

In July, Quinn and Jeanne arrived in Paris and did a round of their artist friends before going on to Venice, Assisi, Boulogne, Perugia and Sienna. Gwen seems to have kept a low profile; in any case she knew they would be back in Paris in September. 'You are free only when you have left all,' she wrote in her pocket diary for 7 July 1923. 'Leave everybody and let them leave you. Then only you will be without fear.'[36] She was still painting the concierge and the nude girl, and she had nearly finished a painting of the same model clothed, which she called *Woman with Hands Crossed*.[37] She was also making, by hand, albums in which she was mounting her drawings, which she took to the Villa Calypso to show Quinn and Jeanne when they came back in mid-September. Also that September she introduced them to Augustus's sons, Robin and David, who were briefly in Paris. She may again have been in confiding mode, since on the back of the page of her diary Jeanne jotted, cryptically, 'Impasse / Infant-Jesus'.[38]

Quinn and Henri-Pierre Roché were soon back in Gwen's studio having another trawl through her recent work. They found a painting propped up, face to the wall, among the ones she had planned to throw away. She willingly gave it to Quinn, but told him he was not to count it as one of the ones she owed him. He also took away a nude which she would really have liked to do again, and some small nude studies. None of these was to be counted as work she owed him, she insisted. But she was pleased to see him take the picture she had discarded, 'it gave me such pleasure when you took the picture turned round!'[39] She obviously thought it had intrinsic value, even though she had clearly not intended to send it to him. After Quinn went back to New York, Roché came several times to the rue Terre Neuve, where she showed him all the paintings she had stored in her attic. He said he and Quinn were sure they could find buyers for them and took her with Jeanne to lunch at l'Éléphant Café, where they tried to discuss the 'surplus paintings', but Gwen was not encouraging. Jeanne shrewdly thought it unlikely she would ever give any of this work up to Roché; Gwen, equally shrewdly, told Jeanne that '*all* her paintings' belonged to Quinn.[40] Of all the time she had spent with him in Paris, she later told him, 'I was most happy with you at the Gervais! You were a charming boy at my side.' She had taken him to visit her elderly neighbours, Monsieur and Madame Gervais, who had been charmed by him. He also accompanied her to see the Mother Superior at the Convent, to dinner at La Pereuse, and to a party. They visited Brancusi, and Quinn finally achieved his ambition of introducing her to De Segonzac – for him, 'the cap that crowned the whole thing'.[41] That had all been 'lovely', Gwen politely assured him, but she was not used to parties. 'I liked the other things we did better.'[42]

Quinn had rushed back to New York in a hurry – too busy, he said, even to buy ties or gloves – leaving Jeanne still in Paris. It was a trying autumn for her. She wrote him an uncharacteristically weary letter on Armistice Day, pleading for more time for her own work, since she was finding the business of negotiating for him and living up to his friends exhausting. She wanted to write more poetry. This was her *métier*, she told him, and to do it well she needed leisure, solitude and time to dream. It would be impossible to hold her own in the company he kept unless within the next year or so she could produce something 'rather fine' of her own. If not, it would be the '*tall timber for me and an attic a la* Gwen John'. If after a year she had produced nothing of value, '*why* the *complete disappearance*'. She would go among simple folk and live as a recluse: if Gwen John could do it, so could she. She was lonely without him. She had been out watching the Armistice Day celebrations in the cold; it was bitter, with snowflakes in the air and she obviously felt desolate.[43] Gwen, it seems, knew nothing of this. She had been taken by Jeanne to a new dentist, a Mr Merril, who now proceeded to torture her on a regular basis, but she was trying in spite of this to keep painting.

Eventually the three paintings were finished. Gwen now sent *Woman with Hands Crossed*, *Girl with a Blue Scarf* and *Young Woman in a Mulberry Dress* to the Autumn Salon, after which they would be taken to Pottier to be dispatched to Quinn, together with the two long-promised nude sketches.[44] She also owed him, Quinn reckoned, five watercolour drawings, to be added to the larger of the two portfolios which he had brought with him to Paris for the purpose.[45] 'I shall take the 3 to Pottier's but the 5 drawings are not ready,' replied Gwen.[46] She now worried that she had not fulfilled her part of their bargain and when a cheque arrived from New York she went off to find Jeanne, who was sitting for Derain, to ask her what to do. Just bank the cheque, advised Jeanne.[47] Rosenberg was in New York exhibiting Picasso, Braque and Marie Laurencin, but by now, Quinn said, he was 'getting very tired of her work and of her being boomed'. Rosenberg had things which had not arrived in New York; they were still at Pottier's waiting to be shipped – an El Greco and Cézanne's wonderful portrait of his father. Quinn alerted Gwen and Jeanne, telling them they should take the opportunity to go and look at them while they were still there.[48] By the time she heard from him Gwen had already seen them. She was deeply affected by them, especially by the Cézanne, telling Quinn, ' "Cézanne's Father" is astonishing! It is so real.' She thought it had been good for her own work to see it, particularly in isolation; a month later she was still reflecting on it, and feeling that she had 'made a step in advance, through them, in my art'.[49] Her paintings now finally seemed to be progressing with the same degree of experimentation and development as her drawings. She wrote to Chloe about them, asking, when she was a child, had she played a game the Johns used to play, 'warmer . . . warmer . . . hot'? She finally felt as if she was beginning to get hot.[50]

19

The Chenil Show

. . . my paintings are such a part of me . . . [1]

In November, Jeanne left Paris to go to England and Ireland. It was January or February 1924 by the time she finally contacted Gwen again to tell her that her Salon paintings had now arrived, together with a sketch of the nude which Jeanne had earmarked as hers even though Quinn was very reluctant to part with it: he had not given it to her, she told Gwen, until she had gone to claim it 'and *actually carried it away*'. He had had to be coaxed, too, to give her some of the drawings; eventually, he let her have a drawing of Tum the cat and one of green leaves in a white vase. They reminded her of Gwen, 'your mind, your sympathy, memories of our happy hours', they were like 'a kind of delicate music that does not break the silence'. She sent Gwen a book of her children's rhymes: nursery rhymes she had written sequels to, which she hoped Gwen would consider illustrating. She said she would pay her for the drawings, both their names would appear on the cover and they would share the profits, and told her how much she missed her and longed to come back to Paris. She felt 'spiritually alone' in New York: 'There is nothing for me in this mechanistic fear-ridden city.' She was always thinking of Gwen, their lunches, the bag Gwen took to silt away treats for the cat; their teas, 'and all the quiet and loveliness life holds for one in Paris'.[2]

Somewhat oddly, it took Gwen several weeks to reply. When she did, she told Jeanne she had been distressed saying goodbye to her; she had missed her very much, and when she realised she had heard nothing from her for a long time she had finally resolved to forget about her. She hoped she would come in the spring, but she no longer felt the same about her. She would do the drawings with pleasure, but she was offended by Jeanne's offer of payment. The dentist had practically ruined the past few months, since all he seemed to do was the same work over and over again, without ever seeming to make a difference. The boring Mrs (Ford Madox) Ford had been to Meudon and wasted three of her afternoons. Furthermore, Kiki the cat had died. Jeanne had sent gifts – a fur jacket and a silk blouse – but Gwen made no mention of them. She did, however, show imaginative interest in the book of nursery rhymes: 'You mustn't mind if they don't tell the same stories as the poems, wouldn't it be only saying the same things over again?' but to do them properly she really needed to know more about the poems. She also passed on, somewhat bossily, a message from the dentist. The next time Jeanne was in Paris his mother would like to see her, 'so when you write please try and remember to give me an answer'.[3]

Jeanne was duly apologetic, reacting for all the world as if she had done something to offend. She could not always be continuously in touch, she explained, since she had so many invalids to look after and a lot of other duties. The winter had been filled with the cares of others. She had not meant to offend her by mentioning payment for the drawings: surely if the book was a success, she would accept half the proceeds? She knew how stressful the dentistry had been, and had tried to stay in Paris until the worst of it was over; she also astutely mentioned that Gwen was not to worry at all about sending more drawings, or about the paintings in the attic. The Primrose League of America wanted to use one of Gwen's drawings of flowers for their new anthology of poems by the members of the League: could they do so? She admitted that she was hurt. 'I shall always love you,' she assured her, 'just as I have loved you in the past and I am very much troubled that I have lost a part of your love. It was and *is* very precious to me.' Finally: '*Poor Kiki!*' – what had been the matter?[4] The rift does not seem to have lasted long, and was probably mostly to do with the dentist, since it emerged that Gwen thought she could probably have got someone to do the work for a third of the price; he had cut horribly into her time and never seemed to finish the job. (She had heard from Thornton, too, in British Columbia, who was having a hard time with the people he was staying with, who were exploitative and unpleasant. He was sick of being poor, he told her, and beginning to find it degrading. 'Anyway I am going to make some money – a bucket full of it.'[5] Perhaps this, arriving as it did at the same time as Jeanne's lavish gifts, had upset her.) But she had been grateful for the gifts, she now told her – she had been wearing the fur – and she was full of praise for Jeanne's poems. She liked very much the idea of contributing drawings to a book of Jeanne's poetry, it was just that the nursery rhymes had rather defeated her. She was clearly relieved that Jeanne seemed to be part of her life again. 'Why can't you come in May?' she asked her. 'And why can't you come if Mr Quinn can't come?'[6]

Effectively, the dentist had interrupted her complex response to Cézanne's portrait of his father. Using the 'convalescent' model again, she had painted her seated, reading a letter or a book; wearing a hat and a cloak. The paintings are monumental, sombre, with Gwen's typical mixture of harmonious delicacy and massive opacity, and they have also discernibly taken something from Cézanne's portrait, in which the figure is described in dynamic repose, the newspaper he is reading blocking the torso and head in subtle separation from haunches, knees and feet. Each part of the body is blocked separately, worked in horizontals rather than verticals so that the form of the figure is twisted very subtly, almost like a spring. The light source casts light across the face, knees and ankles, so that the feeling of energy is accentuated further; the act of reading becomes absolutely active and the figure is, as Gwen described it, astonishingly alive. This is what she seems to have tried for in the many variants she now made of the convalescent seated, reading. Again and again she worked, on one canvas after another, on the business of animating the reading figure by changing the position of the hands, the tilt of the head; the set of the shoulders.[7] She also began a gorgeous tonal study of a younger model – a pretty, piquant child – in subtly harmonised pinks. This painting is fresh and delicate, with all the tenderness of her drawings of Breton children. It was an unusually productive time: this year she would produce three new paintings for Quinn – *The Convalescent* (a young woman reading), *Woman with Cloak*[8] and *Girl in Rose*[9] – as well as many variants in oils of the 'convalescent' and several of the woman wearing a cloak.

Quinn sent her a new instalment of $50, and was full of praise for her paintings. He reminded her about the ones in the attic. He was desperately excited about his latest purchase of a canvas by Rousseau[10] the arrival of which he had celebrated by throwing a party and drinking a quart of pre-war champagne.[11] But despite this apparent surge of enthusiasm and energy, he was ill. Jeanne now revealed that he was suffering from liver trouble, but asked Gwen to say nothing to anyone. For the time being, she said no more. Jeanne too thought the Rousseau painting very beautiful: it was 'not like any lion that ever roared outside Rousseau's imagination'. She was still busy with her nursery rhymes, and although she understood that they might be 'too insignificant' for Gwen, she said that just in case she was still thinking about illustrations, they were intended for very young children and were inspired by her own dissatisfaction as a child with the Mother Goose nursery rhymes, which never seemed to tell you what happened next. She planned to put the original rhyme on the left of the page, with her own on the right. She pinned a blank sheet on to a dummy, to show Gwen where she wanted the drawing. They should be done in as few colours as possible to keep the costs down, and very simply, 'rather suggestive than pictorial'. What she had in mind was something in the style of Gwen's drawings of children in church, and 'the little stupid boy that I have' (possibly a variant of *Boy with a Blank Face*).[12] She realised that her own ideas might be distracting, but in case Gwen needed a trigger, 'For the "Bobby Shafto," I had thought of a fantastic whale, just turning into the drawing, and astride his back, the redoubtable Bobby with silver buckles. All, everything, quite Japanesy and flat.' As usual, she was missing Gwen. She had her paintings of the nude and *Girl with Cat* on the walls of her little 'den', she told her. She wished Gwen could visit her there, they could have roast chicken at her table and tea and cakes in bed.[13]

Gwen now softened, admitting that Jeanne's parcel of presents had not arrived until several days after she had written the disgruntled letter. It was mid-March, and 'exquisite' in Meudon, but her work was still being interrupted by the dentist. Jeanne was, in fact, still under a great deal of pressure. She was writing a new poem, with echoes of Christina Rossetti's 'Winter, My Secret', which hinted at thinly veiled despair: 'You cannot find me any more / Just by opening a door / Nor by creeping in at will / Over any window sill / Nor by any loud halloing / On the way that I am going.'[14] Squashed rather grubbily in Gwen's pocket was the dentist's mother's address. She now fished it out, apologised for the state of it and sent it to Jeanne. She had not managed very many drawings for the nursery rhyme book, she told her, though she had been trying. She thought she could perhaps do some, but they might not be what Jeanne had in mind. Bobby Shafto roaring in in his silver buckles on the back of a whale was not really Gwen's style.[15]

She worked all through May 1923, painting the variants of the 'convalescent' and concentrating on the problems of describing forms. She made brief jottings in her pocket notebook ('Method. P. form. drawn, filled in au besoin').[16] But she had been working intensively all year and now began to think about getting away, noting down a possible itinerary for a trip to Brittany ('Ste Anne d'Array: Donaumenez; Audierne; Concarneau; Dhanger a Quimpere; Pornichel; Pouliguen; La Baule') and in June or early July she disappeared. Soon she was back in Paris. Ursula was there briefly and they managed to meet, though her departure was unintentionally abrupt. They arranged to meet in the rue Terre Neuve if it was fine and if not, at the Bernheim Jeune Gallery. But their sense of what constituted fine weather was obviously fatally at odds, and while Gwen waited in the rue Terre Neuve, Ursula headed for Bernheim Jeune.

By the time Gwen heard from Ursula again, Ursula was back in England. She opened her letter with great pleasure, to be met with a shock for which she was completely unprepared. 'Is it really true that John Quinn is dead?' she wrote immediately back. Could they possibly have made a mistake in the press? This news had passed her by completely. She wrote immediately to Jeanne. 'Is it true he is dead? I am dreadfully unhappy and you must me [*sic*] more unhappy. Will you come over and we can talk of him and you will see how I love you always and have never ceased to though I pretended to (because I was hurt). Your Gwen.'[17]

Jeanne kept Gwen's letter together with her letters from Henri-Pierre Roché, who had written to her as Quinn lay dying, 'Do not die, Jeanne. God is big. I understand your regret that you have not had fully what some other women may have had. Though I know that you have had, and given, much more than any other. What they have had would have been one more worm in your head because love was in you – but for them it has gone, left nothing, because *that* dies at once, is ashes, when love is not there . . . I thank you for telling me as you do about the paintings he keeps with him and those he puts aside, and why.'[18] In her diary for that year, which ends on the date of Quinn's death – 28 July – Jeanne kept a graphic record of his last days. On the final morning she recorded: 'Seven o clock. John died at six-thirty . . .' She had dreamt of him as a baby. In her dream, she picked him up and wrapped him in something and walked the floor with him. 'He slept and waking lay on my breast and clung to it with small clinging fingers – His soul was the child – It had come to my arms . . .' Later that day she

Gwen John's mother, Augusta Smith

Gwen John's father, Edwin John

The four John children with their nurse, *c* 1880

Augustus, Ida (holding David) and Gwen John

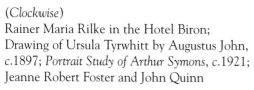

(*Clockwise*)
Rainer Maria Rilke in the Hotel Biron;
Drawing of Ursula Tyrwhitt by Augustus John, c.1897; *Portrait Study of Arthur Symons*, c.1921;
Jeanne Robert Foster and John Quinn

(*Clockwise*)
Chloe Boughton Leigh, c.1907;
Chloe Boughton Leigh, c.1910;
87 rue de Cherche-Midi; 29 rue Terre Neuve

Breton Boy, late 1910s

The Child with a Polo, late 1910s

The Chateau Vauclair

The Victorian Sisters

Madonna and Child
(in a Landscape), c.1928

The church at Meudon

Four Little Girls Kneeling
in a church, c.1910s

A Vase of Flowers, c.late 1910s

Vase of Flowers with Ferns,
c.late 1920s to early 1930s

Rue Terre Neuve, *Meudon*, late 1910s to early 1920s

Cat

Auguste Rodin,
Danseuse cambodgienne, 1906

Auguste Rodin,
by Ernest H. Mills, 1909

Auguste Rodin, *The Whistler Muse*

wrote, 'This is the end of the book this is the end. *The rest is silence.*' The previous day, she had written to Roché to tell him she wished to die. He replied with extraordinary wisdom, 'I receive your terrible-beautiful letter of July 27. he told you: "Goodbye dearest" you tell me: "the year's illness brought perfect love at least." if you go to him, I shall say, "Well done, Jeanne." if you don't, it is the same. please don't leave me without news. do you see Mr. Curtin often? have I to write to you both the same facts? does he show you my letter posted with this one? & the clippings?' De Segonzac, who had just been to see him, had been deeply moved. He was 'the dearest of them all', Roché told her, and had 'understood John'.[19]

Gwen, still shocked, wrote again. 'My sweet, my beautiful little Jeanne, are you very unhappy? Perhaps you arnt [*sic*] because you have force of character and you are religious too. it isn't pious to suffer long. We have to think of the others (Who are, by the way, a part of ourselves) . . .'[20] It crossed with Jeanne's. 'I wish I could come to you now and beg you for comfort and consolation (although I think there is none in the world now). John died on 28th. of July after months of torturing illness.' He had died of cancer of the liver and according to Jeanne, had not known how ill he was, though he had already had operations for the cancer in February 1918 and probably even earlier. They had been straightening up his affairs and discussing the future, and he had talked of marrying her that summer. 'To say I loved him deeply, worshipped him, expresses the faintest shadow of the happiness I had,' she told Gwen. She now revealed that she had been nursing him for three months and had scarcely left his side since she left Gwen the previous November. They had been surrounded in their misery, she told Gwen as she had told Roché, by the works of art he loved, including Gwen's. He grew 'strangely fond of flowers', though he had never seemed to appreciate them before, so she had filled the room with pink peonies, pink and red roses and blue and purple larkspur, in Chinese crackle jars. Generously, she thought of Gwen, assuring her that she would find out whether Quinn had made any provision for his arrangement with her to be continued, when she knew about his will. His estate would go to his sister, Mrs Julia Quinn Anderson, and her daughter Mary Anderson. Jeanne would do her best to buy some of Gwen's paintings from them if she could, as Mrs Anderson was 'a very sweet woman, but she knew nothing of his life, or of his world of art'. She was not, she thought, one of the executors of his will; Roché would be in charge of selling all the paintings, which would probably be sold in France. She had been very ill since Quinn had died. 'I cannot adjust to life; you will understand I know . . .'[21]

Couldn't she come to Paris? Gwen asked; wouldn't it do her good to come over and see her, and Monsieur Roché? She thought so, but she realised Jeanne must know best. Like Roché, she urged her, 'Don't pray to die any more. It is God's will that you live or else you would die you know.' She was full of solace and imaginative, wise thoughts. 'We must go on with our mysterious work. Yours is, just now, only to live and suffer.' She advised her, 'To make it less difficult try & leave that part of you that suffers so and make another part of you go into somebody else's life – it doesn't matter whose life it is a child's even. You need not talk to it but be with it & listen to it (the child or person).' It was her task to suffer, but also to try to conquer her suffering, she told her. 'It is not religious to suffer long'; Jeanne would know that some day, 'for you are extremely religious my pet'.[22]

She was genuinely shocked and saddened by Quinn's loss; he had been part of her life for a long time. She could not, she told Jeanne, touch or think about any of the work which was to have gone to him; she could not think at all about the pictures in the attic: 'I suffer Jeanne.' She had clearly been thinking, too, about how she would cope professionally without him. She told Jeanne that it would greatly console her if she would 'take his place as regards my work'. She offered to send Jeanne everything, and Jeanne could just send her payment occasionally when it was convenient; she need not send anything at all if she didn't want to, but then Gwen would reserve the right to sell things in Paris as and when she wished to.[23] She again encouraged her to come to Paris: they could work together, go for walks with Monsieur Roché and see lots of new pictures.[24]

Ursula had also been thinking about the implications for Gwen of Quinn's death. She wrote to her in September suggesting she might sell *Dorelia in a Black Dress*, which Gwen had given her in 1917. 'Please don't,' replied Gwen. 'I shouldn't take the money.' If Ursula wanted a new portrait she would send her one as soon as she had one ready, but she would not think of selling it to her. She thought she would not be in financial difficulties unless Mrs Foster simply continued to take her work for nothing. She obviously found it difficult to imagine not sending her work, as usual, to New York, and she seems to have taken it for granted that Jeanne had no financial problems. Mrs Foster was proposing to buy all Gwen's work from Quinn's sister, she told Ursula, 'so it might amuse [Jeanne] to take John

Quinn's place'. Gwen naturally wanted this to happen, as then she would not have to worry about selling her work. She was still very preoccupied by Quinn's death. As for Ursula's suggestion that they might go to Assisi together: 'You *know* I can *never* go to Assise [*sic*] or anywhere else because there is nobody to feed the cats.' This was not strictly true – she had been away that summer – but she was clearly unsettled by the recent course of events, and determined not to be diverted.[25]

In the summer she had exhibited at the Salon des Tuileries. Albert Rutherston, visiting Paris with his brother Charles, had been to the exhibition in June or early July and written to her praising her work.[26] Now, in late September, Charles Rutherston began to bother her, writing from England to say that he wanted to buy *The Letter*,[27] a variant of the convalescent paintings, and *Interior*,[28] a variant of the interior of the rue Terre Neuvre with round table and teapot (a more impasto, less detailed version of the early painting she had sent in February 1916 to Quinn).[29] He badgered her until she finally relented, so mithered by him that she let him have them for £15 each, and another he wanted for nothing.[30] This did not bode well for Gwen's future negotiating techniques, a problem Augustus had already anticipated (though he had not yet got wind of the Charles Rutherston episode). Augustus, who was planning a trip to New York, now turned up in Meudon and took her to dinner at the Villa Calypso to discuss Quinn and Jeanne with her, promising that when he got to New York he would talk to Jeanne.[31] To thank him, she sent him a big album of drawings, which delighted him; he was thrilled to have so many, and told her they were better than he had anticipated.[32]

Jeanne now sent a cable, which Gwen interpreted as a promise to take Quinn's place. She had been waiting to hear from her before letting the Salon des Tuileries know whether or not she wished them to sell her work and she now wrote relinquishing that opportunity. She was thrilled to hear from Jeanne, as a continuing professional connection with her was what she most wanted. She could not paint yet, she told her, because 'if I painted it would be to finish some things which were going to "John" and it gives me pain'. Despite her confidence in Jeanne, she realised that her intentions were still not entirely clear. 'I don't understand the cable it's taken down so funny,' she wrote in reply, 'but why do you say you are going to send money I don't need any yet you know'. She urged Jeanne not to worry about money, adding to the general confusion. She said that perhaps for now it was good for Jeanne to be occupied by business matters, since this would divert her from her grief. But at some stage she should try to detach herself from the business and give 'more and more time to dreaming – the kind of reverie we spoke of in that restaurant, the right kind – that leads to your poetry and my painting'. Confusing though it all was for both of them, Gwen seemed most overwhelmingly to treat Jeanne's cable as reassurance; she dreamt about Jeanne, and felt generally reassured.[33]

It may have been that Jeanne, in wanting to be quick to reassure her, had assumed that Quinn's will would make some provision for her to take his place as Gwen's patron, even if it included no specific instructions in that regard. The will, dated 22 July 1924 (six days before the date of Quinn's death), had now been published, and Jeanne had read it. Not only did it make no mention of Gwen; there was effectively no provision for Jeanne, either. Quinn had left his estate to his sister and instructed that his art collection should be 'duly catalogued and sold at public auctions after being properly advertised'. His oil paintings by Augustus John and John B. Yeats went to Mrs Anderson, to go to the Metropolitan Museum of New York or the National Gallery, Dublin if she failed to dispose of them in her will. Other beneficiaries included Quinn's friend and executor Thomas Curtin, who got $15,000; Quinn's sister Clara in the Ursuline Convent at Tiffin, Ohio ($2,500, with further, substantial funds at her disposal should she ever decide to leave the convent); and former mistresses, Dorothy Coates and Ada C. Smith ('As a token of my regard and esteem for her and of her kindness') who got $40,000 and $25,000, respectively. All the rest of the estate and property went to Julia Quinn Anderson and any issue who might survive her.[34]

Jeanne explained to Gwen that Quinn had not known he was going to die, and they had not wanted to rob him of hope by telling him. She had been grieved to discover that there was no provision for Gwen; she also told her that she herself was not in his will. She assured her of her commitment as a friend: 'Your letters have given me a great deal of comfort. I can't thank you for them for they are in my heart. You know that I *do* love you dearly and *always*.' But family concerns, and now John's death, had drained her. She had asked the executors to send Gwen the $250 Quinn had been about to send her when he died; if for any reason it failed to arrive, she would make arrangements for her to be sent 'some temporary funds'. She would arrange in November for Gwen to send, at Jeanne's expense, whatever paintings she had ready, and Jeanne would put them on sale '(as we planned last year)'. She wanted Gwen to go on living in Meudon, to paint in comfort and live as she needed to. One development was that Mr Mitchell Kennedy of the Anderson Galleries in New York had written to Augustus, to ask him if he would authorise Jeanne to act as his New York agent. If this came about, Jeanne would be able to continue to pay Gwen on the same basis as Quinn had (she did not say for how long). Alphonse Kahn wanted to buy some of Gwen's work and would probably come to see her if she sent him her address. Jeanne offered to send Gwen a copy of the will if she wanted to see it, and sent her a velvet dress.[35]

Gwen rose imaginatively to this, in the circumstances, telling Jeanne that she thought it 'so strange he left legacies to old mistresses and not to you – but it only shows he was sure of living!' But she was confused. The money had not arrived, she alerted her. Moreover, 'I wish when you write next you will say more plainly what you want me to do about my work, as I don't understand.' She did not wish Jeanne to be her agent: she thought she meant to continue as her patron, on exactly the same terms as Quinn. She assured her that she was still working on some drawings for Jeanne's book of nursery rhymes, though when she had tried to do illustrations 'in the ordinary sence [*sic*] of the word' they had been 'dreadful failures'. They were not really illustrations as such, but perhaps they would still complement the rhymes. She had finished four, 'a goose, a house, which would do for lollipop house, a cat, and some rabbits'. But she would try to do a few more. If she heard nothing by cable, she would keep them a bit longer. 'Gus has been here, and he will see you soon I think,' she again reassured her.[36]

Still, Jeanne persisted with the unspecific promise that she would take Quinn's place. For the time being, she advised Gwen to send Mrs Anderson just enough work to cover the two instalments outstanding, since any paintings she sent from now on would simply form part of Quinn's estate. They would be sold, and the money would go to Mrs Anderson, who was already a rich woman. In addition to other resources she had a small fortune of her own, and she would now have 'an *income* of $18,000 a year'. In the longer term, she still hoped to find a way of taking Quinn's place. She knew that Gwen's livelihood depended on the connection, but she also cared enormously about her, and did not want to be deprived of their friendship. She told Gwen she wanted to help her 'for my own sake, and because I love you and want you to go on with your painting'. She was more comforted by

Gwen's words, she told her, than by anyone else's. She felt she was dying spiritually, but perhaps it was true that after great grief it was possible to come alive again. She was in Maine with her invalid sister, where she was reading Christina Rossetti's poetry. She and her sister sat looking at the sea. There had been a frost, which had killed all the flowers except a spray of the blue larkspur Quinn had loved. She put some in her letter to Gwen and said they reminded her of Quinn's eyes. She enclosed a letter from Thomas Curtin, and warned her that when she replied she should not say anything she would not want Mrs Anderson to know, as all correspondence had to be put before her and the executors.[37]

Gwen was not even sure how many paintings would reasonably cover the two outstanding instalments. She asked Pottier, who said four pictures would be enough, she should send two now and two later. She was worried about which paintings to send, and wished Jeanne could be there to help her choose,[38] but she was relieved that four paintings would be enough, and touchingly grateful to Jeanne for writing 'so fully and so practically' since as a poet, 'all business must be so tiring to you'.[39] Jeanne responded that three would be ample, and she would bid for them herself at auction.[40] Despite the instructions in Quinn's will, she had been battling to delay the auction. She could not bear the idea of the collection's being dispersed and was worried that an auction at this stage would glut the market and devalue many of the works. She had written an eight-page letter to Thomas Curtin, pleading with him not to sell the collection. Surely, she insisted, Quinn's friends owed it to his memory to do as he would have wished (despite the fact that she knew his wishes, at least as expressed in his will).[41] Furthermore, she calculated that it would be to Mrs Anderson's advantage as she would probably gain something in the region of $100,000 by delaying the sale. In the event, the auction was delayed until 1927. Gwen now began to worry about a little album of drawings which she particularly wanted Jeanne to have. Quinn had taken them out of the album she had made and had had them framed,[42] and she wanted Jeanne to make sure they had either been replaced in the book, or sent to her in their frames. There were in fact two albums, she told her, and she was welcome to both, but she particularly wanted her to have the smaller one as there were more drawings in it. Had Jeanne seen Gus yet? He was trying to get Gwen to send work to England, but she had told him she was waiting to hear from Jeanne.[43]

News of Rutherston's purchases had now reached Augustus, who by the end of December was back in Alderney Manor. He tried to buy back some of the drawings from him, without success. As for the question of Gwen's satisfying Quinn's executors, he thought Jeanne was quite right: 'Two pictures for 250 dollars each is already too much.' (In fact Gwen had sent three, for $500.) That was – by Augustus's calculations – fifty pounds a picture. He told her she should be getting three times that amount, and would easily do so if she sent her work to England, where he already had contacts anxious to acquire her work. She should not have to 'submit to any discomfort or privation any longer. It can't be good for your health or work.' He had put off going to America until the following year, but he would see Jeanne then. He had already heard that there was going to be a great sale of all Quinn's pictures which he wanted to talk to Gwen about, not knowing of the delay, and he promised he would come to Meudon again soon and take her for a meal at the Villa Calypso. He was clearly concerned that her situation was precarious; he also saw an opportunity for her to spread her net a little wider. 'Don't send the executors any more work,' he warned her. 'I'm sure Quinn wanted to help you & get your work as long as you'd let him.'[44] But there was Jeanne to think of. 'I am lonely for you,' she was writing to Gwen, 'and so anxious to come to France and to Meudon. I do not lose John – he seems very near.'[45]

New Year 1925 began with a promise of a present. Augustus had warned Gwen that something excitingly breakable was on its way from England, packed by Dorelia. 'I shall tremble when I open it,' she replied in game acknowledgement. 'Is it a caste of Donatello?' She was not to listen to Albert Rutherston, Augustus told her, he could be wrong about things (he thought Rousseau, for example, was naive). She was glad to know that Augustus agreed with her.[46] She and Mr Rutherston, she now revealed, had spent several afternoons together, and had found themselves mutually contemptuous. He was still in Paris, but she was not planning to spend any more time with him as he was so tiring, and she had not sold him any more paintings, nor a drawing he had wanted. Indeed, she would never have sold him anything if she had met him first. For a while, the issue of her arrangement with the Quinn estate seemed suspended and Gwen simply went back to work. (A pile of broken crockery eventually arrived: 'Dodo,' apologised Augustus, 'was responsible for the packing and says she did it very carefully!')[47]

To Ursula, Gwen confided her frustrations about the difficulty of getting paper for her drawings. She had found some perfect Japanese paper which she had cut up into the right sizes thinking she could easily get more, but when she went back to the shop she found it was all sold. This was very frustrating as it was 'exquisite' for her drawings, and the colours of the paint did not run into one another. Since watercolour is indelible, each brush stroke had to be final and there could be no retouching. The Japanese paper had absorbed the colour perfectly; she had felt quite ill when she realised she would have to use another kind of paper. Ursula advised Ingres paper, washed and dried flat, five or six sheets laid one on top of another – a method Gwen had not tried. 'It is consoling to talk to an artist after all this time,' she told her. 'Your letter is a blessing.' She was still working on the last of the three paintings to be sent to America. Ursula again suggested buying a painting. But 'of course I can't sell to you!' came the reply. Ursula had obviously been worried for her and not entirely confident that Americans were predictable. She sent her a beautiful cerulean blue jacket; Gwen loved the colour and wore it every day. The possibility of penury seemed to worry everyone far more than it did Gwen herself.[48]

The news from New York was not good. Poor Jeanne was suffering further anguish: Thomas Curtin had died, on 2 March, of tuberculosis. She had been working with him on Quinn's papers and they had 'many more plans', but she feared none of these would now come to fruition. Her mind was still on the problem of what to do about Gwen's work and she now proposed selling work for her through Joseph Brummer's Gallery. She still wanted to take Quinn's place, she assured her, and perhaps next year she might be able to think about it, but this year all her money had been taken up by her sister's illness, and now by her brother's, as he had heart trouble. 'If only [Quinn] had realised his condition and made the proper arrangements in his will for you,' she was still lamenting. 'He *loved* you and wanted you to go *on quietly and paint in Meudon*.'[49] She wanted to come to Paris, but she had Quinn's letters to edit first, and she also wanted to produce a book of memoirs by his friends. In fact, she and Gwen appear to have lost touch at this point, possibly because of Jeanne's embarrassment at not being able to take Quinn's place as she had hoped.

That summer, Gwen began to think about the possibility of showing a few paintings in London with Ursula. She was not proposing a large exhibition, so they would not need many paintings; in any case, she thought small exhibitions were much more effective than large ones – she had been to Madge Oliver's recent show, and thought it unintelligent and exhausting.[50] When Ursula replied, she sent news of Madge Oliver's death. This, too, seemed unbelievable. 'Is it really true?' she wrote back, and, with typical candour: '. . . I miss her now she may be gone away though I never thought of her much before!' In June, there was further tribulation. She sat on a needle and spent two days in hospital having it removed from her thigh. Augustus expressed his usual thinly veiled concern: 'I heard you had an operation and found you had swallowed a needle or something. I trust you're all right now.'[51] Ethel Nettleship (Ida's cousin) wanted to see her about the possibility of exhibiting one of her works and one of Augustus's at the Turner Art Gallery in Truro. There were several people in London who wanted her work, he again assured her; now that she could not send to Quinn, she really should think about sending her work to England.

But the removal of the needle put her behind with her work, and now the priest had asked her to do his portrait from a photograph. 'I am ridiculous,' she told Ursula, 'I cannot refuse *anything* that is asked me.' She had been trying unsuccessfully for months to do it, while the 'exquisite summer' was slipping away. Ursula thought she did not have enough work for an exhibition. 'I don't understand . . .' came the reply. 'Can't you get enough things together and have it with me perhaps in the winter? It won't take many things if we have it together.' If it were not for the drawing of the Curé, she could be ready by October. If they were to exhibit in, say, December, it would need to be planned now. It was perhaps already too late. Augustus had offered to arrange an exhibition for her but he was now in Naples; he might be offended if they did it without his patronage, so perhaps, on reflection, they ought to wait. But she was clearly determined.

As the autumn wore on, she found herself doing more watercolour drawings which she thought would probably not be suitable for an exhibition as they were so small. But she did have five canvases ready, which needed only a little retouching. What was the smallest number of pictures they would need, she asked Ursula, for a small exhibition? The Leicester Galleries were a possibility as she had heard they took paintings without commission, otherwise it might not be possible, as the gallery fee would outweigh their income from sales. But she still wanted it to happen. 'If you were energetic,' she insisted, 'you would soon do a few canvases and send some you have. Say in two or three months? . . . Let me know . . .' In the meantime, Augustus had been energetic on her behalf. He had provisionally arranged a 'one man show' for himself and Gwen at the Chenil Galleries, but she said she would still rather exhibit with Ursula. The Chenil exhibition was planned for mid-April 1926, but there was surely still time to include Ursula, who was feebly protesting that she had not been doing many drawings lately. 'You speak as if you only do drawings,' rapped Gwen; 'don't you paint? We decided a long time ago to have an ex. together.' This spirit of energy and activity had extended to 29 rue Terre Neuve itself, which she and a local girl were busy decorating. The 'big room' was now flesh colour and apple green; the kitchen was salmon, the first room white and dark blue and the passage pink and lighter blue. It was a remarkably sociable and busy time. She had had further news of Albert Rutherston, who had a new baby. Gwen was interested, not, she said, because it was Albert's but because 'it is a baby and ugly and tiny'. She hoped it would live. Michel Salaman (Augustus's old friend from their early Slade years, brother of Louise) had clearly been mentioned; after all these years it occurred to her to wonder whether Michel had had babies, too.[52]

It was nearly Christmas. Thornton sent stories from Hope in British Columbia about his new friend Peggy Richmond, aged six, who had taken him for a walk to her father's store. When they got there they found a salesman who had spread out on a table at least three dozen kinds of toys. 'To say that Peggy was delighted is a mild way to put it,' and the traveller 'bore up pretty well under about fifteen different kinds of noise'.[53] Ethel Nettleship now wrote from Cornwall to tell her that after all her efforts, the Turner Gallery had rejected Gwen's pictures as they thought them 'too delicate and slight for a public exhibition'. What Gwen really wanted was to be left to get on and paint. 'The truth is,' she was now agonising, 'I'm afraid I shall have a very tiny show . . . My exhibition is a right mess.'[54]

The Chenil show was held in London from May to July 1926 and in the end included nothing by Augustus; it was billed as 'Paintings and Drawings by Gwen John'. She showed forty-four pictures (including about twenty oil paintings) and four of her hand-made albums of drawings. It was Augustus who thought these would strengthen the show, but although he suggested having the ones she had sent him removed from the albums and mounted they were eventually shown as they were.[55] Chenil was very excited, assuring Gwen that the show would be a financial success before he had even seen her work; characteristically, she saved him a great deal by framing everything herself (he told her he would do the framing, but by then she had already ordered the frames, and typically, it did not occur to her to cancel the order). Ursula, with Gwen's help, wrote the foreword to the catalogue and the show was very successful. Michel Salaman lent *The Pilgrim* (one of her new paintings of a woman wearing a cloak), which he had bought at the beginning of the year, and wrote to tell her he could see so much in it of the Gwen he remembered that it made him want more, though he realised she had probably changed. 'I don't think we change, but we disappear sometimes,' she told him in reply. She meant it literally, not, as has sometimes been assumed, in a spiritual or mystical sense. 'You disappeared a long time.'[56]

Salaman and William Rothenstein both went to see the show the day before the private view and were enchanted and moved. 'It was indeed a chastening joy to stand there amongst those pale, quiet songs of yours – like listening to the still music of the harpsichord – only there is nothing antique or archaistic about your works they are so intensely modern in all but their peacefulness,' Michel told her. He said it took him back to their Slade years, with all their aims and hopes; she now seemed to him to be 'the only one of the eager band who had been utterly faithful to those aspirations, who not only had not failed them but achieved more than we dreamt of'.[57] William Rothenstein especially admired the 'cool nuns, with their quiet and beautiful hands': 'What a rich past, what a sure and sensitive present,' as though 'an exquisite peace, & a perfume which mystics say fills the air for them at times, had entered into your spirit, and quickened it with a new ecstasy'.[58] Gratifyingly, what they both seemed to appreciate was not so much the individual paintings as the atmosphere and mood uniting her work as a whole, which was what she had always aimed for.

Gwen did not go to London to see the show, but seeing her work made people want to re-establish contact with her and acknowledge their feeling that something of her had, over the years, stayed with them in her absence. Everyone became proprietorial. William Rothenstein found himself feeling thankful that 'No shadow, thank Heaven, has ever come between us.'[59] She was clearly touched, and anxious to know what others thought of her work. Frederick and Dorothy Samuel bought one of the variants of *The Pilgrim*: she wrote asking them to tell her what they thought of it. (They told her they admired her ability to convey natural atmosphere and light, and that they could see a clear line of development from her early to her later work.)[60] That November, she loaned *Dorelia in a Black Dress* to the

National Gallery, which yielded £200.[61] (Charles Aitken, the Director, said he thought there was too much space to the left of the canvas: would she agree to their turning it in two inches? The answer was no.)[62] She also showed three paintings at the Manchester Art Gallery, including another of her paintings of Dorelia, *The Student*, which they had purchased the previous year from Charles Rutherston.[63]

At the end of the year, she suddenly decided she would go to see Augustus and the family at Alderney Manor. Dorelia sent instructions about how to get there, and money to buy a fur coat for the journey. It is unlikely that Gwen was fully prepared, after all these years, for the liveliness of Augustus's household, which was usually bursting with people – T.E. Lawrence arriving on his motorbike, or Tallulah Bankhead turning cartwheels in the hall; and everyone staying on and on, oblivious to Augustus's *sotto voce* exhortations to them all to why not just go?[64] It was Christmas time, moreover, and the whole family was there. In the midst of a host of other guests, Gwen arrived, looking tiny and shy. Augustus's daughter Vivien thought she looked like a miniature Augustus, and noticed the extreme pale blueness of her eyes, which seemed to fill with tears as she talked, excitedly and enthusiastically. Gwen asked to see Vivien's paintings, and told her she must work harder and harder, and she insisted on speaking French. The experience must have been overwhelming after the silence of the rue Terre Neuve. Mealtimes seemed particularly noisy and overpopulated, and Gwen retired to her room to eat. She seemed disorientated and a bit culture-shocked. When she did speak English, Augustus noticed with surprise Pembrokeshire vowel sounds he had not remembered from their youth. Augustus was preoccupied with his work and all the other guests, but the bond between them was discernible – his children noticed and remembered it.

She did not stay in England for long and was back in Meudon by Christmas Day. She had not managed to see Arthur and Rhoda Symons but she sent them a Christmas gift, a book about Rousseau which they were delighted with. They wrote promising to come to Paris in the spring, though Rhoda was not making very much progress with her French lessons. Gwen spent Christmas alone, celebrating by going to a concert of beautiful music in Notre-Dame, which she described for Thornton. Christmas in British Columbia had been eventful. He spent it with his friends the Richmond family, and six-year-old Peggy had 'a bewildering lot of toys'. Just before Christmas her favourite doll had broken its head, so he had got it a new one. While it was headless she had been endlessly kind and motherly to it but once the head was replaced she seemed to forget all about it. Her sister Constance had had an adventure in a shop. She had got in a lift with their brother Eilydh, failed to notice when he got out and went 'ever so far down'. She was comforted by a man who gave her chocolate and helped her to find her brother. Thornton recorded all their stories, in careful detail, for Gwen.[65]

20

Véra

Mysteries of technique, mysteries of the heart![1]

At the end of 1926, Rilke died. His *Vergers* were published this year, in an edition together with *Quatrains Valaisans*: Gwen bought or was given a copy (she also owned the 1926 as well as the 1923 edition of his *Cahiers de Malte Laurids Brigge*). His death shocked and upset her, and she felt she needed help in understanding how to pray for his soul. The philosopher Jacques Maritain and his sister-in-law, Véra Oumançoff, both lived in Meudon and since they had also known Rilke she turned to them for advice and they were able to talk to her about him and to comfort her. Véra was an ardent Catholic, a forthright character who was initially kind to Gwen, but she was ultimately unable to provide the artistic sympathy Gwen really needed. Maritain was a Christian philosopher.[2] He seems to have been a kind, shy and unassuming man – the Mother Superior referred to him as 'notre petit frère fatigué'.[3] Gwen made some poignantly observed sketches of him, glimpsed in profile or from over his shoulder, as if she had caught him unawares. A year or so later she introduced him to her nephew Edwin, Augustus's son, now a student in Paris, whose opinion of the 'savant thomiste' was less unequivocal, which infuriated her as she could not bear to see him criticised and would countenance nothing less than unambiguous admiration for him.[4]

Deaths always seemed to recall and echo other deaths. At some deep, oblique level Rilke's death reçalled the sadness and yearning associated with Rodin. While she was still upset and confused about Rilke's death,

Gwen burned herself on a lamp and Véra consoled her. This unexpected demonstration of warmth when she was feeling so vulnerable had a powerful impact. As Véra was also religious, the old confusion of devotional love with emotional yearning now began to resurface. Véra, now, became the object of her emotional desire.

The other powerful element in the old complex nexus of needs was Gwen's chronic need for approval of her work – ironically, since she had never before been so focused, nor more fêted. She was familiarising herself with André Lhote's theories of art, possibly, at this stage, through Constance, who was attending his classes. (Gwen would eventually go too, and they discussed his theories together. These were ongoing discussions: when Constance referred to him in letters it was with easy familiarity.) Lhote taught the paradoxically compatible aims of artistic impersonality in the interests of developing technique, with a view to yielding up within the work the 'mysteries of the heart'. He passed on Poussin's advice to the artist to remain 'above his work in full freedom and clarity of mind'; the rest would follow. But the main and ultimate aim of art should be 'to give pleasure'.[5] Gwen had also begun to be influenced by Rouault, whose work Lhote particularly admired. She was probably also reading Rilke's poetry again, and being drawn into the atmosphere of his symbolic voice. Now – as she had before, to Rodin – she wanted to give her drawings as gifts and began to give them to Véra, intending them to serve as tokens of obedience and love; needing them to be approved of and praised.

She also began to make hundreds of minuscule sketches, often on Grands Magasins du Louvre notepaper, of Saint Thérèse,[6] the 'little flower' and servant to the Madonna and child, with her younger sister. She based these drawings on a studio portrait of the young Saint as a child, posed with her sister in a photographer's studio, before her early death and subsequent sanctification: she scoured Paris to find a copy of this photograph. It shows two little girls posed together in short dresses and pinafores with the usual photographer's props – the curtain, the pot plant – and she drew them over and over again, hundreds of tiny pen and ink sketches, adding, sometimes, the odd minor variant: she sometimes, somewhat weirdly, put a little dog at their feet. She made watercolour and gouache sketches as well as pen and ink ones, using a range of colour schemes. Nobody knows why she sketched them over and over. Perhaps she just felt the basic sketch was successful so she reworked it absentmindedly or for relaxation, like a doodle, to exercise her hand. Maybe she sometimes did it without really thinking.[7]

In 1927, Gwen's paintings were exhibited in New York in the second retrospective exhibition of Quinn's collection. Two of her paintings were also shown in the Vienna Secession that autumn, in the Meisterwerke Englischer Malerei aus Drei Jahrhunderten; and another was exhibited in Toronto. But the focus of her mind was still inward. She went for long walks in the forest of Meudon, taking her notebooks in her pockets to note down ideas for 'motifs' and make quick sketches of the things she saw. Sometimes she got tired and did not come back for three or four days; occasionally she still slept under the stars. On one of these excursions, she wrote a fragmented account of a strange experience – perhaps a dream. It is an odd, mysterious piece of writing, haunting and vivid. She wrote about taking the big road into the forest and suddenly seeing that the other side of the road seemed to be the colour of anemones. She picked big bunches, then she came back, taking the path just by the side of the Observatoire, but now there were no more crocuses and violets. The account was clearly intended for Véra, since she mentions the railings of her house. She came down the steps of the haute Terrasse, she tells her, and stopped there to admire the view . . . 'and I called out "Voila la Seine! Viola la Tour Iffel!" [*sic*] to your *grille* when I saw you, it seemed you both had more colour in your cheeks, and I had as well.'[8] This almost hallucinatory vision seems to conflate a number of vivid experiences: earlier walks in the forest, taking visitors up to the Observatoire and pointing out the view, as well as the purer, more vivid experience of simply seeing anemones as pure colour. It is a sensual, creative vision, perhaps reconciling experiences of almost mystical solitude and intensely sensuous engagement with her work, with comforting memories of being accompanied. It suggests that the charge generated by working creatively very hard, over a long period, was now being reflected back to her by the process of looking itself.

In a complex, oblique and ultimately unfortunate way, Véra Oumançoff played a part in this new atmosphere of charged creativity. After the meeting with her and Jacques Maritain, Gwen talked about Véra to the Mother Superior, who suggested that if she could not always see her, perhaps they could write to each other. A door opened in Gwen's mind, and a flood of inarticulable feeling began to surface. Inevitably, confiding her most deeply felt thoughts to Véra would bring back memories of writing to

Rodin: it was a form of love she had practised endlessly and it enabled her to be searching, reflective, confessional. When she left her at the corner of the rue Terre Neuve one day on their way home from Mass, Véra – in an uncharacteristic display of affection (and perhaps a desire for power) – told Gwen to write whatever she wanted to, whatever she felt. It was an irresistible invitation not only to articulate her chronic desire and despair, but also to turn up regularly at Véra's house with declarations, drawings; even the dictionary.

Véra had commented on one of her drawings; Gwen now wanted to show her everything she did and to take her views into account, as she had absorbed Rodin's criticisms and suggestions. When Véra was with her, she told her, she could see the faults in her drawings without her even having to speak. She searched for a word to express the deep longing that was welling up in her again, and came up with the English word 'yearning'. Véra agreed to meet her once a week, on a Monday, and Gwen set about making drawings especially to take to their meetings: they became the 'déssins de Lundi'. She realised the drawings were tiny, but that should not matter, she told her, as they were actually her gifts to God, and He would not mind the smallness of them. It was odd, hearing Véra talk about her work: Gwen was always surprised by the things she said, but she desperately needed to talk to someone about them. If Véra thought they were bad, she was to say so and Gwen would change them. She had never, she said – exaggerating wildly – had any real criticism of her work, because she always sent it by post to one person and she had never shown her drawings to anyone except the priest. She knew they were not art (Véra's view, presumably) but she was trying to make them into art and hoped she would achieve some proper works of art before long.[9]

Part of the attraction of Véra was surely her proximity – she lived close enough to be visited at least once a week, and Gwen probably saw her regularly at Mass. Maritain, who was teaching at the Paris *Institut*, was undoubtedly less accessible. But the problem was that Véra had neither the slightest artistic understanding, nor any inclination for the intense connection Gwen craved, nor any understanding of the deep, residual feelings which were now resurfacing. She began to feel irritated and even perhaps threatened by the idea that Gwen might be outside her house, waiting for her in the mornings, or looking through the railings to try to catch a glimpse of her at unappointed times. She said as much at the outset:

she could tell Gwen had a fine sensibility, but she should turn it towards Our Lord and the Blessed Virgin. We should suffer for the sins we have committed against God, but to suffer because we have not had a reply to our letters seemed to her absurd. But for a while Gwen remained undaunted.

Although she suggested that Gwen write to her once a week, Véra said she would not reply straight away. She also disapproved of Gwen's habit of drawing in church. She only drew during the *Salut* and the *Retraite*, Gwen said, not during the important Masses. Well, that was not acceptable either, retorted Véra, 'l'eglise est un lieu de *prière* . . .'[10] Involuntary distractions aside, to turn on purpose from thoughts about God seemed to her quite inappropriate. Unfortunately, replied Gwen, not everyone was as good as Véra at praying. Sometimes her moments of distraction seemed to last so long that there was not much time over for prayer itself.[11] (We can only imagine how this went down.) Anyway, the orphans with their black hats with white ribbon and their black dresses with little white collars were so beautiful that if she had to give up drawing them, there would be no charm in her life. This was simply not a sacrifice she was prepared to make, even for her.[12] Véra was unequipped to recognise the complex role Gwen needed her to play as muse, and saw the whole thing only as an embarrassing infatuation, but the more she resisted, the more she seemed to act as a catalyst for unleashed yearning. Gwen now began to fill her notebooks with expressions of longing (in one she filled sixty-nine pages with appeals to her to try to understand how she was feeling).

It is impossible to know how many of these unchecked, spontaneous outpourings Véra actually received. Some of them were more poetic than others, possibly inspired by Rilke's poetry ('Part of my heart imprisons me, I will die of hunger, or be suffocated . . .').[13] Among these appeals, she jotted down thoughts and ideas about her work. Véra kept commenting coolly that she hoped Gwen was enjoying it. She had misunderstood, Gwen told her: painting was not a pleasure. She did it the way she did her housework, which she did regularly and meticulously, because it had to be done. The only difference was that, of the two activities, painting was the more tiring and difficult. The only moments of pleasure were when occasionally she looked at something sometimes and saw it fully, in its essence, before she began thinking about it as a potential painting or drawing.[14]

Her work was all the more tiring now, because she was beginning to get frequent headaches and the first intimations of the stomach problems which would eventually worsen, over the years. Occasionally she would jot down in her notebook an account of something slightly hallucinatory, like the dream of anemones in the woods. In one notebook she scribbled, barely legibly, 'Il faut faire de l'art, et pas attendre qu'il vient doucement de soi même?' (Art has to be made, it's no good waiting for it to emerge gradually from within oneself?) Straight after this, she jotted down something more cryptic, and more disturbing. Je faire [?illegible] marcher des petits bébé [*sic*] qui sont dans ma ventre' (I must keep the little babies in my stomach moving).[15] We cannot know when this was written: in the middle of the night, perhaps? The physicality of it is striking and her expression of it particularly poignant. In 1927 Gwen was fifty-one, and had twelve years to live.

She still talked earnestly about her work, not only to Véra but also to the Curé, who seemed to have strong opinions. He said he thought it was rather misty: surely it would be possible to use stronger colours.[16] But even if you wanted it misty, she patiently explained, there must be rules for that, too; you still had to mix the tones. Anyway, what was wrong with misty painting? Some of the great masters, like Puvis de Chavannes, painted in the mist. In the course of this conversation she also revealed that she had begun to work with a colour wheel, of a kind widely available at the time in Montmartre in shops selling artists' materials. It consisted of several layers of revolving discs of colour charts so that it was possible, by turning the different layers, to arrive at compatible tones. It was a complicated procedure, but she said she was having far fewer headaches now that she had got herself one of these cards. She described it to the Curé: it was a disc with perhaps 85,000 [*sic*] numbers. She could find, by making complicated calculations, the colour and tone complementary to any colour or tone. There were long lists and 72 gammas and quadrants which you had to divide by concentric arcs, and ten radii which had to be divided into twenty parts, representing twenty tones, so that you could find with it the simultaneous successive colours, 'contraste ou contraste mélange' of any colour or tone. Her record of this conversation constitutes a major revelation, not only about the way she was working at the time but also about the extreme complexity and precision with which apparently spontaneous and simple tonal decisions in her drawings were arrived at. She explained to the priest, equally crucially, that though the use of the wheel on the whole made things easier, it was not something she depended on all the time; she still had to draw up some rules which emerged for her in the process of drawing, and out of the 'pleins ou couleurs' (planes or colours, presumably) which she made herself, which she would want to go on doing as well as using the wheel. The numbers that appear on some of her drawings may have related to numbered tones on the wheel. It is possible, though it is equally possible that she devised her own numerical formulae for mixing and distinguishing tones.[17]

She continued to use her notebooks as written sketchbooks, for both drafts of letters (to be sent eventually, or sometimes not at all) and written notes towards her drawings, in which she would first establish the motif, then sketch out in words her preliminary ideas for the colours –

30 Dec

Faded dewberry flowers

blacks	flowers	ground
paynes grey	orange	raw umber
black		

Blackberry flowers

blacks	flowers	ground
vert ch	yel. ok	ok j
black	Nap. yel	ok B
	lem yel.	ok R
	black[18]	

– the recurrence of black, here, is significant: she had begun to experiment with black in a way she had never explored before, probably after studying Rouault's use of it.

As she went on making experiments with paint, she continued to study words. She told Véra she thought the obstacle that seemed to be between them was probably a 'technical' one, to do with words, and the differences in the ways they expressed themselves; but she also thought it had something to do with the problems of art.[19] It was partly a question of finding the right forms of expression. She had looked up 'yearning' in her dictionary and been unable to find it; but it was, she told Véra, a desire for love, perhaps human, perhaps divine, of which one is deprived. Everybody must know what this feels like; it had always been there for her, and it always would be.[20] Perhaps unsurprisingly, Véra remained unmoved. Quite apart from any other connotations, her faith would not have allowed her to encourage any confusion between secular and divine love. Gwen patiently tried to see it all from Véra's point of view, but she was desperate for love. She told Véra that the Enfant Jésus had told her she had suffered enough in the world and she could stop worrying about it all now, so she had done just that, except that she was giving the daughters of Monsieur Joly, the landlord of the rue Terre Neuve, English pronunciation lessons – not an easy task, since it was a big family and the teaching made her very nervous. She made notes to herself about the meanings of words: 'Modifier' in English is to modify, mitigate or abate. 'Mitigate' in French is *mitiger, adoucir, modérer*. 'Abate' in French is *réduir, rabaisser, diminuer, faire cesser*.[21] Véra began to suggest that she ought to perform more social duties, though on reflection she thought better of this and tried to take it back. A good job, said Gwen, because the Enfant Jésus told me I didn't have to worry about the world or concern myself with people, and I shouldn't think you'd want to contradict him.[22] At some subliminal level she was tempting herself to recall the experience of yearning for Rodin, but she also knew that would be impossible to resurrect.

She now began to try to persuade Véra into the role of servant of God or divine messenger, while Véra continued to try to establish more distance between them. This was unhelpful, Gwen protested, because the things she needed to say had to be said at the time, like the drawings she made preparatory notes for in church or on her walks, which needed to be done as soon as she got home. It was much more difficult to do them several days later.[23] Véra was lamentably out of her depth. The paintings and drawings she was in the habit of seeing were probably mostly religious; it is highly unlikely that she had any idea of what Gwen was trying to achieve. Influenced by Rouault's work, at about this time she did a series of six strange, uncharacteristic drawings of the Madonna and child in a rocky landscape, *Vièrge et Enfant se promènent dans un petit pays rocailleux* (this may have risen out of Lhote's lectures).[24] The drawings are done in strong, bold, black lines reminiscent of Rouault's and can be compared – though the subject matter is different – with Rouault's *Studies for a Nude* – rough, quick figures which Lhote particularly admired because they were drawings done with no premeditation. He probably lectured on them; certainly, he wrote about them in his book, *Figure Painting*, where he points out that unlike Seurat, say, or Renoir, Rouault's style of experimentation was about going 'in hot pursuit of an experiment, the good or bad outcome of which cannot be foreseen'. It was, of course, how Rodin had made drawings. Rouault had made his *Studies for a Nude* in the pages of his letter-copying notebook, devoting twenty transparent pages to the same subject. The brush strokes are bold, almost violent, and Lhote thought they expressed 'the turbulent idea of getting closer and closer to an ever-elusive form, the native impulse of which he must ultimately imprison in a surrounding contour'. He saw in Rouault's 'fine daubs' something in common with those of Daumier or Rembrandt who, famously, did not have to seek for line, which for him was 'already stored in his memory'.[25]

When she saw Gwen's *Vièrge et Enfant se promènent dans un petit pays rocailleux*, Véra said she thought it was sentimental. Gwen was completely bewildered. She had expected her to like it because of its religious subject matter; her idea of sentimental, she said, was plaster virgins in churches. This drawing was all done in bold blacks, with the Madonna and Child set against a wild, primitive landscape. It was an experiment which took something not only from Rouault but also perhaps from Augustus's primitive drawings of wild women in open landscapes. It also had a Symbolist quality, like a drawing by Puvis de Chavannes – all this was lost on Véra. 'You seem to think everything is "sentimentalism",' reprimanded Gwen. 'Did you invent the expression yourself?'[26] All the same, she kept on trying to please her, deciding that the failure of the painting must be a matter of technique and resolving to stop using blacks. (It *is* a strange picture but it represented a venture into new territory: who knows where it might have led?) She made a note in her notebook, 'Cease to draw in black (?) Observation. Wandering thoughts weaken your synthesis and undo what you have acquired.'[27]

The deep need for creative reciprocity persisted, together with the confusion of psychic voices. She told Véra she would still bring her a drawing every week, since the drawings were her babies,[28] just as the drawings she had done for Rodin had been their babies. At the same time, Véra was supposed to assist her in the ongoing search to discover what it would really mean to be 'God's little artist':

It is to be on your knees before her.
It is to be ascetic.
It is to be a Christian.
It is to be always gracieuse.
It is to think always of her.
It is to obey her. You cannot do this without
It is to produce pictures. the help of Jesus enfant.
It is to pray for her.
It is to join her to your prayers.
It is giving up old griefs.
It is being a different creature from the past.
It is having a conversation ready.
It is having letters a bouquet of little flowers. [*sic*][29]

Still Véra went on vainly trying to insist that she should treat her just as a friend. 'Don't tell me that,' retorted Gwen, she was not like her friends and had no wish to be like them. They were no doubt capricious, bad tempered and not sentimental enough to suit her.[30] It seemed impossible to accept the nature of the relationship; she was determined to transform it into what she needed, but at the same time increasingly frustrated by the futility of the attempt. In a note signed 'Mary', she scribbled that technique no longer interested her, pictures no longer interested her any more.[31] Another jotting reads, simply, 'Rilke: – une femme' – perhaps the desire to elevate Véra to the status of poetic muse had come directly from reading his poetry. Whatever the reason, Véra was having none of it. Gwen tried out compliments and appeals in her notebooks: her dark red dress suited her; she thought she should always wear dark red dresses. (Red seems an unlikely colour for the devout Véra: was Gwen remembering that Rodin had liked her in red?) She offered to go shopping with her and carry her bags. Véra said she was quite capable of carrying her bags herself. To divert herself, Gwen went to search for an exhibition of Chagall's paintings.[32] When she eventually tracked them down, she was very struck by them, convinced that he was certainly not (as some said) a mere fantasist. Back home with the dictionary, she struggled with the word 'renoncer' – obviously Véra's instruction to her to try to let go. But, 'To obey you wouldn't be "a me renoncer", would it? Perhaps it would, sometimes.' She longed for a more reciprocal, creative engagement. But Véra went on resisting her, responding to Gwen's invitation to visit her on Boxing Day with a note telling her she must absolutely not count on her, she would be resting at home that day.[33]

During that year, though, other things had also begun to take over. In the spring of 1927, Augustus and Dorelia had been given notice that they must either buy Alderney Manor or give it up, so in March 1927 they decided to move on. They went to live at Fryern Court, a mile from Fordingbridge at the edge of the New Forest. There was a small cottage near by, and it occurred to them that perhaps Gwen might like to buy it, and move to England to be near them. Negotiations over Yew Tree Cottage were rapidly completed and that summer Augustus and Dorelia had written to say that the sale had gone through. 'The cottage is yours,' they told her, and she was to send as much money as she could spare; Augustus would lend her the rest. Dorelia was sure the place could be 'made delightful without much money', then Gwen could move in as soon as she liked. Gwen sent them a cheque for £76 and asked them to keep account, they could do the final reckoning when she got the money from her exhibition in New York. Her pictures were now – presumably under the auspices of Augustus – being dealt through the Ferargil Gallery. 'The dealer said my numerous (?) friends are immensely enthusiastic about my coming over,' she told Dorelia. '(I did not know I had 1 friend in America!) Picture gallery directors seem to be imaginative!'[34]

She went over to see Yew Tree Cottage in July 1927, and thought it very lovely, quiet and peaceful, with a pretty border of fir trees on one side of the garden. She was trying to avoid Gus and the others, she told Ursula, because 'my mind is not strong enough to keep its harmony when any difficulties and obstacles come' and she was counting on Ursula not to tell anyone she was there, '*I will not be troubled by people*.'[35] (Strains of the overpopulated winter of 1926.) But if Ursula could be there with her she could imagine painting there, 'as we come into each other's solitude or harmony don't we? We are a part of each other's "atmosphere".' She told Ursula that the cottage was very expensive, but Augustus was putting up most of the money and she would pay him back in the autumn. So far, its only furnishing was a little picture of Augustus's on the dresser and she was too hard up to furnish it herself: did Ursula have anything she didn't need? 'One sometimes has,' she hazarded, 'things put away in the lumber room.' She just needed chairs, a table, a bed and a *sommier* to sleep on if anyone came to stay. Having seen the cottage, she went back to France, planning to return to England a few days later to whitewash the rooms and move in. She thought she would then stay until September, then go back to Meudon for the winter, but she warned Ursula not to mention this last plan as she did not want Augustus to know that she had no intention of spending the winter there. Anything Ursula wished to donate could be sent by train to Fordingbridge.

Gwen went back to Meudon, rescued one of her cats from the Meudon-Versailles tunnel where it had hidden, and did some new drawings. Then she returned to Yew Tree Cottage. There was no sign of Ursula, but a consignment of furniture was now *en route* from Ursula's home in Oxford to Fordingbridge, and Augustus had approved the plan to have Ursula to stay. The cottage now contained some blue cups with white spots and some yellow jugs. There was a dresser ready, and a bed and a *sommier* (which cost more than £5, as much as Gwen had been planning to spend on furnishing the whole place) and a picture by Augustus was on its way from London. For the time being Gwen was going to be sleeping at Fryern Court, due to the lack of furniture. Three days later there was still no sign of Ursula but the consignment arrived: a carpet, counterpane, linen, and an overcoat which (apparently without a trace of irony) Gwen said would be especially useful for going back to France. Yew Tree Cottage, meanwhile, was taking shape; she had had the partitions taken down so that the rooms were now quite large, and installed 'a thing for sharpening pencils'.

She did the whitewashing and enjoyed being there for a few days, but she was bothered by workmen. Gus had disappeared off somewhere, and Yew Tree Cottage was clearly not up to accommodating visitors. She still thought the cottage lovely and the countryside exquisite, but she needed to get back to Meudon to finish her paintings. In Paris, ironically, she would increasingly have more to do with Augustus's sons. Henry had just joined the Church, to the consternation of the other Johns (Augustus had met a friend of his, Tom Burns, at a party at Augustus's studio in Mallord Street and put him in touch with Gwen: he obviously thought she would be an ally);[36] David was occasionally in Paris, asking angry questions about Catholicism, and Edwin would soon be there studying at one of the Académies.

Yew Tree Cottage could never be home. Gwen was entirely settled in Meudon by now, surrounded by neighbours and receiving regular letters and parcels from her friends in England. Anyway, there was another plan afoot. In July, a letter arrived from Chloe's solicitors, generously enclosing a cheque in the sum of £90 and advising Gwen to write and instruct them when she required the balance of £500.[37] This had some bearing on Gwen's whispered aside to Ursula, in a letter she had sent her from Yew Tree Cottage. 'I have another secret to tell you but will tell it when I see you. It is of the same species.'[38]

21

The Hangar

I feel more than ever on the point of knowing how to express things – in painting.[1]

'In about 1929 I saw coming into the church a woman with a felt hat with a wide brim, dressed in a long, dark cape, who slid discreetly to the end of the church, and there, without kneeling like the other worshippers, pulled out a sketchbook and began to draw,' Madame Louise Roche later remembered. Madame Roche lived at 6 rue Babie, a leafy, suburban road with large houses on one side and an old wall on the other, just off the main road leading down from the Terrasse towards Bas-Meudon, a few streets from the rue Terre Neuve. 'In front of her were the orphans of the nuns of the Présentation, the first ones with their little outfits decorated with white collars, the "sisters" with their big cornettes who were called the "Filles de la Charité." They all seemed to serve as models and throughout the service this lady went on drawing without stopping. Quite intrigued by this, I found out who this person was, and discovered with surprise that she was an English woman who had converted to Catholicism.'[2]

In the summer of 1927, while the purchase of Yew Tree Cottage was being completed, Gwen had already discovered that at number 8 rue Babie there was a vacant lot with two buildings on it: a wooden building on stilts and a smaller one, also made of wood. According to Madame Roche, the lot had been vacant for some time – oddly, there was one empty plot in this secluded road. The road was very quiet, the wooden buildings would make good studio spaces and it had another virtue, a leafy garden, with lush foliage and little paths running through it, a potential paradise for cats. Towards the beginning of 1929, Gwen bought the land and wooden buildings, recording somewhat illegibly in an agitated scrawl in her notebook her negotiations with the owner.[3] She thought it was expensive; he challenged her to ask her friends if they thought so. She reported back that yes, they did think so, whereupon the man put the price up. (In fact, she appears to have told no one about the transaction, except Chloe.)

The *propriétaire*'s asking price had been 65,000 francs; instead of which he now wanted 68,000 francs. He said the extra 3,000 were the lawyer's fees. When Gwen argued with him, he talked very energetically for a long time while she stood her ground; she noticed he seemed a bit tired afterwards. She was fearless throughout the negotiations. He said that if he had not done a special deal for her, the lawyer's fees would have been 14,000 francs; if she was not happy with his offer he had another purchaser waiting. This did not fool Gwen, who was fairly sure there was no such person since he had agreed not to advertise it. She went next door and asked Monsieur Roche for advice, and a few days later Louise Roche discovered she had bought the land, complete with the garage, shack or 'hangar', as she came to call it (presumably after Meudon's illustrious Hangar Y, which housed the famous balloon). In the spring of 1929, Madame Roche 'saw arriving in the rue Babie the artist whom I'd seen so often at her work!'

Gwen must have bought the Hangar with the money Chloe sent. She gradually paid her share of Yew Tree Cottage, in dribs and drabs, from the sale of paintings in America, possibly from money saved and eventually out of income from her mother's estate. The purchase of Yew Tree Cottage was unaffected by this new turn of events but the plan to live there would never now materialise, though nobody ever understood quite why. Augustus and Dorelia had already found a friend, Fanny Fletcher, who wanted to live in the cottage and they wrote to say that if Gwen had no objections she would move in. She did so, fairly promptly and opened up tearooms in the property. This occupied only half of the house, they assured Gwen; there was still half at her disposal and the tearooms need not disturb her, she would have her own staircase. Fanny Fletcher would pay Gwen £12 a year, and she would also look after the garden and grow vegetables and flowers. 'She understands you want to be left alone, and you won't be interfered with by customers . . .'[4] Gwen said she had no objection to this scheme, so long as her father could stay there if ever he wanted to.[5]

One deciding factor in the purchase of 8, rue Babie was probably her distress at the demolition work which was going on in the rue Terre Neuve. Substantial work was being carried out further down the hill, which meant that her view of the sloping, crooked street would be ruined by the demolition of beautiful houses and the construction of new apartment blocks in their place. She had a complicated reaction to this: it depressed and worried her substantially and she put aside everything else she was working on to make a whole succession of drawings of the street as it was before the building work began. She wrote to Véra about it, warning her that they would both now be relocated in a 'pays inconnu', which was Purgatory.[6] Still, she now had her land, and the Hangar; and the problem of Yew Tree Cottage seemed to have been settled by Fanny and her tearooms.

Gwen was still preparing for her exhibition in New York, and hurrying to get some pictures done before Christmas, determined (as she had been before, on countless occasions) that this was the last time she would ever promise to have work ready for an exhibition, since when the deadline began to loom she was no longer in the mood to do the things she had promised. Working to any kind of deadline was always a strain for her and her eyes were bad now, which did not help. She must have worried a lot about this because she told not only Dorelia and the Mother Superior but also, uncharacteristically, her father. Her eyesight would be a persistent problem from now on, but it did not stop her from working.

In the summer of 1927 John Quinn's sister, Julia Quinn Anderson, came to see her, bringing her daughter Mary to Meudon. They left bearing a painting. They wanted one of a Japanese doll sitting on the table at the rue Terre Neuve (*The Japanese Doll*)[7] but Gwen wisely told them it was not finished. Reluctant to name a price for the one they took, she left it to Mrs Anderson's discretion. More than a month later, as she was about to leave Paris, Julia sent £50, which she assured Gwen was more than she would have made if they had negotiated through a gallery. She had expected rather more, Gwen told her, whereupon Mrs Anderson again insisted she name her price: she had spent a lot on her vacation and had to be careful, she was in no position to make money as her brother had been.[8] Perhaps she was genuinely financially unsettled by the inheritance of this large, complicated fortune. They did, however, seem to appreciate Meudon and were very impressed by the view from the Terrasse, promising that next time they would come for the whole summer. The next time they came, Gwen said, they would be able to have tea in her garden at the rue Babie, there would be no stairs to climb and her picture would be in the garage (the little shed at the side of the Hangar). 'I have put £100 as the value of the picture,' she suggested, firmly but diplomatically; 'but you need not send me that, I shall be quite satisfied with *whatever* you send me.'[9]

In February 1928, Augustus's son Edwin was in Paris, and came to visit Gwen.[10] (Perhaps it was now that he made a fine watercolour drawing on paper of the Hangar in the snow.)[11] Aunt and nephew struck up a lively relationship, meeting at the Dôme (the café popular with artists in Montparnasse) and arguing affably about the merits of Rouault and other painters. She treated him with tremendous, informal affection and they communicated as familiars: 'My dear little boy (whom I admire very much) *Dome* then Friday.'[12] They probably discussed Picasso, and may have gone together to see some of his work, since when he went home to Fryern Court for Christmas Edwin obviously talked to Dorelia about it and she referred to it when she wrote to Gwen: 'I don't know so much about not smiling at Picasso if his pictures we see are as bad or mad as those ones we saw last time we saw them together.'[13] (Perhaps Gwen now took his work more seriously than she had once done, and more seriously than Dorelia did.)

The purchase of the 'ground' in the rue Babie seems to have been kept a secret from the family in England. In the spring of 1928, Gwen was still writing to Ursula telling her how much she wanted her to visit her in Fordingbridge, though she would not yet be able to stay at the cottage itself as it still had no spare bed. Gwen herself was not planning to go there until she had sold one or two pictures, as she still owed Augustus money for it. There had been a lot of expenses which Augustus had met, and she would have to reimburse him. But the cottage had 'very much beauty' and was bigger than it looked from the outside. 'I sometimes want to be there very much,' she told Ursula. She said she found thinking about it compatible with thinking about her work, though work and the cottage never quite materialised together. She was still working very hard. 'I feel more than ever on the point of knowing how to express things – in painting,' she told Ursula in April. 'It feels as if it is a matter of a week or two, but that is nothing new – and so it will be months or years perhaps before I can do it. One must be patient.' The emphasis was still on experimentation and abstraction. She asked Ursula if she ever bought artificial flowers for her drawings, since 'They are in a way better than the others sometimes.'[14] When neither Augustus nor Dorelia could persuade her to return to Yew Tree Cottage, Fanny Fletcher tried: '. . . do come! Are you painting hard?' She was.[15]

In October, Michel Salaman's sister Louise (now Louise Bishop) brought her eldest daughter Bridget to Paris, and managed to get Gwen to agree to paint a portrait of Bridget, which gave her unending trouble. Bridget, who was very taken with Gwen, posed politely in a plain, smart dress and pearls, and Gwen worked intermittently on the picture, but something about the hands stalled her, and she never did get them right.[16] It seems to have been the last (unfinished) portrait in oils she attempted. She was preoccupied again by her neighbours, and now by a new priest, Abbé Charles Collin, who in Gwen's view was spoiling the church. He said it needed cleaning, and proceeded to try to clean the interior. It had been a wonderful shade of gold, with a hint of rose and a patina of age, but he had ruined it with 'Ripoline' and it was now, said Gwen with glorious indignation, the colour of a stuffed corpse.[17] As if that was not enough, he wanted to place a dreadful bronze at the top, which would never be seen anyway because to see it you would have to make an effort to raise your eyes. On top of all this, he wanted to put up a *fleur-de-lys*. It was all very expensive and there was not a single person who thought it necessary. Both Mlle Parmi and Mme Henri said it was better before, and they had clearly not been influenced in their opinion by each other, since they were sworn enemies.

The new Curé represented an unanticipated change. Gwen now began to turn her attention to him – at first, in a spirit of indignation because she hated everything he was doing. He was changing the pictures between the stations of the cross and he had also been vulgar with the ladies of the congregation, making them laugh on the annual church outing (though she admitted she had been busy entertaining Mrs Anderson that day, so had this story only on hearsay). Indignantly, she relayed all this to Véra, in the next breath urging her to read *Tom Jones* while looking at Hogarth's pictures. She apologised for the stains on her copy of *Tom Jones*, it had got like that because it was damp in her cupboard. She told her the whole house was so damp that there were little streams of water running down the staircase.[18] The rue Terre Neuve, despite its recent redecoration, was not the most comfortable place to live, which may have been another reason for buying the Hangar.

The first thing Gwen did when she moved into number 8 rue Babie was to enclose her new land with a high wall to give her privacy and surround and protect her paths. She then quietly installed herself in the Hangar – the larger of the wooden sheds on stilts. She was so unobtrusive that at first the Roches did not realise anyone was living there. She did not move everything in, and kept on 29 rue Terre Neuve because she wanted to go on working on some paintings there; in fact at first she had no real intention of moving completely to the rue Babie. But she loved the Hangar and its garden, mainly because of the land, and its feeling of seclusion and peace, despite the fact that it lacked home comforts: it was unheated, and fiendishly cold in winter (although the rue Terre Neuve, with damp running down the walls, frost in acacia patterns on the window panes, a difficult staircase and lack of garden, hardly sounds paradisal by comparison). The real joy of the rue Babie was the garden. She left all the trees to 'pousser à leur fantaisie (grow wild to their hearts' content), and soon she had quite a forest of her own, from which some acacias, left to themselves, soon emerged, pointing up magnificently towards the sky. The Hangar was in a beautiful avenue of *tilleuls* which made a leafy lane and between these two islands of greenery there was a sunny garden full of wild herbs. The second wooden building, in the midst of all this, could serve as another idyllic studio. The move, therefore, did nothing to distract her from working – on the contrary, she now worked in both the rue Babie and the rue Terre Neuve. She got to know Monsieur and Madame Roche because she discovered that Monsieur Roche was a keen mathematician and asked him for help deciphering a book about the geometry of art (perhaps Gleizes's book on *Cubism*) as she was having difficulty with the technical terminology.

The pleasure of a garden was immeasurable after a lifetime of living in small, upstairs apartments. She was a painter, not a gardener, Gwen announced to the Roches when she arrived; nevertheless she took a keen interest in the fate of the slugs in Madame Roche's vegetables. She told Madame Roche that Shakespeare had said that killing an insect was like killing a Caesar. What did she do with hers? asked Madame Roche. 'I collect them up carefully in a box,' said Gwen, 'and put it outside in the street.' Her cats were in their element at the rue Babie. By now she had about five at a time, and usually spent more time preparing elaborate meals for them than for herself, going to the market to buy fish heads and preparing special pâtés for them. This fascinated Madame Roche, who later recorded with guarded indulgence her memories of Gwen and the world of number 8 rue Babie. She noticed that one old cat got special attention partly because she had no teeth. This was Valentine, 'a frightful and frightening beast'. Another cat (Louise Roche called him 'the assassin') almost caused a war between neighbours, leaping on defenceless baby birds and finishing them off in the branches of the trees until Gwen attached a bell to his collar, after which all day long from the neighbouring garden Madame Roche could hear the sound of 'the alert being rung'.

Louise Roche wrote her (unpublished) memoirs of Gwen in the 1940s, after Gwen's death.[19] The richness of her observations draws attention to Gwen's unusualness and her idiosyncrasies, which must have been part of her character all her life, but Louise Roche was a subtle and gifted observer (only Ida John could have rivalled her as a storyteller) and something of Gwen's warm spontaneity now surfaces through her eyes, as it had much earlier in her life through Ida's. Gwen was to live out the last decade of her life in the rue Babie, and the similarities between the older Gwen and the young girl who had once moved impetuously into the room in the rue Edgar Quinet, installing Edgar Quinet the cat and eccentrically adapting domestic life to suit herself and her art, were still apparent. Louise Roche found Gwen wise, kind and candid; she was also so struck by her extreme sensitivity that she commented on it to Gwen herself, who told her, 'but I wouldn't be an artist without that'. Madame Roche appreciated this, but it did not always make for easy relations. She also noted that in the course of a single conversation Gwen would change expressions so many times that it was easy to read in her face indications that one had quite unintentionally offended her, and in ways it would have been impossible to offend anybody else.

She had a 'beau caractère', Madame Roche remembered; she never saw her as the least bit sentimental. She was disinterested in the extreme; and anything to do with money particularly exasperated her. When she had to go to Paris to the bank it would preoccupy her sufficiently for her to mention it repeatedly. She was charitable, but discreetly: it would not have done to discuss with her how she spent her money. When she moved to the rue Babie she spent a long time drawing one of the priests who lived in Meudon, 'sans fonction sacerdotal'. He was a historian who had written a life of Elizabeth I, and Gwen had been asked to paint his portrait. For several months, every morning at Mass she made sketches of him as he gave thanks. She was paid a fee but she gave it in its entirety back to the church.

When Gwen first arrived in the rue Babie she went to Communion every day. She told Madame Roche, 'my religion and my art are my whole life'. But she did not practise regularly, and when she had settled in and got back to work on a painting, everything stopped for that. She worked intensively without interruptions until it was finished, and sometimes would not be seen in the church for a month. When Madame Roche questioned her about this, Gwen said she would take advice from the priest. She did so, reporting back that he had had nothing to say on the matter and certainly did not think she had sinned. Madame Roche was quite shrewd about Gwen's unique brand of Catholicism. In some respects she felt she had remained fundamentally Protestant. It was her reaction to the death of the Pope that gave her away. He died at the same time as one of their elderly neighbours, a woman Madame Roche did not find particularly pleasant, whom neither she nor Gwen had even known very well. Madame Roche mentioned that Gwen seemed more affected by this death than by the death of the Pope, a remark which elicited one of Gwen's 'long, frank, challenging' bursts of laughter. Of course she was: 'I knew her. I didn't know the Pope at all. They'll soon find another Pope.'

Gwen's impatience with money had other repercussions. One day after Mass, Gwen and Louise Roche picked up their bread together from the baker's on the way home. 'Well, Mademoiselle,' said the baker, 'I haven't seen this picture you promised me arriving!' Surprised, Madame Roche looked at Gwen and saw her face stiffen, while she forced herself to reply vaguely that she had not had much time but had thought about it a lot. As they went on down the road, she said, 'oh! I'm so perverse, that poor woman thinks she's doing me such a good turn, asking me to sell her a picture, I daren't disillusion her because she's doing it to please me. I'll have to do one for her . . . and I just have so little free time . . . I can see she's really fed up with me, but she doesn't want to give up on the idea, for fear of hurting me.' The next day, Madame Roche went back to the baker's by herself, and asked her how much she was thinking of paying Mlle John for the painting. 'Oh, I don't know, paintings are so dear! Maybe a hundred francs! I might even go up to a hundred and fifty. That little picture I've got in my dining room, you know the one, of a basket with flowers round it, was sixty francs.' 'That's what I thought, Madame. Did you know that Mlle John sells her paintings for more than a thousand francs?' 'More than a thousand francs! She must be so rich!'

She did not produce as many paintings as the baker did loaves, said Madame Roche. The baker thought that had nothing to do with it. 'A thousand francs . . . I'd be better off not saying anything else, no, certainly not, I don't think I'll broach the subject again.' Proud of her success, Madame Roche went off to tell Gwen, who kissed her on both cheeks: 'What a favour you've done me!' Delighted, she came round again later the same day and thanked her all over again. 'And that was the story,' said Madame Roche, 'of how the baker of Meudon never came to acquire a painting by Gwen John.'[20]

It was becoming clear that in the rue Babie she had found her natural home. The stories are all of goodwill, kindness, empathy with all creatures. Her extreme sensitivity and concern for her cats, her little canary, the snails, was part of her uniqueness, and in a sense, an aspect of her wildness. Once she moved to the rue Babie, this side of her became more apparent; she was also in a position to indulge it more. One day Madame Roche suddenly noticed an enormous cage in the garden of number 8; Gwen, from a close vantage point, was watching it anxiously. What was the point of the cage? asked Madame Roche: to catch birds, obviously, but why? Gwen now began to laugh, and begged her not to tell anyone as they would all make fun of her. She had seen Madame C—'s blackbird tragically trapped in its cage all day and bought it to set it free, but now it would not go. She had paid 900 francs for it because it sang, and she thought it sometimes talked as well. 'Nine hundred francs? My poor dear, you've been robbed!' 'I know,' said Gwen, 'that's why I don't want anyone around here to know about it. It's been out once but it just came straight back. I'm worried about the cats, but perhaps in the end it will be glad of its freedom.' It was, in the end, but in the meantime Madame Roche decided it was like human beings, it needed some practice before it learned to value its freedom. About dogs, Gwen seemed to feel the opposite. She found a stray, which she brought to number 8 and shut in the garden until, Louise Roche commented, it 'resumed its life as a vagabond'. Gwen was furious about this, and put up notices all over Meudon appealing for it to be brought back. No dog returned. But her notices were not ignored: the Inspector of Taxes saw one of them and made a note of the address, but finding that no. 8 appeared to be uninhabited, he put a dog tax on number 6 instead. For several years, Monsieur and Madame Roche had to keep making claims to prove they had never kept a dog, to Gwen's great amusement.

The spring of 1929 was wet, and despite her pleasure in her new surroundings she was not sleeping well. Worried she might oversleep and miss Mass, she decided to spend the night in the other building at 8 rue Babie, the wooden cabin a few metres square, really no more than a shed, which she sometimes used as a studio when there was too much sun on the Hangar. The cold and rain woke her in the morning because the cabin had no door. Louise Roche was shocked when she realised what she had done, but she knew that Gwen was essentially fiery, and could see that her advice in the matter would have had no impact at all. On such episodes, Gwen's reputation of reclusiveness and self-neglect is founded. It is unlikely there was much in the way of cooking facilities in the Hangar, and it was ferociously cold in winter. But it meant that in the summer, despite some cold and rainy nights, she could be elemental. This was the woman who, in 1903 when women were still chaperoned, walked from Bordeaux to Toulouse, hurled herself off rocks into deep waters, made love on the floor of Rodin's studio. Now, as she got older, she would sometimes sleep in the forest at Meudon when she was too tired after a day of walking and drawing to go home. But she was beginning to be troubled by stomach pains and she seems to have had recurrent glandular problems. She doesn't appear ever to have consulted a doctor and she craved fresh air. She spent her last years in the glorious surroundings of the rue Babie, sleeping in the little wooden shed some nights exposed to the elements, with her tall acacia trees, her wild garden, her cats running free.

There was no domesticating her now. She was still painting Bridget Bishop's portrait, but it went on giving her trouble – 'does the hand not being finished upset the whole?' Louise asked her, in June 1929. She invited Gwen to stay with her at Fyfield Manor, near Marlborough, but said she presumed she would 'rather die than stay in a conventional home'.[21] The *grippe* had kept Gwen in Meudon that spring, so that by mid-May she had begun to feel as if she had not seen Paris for quite some time. She was making new drawings of the congregation in the church, drawing girls taking their first Communion and having trouble with one particular child, whose face she could not seem to capture. She spent hours at a time in church, while the little girls took their retreat, almost without pausing to eat, trying to get the profile. Her persistence was unflagging; she worked until she was exhausted: it had to be right. One day, Louise Roche remembered, a huge lorry arrived at the rue Babie to collect a painting for an exhibition. At the last moment, Gwen decided that the bottom of the painting needed to be re-done, so the driver waited for several hours in the street, on strict instructions to collect the painting that day, while she made the necessary adjustment. Madame Roche was quick to deduce from this not only Gwen's perfectionism but her stature as a painter; but she also noticed that the sales of her paintings did not seem to interest her at all. She had received advice from America about what she should ask when she exhibited there but she told Madame Roche she thought it was too much. On the other hand, she was clearly proud to be counted among the great painters and wished to maintain her sense of her own standards.[22] (She was a natural pupil for André Lhote, who taught that indifferent painters paint in order to finish a picture; serious painters paint in order to learn more about how to paint.)

The association with Véra now cooled off, though from time to time Gwen would think about her again, and when she did it could still depress her. 'My life is like a long illness,' she wrote in her notebook, her mind on it all again.[23] But she finally decided she had understood Véra. 'I know why you don't like human love,' she told her: 'it's because it's more awkward than the love of Jesus.'[24] She told her she knew she had only learned English to please her mother and she knew how she hated speaking it. Véra had criticised her drawings, the way she dressed, her sentimentality.[25] She refused her gifts of flowers.[26] Ultimately, she became so unfriendly that Gwen decided she could not go on being undermined by her. Michael Holroyd has suggested that Véra had originally hoped to use Gwen to realise her thwarted ambition for nursing the poor.[27] Perhaps, then, she eventually felt a little stupid as well as embarrassed by the attentions of this vulnerable but shrewd and in fact rather powerful person – 'a great lady, in a way', as Jeanne had remarked to Quinn.

Gwen wrote to Tom Burns, the friend of Augustus's son Henry, about Véra, telling him that Véra was apparently angry not to have been filled in on any gossip about Augustus. She said it had not occurred to her to do so, she had not thought Véra would be interested. She decided she had rumbled her: Véra was not in the least straightforward, despite all her pretences. 'Catholics arnt [*sic*] simple though they pretend they sometimes like simplicity.' She had obviously been a Catholic all her life, she was so devious; she also told 'millions of little lies', a skill, Gwen admitted, which had 'a certain charm for me . . .', but she ought to stop writing about her really, she told Tom: 'Letters are rather cowardly things sometimes, like throwing stones that can't be sent back to you (at once).'[28] Louise Roche remembered that Gwen seemed to be quite close to Véra for a while, but that the friendship had not appeared to last for very long. One day Gwen told her she was not seeing Véra any more, she was too authoritarian. Gwen finally dissolved their association in her own mind by writing a pastiche of a Catholic's defence, a kind of trial by jury before God, in which she and Véra find themselves in Purgatory together and Véra is hauled up before her Maker for being unkind to Gwen. She is told that it was He, God the Father, not the Mother Superior, who had brought them together on Earth, and that she should run along and find Mary and be nice to her, she would find her in the Salle Jeanne d'Arc, drawing the children at their catechism: 'Saint Pierre will show you the way. Goodbye.'[29] Eventually, during the early 1930s, Véra moved away from the neighbourhood.

From now on, Gwen began a regular correspondence with the Curé who had taken an interest in her work, Canon Piermé, who had been sent to the neighbouring chapter of the church, at Champigny-sur-Marne. She began to write to him there, appealing to him in her sadness and desolation and telling him how much she longed to see him. She suddenly felt deserted again. Véra was clearly never going to turn into the kind of intimate and muse she craved, and she had lost her confessor and confidant now that the Canon Piermé had gone from her. She was never going to warm to the Abbé Collins, and she yearned for love and attention. Before the Canon Piermé made his departure he appears to have taken advantage of her passionate need for demonstrative love. In a note dated 'Mai 24, 1929', she sent him directions through the forest:

> Cross the Place de l'Observatoire (coming out of the rue Jacques Minot), take the rue Capucines, then go up the first road on the left, which will take you into the forest. When you get to the lodge cottage at the entrance, take the path on the right. After you've walked for a few minutes, you can go under the copse (on your left there's a wall) and you'll see the bluebells, this is the best place to see them because there are never many people there.[30]

Gwen now began to write more openly and insistently to the Canon Piermé, addressing him routinely as 'My dear Master', echoing the way she had addressed Rodin, her '*cher Maître*'. The extent and intensity of this liaison now emerged. She told him he should not worry about the feelings she had confided, they were just the things women felt, 'at the base of all our suffering, all women, for always and always'. They had been on excursions together in the woods in Meudon and the forest near Champigny, where he lived. She had gone there by herself, hoping to see him, and got lost, finding herself in 'strange and beautiful paysages'. When he went on retreats he sent her postcards and letters of solace and affection, which he asked her to keep safely hidden. (They were as safe, she said, as if she had put them in a box and buried them in the garden.) Once, she took her letter to the *concierge de la Presbytère*, asking her to give it to him by hand (further echoes of her relationship with Rodin). She commented on his sermons, advising him that sometimes they were too long, which diminished their effect. Sometimes they moved her to tears: he wrote so well that his phrases stayed in her mind. He wrote encouraging her to reply, telling her not to worry about making mistakes in French, just to write. When she was working, she should think of herself as working for him. This was exactly what she wanted to hear, and she told him that as she worked, she thought partly of him, partly of Jesus. He was pleased she had a special name for him, but then he could not remember what it was, and asked her to remind him. 'Maître!' came the reply.[31]

She began to send him money. She had just been sent a cheque for £11 she told him once, she needed it to live on but when she got some more she would send it to him if she could. At Easter, she wrote assuring him that the whole business of money was simpler than he seemed to think. 'It's quite natural that I bring it to you and it's a shame I've hardly ever got any.' He would get more as soon as she had had her American exhibition but she was five weeks behind schedule with her paintings, so perhaps the dealer would lose patience. There were a lot of things he would have to be patient about, but she was his grateful, humble, obedient Mary – just as she had been for Rodin. She said she kissed his hands and feet in the name of Jesus; he told her Jesus was always with her. She told him not to be afraid she would tell anyone about them, she would not, even if she had anyone to tell; her reticence was a British trait – one did not talk frankly 'chez nous' – and it was also part of her character.[32] The Gervaises, she rather dangerously admitted, had known how upset she was when he went away, but then, so did everyone.

Old Monsieur Gervais died suddenly while he was taking care of his sick wife, which saddened Gwen as she had been very fond of him.[33] She wrote to tell Canon Piermé, who sent words of comfort, assuring her he would pray for her every day. He encouraged her to work hard at her painting, and urged her to read Saint Augustine and not to neglect her Communions. But he now asked her to destroy all his letters and even the envelopes – he was clearly afraid their assignations would be discovered. She was very upset by this request, which she ignored. She was passionate, even into her later years, but this rekindling of desire had a trying effect on her nerves. For years, with Rodin, expressions of ardent desire had involved spiritual understanding as well as physical desire, and the denial of it had been chronically distressing and exhausting. Now – though to a far lesser extent – she was being asked to practise denial over again (which is not to suggest that the canon's motives were pure, nor that he was not taking advantage of her).

Augustus was still, when he got the chance, surreptitiously protective. Gwen sent all her latest thoughts about painting to him and Dorelia, who replied that all her remarks were quite clear, and Augustus said he would follow her advice as soon as he could.[34] He had met Julia Quinn Anderson that autumn, and found her severe and frightening, which somehow got back to her (perhaps he told her himself). She wrote to tell Gwen how hurt she was – perhaps it was because of her prematurely grey hair, a 'great source of grief' to her, or her short-sightedness. (It probably had rather more to do with the cheque she had sent Gwen on 9 July, for 255 francs; a month later, at Gwen's request, she sent a further £20: about another 50 francs.) Thanks to Gwen, Mrs Anderson had established a mutually supportive relationship with the Mother Superior at the Convent, who was now the delighted recipient of her patronage.[35] She said she was sorry she had made the wrong impression on Augustus, and hoped he had by now revised his opinion of her. She would see the New York dealer as soon as she could, though a lot of the dealers were in Europe for the summer and would not be back until late August or early September. Gwen was to let her know when she could send paintings for the next exhibition, and how many she intended to send.[36] Augustus's son Edwin was intermittently in Paris, and he and Gwen were still on familiar terms. Occasionally there would be a falling-out or difference of opinion but for the most part they got on affably, meeting in the Dôme to discuss art and their respective domestic affairs. (Edwin preferred the Deux Magots – the chic, popular haunt of the literati – but

Gwen said the '2 maggots' was too expensive for her that winter.)[37]

On Christmas morning she wrote to Canon Piermé to wish him a Happy Christmas, telling him she had been to Midnight Mass and missed him. She missed him all the time, she told him, and sometimes she was at a loss to know what to do.[38] Her feelings for him were temporarily confused and magnified now that he had disappeared to Champigny, no doubt recalling the anguish she had felt a decade or so before over the priest she had told Jeanne about: uncannily, this was something of a repeat performance. But before long she seems to have stopped thinking about him. In her notebooks, in among her notes and drafts of letters, she made lots of small drawings – of the backs of members of the congregation in their tall hats; vases of flowers; a number of tiny sketches of a young girl holding a baby; hands holding flowers; hands holding a book; and repeated small pen and ink sketches of Bridget Bishop.[39] From now on, she would put down roots – idiosyncratic though they may have been – in the Hangar, safely bound by its new wall and surrounded by tall trees, jealously guarding her new space and her capacity to work as and when she needed to. Independence and solitude were the things she most needed. The rue Babie – with its lush, wild garden, the cats, the trees – provided both; and she would need them more and more.

By the New Year of 1930, work was beginning on the Hangar. The workmen came in to decorate it and make it more habitable, though it was still not really weatherproof. The weather was very cold, and Gwen had the flu again. Chloe sent regular consignments of Typhoo tea, deflecting all promises to pay back the money she had lent Gwen to pay for number 8 rue Babie: '*Of course* don't say or *think* any more about your land. If I was an outside person, unconcerned . . .' Gwen was still offering to send her 'little tiny paintings' instead of letters; Chloe was still tactfully resisting this, possibly because she thought that if Gwen started to send drawings she would stop sending news. By the summer, Chloe was wondering what the bill for the works undertaken on the Hangar would come to, and whether she could make a contribution.[40]

Ursula had promised to visit, and Gwen wanted her to meet Constance, though she had asked Constance, who had become an extremely close confidante, to be discreet with Ursula (perhaps Gwen had told her about the Canon Piermé, or her problems with Véra).[41] Ursula did visit briefly in June, though a day Gwen had planned around tea in the Avenue de l'Observatoire had to be cancelled because Ursula suddenly needed to dash back to attend to her husband, even though as Gwen reasonably pointed out, 'he has you always as it were'. She now wanted her to come back soon and 'finish' her visit. 'To cross [the Channel] is nothing now-a-days, it is so easy and not tiring and you could go straight back to your hotel.' The cancelled day threw her, she had been hoping to go back with Ursula on the boat and dine in one of the little restaurants on the riverside at Bas-Meudon, which were too expensive to justify sampling on her own.

Ursula's visits still meant explorations and pleasure. They also meant an opportunity to talk properly about painting. Gwen sent her a book about Rouault's work. Ursula admired Rouault and Chagall equally, which impressed Gwen because they were such different painters. She herself thought Chagall's work 'calm and natural au fond, though people can't always see that, because of his subjects and his fantasy', and was not surprised to know that Ursula had been so struck by his work that she had dreamt about him. She told her that Edwin had asked her if she thought Chagall was mad; when she said she thought Rouault 'the greatest painter of our day', he gave 'a snigger of contempt'. He went off to check this out at his Académie and came back saying he thought Rouault put everybody else in the shade at the exhibitions: 'Nearly always my opinions are met thus by Edwin – and in a few weeks after he comes to me with the same opinion as if newly discovered.' It was always Gwen who initiated the discussion, she told Ursula: 'he does not talk of his own accord. Boxing interests him more.' Ursula had met him, and told him she liked boxers. She was 'rather sorry' she had done that, said Gwen, who heartily disapproved of boxing (not least because it was a dangerous sport and she was concerned that Edwin might get hurt) but at least Ursula could now 'place' Edwin.[42]

Ursula did come back, so perhaps they did dine in one of the smart riverside restaurants at Bas-Meudon. On her way home she left presents in one of the *grands magasins* for Gwen to pick up, but she was not able to go to collect them immediately, because just after Ursula left 'a terrible event (!) arrived' and took up nearly all her time. Mrs Anderson had obviously done her stuff in New York, because Frederic Newlin Price, Director of the Ferargil Gallery, had sent his colleague Maynard Walker to Europe that summer; now suddenly Mr Walker asked to come and see Gwen, saying he hoped she would have plenty of pictures ready for the show of her work they were planning to hold in the Ferargil Gallery. Thrown into a panic, she played for time by telling him she would be away, and asking him to come to her studio in the rue Babie the following week. He set a date for ten days hence and she worked fiendishly, getting up at first light and working until dark. When he arrived he seemed pleased, she told Ursula, 'but he said it was not enough and I must send at least ten more . . . I have to send the first lot on 15 August and the second on 1 Nov.'[43] She realised American dealers proceeded by charm, but was nevertheless quite touched by Mr Walker, and he by her. His visit to the Hangar, he said, had been 'one of my memorable experiences in life . . . I came away with the feeling that if everything else disappointed me I should still be repaid for my long journey by that one brief hour in which I came to know more of you and your art . . . I thank you most sincerely for allowing me that privilege.' He reassured her that 'New York and America' would love her exquisite work, promising her that everyone at Ferargil would do 'all in their power to help you build your studio at Meudon.'[44]

In fact, Gwen was still finishing the drawings she had started in the rue Terre Neuve, of the view about to be ruined by the new buildings. When these were finally completed they did not spoil the vista as completely as she had feared, but she was still glad she had spent several months on the pictures instead of preparing as she should have been for the Ferargil show.[45] Meanwhile, in an impressive piece of politicking, she wrote to Mr Newlin Price himself: some months ago, she told him, she had sent him a drawing (a self-portrait) which had never been acknowledged. She had registered it and subsequently written to Mrs Anderson about it as it had been preying on her mind. Mrs Anderson had since made no mention of it so she was assuming it was 'all right, but I should be glad of a word from you all the same'. Would he, she asked, at the same time notify her as to his preferred month for holding her exhibition? 'I could wait till next Spring if you think that is the best time for exhibitions . . .'[46]

In this last decade of Gwen's life (the 1930s) she apparently more or less stopped worrying about money. It had never been her main concern, as Louise Roche had remarked, but at the same time she had never been blasé about financial concerns. Her financial responsibilities had underpinned her contract with Quinn and had very much determined her attitude towards his estate immediately after he died. The impossibility of buying the Château Vauclair had been a turning point in her attitude towards money and property, and the muddle over the purchase of Yew Tree Cottage when what she really needed was a garden in Meudon seems to have bothered her hardly at all: she simply went ahead and did what she needed to do. For a while, she was supported by Chloe's long loan; then in April 1930, the last surviving child of Thomas Smith (Gwen's maternal grandfather) died. Gwen's father (who of course knew nothing of the loan from Chloe) wrote to say that the income from their mother's estate was about to be apportioned. Gwen would receive a portion of the capital and some revenue from the auction of property, due to take place in October. He urged her to 'shun any investment of a speculative nature' and invest her shares in securities which would yield a regular income.[47] She received a cheque for £200 that November, and he told her she could expect a considerably larger sum after the property had been auctioned.

In the summer of 1930, Gwen went to Londerzeel in Belgium, to meet Chloe and Grilda who were there seeing the Rembrandts. She took Johnny, a small kitten wearing a pink bow, leaving all the other cats in Meudon with Madame Roche. Chloe and Grilda had been very keen for her to go with them to see all the galleries, but she stayed in Belgium for just two nights, feeling disrupted and disorientated by the trip. She left the kitten with Chloe, who took him to the Convent at Londerzeel, where the nuns adopted him. Back in Golders Green, Chloe sent tea, news and a copy of André Gide's *Dialogues*. She was still worried about Gwen and money. 'It seems dreadful that your shed has to be paid for just now, when you have not much left for yourself!'[48] She hoped Gwen's pictures would sell well in America, but anyway sent another small contribution towards the 'shed'.

In September 1930, Dorelia wrote from Fryern Court. 'Do you really want to buy that cottage because we can easily buy it if not. It seems such a lot of money for you to spend unless you are going to use it here.'[49] The garden was full of flowers and there was a lovely passion flower growing on the south wall. The taxes and bills had amounted to 'almost nothing'. That autumn, the Carnegie Institute sold one of Gwen's paintings (one of the *Girl in a Blue Dress* series). Dorelia sent her a cheque and the painting was shipped to America. Gwen now wanted to know how much she still owed on Yew Tree Cottage: not very much more than she had already paid, said Dorelia, but she did wish she would go there and take advantage of it. She invited her for Christmas at Fryern Court: most of the family would be there and they could get Fanny to vacate her cottage and invite Edwin over from

France.[50] But in fact, Gwen was already more in touch with the family than ever before. Through Tom Burns, she was also now corresponding with her nephew Henry, who put her in touch with Edith Nettleship, who was ill after an operation. Gwen now began to write to Edith, sending French newspapers and books.

Winter in the rue Babie, despite the recent redecoration of the Hangar, was no joke. Gwen had bronchitis, a congested eye, and digestive problems: even tea seemed to upset her and she began to worry that it might be harmful. She asked Chloe, who said she thought it could not possibly harm her. But she did worry about the cold, and sent her an eiderdown and two covers. Even in July, it was cold at night in the Hangar. 'I really think you ought to have it covered in *soon*,' Chloe advised her, 'and have it made as warm as you can for the winter. It seems *dreadful* you waking up shivering.' But Gwen did not want workmen in again, they would be endlessly distracting and she wanted to paint. 'I think anything is better than your being so cold,' persisted Chloe. She worried that Gwen kept getting ill and that the eye did not seem to improve. She was not sure she should be encouraging the idea of sleeping there at all once it got very cold, though it might be different, if it was boarded up. She urged Gwen to get the Hangar made weatherproof, offering to pay for the work herself, 'and *do* try to get some kind of lamp or stove to give a good heat'.[51] Meanwhile, she would try to find her a new coat for the winter.

Gwen was busy with her last known work in oils, a tiny painting of a woman in a high hat seated by a window.[52] She painted six virtually identical versions of this, one in oils and pencil, the other five in a mixture of oils and gouache. As usual, she first made lots of tiny drawings: on one sheet she did fifteen quick preparatory sketches, dating them 1931. She wrote to Frederic Newlin Price to assure him that she had eight works ready to send him but that she was busy with something new, with which she was making new discoveries. She was now working in very generalised forms, with abstract shapes. The woman's skirt merges, in a series of dry stripes, into the upholstery of the seat she is sitting on; the half-open book in her lap seems to emerge out of a fold in her skirt; her lower form is determined by the curve which outlines the seat and is echoed in her enormous curved, low-brimmed hat; her hands are curved like tiny petals or shells. The few broad, curved strokes which determine the rhythm of the painting suggest the woman's form; in stark contrast, the window is a roughly delineated oblong. The perspective of the painting is unorthodox: we see her in profile, but it is unclear precisely how the partially glimpsed chair sits in space. She seems too close to the window, juxtaposed with the chair rather than seated realistically on it. (It is essentially Post-Impressionist, slightly reminiscent in form of a Duncan Grant or a Vanessa Bell painting but the colours and mood are uniquely Gwen John.)

She still felt she was only now beginning to 'know more how to express what I wish to'.[53] She went on scribbling small sketches on hundreds of pages of Grands Magasins du Louvre paper, each blocked into tiny squares with a separate, minuscule drawing in pencil or pen and ink in each square, of trees; flowers; a child with a baby; a house in a garden. She was still experimenting with ways of generalising forms. Meanwhile, in New York, Frederic Newlin Price and his colleagues were determined to get their exhibition. Newlin Price himself wrote on 1 February 1931, an imploring letter in which you can almost hear his distraction: 'People are so disappointed about your exhibition. Please send us a few anyhow to show them – then the *show* can be made next year when you are ready. Please –'[54] When this did not work, Maynard Walker tried. 'We desire your pictures more than ever. We cannot be contented without putting on your show this year. Wouldn't it be possible for you to send us now all that are finished? We know it would be successful and we want very much to present you to America. It will give us great happiness if you can write and let us know that they are shipped.'[55]

She told them there were eight pictures at the shipper's, ready to be sent, but she was not sure how she could finish many more. In March, she suddenly had an idea: Mrs Anderson had mentioned that when she was in London she had seen some of Gwen's pictures, including a little nude in a frame she thought did not suit it, in the Warren Gallery. Chloe was sent off to investigate: perhaps Gwen thought that if she could extricate these pictures, they could be sent to New York. The search proved fruitless. The Warren Gallery's records detailed sixteen pictures but they had all been sent back by request to Augustus, and Dorelia had signed for them. They had probably been forgotten, said Chloe, but were doubtless safely in Mallord Street or at Fryern Court.

Julia Anderson now wanted to know if Gwen could persuade Augustus to grant permission to reprint his letters to Quinn. He had apparently said long before that he would as long as he could see in advance exactly what was to appear in print. She was bitterly disappointed that he now seemed to have changed his mind: could Gwen find a way of persuading him to reconsider?

Gwen had other things on her mind: it would turn out to be a sad and tiring spring. In February she had written to Edith Nettleship (Ida's cousin, who had brought up Ida's fifth child, Henry), asking her to send her a card with news. 'If you can say on it you are getting better you will make me happy.'[56] But soon Henry wrote on her behalf to say that Edith was dying. She had asked him to tell Gwen how very fond she was of her, and that she would write if only she could. She was being kept alive by her spirits, which were high. 'She wanted to put 10/- on the Derby!'[57] Henry thought she had worked so hard in her lifetime that for her, dying was happy, since it meant freedom, and complete rest from pain. She was failing, but still had enough energy to write limericks about the nurses. She was devout, and prayed a lot: 'I think her prayers saved a family from ruin – got them about £200.' Gwen was touched by this, and decided to go to England to see Edith before she died. She made arrangements for the cats, who all stayed behind, including the awful Valentine. Madame Roche looked after them, writing vividly to England with news of all their adventures. Valentine was lost, but then her *miaoulements discordants* began to emerge from the garage, whereupon Louise's son Alexandre had got in through the window and found her. Louise had fed the cats minced meat and bread and shopped for them at the market. She had also taken in the coal, tipped the coalmen and paid the gardener. (A card promptly arrived from England, thanking Alexandre.)[58]

When Gwen contacted Louise Roche again, it was to tell her that Edith had died. Louise comforted her with further news of the cats. All three were well, the little one – 'toujours espiègle et remuant (mischievous and restless)' – just wanted to eat and be stroked. The one she had nicknamed 'l'Invisible' was reassuringly ringing his bell in the grass at number 8, though he was nowhere to be seen. As for old Valentine, she had finally emerged from the garage and was now perching quietly on the boxes. All the cats had had a treat at the weekend, because Louise had sent the children to the butcher, with instructions to watch the meat minced in front of them and that half a pound would be 90 centimes. But the children, unaware that there was a horse butcher, had gone to the usual butcher, holding up the Sunday crowd while he prepared half a pound of best beef. Alexandre had been quite unfazed: he just said, 'Mlle John won't mind. Anyway it's Sunday, why shouldn't the poor things have a treat?' Gwen replied that actually she had been thinking of telling Madame Roche that Valentine usually had pâté de foie gras because she didn't have any teeth, but she thought Madame Roche would probably draw the line at that. Too right, said Madame Roche.[59]

It is unlikely that Gwen found time while she was in England to go to Yew Tree Cottage. As the summer approached she wrote to Winifred, asking her if she would like to take the children there. Her invitation, Winnie replied, had 'warmed me right down deep into the "cockles" of my heart', but she could not manage it just at the moment.[60] Perhaps Papa . . . But Edwin John was busy keeping his eye on the winding up of the Thomas Smith estate. On 14 March he sent Gwen two cheques, one for £730 and the other for £20. He notified the Trustees' solicitors and paid the cheques into Barclays Bank, but Gwen now wrote asking him to liberate £550 of her money. 'You have now received from the Estate £200 and £750 – out of which you have paid £200 to Dorelia,' he replied. 'Will you tell me what you propose doing with the balance of that £550 – after discharging the debt of £20, which you owe?' He advised her to invest the whole of her share in the estate, which would yield a significant income.[61] (She must eventually have persuaded him, because her estate at the time of her death was valued at £438 10s. 8d.) If £200 was left owing on Yew Tree Cottage, she must have repaid her debt to Chloe, at least in part.

In August, she went to Joigny to visit the Mother Superior and the nuns there. Gwen was a real 'amie de la Présentation', said the Mother Superior: she was still in touch with Mrs Anderson, who had been very thoughtful about the children at Joigny.[62] Gwen told the Mother all about her new studio and promised to draw it for her; she was full of admiration for the countryside at Joigny and she brought news of Monsieur and Madame Gervais and the Maritains. Perhaps she went straight on to Londerzeel, because she went there again in September to join Chloe, tempted by promises that she would see her little cat Johnny again (he had changed his name on entering the Convent – like a nun – and was now called Robinson Crusoe).[63]

When she got back to Paris, Gwen may have gone with Constance to some of Lhote's classes: she jotted down some notes which may have been taken from a lecture, dating them precisely and interspersing lists of 'Rules' with her own jottings:

Rules. The drawing is the complimentary [*sic*] of atmosphere.
Rule 2. The atmosphere is the motif & its complimentary seen at a distance.
Rule 3. The blacks is the drawing of the turning of the leaf of the drawing.

On 23 November 1931 she noted, 'Thoughts: Do no more "cogitations." Arrange pictures . . . The transformation of your sins your faults.' But increasingly, the detailed notes she made in her tiny black pocket notebooks were about deciding on subjects and working out tonal and formal relationships in specific drawings:

Dec. 1. 31.

Faded dew-berries
(The road. Brun vibert

Okers [*sic*] darkened with black
(turnings of the leaf – chrome greens
complimenter Sepia Hair
Dissacord : – ombre natur. [*sic*]

Rule 1 the drawing is the discord
Rule 2 The atmosphere is the notes seen at a distance.
Paint the atmosphere & its complimentary.[64]

The summer of 1931 had brought a clatter of news from Rhoda Symons: 'Gwen! Will this ever find you? What has become of you? Won't you send us a little word?'[65] She had been ill but was recovering, Arthur was 'marvellously well' and sent 'fervent admiration'. Perhaps this is why a few new sketches of Arthur Symons now turn up in the pocket notebooks; Gwen may have taken out her old sketches of him and made some new ones as a way of keeping him in mind. As 1931 drew to a close, Ruth Manson – with Rosamund and Rosamund's new daughter France, born the previous winter – set off for the Midi with Ida Brown. They invited Gwen to join them but she was not tempted. She had done an unusual amount of travelling already that year and she was obviously not particularly well. She wrote to Chloe asking her whether she thought she ought to make a will. Chloe said yes, she always thought of doing so herself whenever she was ill.[66] In England there was a specially devised form which had to be signed in the presence of two witnesses, neither of whom should be beneficiaries. But she thought it might be different in France because French laws were different. Gwen should ask a lawyer, priest or banker. The inheritance from the Thomas Smith estate had probably made her consider this; so, too, perhaps, had Edith Nettleship's death. In any event, she made no further mention of it, and for the time being no will was made.

22

For Dieppe

pour Dieppe

matin	St L	1.15
	Meudon	9.5
	Start at	10 to 9
Soir	St L	4h 54
	Meudon	3 25
	start at	10 past 3[1]

Gwen had seemed during the past few years to be working on a smaller and smaller scale, delicately and minutely, perfecting tiny watercolours drawings of plants and flowers and making quick, occasional sketches: of her Meudon neighbours; Saint Thérèse and her sister; a house between trees (at Joigny, or Lanvois); a woman with a baby – possibly Rosamund Manson and France.[2] she was settled, though cold and not particularly well, in the rue Babie and she loved its leafy seclusion. Works were under way on the Hangar to make it more weatherproof. There was plenty of interest in her work – she had potential purchasers in both America and England – but she worked steadily at her own pace, dealing with the cold, failing health and the need to be independent. Chloe regularly sent clothes, advice, money, tea. Thornton, now happily married to a woman he called 'Mum' (a not uncommon form of endearment from husband to wife at that time) sent warm, inventive accounts of his domestic life. The younger generation

– Edwin, Henry, Tom Burns – gravitated towards Gwen, and were welcomed, rebuffed, rebuked, and generally given robust attention. She grumbled about her neighbours, who interrupted her stories to tell their own; but she visited them when they were ill and gave them money and gifts when they needed them.

She read books about, and by, Cézanne and Gleizes, and studied their methods. She read Rilke, she read *Jude the Obscure*. She went on moving, little by little, towards a more abstract freedom and complexity. The tiny black notebook she kept during this time was filled with reflections, notes about new techniques and ideas drawn from Cézanne and Gleizes. The forms of her drawings were becoming increasingly suggestive, blocked in rather than described in line; and she was using stronger colours more subjectively. In one watercolour drawing of Meudon, she showed warm, lit windows, apparently at dusk, and a lake: the lake is a scintillating blue, and the whole drawing seems to reflect her deep love of the place.[3] She had by now moved right away from the draughtsmanship she had learned at the Slade. Fascinated by the theories of Cubism, she was moving steadily towards – even if she never completely attained – an abstract subjectivism. What she was striving after is perhaps most easily visible in her watercolour and gouache sketches of flowers and foliage, in which tonal complementaries are used to create the impression of movement in a glimpse. In her late oil paintings may be discerned the strength of character perceived by Augustus early on, sustained and now developed into a kind of monumentalism in her figures and a contrasting levity in her depictions of them in space. The early sense of inner depth remains, but in the late work it is more fluidly and suggestively realised. In her later years, moreover, she began to develop a less arduous attitude towards her work, painting and drawing for the moment rather than planning ahead. At Pentecost 1932 she recorded in her notebook the death of an unnamed kitten, but it was not the tragedy it would have been in her earlier years. Instead, she related it to her feelings about her own life and work. 'Don't think (as before) to work for years ahead – & the number possible – you work for one moment . . .'

She made notes, in a little pocket notebook from the Bon Marché, on her methods of working; they show her juxtaposing tones to suggest volume and contour:

Turning of the leaf Rouge
Indienne: – Russets – okers. [*sic*]

Complementary of Payn's grey: – ombre brule

complementary of Rouge Indienne: – vert lac

Complementary of Terre de Sienne : – nat. cassells earth.[4]

It is very moving to look at her simple, later watercolours of flowers in pots and to realise that the colour marks are composed of complex combinations of tones, and that the effect of simplicity is conjured by this controlled profusion of mathematically ordered colours. The form was developed from the object, the atmosphere was to be defined by geometrical faceting; space was to be firmly tied to the picture rectangle. Gleizes's theory of Cubism, echoing Cézanne's, was that the painter went round the object, as it were, 'adding up' its most important formal and structural features as disclosed by partial views, eventually constructing a total image. The effect of simultaneity was therefore both geometrically achieved and illusory, arrived at by the juxtaposition of parts: a construction of outlines blended into a formal structure which both had its own aesthetic value, and at the same time analytically described the object.[5] As Gwen had earlier noted to herself, 'the atmosphere can be done round'.[6]

She combined these experiments with the geometry of the picture plane and the construction of forms with her own, instinctive sense of fluidity of line. Her recent freer, more daring and more subjective use of line had been influenced by her fascination with Rouault and Chagall. The effect is limpid, watery, simple; with a hint of fun and a suggestion of wistfulness. The flowers in pots are at once resolved, harmonious; and moving towards something else, pushing out into new forms. Her late work represented an opening up – analagous in mood, if not subject matter with, say, Picasso in playful mode. In the work of her last years she resolved something, achieving a kind of artistic fecundity and an emphasis on organicism. Unlike the series of oil paintings she was working on in the late 1920s – of *Girl in a Blue Dress*, for instance – the late flower drawings reinvoke, in their notes and tones, the rocks and stones of Pembrokeshire, smudged and spotted with lichen; and the watery colours of its foliage and wild flowers.

The soft ochres and greens, the gentle earth tones – sienna, *rouge indienne*, cassells earth, burnt umber – are carried over into her street scenes, which celebrate secluded lanes and corners of Meudon.

She discovered new colours, which lent themselves to new ideas and enabled her to make new connections. In October 1932 she was trying out 'white rose' on two different subjects:

White rose : 1. communiant.
2. bouquet in spotted jug.

White rose called for mixes of green (made by mixing yellow and black), umber and vermilion; and the fully delineated subject then emerged out of the colour mixes:

communiant : –
The green is made with chrome yellow & black.
The white dress is umber nat.
The ground is green & burnt umber.
The carnations of this skeme [*sic*] is in the lake or a blue vermillion.

In a later note, the subject is not mentioned at all:

June 20
White Rose –
ombre nat. Nap. yel
fond ombre brule – green
mode of noir & chrome y.
shadows of Rose noir and ombre brule.

The word 'turning' occurs a number of times, suggesting again that she was focusing on the finest thread, the finest edge; a delicate suggestion of gentle movement and a way of invoking breadth and depth through the gentlest possible treatment of line. With this minuteness and fragility came rigour, discipline, effort:

Oct. 4. 32.

Method : – 1. The Turning
of heads the women
2. the climate
3. the bud
4. 3 Blobs.
5. drawing from the blob.[7]

In these last years in the rue Babie, Gwen worked with the immense rigour necessary to try out her newly acquired technical information, making tiny abstract colour drawings of the organic world around her, seeing in the minuscule cup of a bluebell tones of black, yellow, sienna and grey; and detecting shades of yellow, green and black in the newly discovered white rose.

In her final years she used only pencil and charcoal, watercolour and gouache. She stopped painting in oils, probably because she now lacked the necessary stamina. She never finished her portrait of Bridget Bishop. Despite constant gentle nudgings from Louise Bishop she never solved her problem with the hands, something she seems to have discussed with her nephew Henry, with whom she had also discussed Chagall ('. . . liked so much what you said,' he told her: 'Chagall, superbes, the great *difficulty* of the business, etc.'). The unfinished portrait obviously worried her a great deal. Perhaps Henry mentioned her difficulties with it to Augustus, because he 'Saw daddie . . . Told him re. the hands.'[8] If this finally defeated her, it was not from any diminishing interest in the demands of portraiture. On 13 March 1932 she recorded a feeling of complete, even religious commitment to the demands of her art:

The Book closed.
The New Life
God has taken me.
'To enter into Art as one enters into Religion.'

On the same page, she made careful notes on portraiture:

The making of the portrait : –

1. The strange form.
2. The pose and proportions
3. The atmosphere and notes
4. The finding of the forms (the sphere – the hair – the forehead, the cheek, the eye the nose, the mouth, the neck, the chin, the torso.
5. Blobbing.
6. the sculpting with the hands.[9]

These notes, too, reflect Gleizes's theories, and they translate into the work of oil painting the discoveries she had been making in her drawings. The search for 'strange form' (recalling Edgar Allan Poe) consists of close attention to the pose described in blocks and masses; the creation of atmosphere or mood through 'notes' – or infinitesimally delineated or graded tones – and the gradual 'realisation' of forms, which were to emerge out of, rather than determining, the process. The 'blobbing' meant quick, lightly smudged rather than graphically drawn marks; 'the sculpting with the hands' came last. Though she did not finish any oil paintings during these final years, she never definitively discarded the five she was still working on to send to New York. Instead she turned her attention to her work in watercolour and gouache, which still demanded control, self-discipline and sustained concentration. She told herself to stop being so foolishly distracted by people. She was to stop: '1. sitting before people listening to them in an idiotic way. 2. undergoing their influence – being what they expect – demande. 3. by fear flattering them 4. . . . valuing too much their signs of friendship . . . 5. Thinking too often of people.'[10]

She still saw her nephews whenever they were in Paris, though there appears to have been a temporary rift with Edwin, who wrote to Henry on 17 October 1932: 'Now kindly hear the real reason why she shunned my society (for shun it she certainly did) . . . I indulged in the horrible and degrading pursuit of boxing . . . Anyone who indulged in this bestial pastime seemed to her an appalling thing and to be hardly a fit person to converse with.'[11] But she clearly did not shun it for long, and later made him, with Thornton, joint executor and beneficiary of her will.

In 1932, the Canon Piermé died, leaving Gwen with new feelings of bereavement and spiritual despair. She turned to the Mother Superior of the Convent at Joigny, confiding her distress, though not the reason for it, and going to Joigny in August of that year looking for solace and consolation. She made several drawings of a little house – *Cottage behind a Wall*[12] – in sketches on Grands Magasins du Louvre paper and in a larger gouache drawing which may have been done at Joigny. 'Try to seek happiness by creating joy around you,' counselled the Mother. She reminded her of her first Communion ('How happy I was to lead you to the bon Dieu').[13]

'I want to ask you to remember always,' wrote her father from Tenby, 'that on my decease – you, Thornton, Augustus and Winifred will be entitled to my Estate in equal shares – for your respective lives – with remainder to the children.' He had been ill with severe bronchitis and confined to the house for a few weeks – a 'terrible ordeal for me to endure – being such a lover of outdoor life'.[14] He assumed Gwen had abandoned the idea of living at Yew Tree Cottage, but he hoped she would go back to England soon. Her thoughts now revolved around her work, and the people closest to her. She was unfailingly supportive of Angeline Lhuisset, who now had to live, she told Gwen, like a child: being looked after by her parents, with morphine and hot compresses, in constant fear of a further *crise*. What must you think of me, she asked Gwen – ill one moment, out catching fish, the next?[15] But Gwen understood the deceptive rhythms of serious illness. When Angeline was ill, she was extremely ill, vomiting every day and needing more operations on her stomach. (Her life became almost absurdly sad: her uncle, who lived in Meudon and visited her regularly taking news of Gwen, died the following year. Her brother had a road accident and injured his legs; her sister died, in the winter of 1934, at the age of thirty-five, leaving seven children, the eldest aged nineteen, the youngest aged seven. The following year the children's father died, and the children all had to be found homes.) Gwen wrote solicitously through all of this, sending news, solace, lottery tickets and gifts of money. People mattered, unless they were malicious, or gossips, or pretentious, or unreasonably demanding. If she could unobtrusively help them, she did. (If Angeline was the model for the painting of 'the convalescent' Gwen may have felt she had a particular debt to her.)

Chloe sent tea, news from England and silk stockings from the sales. She also sent a rubber sheet, probably for insulation against the cold and damp. 'Hope you have a good stove now and are keeping *warm* in the cold,' she was insisting in November 1932. 'Please tell me if you would like anything warm, woolly coats or *anything*, as they are cheaper in England, and I think it is so important to try and keep warm in winter.' She wanted to know if Gwen had plenty of blankets and offered a brown fur coat. She was still resisting all Gwen's attempts to pay back some of her loan. '*I must say again* that I do hope you won't think of sending me a cheque, it would be such a pity . . . I could not *bear* to take any from you when you will not really have very much and also it would be a *waste* . . .' : if she invested it she would lose a quarter of the interest in income tax.[16] Grilda continued to nag her to complete the weatherproofing on the Hangar, advising her to consider borrowing money from a building society, as people did in England.[17] In May, Ruth Manson arrived with Rosamund and the toddler France, who saw cats, flowers and stones which left a deep impression; when she got home she was still talking about the garden and the cat going up the steps. They invited Gwen to join them for the summer, promising that if she did she would be left in peace. At Christmas, she sent France a set of pink furniture for her doll's house. This was a success; her mother reported that she 'has a little doll she has put in the bed'.[18]

By the end of the year, everyone was still asking about the American exhibition. But then in January 1933, Dorelia wrote to ask whether she would like to have a show in London as Augustus's agents were anxious to have one, and Gwen had a lot of English admirers. There was also the continuing question of Yew Tree Cottage. Might she now consider selling it? They thought she would easily make back what she paid for it and the money might be useful to her. (This suggests that Gwen had paid in full for Yew Tree Cottage.)[19] But money, by now, did not seem to be much of an issue. She seemed to have become absent-minded about it: when the Mother Superior wrote in January 1933 to thank her for the news of another Meudon neighbour's death, she added that she had been sorry to have to trouble her for her annual gift to the convent of 500 francs. (By the following February Gwen had still not got round to cashing the cheque her father had sent her in December and he wanted to know what had become of it. To placate him, she sent him a letter from a child who lived at 28 rue Terre Neuve: 'bonjour mademoiselle Mary . . . orvoir mademoiselle Mary . . . Je vous remerssie de vos petite fleur mademoiselle Mary'.)[20]

In November, her nephew Edwin wanted her to meet him at the Dôme. But she was busy painting, Gwen said, and about to go into a *retrait*, which meant that 'I don't see anybody . . . till I've done some things (paintings). My "retrait" will last 1 or 2 months. It is to concentrate my mind on these things.'[21] She was still elusive the following summer, when Michel Salaman's son Michael was living in Paris for a while and wanted to visit her. She told him she could not receive him as she was about to go away for the next few months. She may have gone back to Joigny or to visit Ruth Manson, who was in the country for the autumn with Rosamund and France, and urging Gwen to join them: the corn was ripening and everything was beautiful, she should come before it was all over. Or perhaps she was 'away' on another *retrait*, wanting to remain undisturbed while she finished some work.

She sent five pictures to Dorelia for sale in England – *Girl in Grey with White Collar*, *Girl in Grey*, *Flower Picture*, *Little Girl* and *Girl with a Pinkish Brown Shawl*[22] – and told Chloe she was about to send £50 in part payment of her loan. Chloe still would not hear of it, she said Gwen must not think of sending anything unless she ever became '*quite rich*'. There was another £300, Gwen said, vaguely; Chloe was unclear where this was supposed to come from and adamant that she did not want it – 'Of course I would never think of having any of it, as I said a long time ago. *Please do not think any more of it.*'[23] She thought it would be much better if Gwen could use it to build a small house on the sunny side of her garden. She does not seem to have been much encouraged by news of impending new work on the Hangar: 'I am sure it would be far better for your health if you had a warm, comfortable house – with plenty of sun.' She had another, more immediately appealing idea. She had been in Sussex, near Newhaven and it had made her want to cross over to Dieppe 'as the sea was lovely and calm, and we wondered if you would have come there. But I thought the sea would not be calm for very long, and next day there was a wind and huge waves, I was glad I was not on the sea!'[24] Perhaps the idea of the wind and huge waves fired Gwen's imagination. She made a note of the train times on a slip of paper and tucked it inside the cover of her pocket notebook. She was becoming increasingly fragile. In the winter of 1935 she slipped on the ice, severely jarring her leg and left hand. Several months later they were still giving her trouble. She was left-handed, so she must have found it difficult, if not impossible, to draw. It was to Thornton that she confided her most serious worries about her health. He counselled *courage* and fortitude, and sent her encouragement and solace. He said it was poor health that made him despondent: when he felt fit he never felt low, but he reminded her that life was a test and the Johns were strong. 'All resistances are beneficial when we overcome them, and we get all our faculties for this from a long line of ancestors.'[25] But in October 1935 there was another reminder that life was fragile. A letter arrived from Mary Anderson with the news that Julia Quinn Anderson had died, quite suddenly and unexpectedly, of what they had thought was neuritis. The days of the Quinn connection were now, finally, over.

'*Less travaux ont commencé!*' Gwen reported excitedly to Ursula in July 1936 – 'That means they're putting boards to the hangar.'[26] It would all be completed by October, or perhaps even long before. Ursula came to Paris twice that year, once in the summer and again briefly in October. If she had not, Gwen told her, she would have 'gone on and on and never have anything done or even commenced' – she had needed the stimulus of her company. Ursula was still the major inspiration for her work; when she was in Paris they went to galleries, restaurants, shops. They talked about Ensor, Cézanne and Gleizes; they compared drawings and they went to two of André Lhote's classes together. She made notes, similar to the ones she had made before; this time possibly taken directly from Lhote's classes:

1. tones
2. finding of personal forms
3. drawing of per. forms in pencil for eye training
4. background painting (one side)
5. 1. hat or hair. per form – face, per-form
   blocked from hair – then drawn
   2. body per. form, hands per for.
   blocked from body, then drawn.
6. rest of body blocked in &
   rest of background blocked in.[27]

In other jottings, she seems to have been thinking more in terms of her own habitual methods and language:

Method
1. The colour of the light
2. The strange form

3. Blobbing twice –
4. The tones
5. The colours
6. Blobbing 3 times
7. Execution from the blobbing.[28]

She was still thinking about 'strange form' – capturing the essential strangeness or mystery implicit in presenting the human form in a spatial dimension. 'Blobbing 3 times' may suggest the deepening of the tone through several applications of the same brush without adding more pigment. 'Execution from the blobbing' implies that the form would begin to suggest itself from the first few marks, a method consistent with her earlier notes five and six, '5. 1. hat or hair. per form – face, per-form blocked from hair – then drawn 2. body per. form, hands per for. blocked from body, then drawn. 6. rest of body blocked in & rest of background blocked in.' The first note in the notebook (dated 'Nov 3 31') is about the creation of atmosphere: '*Atmosphere umber*.' She would then work with complementaries – the complementary of umber was 'bleu-black'; for the 'turning of the leaf of umber' she would need '1. burnt umber 2. okers' [*sic*].[29] Then she noted down the constituents of umber: Naples yellow; crimson lake; raw sienna; burnt sienna. If the atmosphere was to be 'Brun Vibert', the complementaries would include red ochres. Each possibility is noted, and all the surrounding details listed, sifted and alternatives suggested. It may be that, with failing health as well as an increasing interest in geometric relationships, she needed more than ever to get down in writing all the elements of the drawing she was mapping out in her mind's eye.

Ursula, arriving at the Hôtel le Royal in the Boulevard Raspail, was anxious to be reassured that Gwen was well. 'I have an idea that you are not. I think I dreamed that you were ill.' After they met, she sent no follow-up expressions of anxiety or caution about Gwen's health, so when they met at the Dôme Gwen must have obliged her, as requested, with an appearance of 'robust health'.[30] But she was nervous and slightly *distraite*, and she did write to Ursula afterwards to apologise for being over-sensitive. 'At the Dome you interrupted me and I couldn't say what I wanted to and I felt a sort of angoisse and showed it and you looked sorry as if it was your fault. It wasn't your fault, everybody does that from time to time . . .' She promised the *travaux* would be finished long before Ursula came back in October. In the meantime, she was sleeping in the garden when it was not raining. She had sat on the stone steps to draw a flower and caught 'an interior chill, a lot of pain & fever'.[31] This had been an annoying interruption because she was trying to finish twenty paintings by 11 September. Frederic Newlin Price still had not given up on the idea of an exhibition in New York. When it became clear that she was not going to manage this she sent a telegram to Augustus asking him to send some of her pictures from London, but they did not arrive in time. In the event, the representative sent by the gallery said she had not expected to take them all back with her, so Gwen now had until Christmas to send all twenty.

Somehow a picture of Gwen has grown up, in the years since her death, of a reclusive, solitary person who neglected herself, refused to eat and never exhibited her work. She was ill now – more seriously so than she realised – and since Quinn's death had lost any real sense that she had an appreciative public. But given her failing health and domestic constraints, she seems to have been remarkably vigorous. She told Thornton about her digestive problems but she does not seem to have seen a doctor. Louise Roche thought she began to neglect her health towards the end of her life. In a letter to Ursula, Gwen recommended malt: 'you get it in grains and grind it like coffee. You put it in cold water and let it boil two or three minutes. I make enough for three days to save time and just warm it up. You can drink it with a little milk like café au lait for your petit déjeuner and you will find that it sustains you very much.' Well, this was breakfast; she was not necessarily recommending it as a substitute for lunch, tea and dinner. It was not long since she had tried to persuade Ursula to come with her to one of the expensive restaurants on the riverside in Bas-Meudon, and the malt recipe sounds like an attempt at nutrition rather than avoidance of it. She seems to have done what she could to stay well. She also recommended to Ursula a form of massage: 'Press very firmly, not on temples but down sides of eyes, plutot . . .'[32]

Ursula's visit to Paris energised Gwen remarkably. Letters were exchanged between the Hôtel le Royal and the rue Babie and, after Ursula had left, between England and Meudon. When they went to Lhote's classes Gwen was immensely excited by what she learned from him. She wrote asking Ursula, now back in England, 'What do you think of Lhote's book? Should I get it? I thought I had it but it's *Gleizes*, the book I have – more cubist.' When she did get Lhote's book, she told Ursula it gave her joy. She hoped Ursula had a copy herself, if only for the beautiful reproductions, though she was shocked at his immodesty in including in it so many plates of his own paintings – 'one in colour too. I think it would have been better taste to have left them out.'[33] She also read Fierens's book on Ensor, which impressed her less, but she was interested in Ensor's work, which she went to see. She told Ursula she hoped there would be another exhibition soon, as she wanted her to be able to see the way he used colour. She particularly liked his macabre carnival masques – 'done in pure colours vermilion emerald green etc.'. She was also reading a book about Cézanne, which she offered to lend to Ursula but 'It is *very* precious to me so please send it back or bring it in Oct.'[34]

She discovered a new range of le Franc colours which she introduced to Ursula, telling her that the best way to remember colour tones was by association – 'it is a great help to have each connected with something. Did I put cinabre *claire* for the little ball holding the snowdrop petals? There are 3 cinabres.' Her descriptions of colours are quite lovely: 'Rouge Phenicien is the colour of what we called wild geranium the stems are dark crimson the leaves seem dipped in pale crimson just now the rest of the leaves are somewhat Anglias. Earlier in the summer the leaves are emerald green all over.' Her responses to colour are emotional – 'Rose Erythrine (le Franc) is a very beautiful & brilliant Rose.' Sometimes she simply notes them down for Ursula – 'Laque geranium – fugace'; 'Rouge *rubis*' – colour becomes holistic, tactile, even synaesthetic. At other times, she is merely practical. '4 Anglais is the green on the tubs by your hotel (le Franc)'; 'Ocre [*sic*] jaune *demi brule* is useful to one'; 'Cinabre vert is the green ball holding the snowdrop petals'; 'Vermilion Français is warmer than v. ecartat . . .'[35]

When Ursula went back to England they sent each other drawings for criticism and advice, and Gwen told her she should not be so concerned to make a beautiful drawing that she forgot everything Lhote had taught them about tones, the 'passages' from dark to light and colour contrasts. 'I learnt so much at those two visits,' she told her, 'I didn't know how much till now.' He clarified things she had discovered for herself: 'For instance I said a cat & man it's the same thing it's an affair of volumes. That's saying the same thing as L'Hote [*sic*] said when he said the object is of no importance'[36] – he was recommending a complete departure from representation towards the depiction of the object as an equivalent for the artist's sensation. She was very clear about precisely what she had taken from Lhote's teaching: in the first class, 'that there must be contrasts & "le passage" & a broad way of seeing the tones, no little paquets – "pas de petits paquets" as the students made'. In the second class, she admired 'his big picture of a girl & a tea table & a green curtain'. She felt she had not really appreciated until then how good an artist he was. Everything else she had learned, she generously claimed, had been from Ursula. She just wanted, now, to get on and '"realize" my little paintings'. She took 'realize', she said, wittily, from Cézanne; 'I think *finish* would be a better word in my case.' But she was eager to learn more from Lhote. 'Ill or well I shall go to L'Hote's in Oct,' she resolved, in August 1936.[37] She was still trying to finish enough paintings to send to Frederic Newlin Price, but she dreamt of fresh air, and the sea.

In January 1937 her father, by now turned ninety, sent her a newspaper article about the National Museum of Wales' purchase of *Girl in a Blue Dress* – 'Art of Miss Gwen John: Special Exhibit at National Museum.' The article, typically, focused on Gwen's 'deliberately restricted range of subjects' rather than on her technical experimentation and achievements.[38] Augustus was in Jamaica; before leaving he and Dorelia had again suggested to Gwen that she sell Yew Tree Cottage.[39] But there was too much to think about, and Gwen was not well. She wanted to get to the sea. Michael Salaman still wanted to meet her. She was not in retreat, she told him, merely not very well, she had the *grippe*, 'the real-fever etc.' and was holding her letter out in the wind before sending it to get rid of germs.[40] Still, she told only Thornton the extent of her worries about her health. He assured her the secret would be theirs, but asked her to keep him informed: 'I think secrecy is a valuable aid and force. It was quite right for you not to tell me whether you had recovered the use of your wrist. But secrecy can be carried to a restriction of intercourse. If I get a glimpse I can build up a mental picture.' He told her he had had similar problems, but had found a miracle cure: linseed. It had a spectacular effect on bowel and stomach problems and he recommended it to everyone, whether they needed it or not. If he had known of it years ago the whole course of his life might have been different. 'Upon such small things does life and success depend.' (He recommended it 'whole and dry' with no additives, and told her it was also called *flaz* and *lin* in French; he also assured her that her secret would be safe from 'the old man, who has kept many a secret from us to our mutual benefit':[41] she does not appear to have probed this.)

This is the clearest evidence we have of the serious illness which now caused Gwen's health gradually to deteriorate. Not even Chloe or Ursula realised how ill she was; perhaps she was reluctant to worry them and knew that Thornton would show concern but not panic (it is very unlikely, moreover, that even Gwen knew how ill she really was). All the life-lines still converged. Ursula sent a card from China, then one from Japan, and promised to send some Chinese drawings. Gwen, in turn, sent news from Paris: there was another Cézanne exhibition. She had already been once to the Musée d'Art Français Anciens and wanted to go several times, but she was finding it very painful to stand and walk. It may be that even though her wrist was not completely healed, her fall on the ice the previous winter was not the only reason for her problems: perhaps her intestinal problems now also made it difficult to get about. She assured Ursula, however, that the 'country suit' she had offered to send would be very useful: she obviously expected things to improve. In June, Maynard Walker contacted her again. He had now established his own gallery and wanted to come and visit her. He came to the Hangar, and wrote ecstatically from the Hôtel San Regis before he left, 'I am leaving Paris with the greatest feeling of peace and joy, I think the same spirit that emanates from your paintings is in that garden and surrounds you – I don't know whether you are religious or not but in any case you have a halo – I wish I might help in showing the world such paintings as yours.'[42] Gwen assumed she was still under an obligation to the Ferargil Gallery (where a Mr Sullivan had replaced Maynard Walker). This may have been why she showed Maynard Walker nothing she had done since he had visited her before.[43] But he did suggest that if this arrangement should fall through, perhaps she would be free to send work to him. (She must have warmed to him during his previous visit, otherwise, given her commitment to the Ferargil Gallery, she probably would not have welcomed him to the rue Babie.)

When she wrote to Angeline in January 1938 it was to explain that she had been ill for a long time but she thought she was now better.[44] She had shown Angeline's letter about her brother's orphaned children to another of their neighbours, Madame le Brun, and she now sent greetings from her, too: they were both glad the children would be taken care of. Gwen was still very much a part of life in Meudon, and her friends and neighbours still relied on her (her friend Monsieur Charre had a bad foot and had been unable to get to church because of it; he wrote her a note to say that if she could look in if she was passing it would give him great pleasure).[45] She still mattered in England, too. Dorelia's mother had just died, and her sister, Katie Lethbridge, wrote to thank her for her letter of sympathy, assuring her that there were still plenty of people in England who would like to see her and if she could see her way to visiting they would make sure her cats were well cared for.[46]

But now there was a great sadness. Edwin John died on 7 April 1927 after being seriously ill with bronchitis, leaving, Augustus thought, 'some £50,000' (a terrific sum in 1937) though there would be eroding death duties. Augustus broke the news. He had gone with his son Caspar to the funeral at Gumfreston, the tiny Pembrokeshire village where Edwin had still played the organ every Sunday, walking the mile and a half from Haverfordwest. No one was prepared for his death, even though Edwin was ninety-one. Only recently, Augustus said, he had received one of his little folded letters, 'written as usual from motives of economy on a half-sheet of notepaper', assuring him he was very well.[47] He had written to Gwen on 28 March – he had just been thinking it was about time to hear from her when her 'pretty card made its welcome appearance. Many thanks for it dear.' He thought he was making good progress. Walking was difficult but the doctor thought he was improving. He was banking on that, because 'walking exercize' was, as ever, his chief pleasure.[48]

A month later, Thornton filled her in with further details of their father's will. He was aware that death duties were high in England, but thought they were likely to be paid by the sale of property rather than out of income from the estate. Gwen sent him a book about religious revivals and asked him why he thought phenomena were usually only seen at meetings where people had gone expressly to see them. He said it was probably because they were 'emotionally prepared' for them (and that Hitler would one day be found to be 'the perfect example of the self-hypnotised person'). It was surely better to be governed by reason than by emotion; those who had made great decisions during the last few days had saved bloodshed and suffering on a tremendous scale. He sent news of Louise's baby, who was now walking. 'Mum' had been seriously ill, but had been saved by a chiropractor, which made him wonder if there was one in France whom Gwen could go to. He sent a quotation from one of Winnie's Christian Science newspapers: 'Bear in mind that his presence, his power, his peace are available for you at all times' – easy to remember, he pointed out, because of all the p's. He had been listening to Dr Clem Davis on the radio, and also sent 'something from Dr. Clem': 'He is like a tree planted by the rivers of water, which bringeth forth his fruit in season. His leaf also shall not wither, and whatsoever he doth shall prosper.' He wanted to know whether in her reading Gwen had ever come across the results of Tolstoy's search for 'the rejuvenating and ennobling elements that lie in the depths of the mind'.[49]

In England, Chloe offered to send some warm clothes for Christmas. She had not heard from Gwen for some time: she must have thought she was dead, said Gwen. No, said Chloe, but she had been afraid she was ill. She offered to send her a pink almond tree as they were lovely and bloomed so early, the leaves emerging later.[50] Ursula had been in Morocco, and sent evocative descriptions of towns surrounded by high walls, tall palm trees and people moving about silently in flowing white clothes. Back in England in June, she made up a large parcel of clothes for Gwen – suits, dresses, a *corselet*, blouses and a hat. She had made up the parcel ages ago, but only just discovered that it had not been sent. She sent it now, in obvious haste, but she did not forget what had always been the essential thing: 'I am very glad you are painting.'[51]

On 10 September 1939, Gwen made her will in Meudon with a local lawyer, Adrien Bachelez.[52] Then she went to Dieppe. Perhaps she was still thinking about Chloe's description of the wind on the sea; she may even have arranged to meet her there. Britain and France had just declared war on Germany so possibly she was anxious about that. Or she may have left in a state of confusion. She apparently took no luggage, but Augustus's story that she left instructions for the cats to be looked after is uncorroborated.[53] In May, Dorelia had proposed the sale of Yew Tree Cottage for what it had cost, £500. She wanted to buy it back so that Fanny Fletcher would have somewhere to live if anything happened to Dorelia and suggested paying Gwen £200 immediately and the rest in about a year, mentioning that it would help for tax purposes if they could declare it as a gift.[54] The cottage was duly contracted to be sold to Dorelia for the sum of £500 and she paid Gwen £200 that June. Her daughter Vivien had heard – from Edwin, presumably – that Gwen had not been well; when Dorelia wrote to say she hoped she was better, clearly nobody knew how ill she really was.

On 20 September Monsieur Jean Jousset, a Dieppe lawyer, wrote to Edwin. 'A few days ago, I was summoned to the hospital at Dieppe by Miss

Gwendolen Mary John, your aunt, who wished me to draw up her last will and testament and to give me various instructions.'[55] Her will established Edwin as her residuary legatee. She had bequeathed to him everything, including her property at Meudon, except for half of her current account at the Chase Bank, which she left *à titre particulier* to Thornton. The lawyer asked to be supplied with precise details of Gwen's civil status, which were unclear. She had collapsed in the street and been taken to the local hospital where, realising she was dying, she called for a lawyer to whom she gave her will and burial instructions. She died in the Hospice de Dieppe, aged sixty-three, at 8.30 on the morning of 18 September 1939.[56]

Her nephew Edwin went to the Hangar that September to wind up her affairs. Stacked up in the abandoned Hangar and shed were all her paintings and 'a mass of beautiful drawings' in different media: pencil, charcoal, gouache and watercolour, which he took back with him to show Augustus in London.[57] Augustus was deeply impressed and moved by these pictures, and he and Edwin began to make arrangements to exhibit Gwen's work. A number of galleries showed interest, and the Matthiesen Gallery in London was chosen to represent her estate. In 1940 Matthiesen held an exhibition of her paintings and drawings in the Wildenstein Gallery in Bond Street. Augustus, 'flummoxed by their beauty',[58] offered to pay for the pictures to be mounted and framed. Because of the war it was impossible to show more of her work for another six years.

Michael Holroyd has commented on the difficulty for Edwin of dealing with Gwen's affairs with Augustus attempting to mastermind responsibility. 'Edwin, as the executor and chief legatee, was in authority, . . . Augustus himself felt an instinctive protectiveness towards Gwen arising from their childhood days together.'[59] In 1946 Edwin gave Matthiesen permission to hold a large memorial exhibition of Gwen's paintings and drawings in London, and Augustus (who had written an article on Gwen for the *Burlington Magazine* in 1942) agreed to write a foreword to the catalogue. Augustus was unhappy with the catalogue and blamed Edwin, who was 'perplexed to know what it is that is expected of me'.[60] Augustus then had the idea of writing a memoir of Gwen, partly to make amends for the fact that 'I blame myself continually for having even appeared to be unkind to her at times . . .'[61] But he allowed that if there was anyone else able to write it, he would gratefully hand over the task. Romilly John's wife suggested herself, but this idea did not satisfy him. A proposition for a volume by Wyndham Lewis about both Gwen and Augustus came to nothing.

Augustus eventually wrote about Gwen in his memoirs, *Chiaroscuro* and *Finishing Touches*. There are inaccuracies in his accounts of her but his love and affection shine through. John Rothenstein recalled seeing him 'peer fixedly, almost obsessively, at pictures by Gwen as though he could discern in them his own temperament in reverse'.[62] Augustus always maintained that he and Gwen were 'not opposites but much the same really, but we took a different attitude'.[63] In his later years he still felt rueful, and was once heard lamenting that 'Fifty years after my death I shall be remembered as Gwen John's brother.'[64] She is remembered both as Augustus John's sister and as a substantial painter whose work is quite different from his. Her work is her memorial, her life was her own. She lived it uniquely, with dedication and daring. 'Thought:' she headed one of her many draft jottings to herself –

> 'You make your life
> let it be consciously, with *fearlessness*.'[65]

Abbreviations

MR	The Musée Rodin Archives, Hôtel Biron, Paris: *Extraits* and letters of Gwen John.*
NLW	The National Library of Wales, Department of Manuscripts and Records, Aberystwyth: Gwen John Papers.
NYPL, JQMC	The New York Public Library, Manuscripts and Archives Division, New York: The John Quinn Memorial Collection, Astor, Lenox and Tilden Foundations.
NYPL, Foster-Murphy Papers	The New York Public Library, Manuscripts and Archives Division, New York : The Foster-Murphy Papers, Astor, Lenox and Tilden Foundations.
Tate, TAM	The Tate Archives, London (Tate Archives Microfilm).

*The letters and other papers of Gwen John in the Musée Rodin Archive are uncatalogued and usually undated by Gwen John, except by day of the week. Thus the convention eg. 'MR, Jeudi soir' has been used to identify as precisely as possible her letters to Rodin held in the Musée Rodin Archive. All translations from the French are by the author.

Notes

PREFACE

1. NLW 22313D, ff. 112–14; NLW 23508D, f. 60–9 Louise Roche, unpublished 'Reminiscences of Gwen John'.
2. Auguste Rodin, *Rodin on Art and Artists* (in conversation with Paul Gsell) (New York, Dover Publications, 1983), p. 45.
3. NLW 22293C f. 43–7.
4. Gwen John to Edwin John, Nov. 1933. 'I don't see anybody . . . till I've done some things (paintings). My "retrait" will last 1 or 2 months. It is to concentrate my mind on these things.' By kind permission of Sara John.
5. Augustus John to Vivien White, quoted in Michael Holroyd, *Augustus John: The New Biography* (London, Chatto & Windus, 1996), p. 557.
6. Edwin John to Augustus John, quoted in Cecily Langdale, *Gwen John* (New Haven and London, Yale University Press, 1987), p. 130, note 1.
7. NLW 22312C, f. 67.
8 MR, Gwen John to Rodin, Lundi nuit.
9. Quoted in Matthiesen Ltd, *Gwen John* Memorial Exhibition Catalogue, Matthiesen Ltd, London, 1946, p. 7.

1 CHILDHOOD

1. Letter from Betty Cobb, 21 June 1966, Tenby Museum.
2. NLW 22288A, f. 13.
3. Michael Holroyd, *Augustus John: The New Biography* (London, Chatto & Windus, 1996), pp. 4–5.

4. Augustus John, *Chiaroscuro: Fragments of Autobiography* (London, Arrow, 1962; first published, Jonathan Cape, 1952), p. 14.
5. *Haverfordwest in Old Photographs*, collected by the Dyfed Cultural Services Department (Stroud, Alan Sutton, 1992), p. 9.
6. Ibid., pp. 9–16.
7. G. Douglas James, *The Town and County of Haverfordwest and its Story* (Haverfordwest, J.W. Hammond, 1958), pp. 9–12.
8. Ibid., p. 130.
9. Ibid., p. 112.
10. Ibid., p. 130.
11. Ibid., pp. 144–5.
12. J.W. Phillips and Fred Warren, *The History of Haverfordwest*, originally written by the late John Brown, revised and added to by J.W. Phillips and Fred Warren (Haverfordwest, LL. Brigstocke, 1914) p. 76.
13. W.D. Phillips, *Old Haverfordwest*, a reprint of articles which appeared in the *Pembroke County Guardian*, 1924–5, with added illustrations (Haverfordwest, J.W. Hammond & co., n.d.)
14. J.W. Phillips, *History of Haverfordwest*, p.76.
15. Ibid., p. 23.
16. Haverfordwest Public Library.
17. Ibid.
18. Holroyd, *Augustus John*, p. 10.
19. Letter from Betty Cobb, 21 June 1966, Tenby Museum.
20. *Figures in a Landscape*, Tenby Museum. Acquired from Hughes in 1984.
21. Holroyd, *Augustus John*, p. 10.
22. Ibid.
23. Ibid.
24. Augustus John, *Chiaroscuro*, p. 11.
25. Ibid., p. 18.
26. Alison Thomas, *Portraits of Women: Gwen John and her Forgotten Contemporaries* (Cambridge Polity Press, 1996; first published 1994), p. 71.
27. Tate, TAM 21C: NYPL, 20/22, Jeanne Robert Foster to John Quinn, 4 October 1920.
28. Augustus John, *Chiaroscuro*, p. 16.
29. Ibid., p. 18.
30. Holroyd, *Augustus John*, p. 5.
31. Ibid.
32. Augustus John, *Chiaroscuro*, p. 12.
33. Holroyd, *Augustus John*, p. 5.
34. Ibid., p. 6.
35. Augustus John, *Chiaroscuro*, p. 13.
36. Holroyd, *Augustus John*, p. 11; p. 632 note 17. 'The death certificate inaccurately gives her age as thirty-four.'

37. Letter from Betty Cobb, 21 June 1966, Tenby Museum.
38. NLW 22307C, f. 92.
39. Augustus John, *Chiaroscuro*, p. 11.
40. Holroyd, *Augustus John*, p. 7.
41. Augustus John, *Chiaroscuro*, pp. 28–9.
42. Tenby Museum.
43. Augustus John, *Chiaroscuro*, p. 26. [In his memoirs, Augustus incorrectly refers to *Memoirs of the Duc de Grammont*.]
44. Ibid., p. 22.
45. Holroyd, *Augustus John*, pp. 18–19.
46. Augustus John, *Chiaroscuro*, p. 27.
47. Ibid.
48. Tenby Museum.
49. *Landscape at Tenby, with Figures*, Tenby Museum; Cecily Langdale, *Gwen John* (New Haven and London, Yale University Press, 1987), p. 9; p. 133, no. 2.
50. Augustus John, *Chiaroscuro*, p. 216.
51. Ibid., pp. 28–9.
52. Holroyd, *Augustus John*, plates section between pp. 94 and 95.
53. Augustus John, *Chiaroscuro*, p. 43.
54. Holroyd, *Augustus John*, p. 14.
55. Thomas, *Portraits of Women*, p. 35.
56. See chapter 8, note 15 below.
57. NLW 22306D, ff. 22–3; NLW 23510D, no. 18.
58. *Winifred John in a Large Hat*, Cecily Langdale: *Gwen John*, p. 185, no. 159.
59. *Winifred John in a Flowered Hat*, Cecily Langdale : *Gwen John*, pp. 184–5, no. 160.
60. *Portrait of the Artist's Sister Winifred*, Cecily Langdale : *Gwen John*, p. 11, no. 6.
61. *Portrait of Winifred John*, Cecily Langdale : *Gwen John*, p. 185, no. 163.
62. Tenby Museum.
63. Augustus John, *Chiaroscuro*, p. 28.
64. NLW 22777D, ff. 148–9.
65. Holroyd, *Augustus John*, p. 15.
66. NLW 22312C, ff. 18–19.
67. Letter from Betty Cobb, 21 June 1966, Tenby Museum.

2 THE SLADE

1. University College London Library, Manuscripts and Rare Books, BA 27.
2 Alison Thomas, *Portraits of Women: Gwen John and her Forgotten Contemporaries* (Cambridge, Polity Press, 1996; first published 1994), p. 33.
3. Augustus John, *Chiaroscuro: Fragments of Autobiography* (London, Arrow, 1962; first published, Jonathan Cape, 1952), p. 43.

4. Ibid. pp. 25–6.
5. Ibid. p. 218; Augustus John, *Finishing Touches*, ed. D. George (London, The Readers' Union, 1966), pp. 79–81.
6. Thomas, *Portraits of Women*, p. 64.
7. Augustus John, *Chiaroscuro*, p. 43.
8. Thomas, *Portraits of Women*, p. 35.
9. Ibid., p. 21.
10. Ibid., p. 66.
11. Ibid., pp. 38–9; Michael Holroyd, *Augustus John: The New Biography* (London, Chatto & Windus, 1996), pp. 60–1.
12. UCL Library, Manuscripts and Rare Books, BA 27.
13. Thomas, *Portraits of Women*, p. 64; UCL Library, BA 27.
14. NLW 19645C, f. 6.
15. Malcolm Yorke, *Matthew Smith: His Life and Reputation* (London, Faber and Faber, 1997), p. 43.
16. Ibid., p. 31.
17. Ruth Butler, *Rodin: The Shape of Genius* (New Haven and London, Yale University Press, 1993), p. 552, note 12.
18. Augustus John, *Chiaroscuro*, p. 41; Augustus John, *Finishing Touches*, p. 91. (In his memoirs Augustus wrote 'Vesta Victoria'.)
19. *Portrait Group*, Cecily Langdale, *Gwen John* (New Haven and London, Yale University Press, 1987), p. 187, no. 168.
20. *Portrait of Winifred John*, Cecily Langdale, *Gwen John*, p. 186, no. 163.
21. Edna Waugh, *Gwen John*, in Thomas, *Portraits of Women*, plates section, pp. 148–9.
22. Augustus John, *Sister of Augustus John on a Day Bed*, Brighton Museum and Art Galleries, c. 1895.
23. Augustus John, *Chiaroscuro*, p. 46; Bruce Arnold; *Orpen: Mirror to an Age* (London, Jonathan Cape, 1981), p. 80.
24. Bruce Arnold, *Orpen: Mirror to an Age*, p. 80.
25. Yorke, *Matthew Smith*, p. 33.
26. Ibid., p. 37.
27. Ibid., p. 38.
28. Simon Watney, *English Post-Impressionism* (London, Cassell, 1908), p. 20.
29. Augustus John, *Chiaroscuro*, p. 37.
30. Yorke, *Matthew Smith*, p. 34.
31. Augustus John, *Chiaroscuro*, p. 36; Ibid.
32. *Self-Portrait*, National Portrait Gallery; Cecily Langdale, *Gwen John*, p. 16, no. 17.
33. *Self-Portrait in a Red Blouse*, Tate Gallery, London; Cecily Langdale, *Gwen John*, pp. 18; 135, no 9.
34. John Rothenstein, *Modern English Painters* (London, Eyre & Spottiswoode, 1952), p. 163.

35. Malcolm Yorke, *Matthew Smith*, p. 39.
36. Michael Holroyd, *Gwen John: Artist in Exile* (Anthony d'Offay exhibition catalogue, 1982), p. 2.
37. Michael Holroyd, *Augustus John: The New Biography* (London, Chatto & Windus, 1986), p. 37.
38. Yorke, *Matthew Smith*, p. 39.
39. Ibid., p. 36.
40. Thomas, *Portraits of Women*, p. 64.
41. *Portrait of Mrs. Atkinson*, Metropolitan Museum of New York, Cushing Bequest. With thanks to Tony Askin. Cf. Cecily Langdale, *Gwen John*, p. 6, no. 4.
42. Metropolitan Museum of New York. With thanks to Tony Askin.
43. Watney, *English Post-Impressionism*, p. 19.
44. Robin Spencer, *Whistler: The Masterworks* (London, Studio Editions, 1990), p. 14.
45. Tate exhibition guide to 'The Age of Rossetti, Burne-Jones and Watts', October 1997–January 1998.

3 INTERIOR WITH FIGURES

1. Michael Holroyd, *Augustus John: The New Biography* (London, Chatto & Windus, 1996), pp. 73–4.
2. Ibid., p. 68.
3. Augustus John [AJ] Papers, NLW 22798B, ff. 16–17.
4. Ibid., ff. 18–19.
5. Ibid., ff. 16–17.
6. Ibid., ff. 18–19.
7. Ibid., ff. 20–1.
8. Ibid., ff. 22–4.
9. Ibid.
10. Ibid., f. 25.
11. *Interior with Figures*, Cecily Langdale, *Gwen John* (New Haven and London, York University Press, 1987), p. 10, no. 7.
12. Alicia Foster, 'She Shopped at the Bon Marché', *Women's Art* Magazine, 65, July/August 1995, pp. 10–14.
13. AJ Papers, NLW 22798B, f. 28.
14. Ibid., f. 30.
15. Robin Spencer, *Whistler: The Masterworks* (London, Studio Editions, 1990), pp. 40–1.
16. Ibid., p. 29.
17. Holroyd, *Augustus John*, p. 73.
18. Augustus John, *Chiaroscuro: Fragments of Autobiography* (Arrow, 1962; first published Jonathan Cape, 1952), p. 59.

19. Spencer, *Whistler*, pp. 22–3.
20. Ruth Butler, *Rodin: The Shape of Genius* (New Haven and London, Yale University Press, 1993), pp. 381–2, 394–6.
21. Holroyd, *Augustus John*, p. 72.
22. Ibid., pp. 70–4.
23. AJ Papers, NLW 22798B, f. 30.
24. Holroyd, *Augustus John*, pp. 73–4.

4 THE WAIF OF PIMLICO

1. NLW 14930C, f. 20.
2. Michael Holroyd, *Augustus John: The New Biography* (London, Chatto & Windus, 1986), pp. 70, 74.
3. Augustus John, *Finishing Touches*, ed. D. George (London, The Readers' Union, 1966), pp. 79–81.
4. NLW 14930C, f. 20.
5. Holroyd, *Augustus John*, pp. 80–1.
6. Ibid., p. 81.
7. Ibid., p. 85.
8. NLW 14930C, f. 29.
9. Holroyd, *Augustus John*, p. 87.
10. Ibid., pp. 88, 115.
11. Ibid., p. 89
12. Ibid., p. 115.
13. Cecily Langdale, *Gwen John* (New Haven and London, Yale University Press, 1987), p. 134, no. 6; p. 135, no. 9.
14. Holroyd, *Augustus John*, p. 112.
15. Cecily Langdale, *Gwen John*, p. 23, plate 24.
16. NLW 14930C, ff. 22–3.
17. *Self-Portrait in a Red Blouse*, Tate; Cecily Langdale, *Gwen John*, p. 18; p. 135, no. 9.
18. Frederick Brown, *Portrait of the Artist*, Ferens Art Gallery, Hull City Museums and Art Galleries; Cecily Langdale, *Gwen John*, p. 18, plate 18a.
19. NLW 14930C, ff. 22–3.
20. Cecily Langdale, *Gwen John*, pp. 135, no. 9.
21. Holroyd, *Augustus John*, p. 94.
22. Bruce Arnold, *Orpen: Mirror to an Age* (London, Jonathan Cape, 1981), p. 114.
23. NLW 21468D, ff. 13–14.
24. Holroyd, *Augustus John*, p. 135.
25. Ibid., p. 133.
26. Ibid., p. 135.

5 THE ROAD TO ROME

1. NLW 21468D, ff. 7–8.
2. Michael Holroyd, *Augustus John: The New Biography* (London, Chatto & Windus, 1996), p. 134.
3. NLW 22799D, f. 77.
4. Holroyd, *Augustus John*, p. 127.
5. Ibid., pp. 133–4.
6. Ibid., p. 136.
7. Ibid. Cf. *Gwen John* : exhibition catalogue, Arts Council, 1968, Introduction by Mary Taubman.
8. NLW 22307C, ff. 8–11.
9. Ibid., ff. 116–17.
10. Holroyd, *Augustus John*, p. 136.
11. NLW 21468D, ff 15–19.
12. Ibid., f. 20.
13. Ibid., ff. 19–20.
14. Ibid. ff. 2–6.
15. Holroyd, *Augustus John*, pp. 137–8.
16. NLW 22307C, ff. 19–20.
17. NLW 22311C, f. 135.
18. NLW 22307C, ff. 10–11.
19. NLW 22279B.
20. *The Student*, City of Manchester Art Gallery; Cecily Langdale, *Gwen John* (New Haven and London, Yale University Press, 1987), p. 20, no. 11.
21. Rainer Maria Rilke : 'Will I have expressed it before I leave . . .' from *French Poems*, trans. A. Poulin, Jr., in *Rilke* (London, Everyman, 1996), p. 75.
22. *Dorelia by Lamplight, at Toulouse*, Cecily Langdale, *Gwen John*, p. 19; p. 136, no. 10.
23. M. Chamot, *Country Life*, 19, June 1926, pp. 884–5.
24. John Rothenstein, *Modern English Painters* (London, Eyre & Spottiswoode, 1952), p. 167. (Rothenstein abbreviates the title to *Dorelia at Toulouse*.)
25. NLW 21468D, ff. 7–8.
26. Ibid.
27. Ibid., ff. 9–10.
28. Ibid., ff. 11–12.
29. NLW 22776D, ff. 24–5.
30. NLW 22305C, ff. 96–8.
31. Ibid.
32. Ibid.
33. NLW 22307C, ff. 12–16.
34. Ibid., f. 23.

35. See National Library of Wales: *Gwen John Papers, A Schedule of Papers Purchased in 1984 and 1987*, compiled by Ceridwen Lloyd – Morgan (The National Library of Wales, 1988), p. 18, note 1.
36. NLW 22789D, ff. 58–9.
37. NLW 22305C, ff. 5–6.
38. NLW 22789D, f. 60. Emphasis in the original.
39. NLW 22308C, f. 11.
40. NLW 22789D, f. 62.
41. Ibid.
42. Ibid.
43. Ibid., f. 63.
44. NLW 22307C, ff. 27–8.
45. Ibid., f. 26.

6 RODIN

1. MR, Gwen John to 'Julie' (ie Rodin), Mardi nuit.
2. MR, Vendredi. She usually earned 3 francs a session.
3. Rainer Maria Rilke, *Die Aufzeichnungen des Malte Laurids Brigge* (The Notebooks of Malte Laurids Brigge) (New York, Vintage, 1985), pp. 1–44.
4. National Museum of Wales Archive; Cecily Langdale, *Gwen John* (New Haven and London, Yale University Press, 1987), p. 189, no. 173.
5. MR, Lundi après-midi.
6. Rilke, *Notebooks*, pp. 1–44
7. MR, Lundi nuit.
8. Ibid.
9. NLW 22155B, ff. 1–2.
10. Frederic Grunfeld, *Rodin: A Biography* (Oxford, Oxford University Press, 1987), p. 478.
11. Ibid., p. 598.
12. Ibid., p. 478.
13. MR, Vendredi soir.
14. NLW 22155B, ff. 1–2.
15. NLW 21468D, ff. 13–14.
16. NLW 22155B, ff. 1–2.
17. NLW 21468D, f. 14.
18. MR, Jeudi soir.
19. MR, Dimanche matin.
20. Auguste Rodin, *Rodin on Art and Artists (Conversations with Paul Gsell)* (New York, Dover, 1983), p. 10.
21. Grunfeld, *Rodin*, p. 478.
22. MR, postcard, 2 August 1904.
23. Ruth Butler, *Rodin: The Shape of Genius* (New Haven and London, Yale

University Press, 1993), p. 28.

24. MR, postcard, 23 September 1904.
25. Rainer Maria Rilke, *Rodin* (Berlin, Julius Bard, 1903).
26. Rilke, *The Notebooks*, pp. 1–44.
27. Bernard Champigneulle, *Rodin* (London, Thames & Hudson, 1967), pp. 232, 239.
28. NLW 21468D, f. 15.
29. MR, n.d.
30. Rodin, *Rodin on Art and Artists*, pp. 21–2, 92–5.
31. MR, Samedi, six heures.
32. Ibid.
33. Puvis de Chavannes's 1867 sequence of variants (designed for an interior) depicted *History*; *Reminiscence*; *Imagination*; *Vigilance*. The original French title of *Reminiscence* was *Le Recueuillement* (meditation, contemplation, composure). Tate exhibition guide to 'The Age of Rossetti, Burne-Jones and Watts', October 1997–January 1998.
34. Rodin, *Rodin on Art and Artists*, p. 58.
35. MR, Samedi, six heures.
36. NLW 21468D, f. 15.
37. Butler, *Rodin*, p. 382.
38. Ibid., pp. 394–6.
39. Grunfeld, *Rodin* p. 522: quoting from Rodin, *Les Cathédrales de France* (Paris, 1914).
40. Rodin, *Rodin on Art and Artists*, p. 47.
41. Ibid., p. 80.
42. MR, Samedi soir.
43. Cecily Langdale: *Gwen John* (New Haven and London, Yale University Press, 1987), p. 31, no. 35.
44. MR, Samedi soir.
45. Butler, *Rodin*, p. 436.
46. Helen Pinet, *Rodin et ses Modèles* (Paris, Musée Rodin, 1990).
47. Butler, *Rodin*, p. 437.
48. Rodin, *Aquarelles et Dessins Érotiques* (Paris, Musée Rodin, 1996).
49. Butler, *Rodin*, p. 437.
50. Ibid., p. 440.
51. Ibid., pp. 440–1.
52. MR, 7 rue St Placide, Mardi soir.
53. Ibid.
54. MR, Vendredi nuit; Dimanche soir.
55. MR, Lundi soir.
56. MR, Mercredi.
57. MR, Jeudi matin.
58. MR, La nuit de lundi.

59. MR, Mardi soir.
60. MR, Jeudi soir.
61. MR, Mercredi soir.
62. Ibid.
63. MR, Dimanche matin.
64. MR, Mardi soir.
65. Ibid.
66. MR, Jeudi soir.
67. Ibid.
68. GJ referred often in her letters to the Bon Marché. See also Alicia Foster, 'She Shopped at the Bon Marché', *Women's Art* Magazine, 65, July/August 1995, pp. 10–14; also Michael B. Miller, *The Bon Marché: Bourgeois Culture and the Department Store, 1869–1920* (Princeton, Princeton University Press, 1981).
69. Rodin, *Rodin on Art and Artists* pp. 18–20; Grunfeld, *Rodin*, pp. 82–4.
70. MR, Lundi soir.
71. MR, Vendredi nuit.
72. MR. See Curators of the Musée Rodin, *Rodin, Whistler et la Muse* (Paris, Musée Rodin Publications, 1995), p. 144–7, nos D. 5079–85. With thanks to Claudie Judrin.
73. MR, Vendredi.
74. MR, Lundi nuit.
75. MR, n.d. Beginning missing, on squared paper.
76. MR, various.
77. MR, Mardi nuit.
78. Ibid.
79. MR, Lundi nuit.
80. Ibid.
81. MR, Jeudi soir.
82. MR, Vendredi matin.
83. Ibid.
84. MR, Mercredi soir.
85. Ibid.
86. MR, Dimanche.
87. Ibid.
88. Ibid.
89. MR, Samedi après-midi.
90. MR, Mercredi soir.
91. Butler, *Rodin*, pp. 48–9.
92. Ibid., pp. 49–50.
93. Ibid., pp. 51–4.
94. Ibid., p. 368.
95. MR, Mardi soir.

96. MR, Vendredi.
97. NLW 22310C.
98. MR, 7 rue St Placide, Lundi soir (various).
99. MR, Mardi nuit.
100. MR, Mardi soir. Runs on from Mercredi matin [*sic*].
101. MR, Lundi nuit.
102. MR, Jeudi soir.
103. MR, Mercredi nuit.
104. MR, Vendredi nuit.
105. Ibid.
106. MR, Vendredi soir, cf. Ottilie Roederstein, *Portrait* (Gwen John), Cecily Langdale, *Gwen John*, p. 30, no. 34.
107. NLW 21468D, ff. 20–2.
108. MR, Vendredi après-midi.
109. MR, Lundi soir.
110. Grunfeld, *Rodin*, pp. 598–9.
111. MR, Mardi soir.
112. MR, Mercredi soir.
113. MR, Mardi matin.
114. MR, Dimanche matin.
115. MR, Jeudi soir.
116. MR, Dimanche nuit.
117. Michael Holroyd, *Augustus John: The New Biography* (London, Chatto & Windus, 1996), p. 183.
118. Ibid., p. 193.
119. NLW 21468D, f. 16.
120. NLW 22798B, ff. 77–8.
121. NLW 22305C, f. 105.
122. NLW 222798B, f. 4.
123. NLW 22782D, ff. 84–5, 90–1.
124. NLW 222798B, f. 4.
125. MR, Dimanche soir.
126. NLW 22155B, ff. 5–6; cf. 22308C, f. 8.
127. Ibid., ff. 5–6.
128. *The Artist in her Room in Paris*, Cecily Langdale, *Gwen John*, p. 30; p. 139, no. 18. Cf. Sara John, 'Shades of Meaning: Gwen John (1876–1939)', *Country Life*, 12 August 1982, p. 462.
129. MR, Mardi soir.
130. Ibid.
131. Butler, *Rodin*, p. 377.
132. MR, Jeudi nuit.
133. Ibid.
134. MR, 7 rue St Placide, Jeudi soir.

135. MR, 7 rue St Placide, Dimanche.
136. Augustus John, *Chiaroscuro: Fragments of Autobiography* (London, Arrow, 1962; first published, Jonathan Cape, 1952, p. 218).
137. MR, Jeudi soir.
138. MR, Dimanche nuit.
139. MR, Dimanche soir.

7 LA CHAMBRE SUR LA COUR (7 RUE ST PLACIDE)

1. MR, Gwen John to Rodin, 7 rue St Placide, Lundi soir.
2. See Chapter 6 note 68, above.
3. MR, Vendredi soir.
4. MR, Mardi soir.
5. MR, Mardi après-midi.
6. MR, Vendredi soir.
7. MR, Lundi soir.
8. Ibid.
9. MR, 7 rue St Placide, Lundi soir.
10. NLW 22310C.
11. NLW 22155B, ff. 5–6.
12. MR, Vendredi soir.
13. MR, 7 rue St Placide, Dimanche.
14. MR, among loose 'Fragments'; n.d.
15. MR, Samedi.
16. MR, Vendredi soir.
17. MR, Dimanche.
18. MR, Vendredi soir.
19. MR, 7 rue St Placide, Samedi.
20. MR, Mercredi nuit.
21. MR, Jeudi soir.
22. MR, Dimanche soir.
23. NLW 22310C, f. 4.
24. MR, 7 rue St Placide, Vendredi soir.
25. Ibid.
26. MR, Samedi nuit.
27. MR, Vendredi.
28. Ruth Butler, *Rodin: The Shape of Genius* (New Haven and London, Yale University Press, 1993), pp. 376–8.
29. Rainer Maria Rilke, *Auguste Rodin* (Berlin, 1903).
30. Butler, *Rodin*, p. 375.
31. Rainer Maria Rilke, *Letters to a Young Poet* (New York, Norton, 1934; revised edn, 1993), p. 26.
32. Ibid., pp. 18–19.

33. Ibid., pp. 36–7.
34. Ibid., p. 48.
35. Ibid., p. 55.
36. Ibid., p. 39.
37. Ibid., p. 66.
38. MR, 7, rue St Placide, Lundi soir.
39. *La Chambre sur la Cour*, Cecily Langdale, *Gwen John* (New Haven and London, Yale University Press, 1987), p. 34, no. 15.
40. *A Lady Reading*, Tate Gallery; Cecily Langdale, *Gwen John*, p. 38, no. 24.
41. Rilke, *Letters to a Young Poet*, pp. 68–9. NLW 21468D, f. 22.
42. Ibid., pp. 68–9.
43. NLW 21468D, f. 38.
44. MR, Jeudi soir.
45. MR, 7 rue St Placide, Dimanche.
46. Ibid.
47. Ibid.
48. MR, 7 rue St. Placide, Lundi soir.
49. Ibid., Mercredi soir.
50. Ibid.
51. Ibid., Jeudi soir.
52. Ibid., Lundi soir.
53. Ibid., Dimanche soir.
54. Ibid., Mercredi soir.
55. Ibid.
56. MR, Mercredi.
57. MR, Dimanche.
58. Butler, *Rodin*, p. 377.
59. MR, Mercredi soir.
60. MR, Jeudi soir.
61. MR, 7 rue St Placide, Mardi soir.
62. Ibid.
63. MR, Lundi soir.
64. MR, Jeudi soir.
65. MR, Mardi soir.
66. MR, Le matin de mardi.
67. MR, 7 rue St Placide, Le soir de mercredi.
68. MR, le matin [*sic*].
69. MR, Mardi soir.
70. MR, Jeudi matin.
71. MR, Mardi soir.
72. NLW 22307C, f. 119.
73. Ibid.
74. Ibid., f. 125.

75. MR, Jeudi soir. Runs on from Mercredi soir.
76. MR, Mercredi soir.
77. MR, Dimanche. Runs on from Jeudi.
78. MR, Samedi matin.
79. Michael Holroyd, *Augustus John: The New Biography* (London, Chatto and Windus, 1996), p. 216.
80. Butler, *Rodin*, p. 389 ff.
81. Michael Holroyd, *Bernard Shaw* (London, Vintage, 1998), p. 353.
82. MR, Vendredi soir.
83. MR, Samedi, 3 heures.
84. MR, various.
85. MR, Vendredi soir.
86. Ibid.
87. MR, Dimanche matin; runs on to Dimanche soir.
88. MR, Jeudi matin.
89. Ibid.
90. Ibid.
91. Ibid.
92. Ibid.
93. MR, Mercredi soir.
94. NLW 22798B, ff. 4–5.
95. NLW 22788C, ff. 3–4.
96. MR, 7 rue St Placide, Mercredi soir.
97. MR, n.d., among a clutch of loose papers labelled (by a secretary or reader) 'Mary John Copies de textes divers'.

8 IDA

1. NLW 23549D, ff. 16–18.
2. MR, *Extraits*.
3. MR, Mardi soir.
4. NLW 22310C, f. 9.
5. MR, Lundi nuit.
6. MR, 7 rue St Placide, Samedi soir.
7. MR, Jeudi.
8. MR, Mercredi soir.
9. NLW 22310C, f. 11.
10. MR, Lundi soir.
11. MR, Jeudi soir.
12. MR, Lundi soir.
13. Michael Holroyd, *Augustus John: The New Biography* (London, Chatto & Windus, 1996), pp. 209–10.
14. MR, Mardi nuit. Runs on from 'Lundi soir'.

15. MR, 87, rue du Cherche-Midi au 4ieme porte a gauche.
16. MR, Jeudi soir. Runs on from Mardi.
17. MR, n.d.
18. *Woman Dressing*, Cecily Langdale: *Gwen John* (New Haven and London, Yale University Press, 1987), p. 37, no. 184.
19. NLW 22304C, f. 54.
20. Ibid.
21. MR, Jeudi soir.
22. Cecily Langdale, *Gwen John*, p. 137, no. 14.
23. NLW 22304C, ff. 54–6.
24. NLW 22279D, ff. 36–45.
25. NLW 23549C, ff. 16–18.

9 THE ARTIST'S ROOM (87 RUE DU CHERCHE-MIDI)

1. NLW 21468D, ff. 28–9.
2. NLW 22279D, ff. 46–8.
3. Ibid.
4. Michael Holroyd, *Augustus John: The New Biography* (London, Chatto & Windus, 1996), p. 235.
5. Ibid., p. 234.
6. MR, *Extraits* (various).
7. Alison Thomas, *Portraits of Women: Gwen John and her Forgotten Contemporaries* (Cambridge, Polity Press, 1996; first published 1994), p. 125.
8. MR, Dimanche soir.
9. *Self-Portrait*, Cecily Langdale, *Gwen John* (New Haven and London, Yale University Press, 1987), p. 35, no. 185.
10. MR, 87 rue du Cherche-Midi, Dimanche soir.
11. MR, St Cloud, Samedi soir.
12. MR, 3 rue Royale, St Cloud, Mercredi.
13. MR, Vendredi soir.
14. MR, 3 rue Royale, St Cloud.
15. MR, n.d. 'La continuation de la lettre apropos de la contesse.'
16. MR, Lundi nuit.
17. MR, 3 rue Royale, St Cloud, Mercredi.
18. MR, Jeudi soir.
19. MR, 87 rue du Cherche-Midi, Dimanche.
20. MR, n.d.; NLW 21468D, f. 33.
21. MR, n.d. (loose page, v. crumpled, large).
22. Ibid.
23. NLW 22310C, telegram, 8 September 1907.
24. Ibid., 14 September 1907.
25. MR n.d., beginning missing.

26. *Autoportrait à la Lettre*, MR, no. D7210; Cecily Langdale, *Gwen John*, frontispiece.
27. MR, Lundi 7 heures.
28. Frederic Grunfeld, *Rodin: A Biography* (Oxford, Oxford University Press, 1987), pp. 543–4. Rodin's gown is on display at the Villa des Brillants, Meudon.
29. *A Corner of the Artist's Room in Paris* (with open window), Sheffield City Art Galleries, Cecily Langdale, *Gwen John*, p. 30, no. 32; *A Corner of the Artist's Room in Paris* (with closed windows), Cecily Langdale, *Gwen John*, p. 138, no. 183.
30. NLW 21468D, f. 52v.
31. MR, Mardi soir.
32. MR, 'Christmas Day'.
33. NLW 21468D, f. 18.
34. Ibid.
35. Ibid.
36. Ibid., ff. 21–2.
37. Ibid., f. 18.
38. Ibid., ff. 2–3; MR, n.d. (beginning missing).
39. MR, 'la nuit'.
40. MR, Mardi soir.
41. MR, n.d.
42. NLW 21468D, ff. 28–9.
43. MR, Whistler Muse file.
44. Ruth Butler, *Rodin: The Shape of Genius* (New Haven & London, Yale University Press, 1993), p. 396, footnote 44.
45. Thomas, *Portraits of Women*, p. 127.
46. MR, Mardi soir.
47. NLW 22303C, f. 75.
48. Butler, *Rodin*, p. 371.
49. Ibid.
50. Ibid.
51. Ibid., p. 372.
52. *Correspondance de Rodin*, Vol. III (Paris, Editions du Musée Rodin, 1987), p. 24.
53. Ibid., p. 34.
54. Ibid., p. 64.
55. NLW 21468D, f. 22.
56. Cecily Langdale, *Gwen John*,, p. 138.
57. NLW 21468D, f. 25a–b.
58. NLW 22316C, f. 1.
59. NLW 22307C, ff. 119–23.
60. NLW 21468D, f. 25a–b.

61. Ibid., f. 26. Gabriel de Lavergne, vicomte de Guilleragues, *The Love Letters of a Portuguese Nun* (London, The Harvill Press, 1996; first published anonymously, 1669).
62. Rainer Maria Rilke, *The Notebooks of Malte Laretids Brigge* (New York, Vintage, 1985), p. 207.
63. NLW 21468D, ff 27–9.
64. Butler, *Rodin*, p. 459.
65. Ibid., p. 458.
66. MR, Samedi soir.
67. MR, Jeudi matin, 2 heures.
68. MR, Dimanche matin.
69. MR, Mardi soir.
70. NLW 22293C, f.7.
71. NLW 21468D, ff 30–3.
72. MR, Dimanche soir.
73. MR, Lundi matin.
74. MR, Samedi soir.
75. *Nude Girl*, Cecily Langdale, *Gwen John*, p. 39, no. 19.
76. *Girl with Bare Shoulders*, Cecily Langdale, *Gwen John*, p. 40, no. 20.
77. Wyndham Lewis, 'The Art of Gwen John', *The Listener*, 10 October 1946, p. 484. *Nude Girl* was presented in 1917 by the Contemporary Art Society to the Tate Gallery.
78. MR, Dimanche matin.

10 OSEZ! OSEZ!

1. NLW 21468D, f. 38.
2. MR, Gwen John to Rodin, Lundi soir.
3. NLW 22293C, f. 6.
4. Ibid., f. 12v.
5. Ruth Butler, *Rodin: The Shape of Genius* (New Haven and London, Yale University Press, 1993), pp. 459–61.
6. Ibid., pp. 461–2.
7. MR, Jeudi matin, 2 heures.
8. Archives of the National Museum of Wales, Cardiff, NMW A3517.
9. MR, Mercredi soir.
10. MR, Lundi soir.
11. NLW 22281B, f. 1v.
12. NLW 21468D, ff. 30–1.
13. Ibid., ff. 32–3.
14. *Head of a Young Woman*, Cecily Langdale, *Gwen John* (New Haven and London, Yale University Press, 1987), p. 192, no. 187.
15. *Woman Leaning on her Hand*, Cecily Langdale, *Gwen John*, p. 192, no. 188.

16. NLW 21468D, ff. 36–7.
17. Ibid.
18. Ibid.
19. NLW 21468D, f. 41.
20. MR, 6 rue de l'Ouest, Samedi soir.
21. Ibid., Mercredi matin.
22. Ibid., Vendredi matin.
23. MR, Monneville/Oise, Vendredi.
24. MR, 6 rue de l'Ouest, Mardi matin.
25. MR, Mercredi nuit, 8 heures.
26. MR, Jeudi soir.
27. Ibid.
28. NLW 21468D, f. 41.
29. MR, Dimanche soir.
30. MR, Vendredi soir.
31. MR, 6 rue de l'Ouest, Mercredi.
32. NLW 21468D, f. 38.
33. Ibid., ff. 52v–54.
34. Ibid., f. 41.
35. Ibid., f. 38.
36. Ibid.
37. Ibid.
38. NLW 21468D, f. 41.
39. Ibid., f. 45.
40. Ibid.
41. NLW 22309C, f. 98.
42. A *Woman Sewing*, Cecily Langdale, *Gwen John*, p. 39, no. 22.
43. Cecily Langdale, *Gwen John*, p. 38.
44. NLW 21468D, f. 52v.
45. Ibid.
46. *Chloe Boughton-Leigh*, Leeds City Art Galleries, Cecily Langdale, *Gwen John*, p. 31, no. 21. With thanks to Alex Robertson.
47. NYPL, JQMC, Box 23, reel A2, Gwen John to John Quinn, 9 March; 10 July; 12 August 1914.
48. NLW 22281B, quotation unattributed.
49. Ibid., f. 1.
50. Ibid., f. 2v.
51. Ibid., f. 1.
52. Ibid., f. 2.
53. NLW 22310C, ff. 76–110.
54. MR, Jeudi l'après-midi.
55. NLW 22310C, f. 102.
56. NLW 21468D, f. 38.

57. NLW 22294B.
58. *Ophelia : Portrait Imaginé*, Cecily Langdale, *Gwen John*, p. 32, no. 192.
59. *Étude pour 'Les Suppliantes'* Cecily Langdale, *Gwen John*, p. 32, no. 191.
60. Butler, *Rodin*, p. 184.
61. Ibid., p. 276.
62. NYPL, JQMC, Box 23, reel A2, Gwen John to John Quinn, 28 July 1910.
63. NLW 21468D, f. 53.
64. Ibid., ff. 59–60.
65. NLW 22309C, ff. 1–3.
66. *Girl Reading at the Window*, Museum of Modern Art, New York; Cecily Langdale, *Gwen John*, p. 38, no. 54.
67. NLW 21468D, f. 57.
68. MR, Whistler Muse file.

11 29 RUE TERRE NEUVE

1. NLW 22293C, f. 30.
2. NLW 21468D, ff. 53–5.
3. Musée d'Art et d'Histoire, Maison d'Armande Béjart, Meudon. See also Emile de Labedollière, *Histoire des environs du nouveau Paris: Histoire de Meudon* (Paris, Georges Barba, n.d.).
4. NLW 21468D, ff. 170–2.
5. The Archives of the National Museum of Wales, Cardiff; Cecily Langdale, *Gwen John* (New Haven and London, Yale Univesity Press, 1987), pp. 198–201, 224–5.
6. NLW 21468D, ff. 53–5.
7. MR (among letters relating to Rose Beuret), Dimanche soir.
8. NLW 22293C, f. 9.
9. NLW 22307C, f. 125.
10. NLW 22293C, f. 12v.
11. *The Convalescent* variants: Cecily Langdale, *Gwen John*, p. 161, no. 223; pp. 166–70, nos 111–20.
12. *A Lady Reading*, Cecily Langdale, *Gwen John*, p. 38, no. 24.
13. NLW 21468D, f. 63.
14. NYPL, JQMC, Box 23, reel A2, Gwen John to John Quinn, 22 August 1911.
15. NLW 22309C, f. 13.
16. NLW 21468D, f. 62-3.
17. Ibid., f. 63.
18. NLW 22293C, f. 20.
19. NLW 22280B, f. 16v (Youimoto Yashi is unidentified).
20. NLW 21468D, f. 63.
21. *Girl Reading at the Window*, Museum of Modern Art, New York; Cecily Langdale, *Gwen John*, p. 38, no. 25.

22. John Rothenstein, *Modern English Painters* (London, Eyre & Spottiswoode, 1952), p. 166.
23. NLW 21468D, ff. 63–5.
24. Ibid., f. 66.
25. NYPL, JQMC, Box 23, reel A2, Gwen John to John Quinn, 28 November 1911.
26. NLW 22281B, f. 3.
27. NLW 22295B, f. 5v.
28. NLW 22281B, f. 10.
29. NLW 21468D, f. 62.
30. NLW 22293C, f. 31.
31. Ibid.
32. NLW 22293C, f. 30.
33. Ibid.

12 THE NUN

1. NLW 21468D, f. 72.
2. MR, Lovell, Fenella, to Rodin, 20 February 1912.
3. NLW 23549D, f. 22.
4. NLW 22281B, f. 4v.
5. NLW 21468D, f. 68.
6. NLW 22293C, ff. 43–7.
7. Ibid., f. 34.
8. J.S.W., 'A Visit to Rodin', *Manchester Guardian*, 9 April 1912, p. 10 (MR, Whistler Muse file).
9. Ruth Butler, *Rodin: The Shape of Genius* (New Haven and London, Yale University Press, 1993), p. 468.
10. NLW 22303C, f. 106.
11. Ibid., ff. 110–21.
12. Butler, *Rodin*, p. 472.
13. NLW 21468D, f. 180.
14. Butler, *Rodin*, pp. 474–5.
15. NLW 22307C, f. 39.
16. MR, 1912, Lovell, Fenella, to Rodin, 9 July 1912; 17 July 1912.
17. NLW 22303C, f. 124.
18. NYPL, JQMC, Box 23, reel A2, Gwen John to John Quinn, 5 August 1912.
19. Ibid.
20. NLW 22309C, f. 4.
21. NYPL, JQMC, Box 23, reel A2, Gwen John to John Quinn, 5 August 1912.
22. Cecily Langdale, *Gwen John* (New Haven and London, Yale University Press, 1987), p. 128; NYPL, JQMC, Box 23, reel A2, Gwen John to John Quinn, 28 November 1911.

23. Tate, TAM, II–94, Gwen John to John Quinn, 838–1, 17 November 1912.
24. Tate, TAM 21C, 9/22, Jeanne Robert Foster to John Quinn, 31 October 1921. Cf. Chapter 17, note 36.
25. NLW 21468D, f. 72.
26. Ibid.
27. NLW 22293C, f. 133.
28. Ibid., ff. 43–7.
29. Ibid.
30. NLW 22307C, f. 40.
31. NYPL, JQMC, Box 23, reel A2, Gwen John to John Quinn, 25 January 1913.
32. Cecily Langdale, *Gwen John*, p. 70.
33. NYPL, JQMC, Box 23, reel A2, Gwen John to John Quinn, 24 January 1913.
34. NLW 22309C, f. 8.
35. Ibid., ff. 8–9.
36. NYPL, JQMC, Box 23, reel A2, Gwen John to John Quinn, 9 and 20 February 1913.
37. Ibid., Gwen John to John Quinn, 27 June.
38. Ibid., Gwen John to John Quinn 15 July 1913.
39. Ibid.
40. NLW 22309C, f. 10.
41. Cecily Langdale, *Gwen John*, pp. 163–4: Cecily Langdale has catalogued *A Woman in a Red Shawl* in 'Lost Pictures' (p. 182). She comments: 'Quinn probably never received the painting from the artist. No picture of its description appears in the Quinn estate catalogue or inventory. Although there is a group of paintings of a woman in a red shawl dating to the late 1910s or early 1920s [she lists four: pls 151; 227–9, nos 102–3] there is no known picture of 1913 or earlier which such a title would suit.'
42. NYPL, JQMC, Box 23, reel A2, Gwen John to John Quinn, 3 June 1916.
43. Tate, TAM 21C, Jeanne Robert Foster to John Quinn, 20/22, 4 October 1920. Cf. Chapter 16, note 54 below.
44. NLW 22309C, ff. 141–4.
45. NLW 22303C, f. 138.
46. Ibid., f. 148v–9.

13 WAR

1. NLW 22296D, f. 44.
2. NLW 22305C, f. 113.
3. *Study of a Woman* subsequently entitled *Chloe Boughton-Leigh*, Cecily Langdale, *Gwen John* (New Haven and London, Yale University Press, 1987), p. 31; p. 140, no. 21.
4. NLW 22304C, f. 57.
5. Ibid., f. 184.

6. Cecily Langdale, *Gwen John*, p. 142; Gwen John to John Quinn, 17 July 1924.
7. NYPL, Foster-Murphy Papers, Box 8, f. 476.
8. NLW 22309C, f. 20.
9. NLW 22305C, f. 115.
10. NLW 22155B, f. 9.
11. Ibid.
12. Ibid., f. 9v.
13. NLW 21468D, f. 76–8 [*sic*].
14. Ibid., ff. 78v–78, 77v [*sic*].
15. Cecily Langdale, *Gwen John*, p. 182.
16. NYPL, JQMC, Box 23, reel A2, Gwen John to John Quinn, 27 September 1914.
17. Ibid., 21 December 1914 (Jean Seaghan MacBride, b. 26 January, 1904).
18. NLW 22305C, f. 119.
19. Ibid., f. 118.
20. NLW 21468D, f. 80.
21. NLW 21468D, ff. 83–4.
22. NLW 22311D, f. 52.
23. NLW 22307C, ff. 47–9.
24. NLW 22310C.
25. Ruth Butler, *Rodin: The Shape of Genius* (New Haven and London, Yale University Press, 1993), pp. 492–3.
26. Ibid., p. 494, footnote 4.
27. Ibid., p. 492.
28. NYPL, JQMC, Box 23, reel A2, John Quinn to Gwen John, 4 February 1916.
29. NLW 22306D, f. 7v.
30. NLW 22305C, ff. 121–121v.
31. NLW 22309C, ff. 23–7.
32. Cecily Langdale, *Gwen John*, p. 61; pp. 150–1, nos 49–52.
33. *La Petite Modèle*, Cecily Langdale, *Gwen John*, p. 79, no. 62.
34. NLW 21468D, ff. 85–7.
35. NYPL, JQMC, Box 23, reel A2, Gwen John to John Quinn, 5 May 1915.
36. NYPL, JQMC, Box 27, Maud Gonne to John Quinn, 2 July 1915.
37. NYPL, JQMC, Box 23, reel A2, Gwen John to John Quinn, 5 May 1915.
38. NLW 22311D, ff. 54–66v.
39. NYPL, JQMC, Box 23, reel A2, Gwen John to John Quinn, 26 July 1915.
40. NLW 22296D, f. 27.
41. NLW 22307C, f. 126.
42. NLW 22309C, f. 52.
43. NYPL, JQMC, Box 23, reel A2, Gwen John to John Quinn, 12 February 1916.
44. Ibid., 15 February 1916.

45. NLW 22309C, f. 42.
46. The Metropolitan Museum of New York Archive, ref. no. 55 : 7.6. / 55/ 7.4. With thanks to Tony Askin.
47. NYPL, JQMC, Box 23, reel A2, Gwen John to John Quinn, 17 March 1916.
48. Ibid., 3 June 1916.
49. NLW 21468D, f. 131.
50. It is impossible to know how many of these drawings Gwen did before she lost interest in them, but twenty-four are listed in the Gregg inventory of the Quinn collection (Cecily Langdale, *Gwen John*, p. 203). Six or more were given to the Metropolitan Museum of New York by Frederic Newlin Price, owner of the Ferargil Gallery. (The Metropolitan Museum of New York Archive, ref. no. 55.17.16.) and three to the Museum of Modern Art, New York by Georgette Passedoit, a friend of Quinn's who was in Paris teaching blind men to read (NLW 22309C, f. 48).
51. *Girl in Blue*, Cecily Langdale, *Gwen John*, p. 78, no. 82.
52. *Portrait of a Girl, with Hands Clasped*, Cecily Langdale, *Gwen John*, p. 88; p. 154, no. 63. *Girl in Rose*, Cecily Langdale, *Gwen John*, p. 74; p. 154, no. 65.
53. NLW 22296D, f. 42.
54. Ibid., ff. 45–7.
55. NLW 22307C, f. 127.
56. NLW 21468D, f. 131.
57. NLW 22296D, f. 44.
58. NLW 21468D, f. 131.
59. NLW 22304C, f. 68.

14 17 NOVEMBER 1917

1. NLW 21468D, f. 95.
2. NLW 22293C, f. 76.
3. NLW 21468D, ff. 104–8.
4. Ruth Butler, *Rodin: The Shape of Genius* (New Haven and London, Yale University Press, 1993), pp. 508–10.
5. *Sunday Herald*, 8 January 1922 (MR, Whistler Muse file). Cf. also Curators of the Musée Rodin, *Rodin, Whistler et la Muse* (Paris, Musée Rodin, 1995).
6. Augustus John, *Chiaroscuro* (London, Arrow, 1962; first published, London, Jonathan Cape, 1952), p. 218.
7. NYPL, JQMC, Box 23, reel A2, John Quinn to Gwen John, 8 January 1917.
8. NLW 22309C, f. 60.
9. NLW 22284B, 6 October 1917.
10. NYPL, JQMC, Box 23, reel A2, John Quinn to Gwen John, 11 April 1917.
11. NLW 21468D, f. 93.
12. Ibid., f. 95.

13. NYPL, JQMC, Box 23, reel A2, Gwen John to John Quinn, 11 April 1917.
14. NLW 21468D, f. 95.
15. Ibid., f. 100.
16. NYPL, JQMC, Box 23, reel A2, Gwen John to John Quinn, 6 June 1917.
17. NLW 22309C, f. 66.
18. NYPL, JQMC, Box 27, Maud Gonne to John Quinn, 24 November 1916.
19. Ibid., John Quinn to Maud Gonne, 29 September 1916.
20. Ibid., Maud Gonne to John Quinn, received 6 December 1916.
21. NYPL, JQMC, Box 23, reel A2, Gwen John to John Quinn, 8 January 1917.
22. Ibid., Gwen John to John Quinn, 11 April 1917.
23. NYPL, JQMC, Box 27, John Quinn to Maud Gonne, 14 March 1917.
24. Ibid., 2 June 1917.
25. Ibid., Maud Gonne to John Quinn, 8 December 1917.
26. *Girl in a Blue Apron with a Cat on Her Lap,* Cecily Langdale, *Gwen John*, p. 156, no. 72.
27. *Young Woman Holding a Black Cat,* Cecily Langdale, *Gwen John*, p. 156, no. 73.
28. NLW 223042, ff. 70–3. Verhausen: unknown. Gwen may have meant Émile Verhaeren, one of the signatories to the subscription committee for Rodin's *The Thinker*. (See Frederic Grunfeld: *Rodin: A Biography* (Oxford, Oxford University Press, 1987) p. 503.)
29. NLW 21468D, f. 110.
30. NLW 22307C, f. 58.
31. NLW 21468D, f. 113.
32. Ibid.
33. NLW 22293C, ff. 80–85.
34. NLW 21468D, f. 115.
35. Ibid.
36. Ibid.
37. NYPL, JQMC, 24 October, Ezra Pound to John Quinn, received 11 November 1918.
38. NLW 21468D, f. 119.
39. NYPL, JQMC, cable 12 November 1918, John Quinn to Ezra Pound.
40. NLW 223100, ff. 68–71.
41. Cecily Langdale, *Gwen John*, p. 152–3.
42. NLW 21468D, ff. 123v–122v. [*sic*]
43. Ibid.
44. NYPL, JQMC, Box 23, reel A2, Gwen John to John Quinn, 13 October 1918.
45. NLW 22309C, f. 75.
46. NYPL, JQMC, Box 23, reel A2, John Quinn to Gwen John, February 1919.

47. *Little Girl with a Large Hat and Straw-Coloured Hair*, Cecily Langdale, *Gwen John*, p. 218, no. 295.
48. *Le Petit Garcon Sentimental*, Cecily Langdale, *Gwen John*, p. 211, no. 266; *The Little Boy*, Cecily Langdale, *Gwen John*, p. 212, no. 270.
49. *A Rag Doll*, Cecily Langdale, *Gwen John*, p. 212, no. 271.
50. *Elisabeth de Willman Grabowska*, Cecily Langdale, *Gwen John*, p. 213, no. 273.
51. NLW 22305C, ff. 123–4.
52. NYPL, JQMC, Box 23, reel A2, Gwen John to John Quinn, 12 November 1918.

15 THE CHÂTEAU VAUCLAIR

1. NLW 22393C, f. 88.
2. NLW 22309C, ff. 123–4.
3. NLW 22300B, f. 8.
4. With very grateful thanks to M. and Mme. Burguier de Gérmond. See also André Guigot, *Pléneuf-Val-André depuis la Nuit des Temps* (Pléneuf-Val-André, André Guigot, 1985), p. 62.
5. NLW 22393C, f. 88.
6. Ibid.
7. NYPL, JQMC, Box 23, reel A2, Gwen John to John Quinn, 22 February 1919.
8. NLW 22296D, f. 69.
9. Ibid., ff. 62–3, 93.
10. NYPL, JQMC, Box 23, reel A2, Gwen John to John Quinn, 25 April 1919.
11. Ibid.
12. Ibid., 18 June / 28 June / 27 September.
13. Cecily Langdale, *Gwen John*, p. 117.
14. *Girl with Cat*, Metropolitan Museum of New York, with thanks to Tony Askin; Cecily Langdale, *Gwen John*, p. 72; p. 156, no. 70.
15. NLW 22303C, ff. 176–7.
16. NLW 22305C, f. 127.
17. NLW 22306D, ff. 22–3.
18. NLW 22311C, f. 122.
19. NYPL, JQMC, Box 23, reel A2, Gwen John to John Quinn, 27 September 1919.
20. Ibid.
21. NLW 22305C, f. 129.
22. NLW 22304C, f. 77.
23. NLW 22303C, ff. 176–7.
24. Ibid., ff. 178–81.

25. NLW 22311C, ff. 21–3.
26. It is not known which variant of *L'Enfant à la Poupée* Gwen John gave to Arthur Symons. See Cecily Langdale, *Gwen John*, pp. 68, 212–13, nos. 272–4, for other variants.
27. NLW 22304C, f. 79.

16 JEANNE

1. NLW 22305C, ff. 40–1.
2. NYPL, Foster-Murphy Papers, Box 3, f. 155.
3. Tate, TAM, 21C, 10/22, 16 September 1920. Jeanne Robert Foster refers to Déshanel [Unknown: a personal friend or acquaintance?].
4. Quoted in John Tyrell, *Ezra Pound: The Solitary Volcano* (London, Bloomsbury, 1987), p. 123.
5. NLW 2300B, ff. 35v–37v.
6. NLW 22311C, ff. 32–3.
7. *Faded Dahlias in a Grey Jug*, Cecily Langdale, *Gwen John* (New Haven and London, Yale University Press, 1987), p. 227, no. 331.
8. *Brown Bowl and Flowers in a Brown Vase*, Cecily Langdale, *Gwen John*, p. 103; p. 227, no. 332.
9. Cézanne dreamed of combining the exquisite *sensation* of Impressionist art with something more solid and durable. See e.g. Clive Bell, *After Cézanne* (London, Chatto & Windus, 1929; first published 1922), p. 63.
10. *Les Chapeaux à Brides*, Cecily Langdale, *Gwen John*, p. 110; p. 228, no. 337.
11. *Two Little Girls in Hats, in Church*, Cecily Langdale, *Gwen John*, p. 110; p. 226, no. 327.
12. *Profile of Bourgeois Couple*, Cecily Langdale, *Gwen John*, p. 117; p. 196, no. 202.
13. *Still Life with a Vase of Flowers and an Inkwell*, Cecily Langdale, *Gwen John*, p. 110; p. 176, no. 143.
14. André Lhote, *Figure Painting*, trans. W. J. Strachan (London, A. Zwemmer, 1953; first published Paris, Editions Floury, 1950), p. 21.
15. Nicholas Watkins, *Interpreting Bonnard: Color and Light* (London, Tate Publications, 1997), p. 38. Cf. also Julian Bell, *Bonnard* (London, Phaidon, 1994).
16. *Rue Terre Neuve, Meudon*, Cecily Langdale, *Gwen John*, p. 161, nos. 90–1.
17. *Rue Terre Neuve*, Cecily Langdale, *Gwen John*, p. 222, no. 306.
18. *Rue Terre Neuve, Meudon*, Cecily Langdale, *Gwen John*, p. 161, nos. 90–1.
19. *Street at Night*, Cecily Langdale, *Gwen John*, p. 114; p. 200, no. 222.
20. Tate, TAM 21C 11/22 Jeanne Robert Foster to John Quinn, 16 October 1920.
21. NLW 22311c, f. 83v.
22. NLW 22285B, ff. 1–6.

23. NLW 22293C.
24. NLW B1987/2.
25. NLW 2300B, ff. 34–5.
26. NLW 22311C, ff. 110–16.
27. NYPL, JQMC, Box 23, reel A2, Gwen John to John Quinn, 4 April 1920.
28. Ibid.
29. NLW 22306D, ff. 24–9.
30. NLW 22307C, ff. 69–72.
31. NLW 22304C, f. 83.
32. Ibid., ff. 85–7.
33. NYPL, JQMC, Box 23, reel A2, Gwen John to John Quinn, 4 April 1920.
34. NLW 22311C, ff. 27–8.
35. Ibid., f. 36.
36. NYPL, JQMC, Box 23, reel A2, Gwen John to John Quinn, 15 June 1920.
37. Ibid., Gwen John to John Quinn, June 1920.
38. NLW 22305C, f. 133.
39. NLW 22311C, f. 36.
40. NYPL, JQMC, Box 23, reel A2, Gwen John to John Quinn, 10 July 1920.
41. Ibid., 18 July 1920.
42. Ibid., 2 September 1920.
43. NYPL, Foster-Murphy Papers, Box 3, f. 155.
44. Ibid., Box 4, f. 265.
45. Ibid., Box 3, f. 95.
46. Ibid., Box 4, f. 268.
47. Ibid., f. 291.
48. Ibid., f. 243; Box 3, f. 154.
49. Ibid., Box 3, f. 155.
50. Ibid.
51. Ibid., f. 115, dated (erroneously, by Jeanne Robert Foster) 14 September 1921.
52. Tate, TAM 21C 11/22, Jeanne Robert Foster to John Quinn.
53. NYPL, Foster-Murphy Papers, Box 3, f. 155, dated (erroneously, by Jeanne Robert Foster) 14 September 1921.
54. In the Foster-Murphy Papers, Jeanne has erroneously dated this 4 September: Box 4, f. 271.
55. Ibid., f. 270 (erroneously) dated 4 September 1921.
56. Here the text breaks off in the Foster-Murphy Papers and continues in Tate, TAM 21C 20/22 (accurately) dated 4 October 1920.
57. Tate, TAM 21C: material ends here and is resumed in Foster-Murphy Papers, Box 4, f. 271.
58. Tate, TAM 21C 21/22: 'NOTE: Page missing that gave the name of the priest and more details of his love for her etc. This page must have been vandalized during the years by one of the staunch Papist professors. I hope I

may find the page but I have examined the file where the papers have been for over 40 years – paper by paper and I have not found it. But I will search again. Jeanne R. Foster, April 3, 1969.'

59. NLW 22309C, f. 86.
60. Tate, TAM 21C 11/22, Jeanne Robert Foster to John Quinn.
61. Ibid., 9/22, 31 October, Jeanne Robert Foster to John Quinn.
62. NLW, Sound and Moving Image Collection, RM 34/01, 19/7/74, BBC Wales. Interview with Edwin John, whose view was that the theory that Gwen John went to France to escape Augustus was conjecture: 'She liked France. She liked Paris.'
63. Tate, TAM 21C 9/22, 31 October, Jeanne Robert Foster to John Quinn.
64. Tate, TAM 21C 10/22, Jeanne Robert Foster to John Quinn; NLW 22309C, f. 98.
65. Tate, TAM 21C 10/22; NYPL, Foster-Murphy Papers, Box 8, f. 476. Marie Laurençin acquisitions listed are: *Summer*; *The Little Nude*; *Black Eyes*.
66. Tate, TAM 21C 10/22.
67. NLW 22311C, f. 112.
68. NLW 2230C, f. 67.
69. NLW 22311C, f. 37.
70. NLW B1987/2, ff. 52–3.

17 RECOVERY

1. NLW 22276A, f. 15.
2. *Girl in Blue*, Cecily Langdale, *Gwen John* (New Haven and London, Yale University Press, 1987), p. 159, no. 82.
3. NLW 22308C, ff. 1–4.
4. NLW 22304C, ff. 88–91.
5. NLW 22276A, f. 2.
6. Tate, TAM 21C 17/22, Gwen John to Jeanne Robert Foster.
7. NLW 22276A, f. 2.
8. Ibid., f. 3.
9. Ibid., f. 5.
10. Ibid., f. 7.
11. Ibid., f. 24.
12. Ibid., f. 9.
13. Ibid., ff. 23–4.
14. NLW 222309C, f. 86.
15. Ibid.
16. Ibid.
17. Ibid., ff. 86–99.
18. NLW 22306D, f. 30.
19. NLW 22311C, f. 39.

20. NLW 22276A, f. 15.
21. Ibid., f. 23.
22. Ibid., f. 25.
23. Cecily Langdale, *Gwen John*, p. 220, no. 301; p. 221, nos 302–4; NLW 22297, f. 69.
24. Tate, TAM 21C 8/22, Jeanne Robert Foster to John Quinn.
25. NLW 22311C, f. 41.
26. Ibid., f. 118.
27. NYPL, JQMC, Box 27, John Quinn to Maud Gonne, 29 August 1921.
28. NLW 22309C, f. 93.
29. NLW 21468D, f. 126.
30. NLW 22305C, f. 42.
31. NLW 22309C, f. 93.
32. Tate, TAM 21C 18/22.
33. Ibid., 10/22.
34. NYPL, Foster-Murphy Papers, Box 4, f. 272.
35. Tate, TAM 21C 7/22, Jeanne Robert Foster to John Quinn.
36. Ibid., 9/22. Gwen later (in 1939) told Ursula that she had met Ezra Pound (NLW 21468D, f. 180) so she may have met him during this time, if not necessarily on that day.
37. Tate, TAM 21C 18/22.
38. NLW 22276A, f. 25.
39. NLW 22309C, f. 97.
40. Tate, TAM 21C 18/22, Gwen John to John Quinn, 11 December 1921.
41. Tate, TAM II–151, 838.2. John Quinn to Gwen John, 30 December 1921.
42. NLW 22309C, f. 97.
43. Tate, TAM 21C 18/22, Gwen John to John Quinn, 11 December 1921.
44. NLW 21468D, ff. 129–30.
45. Alison Thomas, *Portraits of Women: Gwen John and her Forgotten Contemporaries* (Cambridge, Polity Press, 1996; first published 1994), pp. 164–5.
46. NLW 21468D, ff. 129–30.
47. Ibid., f. 129.

18 GOD'S LITTLE ARTIST

1. Loose folio in pocket notebook, NLW 22276A, f. 101.
2. NYPL, JQMC, Box 23, reel A2, Gwen John to John Quinn, 27 March 1922.
3. NYPL, Foster-Murphy Papers, Box 4, f. 275.
4. Cecily Langdale, *Gwen John* (New Haven and London, Yale University Press, 1987), p. 172, nos 128–30.
5. NLW 22276A, ff. 197–202.
6. NLW 22268B, f. 1.

7. NLW 22303C, ff. 1–2.
8. NLW 22305C, f. 45.
9. Ibid., ff. 45–7.
10. Ibid.
11. NLW 22309C, ff. 100–19.
12. NYPL, Foster-Murphy Papers, Box 6, f. 357.
13. NLW 22309C, f. 106.
14. Ibid., ff. 100–19.
15. NYPL, JQMC, Gwen John to John Quinn, 9 May 1922.
16. *La Concierge*, Cecily Langdale, *Gwen John*, p. 173, no. 132.
17. *Girl in a Mulberry Dress*, Cecily Langdale, *Gwen John*, p. 90, nos 132–3; pp. 174–6, nos 134–142A.
18. *Girl with a Blue Scarf*, Cecily Langdale, *Gwen John*, p. 173, no. 133.
19. NYPL, JQMC, Box 23, reel A2, Gwen John to John Quinn, 27 March 1922.
20. Ibid., 9 May 1922.
21. NLW 22276A, f. 1.
22. NLW 223096, f. 106.
23. NYPL, Foster-Murphy Papers, Box 6, f. 357, Gwen John to John Quinn, 4 September 1922.
24. NLW 22390C, f. 113.
25. NLW 22276A, ff. 106–106v.
26. NYPL, JQMC, Box 23, reel A2, Gwen John to John Quinn, 3 September 1922.
27. NLW 22309C, f. 115.
28. Tate, TAM 21C 21/22.
29. Ibid.
30. Ibid., 6 December 1922.
31. NLW 22309C, ff. 120–7.
32. NYPL, JQMC, Box 23, reel A2, Gwen John to John Quinn, 1 March 1923.
33. Tate, TAM 21C 7/22.
34. NYPL, Foster-Murphy Papers, Box 4, f. 275. Diary for 9 January 1922– 28 July 1924, p. 73.
35. Tate, TAM 21C 16/22, Augustus John to Jeanne Robert Foster, 1, West 67th St, New York, 21 May.
36. NLW 22277A, f. 7.
37. *Woman with Hands Crossed*, Cecily Langdale, *Gwen John*, p. 91; p. 173, no. 131.
38. NYPL, Foster-Murphy Papers, Box 4, f. 276.
39. Ibid., Box 6, Gwen John to John Quinn, 15 November 1923.
40. Tate, TAM 21C 8/22, Jeanne Robert Foster to John Quinn, 11 November 1923.
41. Tate Archives, II–178, 838–2, John Quinn to Gwen John, 12 November 1923.

42. NYPL, JQMC, Box 23, reel A2, Gwen John to John Quinn, 29 October 1923. B.L. Reid, John Quinn's biographer, comments, re. this occasion, 'with [Gwen], apparently, Quinn had been able to dissemble the state of his nerves and his general health. His own letters to her were now beginning "My dear Gwen."' B.L. Reid, *The Man from New York: John Quinn and his Friends* (Oxford, Oxford University Press, 1968), pp. 590–1.
43. Tate, TAM 21C 8/22, Jeanne Robert Foster to John Quinn, 11 November 1923.
44. NLW 22308C, f. 75.
45. NLW 22309C, f. 126.
46. NYPL, Foster-Murphy Papers, Box 6, f. 355, Gwen John to John Quinn, 19 December 1923.
47. Ibid., f. 359, 21 November 1923.
48. NLW 22309C, f. 126.
49. NYPL, Foster-Murphy Papers, Box 6, f. 355, Gwen John to John Quinn, 19 December 1923.
50. NLW 22304C, f. 92.

19 THE CHENIL SHOW

1. Tate, TAM 21C 15/22, n.d.
2. NLW 22305C f. 48.
3. Tate, TAM 21C 12/22, 20 February 1924.
4. NLW 22305C, ff. 56–9.
5. NLW 22307C, ff. 73–4.
6. Tate, TAM 21C 14/22, 15 March 1924.
7. Cecily Langdale, *Gwen John* (New Haven and London, Yale University Press, 1987), pp. 167–70, nos 111–20.
8. *Woman with Cloak*, Cecily Langdale, *Gwen John*, p. 166.
9. *Girl in Rose*, Cecily Langdale, *Gwen John*, p. 74; p. 154, no. 65.
10. Henri Rousseau, *The Sleeping Gypsy* (Museum of Modern Art, New York). See Cecily Langdale, *Gwen John*, pp. 49, 127 note 36. .
11. NLW 22309C, ff. 128–33.
12. *Boy with a Blank Face*, Cecily Langdale, *Gwen John* p. 223, no. 309.
13. NLW 22305C, f. 56.
14. Ibid., f. 62.
15. Tate, TAM 21C 13/22, Gwen John to Jeanne Robert Foster, 22 April 1924.
16. NLW 22276A, f. 31.
17. NYPL, Foster-Murphy Papers, Box 6, unfiled, inserted after f. 360, Gwen John to Jeanne Robert Foster [n.d.] August 1924.
18. NYPL, Foster-Murphy Papers, Box 9, f. 560.
19. Ibid., f. 557, 8 August.
20. Tate, TAM 21C 13/22, Gwen John to Jeanne Robert Foster, 11 August 1924.

21. NLW 22305C, f. 66.
22. Tate, TAM 21C 17/22 [runs on to] 18/22, Gwen John to Jeanne Robert Foster, 28 August [1924].
23. Ibid., 13/33, n.d.
24. Ibid., 13/22.
25. NLW 21468D, f. 132, 17 September.
26. NLW 22303C, ff. 168–9.
27. *The Letter*, Cecily Langdale, *Gwen John*, p. 167, no. 113.
28. *Interior*, Cecily Langdale, *Gwen John*, p. 75; p. 171, no. 123.
29. Cecily Langdale, *Gwen John*, p. 150.
30. Tate, TAM 21C 17/22, Gwen John to Jeanne Robert Foster, 6 December.
31. Ibid., 15/22.
32. NLW 22305C, f. 135, 18 October.
33. Tate, TAM 21C 11/22, Gwen John to Jeanne Robert Foster, 28 September 1924.
34. NYPL, Foster-Murphy Papers, Box 8, f. 461.
35. NLW 22305C, f. 67.
36. Tate, TAM 21C 15/22, Gwen John to Jeanne Robert Foster, n.d.
37. NLW 22305C, f. 73.
38. Tate, TAM 21C 11/22, Gwen John to Jeanne Robert Foster, 28 September.
39. Ibid., 14/22, 19 November 1924.
40. NLW 22305C, f. 75, 28 November.
41. NYPL, Foster-Murphy Papers, Box 3, f. 144.
42. NLW 22305C, f. 75.
43. Tate, TAM 21C 17/22, Gwen John to Jeanne Robert Foster, 6 December.
44. NLW 22305C, f. 136.
45. Ibid., f. 75.
46. NLW 22155B, f. 11.
47. NLW 22305C, ff. 138–41.
48. NLW 21468D, ff. 133–5.
49. NLW 22305C, ff. 81–5.
50. NLW 21468D, f. 138.
51. NLW 22305C, f. 141.
52. NLW 21468D, ff. 140–8.
53. NLW 22307C, ff. 76–8.
54. NLW 21468D, ff. 140–8.
55. NLW 22305C, f. 142; Cecily Langdale, *Gwen John*, p. 241.
56. NLW 22311C, ff. 11–16, quoted in Cecily Langdale, *Gwen John*, p. 80.
57. Ibid., f. 15, quoted in Cecily Langdale, *Gwen John*, p. 80.
58. Ibid., ff. 3–4, quoted in Cecily Langdale, *Gwen John*, pp. 79–80.
59. Ibid., ff. 1–4, quoted in Cecily Langdale, *Gwen John*, pp. 79–80.
60. Ibid., ff. 18–19.
61. Ibid., ff. 77–9.

62. NLW 22304C, f. 1.
63. *The Student*, Cecily Langdale, *Gwen John*, p. 20, no. 11.
64. NLW Sound and Moving Image Collection, RM 38/01, 19/7/74, BBC Wales, Interview with Vivien White.
65. NLW 22307C, ff. 84–6.

20 VÉRA

1. André Lhote, *Figure Painting*, trans. W.J. Strachan (London, A. Zwemmer, 1953; first published, Paris: Editions Floury, 1950), p. 6.
2. Jacques Maritain (1882–1973) was probably the foremost living representative of Thomist philosophy in the 1920s and 1930s. A deeply spiritual man, he wrote about art and poetry as well as religion. I am very grateful to Sara John for drawing my attention to *The Person and the Common Good* (Indiana, University of Notre Dame Press, 1947) and *Creative Intuition in Art and Poetry: The A.W. Mellon Lectures in the Fine Arts* (New York, Meridian, 1974; first published 1953). Maritain gave the A.W. Mellon Lectures at the National Gallery of Art, Washington in spring 1952. They undoubtedly consolidated earlier ideas and in them he investigates art as 'an inner quality . . . that raises the human subject and his natural powers to a higher degree of vital formation and energy,' through discipline and application (p. 35). Art could be perfected through exercise and discipline, but at the same time 'it depends on a certain natural freedom of the soul (p. 102). This idea of art as an interior quality, to be perfected through the exercise of humility and inner strength, is comparable with the idea of art, and the need to be *recueillie*, which Gwen had earlier absorbed from Rodin.
3. NLW 22301B, f. 24.
4. NLW 22300B, ff. 18–19.
5. Lhote, *Figure Painting*, p. 6
6. St Thérèse of Lisieux (1873–97) made her first communion on 8 May 1884. In 1886 she became a Child of Mary. Following an audience with the Pope, on 9 April 1888, aged fifteeen, she entered the Carmel at Lisieux. She was a gifted and vivid writer. I am very grateful to Sara John for drawing my attention to *Collected Letters of Saint Thérèse of Lisieux* (London, Sheed & Ward, 1979; first published, 1949).
7. NLW 22297B.
8. NlW 22278A, F. 71.
9. NLW 22301B, ff. 21–52.
10. NLW 22308D, f. 143.
11. NLW 22301B, f. 4.
12. NLW 22278A, f. 4.
13. Ibid., f. 8.
14. NLW 22287A, f. 46.

15. Ibid., f. 84.
16. Ibid., f. 55.
17. Ibid., ff. 55v–54v [*sic*].
18. NLW 22301B, f. 41.
19. NLW 22302C, f. 31.
20. NLW 22301B, f. 26.
21. NLW 22302C, f. 76.
22. NLW 22301B, f. 27.
23. Ibid.
24. *Madonna and Child (in a Landscape*), Cecily Langdale, *Gwen John* (New Haven and London, Yale University Press, 1987), p. 112; p. 228, no. 336; sketches in NLW 22297B, f. 3. Jacques Maritain had in 1924 written an essay on Rouault, published in *Art and Poetry*, (New York, New Philosophical Library, 1943), but on the evidence of the conversations recorded by Gwen, it seems unlikely that she and Véra discussed this.
25. Lhote, *Figure Painting*, p. 125.
26. NLW 22301B, f. 25v.
27. NLW 22288A, ff. 31–2.
28. Ibid., ff. 37–41.
29. Ibid., f. 66.
30. NLW 22278A, f. 67.
31. Ibid., f. 64.
32. Ibid., f. 84v. Jacques Maritain mentions Chagall in 'The Preconscious Life of the Intellect', the third lecture collected in *Creative Intuition in Art and Poetry*. He includes him among artists whose work conveys 'poetic intuition', together with Rouault, Satie, Debussy, Hopkins, Apollinaire, T.S. Eliot and 'the great originator, Baudelaire' (p. 56).
    In 1948, Raisa Maritain also wrote about Chagall, in *Chagall ou l'orage enchanté* (Geneva and Paris, Editions des Trois Collines, 1948).
33. Ibid. NW, ff. 125–8.
34. NLW 22308D, ff. 21–22v.
35. NLW 21468D, ff. 159–60.
36. NLW 22305D, f. 15.
37. NLW 22304C, f. 109.
38. NLW 21468D, f. 160.

21 THE HANGAR

1. NLW 21468D, ff. 165–9.
2. NLW 22313D, ff. 112–14; NLW 23508D, ff. 60–9 Louise Roche, unpublished 'Reminiscences of Gwen John'.
3. NLW 22287A, f. 60v.
4. NLW 22308D, ff. 26–7.

5. NLW 22303C, ff. 188–91.
6. NLW 22302B, f. 61.
7. *The Japanese Doll*, Cecily Langdale, *Gwen John* (New Haven and London, Yale University Press, 1987), p. 82; pp. 171–2, nos 126, 127.
8. NLW 22304C, ff. 9–14.
9. Ibid., ff. 38–9.
10. NLW 22300B, f. 21.
11. Edwin John, *8 rue Babie, Meudon*, Cecily Langdale, *Gwen John*, p. 115.
12. Gwen John to Edwin John, Wednesday, n.d. (envelope postmarked 21.11.28). By kind permission of Sara John.
13. NLW 22308D, f. 36.
14. NLW 21468D, ff. 165–9.
15. NLW 22305D, f. 36.
16. Ibid., f. 46.
17. NLW 22289A, f. 49.
18. Ibid., f. 57.
19. NLW 22313D, ff. 112–14; NLW 23508D, ff. 60–9 Roche, unpublished Reminiscences.
20. Ibid.
21. NLW 22304C, f. 49.
22. NLW 22313D, ff. 112–14; NLW 23508D, ff. 60–9 Roche, unpublished Reminiscences.
23. NLW 22289A, f. 41v.
24. Ibid., f. 59v.
25. NLW 22288A, f. 20v.
26. NLW 22301B, f. 106.
27. Michael Holroyd, Introduction to the Anthony d'Offay exhibition catalogue *Gwen John*, London, 1 July–22 August 1982, p. 34.
28. NLW 22289A, ff. 63v–60v [*sic*].
29. NLW 22301B, f. 99.
30. Ibid., ff. 100–1.
31. NLW 22303C, ff. 24–37.
32. Ibid., ff. 44–59.
33. NLW 22308C, f. 174.
34. Ibid., f. 29.
35. NLW 22307D, f. 100.
36. NLW 22304C, ff. 16–21.
37. NLW 22300B, ff. 18–19.
38. NLW 22303C, f. 22.
39. NLW 22297B.
40. NLW 22304C, ff. 117–20.
41. NLW 22300B, f. 41.
42. NLW 21468D, ff. 171–8. See also Gwen John to Edwin John, December,

1932 on the dangers of boxing. Gwen thought the qualities needed 'courage – decision etc.' could be 'turned into another channel'. By kind permission of Sara John.
43. NLW 22303C, ff. 174–5.
44. NLW 22311D, ff. 99–102.
45. NLW 22300B, f. 46.
46. NLW 22308B, f. 42.
47. NLW 22306D, f. 54.
48. NLW 22304C, ff. 122–33.
49. NLW 22308D, f. 40.
50. NLW 22305D, f. 146.
51. NLW 22304C, ff. 122–33.
52. Cecily Langdale, *Gwen John*, p. 232, no. 351.
53. NLW 22300B, f. 65.
54. NLW 22308D, ff. 186–7.
55. NLW 22311D, f. 103.
56. NLW 22300B, f. 55.
57. NLW 22307C, ff. 1–4.
58. NLW 22309C, ff. 156–60.
59. Ibid.
60. NLW 22307C, ff. 128–9.
61. NLW 22306D, ff. 65–6.
62. NLW 22308D, ff. 104–9.
63. NLW 22303C, f. 185.
64. NLW 22278A, ff. 1–3.
65. NLW 22311D, f. 44.
66. NLW 22304C, f. 147.

22 FOR DIEPPE

1. NLW, loose folio inside cover of Gwen John's notebook 22278A.
2. NLW 22278A.
3. Untitled, undated drawing, probably of Meudon or environs, c. 1930s.
4. NLW 22278A, ff. 7–9.
5. Werner Haftman, *Painting in the Twentieth Century* (New York, Holt, Rinehart & Winston, 1965), p. 99.
6. NLW 22285B, f. 6.
7. NLW 22278A, ff. 7v–10. Gwen may have been inspired by Rodin to think about 'turning' the edge of a leaf. He told Paul Gsell that when, as an apprentice, he first began modelling foliage, a colleague pointed out that all his leaves looked flat. 'Make some with the tips pointed at you, so that, in seeing them, one has the sensation of depth.' Rodin took his advice and was 'astounded' by the difference. Auguste Rodin, *Rodin on Art and Artists:*

Conversations with Paul Gsell (New York, Dover Publications, 1983), p. 22.
8. NLW 22307C, f. 5.
9. NLW 22278A, ff. 5–6.
10. Ibid.
11. NLW 22307C, f. 7.
12. *Cottage behind a Wall*, Cecily Langdale, *Gwen John* (New Haven and London, Yale University Press, 1987), p. 231, no. 350.
13. NLW 22308C, f. 115.
14. NLW 22306D, f. 83.
15. NLW 22307C, ff. 159–62.
16. NLW 22304C, ff. 151–61.
17. Ibid., ff. 196–7.
18. NLW 22308D, f. 63.
19. NLW 22308C, f. 47.
20. NLW 22305C, ff. 7v–8.
21. Gwen John to Edwin John, November 1933. By kind permission of Sara John.
22. NLW 22308D, f. 50.
23. NLW 22304C, f. 170.
24. Ibid., f. 164.
25. NLW 22307D, f. 88.
26. NLW 21468D, f. 179.
27. NLW, loose folio in 22278A. (The numbering of points and the way words are curtailed, suggest she might have been taking notes at a lecture.)
28. NLW 22278A, f. 10v.
29. Ibid., f. 1.
30. NLW 22311D, ff. 89–90.
31. NLW 21468D, ff. 181–3.
32. Ibid., ff. 184–7.
33. Ibid., f. 179.
34. Ibid., ff. 181–3, Paul Fierens, *James Ensor* (Paris, Éditions Hypérion, MCMXLIII).
35. Ibid., ff. 184–7.
36. Ibid., f. 180.
37. Ibid., ff. 181–3.
38. NLW 22306D, ff. 117–18.
39. NLW 22308D, f. 51.
40. NLW 14931C, f. 3.
41. NLW 22307C, f. 92.
42. NLW 22311D, f. 108.
43. Cecily Langdale, *Gwen John*, p. 118.
44. NLW 22300B, ff. 31–3.
45. NLW 22305D, ff. 24–6.

46. NLW 22307C, f. 139.
47. NLW 22305D, f. 147.
48. NLW 22306D, ff. 129–30.
49. NLW 22307C, ff. 102–9.
50. NLW 22304C, ff. 175–7.
51. NLW 22311D, f. 94.
52. Cecily Langdale, *Gwen John*, p. 119; p. 130, note 43.
53. Augustus John, *Chiaroscuro: Fragments of Autobiography* (London, Arrow, 1962; first published Jonathan Cape, 1952), p. 224.
54. NLW 22308D, ff. 55–6.
55. NLW 22312C, f. 2.
56. Michael Holroyd, *Augustus John: The New Biography* (London, Chatto & Windus, 1996), p. 556.
57. Ibid., p. 571.
58. Ibid.
59. Ibid., p. 572.
60. Ibid.
61. Ibid.
62. Ibid., p. 49.
63. Ibid., p. 46.
64. Ibid., p. 49.
65. NLW 22303C, f. 170v.

Bibliography

ARCHIVAL SOURCES

The Musée d'Art et d'Histoire, Meudon
The Musée Rodin, Paris: Gwen John Papers
The National Library of Wales, Aberystwyth: Gwen John Papers
The National Museum of Wales, Cardiff: Gwen John, works on paper
The New York Public Library: The Foster-Murphy Papers, Astor, Lenox and Tilden Foundations; The John Quinn Memorial Collection, Astor, Lenox and Tilden Foundations
The Tate Archives, London: Gwen John Papers; John Quinn Papers
University College London Library: *The Slade Animal Land*

PRINTED BOOKS

Bruce Arnold: *Orpen: Mirror to an Age* (London, Jonathan Cape, 1981)
Clive Bell: *After Cézanne* (London, Chatto & Windus, 1929; first published 1922)
Julian Bell: *Bonnard* (London, Phaidon, 1994)
Ruth Butler: *Rodin: The Shape of Genius* (New Haven and London, Yale University Press, 1992)

Bernard Champigneulle: *Rodin*, translated from the French by J. Maxwell Brownjohn (London, Thames & Hudson, 1967)

Susan Chitty, *Gwen John, 1876–1939* (London, Sydney, Auckland, Toronto: Hodder & Stoughton, 1981)

Catherine Dessus: *Decouvrir Meudon* (Meudon, Editions O'Val, 1996)

Dyfed Cultural Services Department: *Haverfordwest in Old Photographs* (Stroud, Alan Sutton, 1992)

Fine, Elsa Honig: *Women and Art* (Montclair, New Jersey, 1978)

Alicia Foster: *Gwen John* (London, Tate Gallery Publishing, 1999)

Germaine Greer: *The Obstacle Race* (London, Picador, 1981; first published Secker & Warburg, 1979)

G. Douglas James: *The Town and County of Haverfordwest and its Story* (Haverfordwest, J.W. Hammond, 1958)

A. D. Fraser Jenkins: *Gwen John at the National Museum of Wales* (Cardiff, 1976)

Frederic Grunfeld: *Rodin: A Biography* (Oxford, Oxford University Press, 1987)

André Guigot: *Pléneuf-Val-André: Depuis la Nuit Des Temps* (in 2 vols.) (Pléneuf-Val-André, André Guigot, 1985)

Werner Haftman: *Painting in the Twentieth Century* (New York, Holt, Rinehart & Winston, 1965)

Michael Holroyd: *Augustus John: The New Biography* (London, Chatto & Windus, 1996)

Augustus John: *Chiaroscuro: Fragments of Autobiography* (London, Arrow, 1962; first published, London, Jonathan Cape, 1952)

Augustus John: *Finishing Touches*, ed. D. George (London, The Readers' Union, 1966)

Sara G. John: *Edwin John*, in *Works from the Collection of Edwin John* (London, Anthony d'Offay Gallery, 2000)

Sara G. John: *Gwen John – A View From the Twenty-First Century*, in *Works from the Collection of Edwin John* (London, Anthony D'Offay Gallery, 2000)

Sara G. John: 'Shades of Meaning: Gwen John (1876–1939)' in *Country Life* (12 August, 1982)

Emile de Labedollière: *Histoires des Environs du Nouveau Paris: Histoire de Meudon* (Paris, Georges Barba, n.d.)

Cecily Langdale, *Gwen John* (New Haven and London, Yale University Press, 1987)

Cecily Langdale, *Gwen John (1876–1939)* in *Works from the Collection of Edwin John* (London, Anthony D'Offay Gallery, 2000)

Cecily Langdale and David Fraser Jenkins, *Gwen John: An Interior Life* (Phaidon Press & Barbican Art Gallery, 1986; first published 1985)

Omar Khayyam: *Rubiyat*, rendered into English verse by Edward Fitzgerald (London, John Lane, MDCCCCV)

Gabriel de Lavergne, Vicomte de Guilleragues: *The Love Letters of a Portuguese Nun* (London, The Harvill Press, 1996; first published anonymously in 1669)

André Lhote: *Figure Painting*, translated by W.J. Strachan (London, A. Zwemmer, 1953; first published, Paris, Editions Floury, 1950)

André Lhote: *Treatise on Landscape Painting*, translated by W.J. Strachan (London, A. Zwemmer, 1950; first published, Paris, Editions Floury, 1939)

Ceridwen Lloyd-Morgan; *Gwen John: Papers at the National Library of Wales* (Aberystwyth, The National Library of Wales, 1995)

Michael B. Miller: *The Bon Marché: Bourgeois Culture and the Department Store, 1869–1920* (New Jersey, Princeton University Press, 1981)

Jacques Maritain: *Creative Intuition in Art and Poetry: The A.W. Mellon Lectures in the Fine Arts* (New York, Meridian, 1974; first published, 1953)

Jacques Maritain: *The Person and the Common Good* (Indiana, University of Notre Dame Press, 1947)

Edgar Munhall, *Whistler and Montesquoin* (The Frick Collection/ Flammarion, 1995)

Antoinette le Normand-Romain & Helene Marraud: *Rodin à Meudon: La Villa des Brillants* (Paris, Musée Rodin, 1996)

J.W. Phillips & Fred Warren: *The History of Haverfordwest*, originally written by the late John Brown, revised and added to by J.W. Phillips & Fred Warren (Haverfordwest, Ll. Brigstocke, 1914)

W.D. Phillips: *Old Haverfordwest*, a reprint of articles which appeared in the *Pembroke County Guardian*, 1924–5, with added illustrations (Haverfordwest, J.W. Hammond & Co., n.d.)

Helene Pinet: *Rodin et ses Modéles: Le Portrait Photographié* (Paris, Musée Rodin, 1990)

Helene Pinet: *Rodin: The Hands of Genius*, translated by Caroline Palmer (London, Thames & Hudson, 1997; first published, Paris, Gallimard, 1988)

B.L. Reid: *The Man from New York: John Quinn and his Friends* (New York, Jonathan Cape, 1968)

Rainer Maria Rilke: *Lettres à Rodin*, Preface de Georges Grappe (Luisant, Durand, 1998)

Rainer Maria Rilke: *Letters to a Young Poet* (New York, Norton, 1934; revised edn. 1993)

Rainer Maria Rilke: *Rilke* (London, Everyman, 1996)

Rainer Maria Rilke: *The Notebooks of Malte Laurids Brigge* (New York, Vintage, 1985)

Rainer Maria Rilke: *Auguste Rodin* (Berlin, Julius Bard, 1903)

Curators of the Musée Rodin: *Rodin, Whistler et la Muse* (Paris, Musée Rodin, 1995)

Auguste Rodin: *Correspondances de Rodin* (in 4 vols.) (Paris, Editions du Musée Rodin, 1987)

Auguste Rodin: *Rodin, on Art and Artists: Conversations with Paul Gsell* (New York, Dover, 1983)

John Rothenstein: *Modern English Painters* (London, Eyre and Spottiswoode, 1952)

Saint Thérèse of Lisieux: *Collected Letters of Saint Thérèse of Lisieux* (London, Sheed and Ward, 1979; first published, 1949)

Robin Spencer: *Whistler: The Masterworks* (London, Studio Editions, 1990)

Mary Taubman; *Gwen John* (London, Scolar Press, 1985)

Hilary Taylor: *James McNeill Whistler* (London, New Orchard Editions, 1978)

Alison Thomas: *Portraits of Women: Gwen John and her Forgotten Contemporaries* (Cambridge, Polity Press, 1996, 1st published 1994)

John Tytell: *Ezra Pound: The Solitary Volcano* (London, Bloomsbury, 1987)

Nicholas Watkins: *Bonnard: Color and Light* (New York, Stewart, Tabori & Chang, 1997)

Simon Watney: *English Post Impressionism* (London, Cassell, 1980)

Sheila Yeger; *Self Portrait* (Charlbury, Oxon, Amber Lane Press, 1990)

Malcolm Yorke: *Matthew Smith: His Life and Reputation* (London, Faber & Faber, 1997)

Index

Académie Carmen, Paris 22, 24, 27
Académie Julien, Paris 23, 24
Action Française 100
Aeschylus: *Orestis* 112
Aitken, Charles 177, 248
Alcoforado, Mariana 104
Alderney Manor, Dorset 150, 201, 248, 260
Aldrich, T. H.: 'Unsung' 4
Anderson, Julia (*née* Quinn): inherits Quinn's estate 237, 240, 241, 242; buys picture from GJ 265–6; AJ finds severe and frightening 276; supports Convent 276, 284; tells New York dealers of GJ's work 276, 278; wants AJ's permission to reprint his letters to Quinn 282–3; death 296
Anderson, Mary 237, 265, 296
Anderson Galleries, New York 241
Apollinaire, Guillaume 124
Aquinas, St Thomas 184
'Armory Show' (1913) 146–7
Association of American Painters and Sculptors 147
Atkinson, Mrs (cleaning lady): GJ's portrait 21

Bachelez, Adrien 303
Ballets Russes 140
Balzac, Honoré de 58
Bankhead, Tallulah 248
Baudelaire, Charles 57, 200, 210, 216
Beckett, Ernest William (Lord Grimthorpe) 53
Benedict XV, Pope 158
Bénédite, Leonce 167
Bernheim Jeune Gallery, Paris 55, 193, 236
Beuret, Rose 61, 66, 105, 110, 123, 130, 157, 166
Binyon, Laurence 210
Bishop, Bridget 267, 277; GJ's portrait 267, 272, 291
Bishop, Louise (*née* Salaman) 16, 29, 30, 32, 267, 291
Blackie (cat) 208
Blake, William 223
Blanche, J. L. 100
Blavatsky, Madame: *Isis Unveiled* 8

Bone, Muirhead 125
Bonnard, Pierre 23, 152, 168, 193, 195
Boughton-Leigh, Chloe: GJ's first portrait (1907) 87–8, 97, 98, 124; friendship with GJ 88–9, 97, 141, 146; second portrait (*Study* of a *Woman*) 150, 152, 158; third portrait (1910) 119–20, 123, 125, 186; nurses in the war 158; sends GJ money, advice and presents 165, 166, 188–9, 190, 262, 277, 280, 281, 286, 287, 293–4, 295, 303; searches Warren Gallery records for GJ's pictures 282
Boughton-Leigh, Grilda 15, 16, 49, 63, 87, 123, 141, 150–1, 158, 166, 280, 294
Bourdin, Monsieur 185, 187
Bowser, Isobel 49; GJ poses for 63, 91, 97, 98, 116, 117; concerned about GJ's health 115, 116; in Pont l'Abbé 141; illness and death 186, 188, 189
Brancusi, Constantin 124, 202, 225, 230
Braque, Georges 225, 231
Brontë, Charlotte (Currer Bell): *Jane Eyre* 8
Broucke, Leonard 39–40, 44–5, 46
Brown, Anna 49
Brown, Frederick xiii, 16, 18, 34
Brown, Ida 49, 54–5, 115, 210–11, 286
Brummer (Joseph) Gallery, New York 244
Burke, Edmund: *The Sublime and the Beautiful* 41
Burlington Magazine 304
Burns, Tom 261, 281, 288; GJ to 273–4
Butler, Ruth: *Rodin* 55–6
Cantal, Lucien 100
Carfax Gallery, London 35
Carlyle, Richard: *Key Arch* 8
Carlyle, Thomas 82, 136
Carnegie Institute 280
Carodna, General 163
Carroll Gallery, New York 159
Catherine, St, of Sienna 184
Cézanne, Paul xv, 185, 186, 194, 224, 226, 288, 289, 296, 299, 300; portrait of his father 231, 234
Chagall, Marc 259, 278, 289, 291
Chamot, M. 41
Chelsea Art School, London 40
Chenil Galleries, London: GJ's pictures exhibited: *Dorelia by Lamplight, at Toulouse* 41; 'Paintings and Drawings of Gwen John' (1926 exhibition) 246–7; *Study of a Woman* 150, 158
Choiseul, 'Duchesse' Claire de: laision with Rodin 96, 105, 110–12, 122, 139, 140–1, 149
Cladel, Judith 157, 166
Clarke-Hall, Edna (*née* Waugh) 14–15, 222
  Gwen John 18
Claudel, Camille xii, 55, 123–4
  La Suppliante 123
Coates, Dorothy 240
Cocteau, Jean 110
Colarossi's school, Paris 24, 88
Collin, Abbé Charles 267, 274
Colour (magazine) 173–4
Conder, Charles 32, 34, 44
Conrad, Joseph 141
Constan, Benjamin 24
Contemporary Art Society 124, 125
Cornford, Frances (*née* Darwin) 103
Country Life 41
Craftsman 148
Cubism 288, 289
Curtin, Thomas 237, 240, 242, 244
Dante Alighieri 57

Daumier, Honoré de 258
Davies, Arthur B. 224, 225
Davis, Dr Clem 302–3
Degas, Edgar 41, 143, 200
De la Fresnaye, 215
Denis, Maurice 23
Derain, André 124, 159, 161, 202, 215, 218, 221, 225, 231
Déshanel, 191, 196
Detroit Sunday News 202
De Zayas Gallery, New York 206, 207, 214
Dieppe, France 295, 303–4
Donne, John 223
Dostoevsky, Fyodor 11, 134, 146
The Idiot 165
Dowdall, Harold Challoner 33
Dowdall, Mary ('the Rani') 33
Duchamp, Marcel 161
Duchamp-Villon, Raymond 159, 161, 225
Dufy, Raoul 159, 161, 208, 215
Duncan, Isadora 110, 111
Durand-Ruel, James 143, 147, 148
Dürer, Albrecht 132, 133

Edgar Quinet (cat) 44, 49, 56, 58, 63, 64, 66, 68, 75, 77–8, 83, 86, 92–4
Eliot, T. S. 124
Ensor, James 296, 299
Epstein, Jacob 141, 224
Euripides 60, 112
Medea 70
Evans, Benjamin 32
Everett, Augusta 18, 20, 22, 29

Faber (Jacques Fabri) 69
Fairfax, Eve 53
Ferargil Gallery, New York 163, 260, 278–9, 301
Fletcher, Fanny 264, 267, 281, 303
Flodin, Hilda 48, 50, 54, 59–60, 64, 66, 67, 69, 76–7
Ford, Ford Madox 202; his wife 233
Foster, Jeanne Robert 202; relationship with Quinn 203; meets GJ 201, 202, 203–4; friendship blossoms 204–8; returns to New York 208; corresponds with GJ 211; returns with Quinn to Meudon 217–18; sits to GJ 218–19, 220, 221; invites the Pounds 220; dislikes Derain's work 221, 223; on her love for Quinn 224; writes article on GJ 225; illness 227; wants GJ to illustrate her books 228, 232, 235; returns to Paris 229, 230–1; rift with GJ 232–4; and Quinn's illness and death 235, 236–8; as GJ's patron in Quinn's place 239–42, 243, 244; on Véra Oumançoff 273
books of poems: *Rock Flower* 228, 229; *Wild Apples* 202
Fryern Court, near Fordingbridge 260
Futurists 137

Gaudier-Brzeska, Henri 224
Gauguin, Paul 183
Gerhardie, Miss (German artist) 48–9, 63
Gertler, Mark 142
Gervais, Monsieur and Madame 132, 230, 275–6, 284
Gil Blas 100
Gillet, Louis 51
Gleizes, Albert 159, 161, 211, 288, 289, 292, 296, 298
Cubism 268, 289, 298
Gonne, Maud xiv; and Quinn 124, 154, 158, 170, 217; meets GJ 160; makes GJ aware of seriousness of war 154, 160–1; tries to get back to Ireland 171–2; arrested 176, 178
Gonne, Seaghan 154, 160
Gore, Spencer 87, 142

Grabowska, Elisabeth de Willman 177, 178, 179, 190
Grabowska, Madame de Willman 177
Grande Revue 100
Guioché, Eugène 117, 157

Hamilton, Anthony, Count: *Memoirs of the Comte de Grammont* 8
Hamonet, Marie 178
Hardy, Thomas 11
Jude the Obscure 288
Hart, Miss (artist) xiii, 49, 55, 63, 80
Hastings, Beatrice 158
Hatch, Ethel 14
Haverfordwest, Wales 1, 2–4
Hébert, Ernest 85
Hindenburg, Helene de Nostiz-Wallwitz 101, 102; Rodin to 100, 102
Hogarth, William: *Analysis of Beauty* 41
Holroyd, Michael 273
Augustus John 38, 304
Horden, Suzanne 48, 63, 64
Hudson, T. J.: *The Law of Psychic Phenomena* 38
Huneker, James 142
Hunter, Mary 53, 157

Impressionists, French 20
Innes, James Dickson 142, 225
International Society of Sculptors, Painters and Gravers: Monument Committee 53, 100, 167

James, William 69
Jeffreys, Dolly 15–16
John, Augusta (*née* Smith) 2, 3, 4–7
Figures in a Landscape 4
Landscape with Cows 4–5
Oranges and Lemons 4
John, Augustus: childhood 2, 8, 9, 10; on his father 7; at the Slade 13, 14, 15, 16, 17; draws Winifred (*Sister of Augustus John on a Day Bed*) 18; on Tonks 19; takes Charlotte St studio 23; and Whistler 26; worries about GJ 29; bohemian life in London 30–1; in France 31; marriage 32; in Liverpool 32–3; exhibits at Carfax Gallery 35; and Dorelia 35–6, 37–8, 42, 43, 44–6; starts Chelsea Art School 40; concerned for GJ 43–4; visits GJ in Paris 65; discovers St Honorine 78; a new affair 84; and Ida's death 89, 90–1; mentions GJ's work to Quinn 124; elected to Society of Twelve 125; sends GJ money 125; worries about her 137, 145; praises her pictures 150; letters to GJ in war 153, 154–5, 158; reports on Rodin's Whistler monument 167; as war artist 172, 180; visits GJ after Rodin's death 173–4; after Armistice 181; in Normandy 186–7; encourages GJ after Isobel Bowser's death 188, 191–2; not interested in buying Château Vauclair 199, 200; and the Symonses 201, 208, 215; disgruntled with Quinn 216, 219; his appearance 219; sees GJ's pictures in New York 229; draws Quinn 229; thrilled with GJ's drawings 239; and Quinn's death 240, 241; and GJ's lack of negotiating skills 239, 242–3; arranges show for GJ 245–6; and GJ's visit to Alderney Manor 248; moves to Fryern Court 260; buys Yew Tree Cottage for GJ 260–1, 266, 300; meets Julia

Anderson 276; refuses publication of his letters to Quinn 282–3; and his father's death 302; after GJ's death 304–5; mother's picture attributed to 5; on GJ xv, 9, 10, 12–13, 16, 35, 141, 304
John, Caspar 35, 40, 65, 78, 80, 302
John, David 33, 40, 65, 78, 80, 181, 229, 261
John, Edwin (GJ's nephew) 78, 80; in Paris 261; relationship with GJ 266, 276–7, 278, 288, 292, 294; introduced to Maritain by GJ 250; interest in boxing 278, 292; as GJ's executor xv, 303–4
John, Edwin William (GJ's father) 5, 6, 10; musical interests 5, 7; and the children 1, 7–8, 12; relationship with GJ 9–10, 13, 265; visits GJ in Paris 27, 118–19; sends her his 'self-photography' 11, 158, 187; disappointed at AJ's failure to be elected to Royal Academy 200; laments industrial crisis 215; sends GJ income from Thomas Smith estate 280, 284; on his will 293; communications with GJ 294, 300, 302; death 302
John, Gwen(dolene) Mary:
1876–1904: birth 4; childhood 1–2, 5, 6–7, 8–9, 12; education 3, 8, 12; at the Slade 10, 13, 14–15, 16–22; early portraits 11–12, 17–18; moves with AJ to Fitzroy St 18; in Paris with Ida and Gwen Salmond 23–8; and Whistler 25–6, 27; her father's visit 27; begins modelling 27, 28; in Howland St basement 29; at Peveril Tower 29–30; with AJ in Rothenstein's flat 30–1; at Le-Puy-en-Velay 31; thwarted in love 31–2; 'aids and abets' AJ's marriage to Ida 32; exhibits at New English Art Club 32; pram-pushing in Liverpool 33; writes to Michel Salaman 33–4; pictures not hung at NEAC 34–5; exhibits at Carfax Gallery 35; friendship with Dorelia McNeill begins 35, 36, 37; on the road to Rome 38–40; intensive painting in Toulouse 40–3, 44; arrives in Paris 43–4; takes rooms at Hôtel Mont Blanc (blvd Edgar Quinet) 44, 47; persuades Dorelia to return to AJ 44–6; painting in Paris 47–8; looks for work as model 48; her circle of lady clients 48–9, 54–5
1904–1910: becomes Rodin's model and scribe 50–2; affair with Rodin 52–3, 56–62, 67, 68–71; poses for Rodin's 'Whistler Muse' 54, 56, 78–9; becomes orderly and harmonious 52, 56; her lady clients 63–4; life at Hôtel Mont Blanc 64–5; entertains AJ, Ida and Dorelia 65–6; prefers to model for Rodin than paint 67, 72–3; moves to rue St Placide 68; and Rilke 71–2, 73; starts painting again 73, 74; life at rue St Placide 74–5; affair continues 74–7, 79–80; posing for Rodin and Flodin 76–7; visited by Ida, Dorelia and children 80; dreams 80–1, 82–3; writes novel 82; leaves rue St Placide 83–4; quarrels with Nuala O'Donel 84; moves to rue du Cherche-Midi 85–6; and Ida's death 90, 91;

difficulty in working 91; and her cat's disappearance 92–4; difficulties with Rodin 94–6, 99–100, 101–3, 104–6, 114–16, 121–2; paintings accepted by NEAC 97–8; and Rilke's return to Paris 103, 104; moves to rue de l'Ouest 107–8, 109; and Rodin's liaison with Claire de Choiseul 105, 110, 112; further modelling 116–17; and her father's visit 118–19; meets Picasso 119; and Camille Claudel 123–4; Quinn interested in buying her work 124–5

1910–1921: moves to Meudon 127–32; corresponds with Quinn 132–2, 135, *see* Quinn, John; need for solitude 136, 137, 138, 139; begins visiting Convent 138; end of affair with Rodin 139–40, 149; sends Quinn *Girl Reading at the Window* (*see below*) 141–2; further dealings with Quinn 142–5, 146–8, 152–3, 158–9; begins 'Nun' picture 143, *see Mère Poussepin* (*below*); insomnia and headaches 145; misunderstanding with Rilke 149; in wartime France 153–60, 163–4; sends Quinn *Seated Woman in Blue*, *Interior* (*see below*) and drawings of generals 162–3; goes to Finistère 164, 165; joins in Meudon life 165; and Rodin's death 173, 174, 176, 188, 189; under bombardment 174–6; goes to Pléneuf 177–8; in Paris for Armistice 180; moves to Château Vauclair 181–5, 198–200; longs to own it 187–8, 191; and Isobel Bowser's death 188–90, 198; turns to Constance Lloyd 191–2, 198; friendship with Symonses 192–3; illness 192, 196; Jeanne Foster's arrival and visit 201–8; puts 29 rue Terre Neuve in order 210; further illness 214; stays with Symonses in England 216–17; meets Quinn 217–18; paints Jeanne Foster 218–19; too busy to meet the Pounds 220; a new optimism 222

1922–1939: working hard as 'God's little artist' 223–4; sends paintings to Quinn 224, 226–7, and Jeanne Foster 228; gives pictures to Quinn 229–30; tortured by dentist 231, 233, 234, 235; rift with Jeanne 232–4, 235; Quinn's death and its ramifications 236, 238–43; exhibits at Salon des Tuileries 239; badgered by Charles Rutherston to sell paintings 239; sends AJ album of drawings 239; sits on a needle 245; exhibits at Chenil Galleries 245–7, and Manchester Art Gallery 248; visits AJ and family 248; and Rilke's death 250; relationship with Véra Oumançoff 251, 252–4, 256–60, 273–4; further exhibitions 252; illness 254–5; and Yew Tree Cottage 260–1; buys the 'Hangar' 263–4, 266, 267–8; visited by Julia Anderson 265–6, and Edwin John 266; Louise Roche's memories of life at the Hangar 268–73; begins correspondence with Canon Piermé 274–5, 276, 277; relationship with

Edwin 276–7, 278, 292; and Ursula's visits 277–8; and Ferargil Gallery exhibition 278–9; illness 281; last oil painting 281–2; in England to see Edith Nettleship 283, 284; inherits from Thomas Smith estate 280, 284, 286; and death of Canon Piermé 292–3; helps Angeline Lhuisset 293; injures herself 295; and Ursula's visit 297–9; illness 300–1; writes will in Dieppe 303–4; death 304
appearance and voice 10, 34, 248
Catholicism 121–2, 135–6, 138, 141, 145–6, 148, 166, 174, 190, 223, 270, 273–4
cats *see* Blackie; Edgar Quinet; Johnny, aka Robinson Crusoe; Kiki; 'L'Assassin'; 'L'Invisible'; Tigre; Tum; Valentine
character and personality xvi, 1, 10, 12, 16, 30, 52, 109, 269, 279–80
friendships *see* Boughton-Leigh, Chloe *and* Grilda; Clarke-Hall, Edna (*née* Waugh); Gervais, Monsieur and Madame; Lhuisset, Angeline; Lloyd, Constance; Oumançoff, Véra; Rilke, Rainer Maria; Roche, Louise; Salmond, Gwen; Symons, Arthur *and* Rhoda; Tyrwhitt, Ursula; Waugh, Rosa
influences xv; Cézanne 234, 288, 300; Chagall 289; Dürer 132, 133; Ensor 299; Gleizes 211, 288, 289, 292; Japanese drawings 113, 193; Lhote 195, 251, 257, 273, 285, 296, 299–300 ; McEvoy 20; Picasso 119; Rodin xiv, 52–3 , 56, 60, 61, 68, 113–14, 193, 194, 195, 225; Rouault 256, 257–8, 289; Tonks 19–22 ; Whistler 25, 27
literary interests and books read 7–8, 11, 19, 27–8, 41, 57–8, 60, 69, 70, 80, 112, 122, 133, 145, 146, 165, 184, 210, 223, 2 80, 288
painting methods and techniques xiv–xv, 19– 22, 41–2, 74, 88, 96–7, 117–18, 121, 148,151–2, 167–9, 179–80, 185–6, 193–8, 211– 14, 226, 227–8, 243–4, 255–6, 281–2, 288– 92, 296–7; *see also* influences (*above*) *and specific works below*
relationship with AJ xii, 10, 12–13, 43, 248, 304–5
relationship with her father 7, 9–10, 13
views on artists 41; Cézanne 231; Chagall 259, 278, 291; Ensor 299; Marie Laurencin 214, 227; Lhote 299–300; Matisse 137, 204; Picasso 119, 208, 221, 266; Puvis de Chavannes 143; Renoir 143; Rouault 161, 257, 258, 278; Rousseau 133
Works:
The Artist in her Room in Paris (1907–9) 66
'Au Chat' (poem) 93
Autoportrait à la Lettre (c. 1907–9) 95
Boy with a Blank Face (c. 1920s) 235
Brown Bowl and Flowers in a Brown Vase (c. 1920s) 193–4
The Brown Teapot (c. 1915–16) 159
La Chambre sur la Cour (c. 1907–8) 73, 83, 97, 98, 103, 124
Les Chapeaux à Brides (c. late 1920s) 194
Chloe Boughton-Leigh (1907) 87–8, 97, 98, 107, 124

Chloe Boughton-Leigh (1910) 119–20, 123, 125, 186
La Concierge (c. 1923–4) 226, 227
The Convalescent (c. late 1910s to mid-1920s) 186, 188, 189, 234
A Corner of the Artist's Room in Paris (c. 1907–9) 87, 96–7, 186, 195
Cottage Behind a Wall (c. early 1930s) 293
Dorelia by Lamplight, at Toulouse (1903–4) 41
Dorelia in a Black Dress (1903–4) 41, 170, 238, 247–8
drawings 122, 144; of children 104, 144–5, 164, 178–9; of generals 163, 164; of Saint Thérèse of Lisieux 177, 251–2
L' Enfant à la Poupée (c. late 1910s) 190
Ètude pour les Suppliantes (c. 1910) 123
Faded Dahlias in a Grey Jug (c. 1925) 193, 197
Flower Picture (n.d.) 295
Girl in Blue (c. 1921) 164, 211, 214, 217, 221, 223, 224
Girl in a Blue Apron with a Cat on Her Lap (c. late 1910s–early 1920s) 173
Girl in a Blue Dress series (c. 1914–15) 151–2, 280, 300
Girl in Grey (c. late 1910s–early 1920s) 295
Girl in Grey with White Collar (c. late 1910s–early 1920s) 295
Girl in Mulberry Dress (c. 1923–4) 226
Girl in Rose (c. late 1910s) 165, 234
Girl Nursing a Doll (c. late 1910s) 179
Girl Reading at the Window (1911) 126, 133–5, 141, 142, 143, 146
Girl with Bare Shoulders (c. 1909–10) 107, 114, 116, 119, 124
Girl with a Blue Scarf (c. 1923–4) 226, 227, 231
Girl with Cat (c. late 1910s–early 1920s) 185, 229, 235
Girl with a Pinkish Brown Shawl (n.d.) 295
Head of a Young Woman (c. 1909) 114
Interior (c. 1915–16) 159, 161, 162, 164, 203
Interior (c. 1915–16) 169
Interior (c. 1915–16) 239
Interior with Figures (c. 1898–9) 25, 34, 87, 97
The Japanese Doll (c. early–late 1920s) 265
A Lady Reading (c. 1910–11) 73, 133, 134, 135, 186
Landscape at Tenby, With Figures (c. 1895–8) 9, 11
The Letter (late 1910s–early 1920s; perhaps 1924) 239
The Little Boy (c. late 1910s) 179
Little Girl (n.d.) 295
Little Girl with a Large Hat and Straw-Coloured Hair (c. late 1910s) 179
Mère Poussepin (the 'Nun') (c. early–late 1910s) 143, 144, 148–9, 150–1, 159, 161, 169, 170, 190, 200, 205, 207, 214, 221–2, 223, 224, 226–7, 229
Nude Girl (c. 1909–10) 107, 114, 116, 119, 124, 125, 186, 216
Ophelia: Portrait Imaginé (c. 1910) 123
Le Petit Garçon Sentimental (c. late 1910s) 179
La Petite Modèle (c. late 1910s) 159–60, 161–2, 164, 185
The Pilgrim (c. late 1920s–early 1920s) 247

Portrait Group (c. 1897–8) 17
Portrait of the Artist's Sister Winifred (c. 1898) 11, 32
Portrait of a Girl, with Hands Clasped (c. late 1910s) 165
Portrait of Mrs. Atkinson (c. 1897–8) 21
Portrait of Winifred John (c. 1895–8) 11
Profile of a Bourgeois Couple (c. 1910s) 194
A *Rag Doll* (c. late 1910s) 179
Rue Terre Neuve (c. 1921) 195–6
Rue Terre Neuve, Meudon (c. late 1910s–early 1920s) 195, 196
Seated Girl (*Girl Nursing a Doll*) (c. late 1910s) 179
Seated Woman in Blue Dress (c. 1914–15) 162
self-portraits 28, 73
first self-portrait 11–12
Self-Portrait (1900) 11, 19, 32
Self-Portrait (c. 1907–9) 92
Self-Portrait in a Red Blouse (1903) 19, 33–4, 35, 186
Still Life with a Vase of Flowers and an Inkwell (c. late 1920s) 194
Street at Night (c. 1910s) 196, 197
The Student (c. 1903–4) 41, 248
Study of a Woman (c. 1923–4) 150, 152, 158
The Teapot (c. 1915–16) 159
Two Little Girls in Hats, in Church (c. 1920s) 194
Winifred John in a Flowered Hat (c. 1895–8) 11
Winifred John in a Large Hat (c. 1895–8) 11
Woman Dressing (c. 1907) 87
A *Woman in a Red Shawl* (c. 1913) 146, 147, 148
Woman Leaning on her Hand (c. 1909) 114
A *Woman Sewing* (c. 1910) 119, 125
Woman with Cloak (late 1910s–early 1920s) 234
Woman with Hands Crossed (c. 1923–4) 229, 231
Young Woman Holding a Black Cat (c. late 1910s–early 1920s) 173
Young Woman in a Mulberry Dress (c. 1923–4) 231
John, Henry 84, 89, 181, 261, 281, 283, 288, 291; Edwin John to 292
John, Ida (*née* Nettleship): at the Slade 15, 16; in Paris with GJ and Gwen Salmond 23–5, 26, 27–8; back in London 29; marries AJ 32; with AJ in Liverpool 32–3, 34; and David's birth 33; and Dorelia and the *ménage à trois* 36, 37, 38, 40, 44, 45, 46; in Paris 65, 66, 78, 80, 84; as storyteller 269; and Henry's birth 89; death and cremation 89, 90–1
John, Kathie 304
John, Mary (*née* Davies) 5
John, Pyramus 65, 84
John, Robin 65, 229
John, Romilly 78, 84
John, Thornton 2, 5, 6–7, 104, 155–6, 176, 181, 200, 233–4, 246, 248–9, 287; and GJ 10, 124, 141, 146, 173, 176, 292, 295–6, 300–1, 302–3, 304
John, Vivien *see* White, Vivien
John, William 5
John, Winifred *see* Shute, Winifred
Johnny, aka Robinson Crusoe (cat) 280, 284
Joly sisters 132, 160, 257
Jousset, Jean 303–4
Joyce, James 124

Kahn, Alphonse 241
Kappus, Franz Xaver 71; Rilke to 71–2, 73–4

Kennedy, Mitchell 241
Kiki (cat) 190, 211, 233
Knewstub, Jack 142
Kuhn, Walter 167, 207, 219

Lagout, Iréne 225
Lamb, Henry 91
Langdale, Cecily 119, 151, 178
'L'Assassin' (cat) 269
Laurencin, Marie 124, 201, 206, 207, 208, 209, 214–15, 219–20, 225, 227, 231
Lavergne, Gabriel de: *The Love Letters of a Portuguese Nun* 104
Lawrence, D. H. 11
Lawrence, T. E. 248
Leclerc, Maître 187
Le Figaro 140
Leicester Galleries, London 245
Le-Puy-en-Velay, France 31
Lethbridge, Katie 301–2
Lewis, Percy Wyndham 80, 107, 225, 305
Lhote, André 195, 251, 257, 258, 273, 285, 296, 298, 299–300
  Figure Painting 258
Lhuisset, Angeline 132, 142, 144, 151, 186, 293, 301
'L'Invisible' (cat) 283
Litalien, Odette 178
Lloyd, Constance: on GJ 15; in Paris 48, 49, 63, 65; poses nude for GJ 54; appearance 80; GJ poses for 91, 92; friendship with GJ 191–2, 198, 210, 277; goes to Lhote's classes 195, 251, 284–5; dislikes Laurencin 214, 219–20
Lloyd George, David 171, 186
London art galleries: Carfax 35; Chenil 41, 150, 158, 246–7; Leicester 245; Matthiesen 304; National 177, 247–8; Redfern 222; Warren 282; Wildenstein 304
Lovell, Fenella 103, 106–7, 114, 116, 119, 137, 141; GJ's portraits *see Girl with Bare Shoulders*; *Nude Girl*
Ludlow, Miss (artist) 98, 115

McBride, John 171
McEvoy, Ambrose 17, 20, 31–2, 91, 161
McEvoy, Charles 23
McEvoy, Mary (*née* Edwards) 32
McNeill, Dorelia: meets and captivates the Johns 35–6; their *ménage à trois* 37–8; walks with GJ to Toulouse 38–41; painted by GJ 41–2, 43; disappears with Broucke 44; persuaded to return 44–6; first child 65; with family and GJ in Paris 65, 66, 69; second child 78; invites GJ to St Honorine 78; in Paris 80, 84; sends crockery to GJ 243; and Yew Tree Cottage 260, 264, 267, 280, 294, 300, 303; opinion of Picasso 266
Mallarmé, Stéphane 11, 22, 57
Manchester Art Gallery 248
Manchester Guardian 138
Mangin, General 163
Mansfield, Katherine 11
Manson, France 286, 287, 294, 295
Manson, Rosamund 141, 177, 286, 287, 294, 295
Manson, Ruth 141, 149, 154, 155, 165, 175, 177, 183, 189, 218, 285–6, 294, 295
  Effet de Neige 152
Maritain, Jacques 250, 253, 284
Marlowe, Christopher 8
Martin, Marcelle 111
Matching Green, Essex 38, 46, 65
Matisse, Henri 110, 137, 159, 202, 204, 208, 215, 225
Matthiesen Gallery, London 304

Merril, Mr (dentist) 231, 233, 234, 235
Meudon, France 127–8, 129, 131–2, 135, 144–5, 154, 165, 175–6, 252; Convent of the Soeurs de Charité Dominicaines . . . 120–1, 128–9, 135, 138, 143, 148–9, 276, 284, 292–3, 294; 29 rue Terre Neuve 127, 129, 134, 159, 175, 202, 210, 265, 267; the Hangar 129, 263–4, 266, 268–9, 271, 272, 277, 281, 287, 297–8, 304; Villa des Brillants 51, 127, 130, 157
Modigliani, Amedeo 158
Monet, Claude 111
Moore, Vice-Admiral Sir Archibald 163
Musée de Luxembourg, Paris 167

National Gallery, London 177; exhibits *Dorelia in a Black Dress* 247–8
NEAC *see* New English Art Club
Nettleship, Ada 25, 32, 89; Ida John to 23, 24, 25, 26
Nettleship, Edith 283
Nettleship, Ethel 245, 246, 281
Nettleship, Ida *see* John, Ida
Nettleship, Jack 15, 32
Nettleship, Ursula, Ada Nettleship to 89, 90
New Age 155, 158
New English Art Club (NEAC) 32, 34–5, 40, 117, 118, 125, 177; GJ's pictures exhibited: *La Chambre sur la Cour* 97, 98, 103, 124; *Girl Reading at the Window* 135; *A Portrait* (1911) 124; *Portrait of Chloe Boughton-Leigh* (1907) 97, 98, 124; *Self-Portrait* (1900) 32
New York art galleries: Anderson 241; Brummer 244; Carroll 159; De Zayas 206, 207, 214; Ferargil 163, 260, 278–9, 301; Sculptors' 224, 226
New York Times 140
Nijinsky, Vaslav 140
Novalis 184, 228

O'Donel, Nuala xiii, 48, 63–4, 68, 76, 77, 79, 83, 84–5, 88, 92, 97
Of, George 152
Oliver, Madge 245
Orpen, William 18, 32, 34–5, 40, 161, 167
Oumançoff, Véra 123, 250, 251, 252–4, 258–60; GJ to 256–7, 265, 267, 273–4

Pach, Walter 152, 159, 224
Paris 23, 47–8, 154; Académie Carmen 22, 24, 27; Académie Julien 23, 24; Bernheim Jeune Gallery 55, 193, 236; Colarossi's school 24, 88; Hôtel Biron 110, 139, 140, 156; Hôtel Mont Blanc (19 blvd Edgar Quinet) 44, 47, 48, 64–5; Musée de Luxembourg 167; 87 rue du Cherche-Midi 85–7, 96, 107–8; 12 rue Froidevaux 24, 28; 6 rue de l'Ouest 109, 117, 129; 7 rue St Placide 68–70, 75, 83–4; Salon des Tuileries 239
Pembrokeshire Herald 3–4
Peveril Tower, Swanage 29, 32
Picasso, Pablo: arrives in Paris 119; GJ's views on 119, 208, 221, 266; patronised by Quinn 124, 159, 161, 215, 221, 224, 225; GJ's stylistic similarities 87, 119, 185, 195; meets Jeanne Foster 202; exhibited by Rosenberg 208, 231
Works:
The Actor 119
Child with Dove 179

La Estera 119, 122
The Frugal Repast 119
Woman with a Crow 119
Piermé, Canon (Curé) 255, 274–6, 277, 292
Pissarro, Camille 195
Pius XI, Pope 270
Pléneuf, France 177–8, 179, 181, 187, 199; Château Vauclair 178, 180, 181–5, 199–200
Plume, La 55
Poe, Edgar Allan 11, 74, 88, 103, 186, 292
Pont l'Abbé, France 141, 149
Pont-Aven, France 183
Post-Impressionism 21, 180, 196, 282
Pottier (packager) 161, 162–3, 217, 221, 224, 226, 227, 231, 242
Pound, Dorothy 220
Pound, Ezra xiv, 124, 176, 202, 220
Poussin, Nicolas 251
Price, Frederic Newlin 278, 279, 281, 282, 298
Prouvost, Camille 208
Prusts, the 8
Puvis de Chavannes, Pierre 15, 22, 27, 52, 143, 255, 258

Quinn, Clara 240
Quinn, John 124; awaits picture from GJ 124–5; his judgement worries her 133, 134, 144; buys *Girl Reading at the Window* 125, 142, 143; misses GJ in Paris 142; offers her regular money on account 142–4; receives drawings 144–5; plans exhibition 146–8; receives *Study of a Woman* and two drawings 152, 152–3; sends GJ money and news of New York art scene 158–9, 161; encourages her friendship with Maud Gonne 160, 171–2; buys *Seated Woman in Blue Dress* and *Interior* 162–3, 164; does not appreciate GJ's drawings 163, 164; is sent *Portrait of a Girl with Hands Clasped* and *Girl in Rose* 165; buys albums of drawings 167, 168; his letters 171; buys AJ's portrait of Symons 172; pleads for Maud Gonne's release 176; pleased with drawings from GJ 178; sends GJ camera 184, 201; wants affidavit authenticating her pictures 184, 185, 187; awarded Legion of Honour 187; and GJ's desire to buy Château Vauclair 198, 200; wants to buy *Mère Poussepin* 200, 207, 214; 'a man of taste' 200; sends GJ money 201–2, 214; and Jeanne Foster 201, 202, 203; has become important to GJ 204; views on Laurencin 214–15, 219, 221; meets GJ 217–18; squabbles with Jeanne over GJ's paintings 218; meets Symonses 216; influenced by Kuhn 219; under terrible strain 221; would sacrifice Picassos 221; acquires *Mère Poussepin* 221–2, 223, 224, 227; illness 224; buys *Girl in Blue* 224; organises exhibitions 224–5; energetic networking 225; blames Rhoda Symons for profligacy 225–6; worred about Laurencin 227; awaiting pictures from GJ 228–9; drawn by AJ in New York 229; in Paris 229; takes GJ's pictures 230; introduces her to Segonzac 230; back to New York 230; sends money 231; suggests GJ see Cézanne's work 231; reluctant to give up GJ

drawings to Jeanne Foster 232; buys *The Convalescent, Woman with Cloak* and *Girl in Rose* 234; illness and death 235, 236–8; will 237, 240, 241, 242, 244, 244, 279–80
AJ's letters to 282–3
GJ's letters to 132–3, 135, 141–2, 154, 160, 162, 163–4, 170, 171–2, 178, 180, 182, 183, 184, 185, 187–8, 198, 199, 201–2, 208, 214, 229
Jeanne Foster to 204–7, 218, 230–1

Redfern Gallery, London 222
Redon, Odilon 161
Rembrandt van Rijn 132, 134, 258
Renard, Captain Charles 129
Renoir, Pierre Auguste 143, 159, 258
Réole, France 39–40, 44
Reynolds, Sir Joshua 41
Richardson, Samuel 11
Clarissa 57–8
Pamela 58, 82
Richmond, Constance 249
Richmond, Eilydh 249
Richmond, Peggy 246, 248–9
Rilke, Clara (*née* Westhoff) 110, 149
Rilke, Rainer Maria 11; as Rodin's secretary 51; with Rodin 66, 71; on Rodin's *Gates of Hell* 56; advice to Kappus 71, 72, 73–4; friendship with GJ 69, 71, 72, 73, 103; invited back by Rodin 102; lends GJ *Love Letters of a Portuguese Nun* 104; discovers the Hôtel Biron 110; on Rodin and his gramophone 111; on the 'Duchesse' de Choiseul 111, 141; misunderstanding with GJ 149; on the postwar world 191; death 250; GJ and his poetry 251, 254
Works:
Die Aufzeichnungen des Malte Laurids Brigge 47, 51, 250
Quatrains Valaisans 250
Letters to a Young Poet 71–4
Verger 250
'Will I have expressed it before I leave. . .' 41
Roche, Alexandre 283, 284
Roché, Henri-Pierre 124, 217, 229, 230, 236, 237, 238
Roche, Louise xii, 263, 264, 268–73, 270, 280, 283, 284, 298
Roche, Louis 268
Rodin, Auguste 22; and Rose Beuret 61; affair with Camille Claudel 123; in London 53–4; starts Whistler monument 53, 54, *see below*; hires GJ as model and scribe 50–1, 54; affair with GJ 52–3, 56–7, 59–62, 66–7, 69–70, 74–6, 79–80, 94–5, 99, 101, 102–3, 136; use of models 55–6; literary tastes 57–8; urges GJ to draw 58, 67; women in love with 63–4; and Rilke 51, 66, 71, 102; in London 67; erotic drawings 55, 76–7; praises GJ's novel 82; sends telegram at Ida's death 91; encourages Ursula Tyrwhitt 91; awarded Ph.D. by Oxford University 95, 138; liaison with 'Duchesse' de Choiseul 95–6, 105, 110–12; continues to give GJ money 98; in love with Nature 99–100; confides in Helene de Nostiz-Wallwitz Hindenburg 101; on women as his Muses 101–2; attitude to GJ 102–3, 105–6, 109; sculpts Fenella Lovell 106; finds studio space in Hôtel Biron 110; GJ wants to pose for 114–15; finds GJ new clients 116–17, 121–2;

studio flooded 126; life at Villa des Brillants 127, 130, 131; contacted by Fenella Lovell 137, 141; end of liaison with 'Duchesse' 139, 140–1; failing health 140; attacked for praising Nijinsky 140; saddens GJ with his *faiblesse* 149; writes to GJ 156; frightened by the war 156; flees France 157; Pope sits to him 158; marries Rose Beuret 166; illness and death 166–7, 173
influence on GJ xiv, 52–3, 56, 60, 61, 68, 113, 193, 194, 195, 225
GJ's letters to xiii, xv, 51–2, 57, 59, 60, 62–3, 64, 69, 74, 85, 91, 108, 139–40
Works:
Les Cathédrales de France 54
'Duchesse' Claire de Choiseul 105
The Gates of Hell 56
Mignon 61
Shaw 79
Whistler Monument 53, 54, 78–9, 100, 112, 1 17, 121, 126, 138–9, 156, 167
Roederstein, Ottilie xiii, 49, 63, 98–9
Rosenberg, Harold 208, 215, 227, 231
Rossetti, Christina 242
'Winter, My Secret' 235
Rothenstein, Arthur 161
Rothenstein, John 305
Modern English Painters 41
Rothenstein, William: and AJ 15, 30–1, 35, 38, 91; on GJ's *Self-Portrait in a Red Blouse* 19; NEAC judge 32; praises GJ's pictures 98, 247
Rouault, Georges 124, 161, 225, 251, 256, 257, 258, 266, 278, 289
Studies for a Nude 257–8
Rousseau, Henri 124, 132–3, 234, 235, 243, 248
Ruskin, John 27
Russell, Bertrand 184
Rutherston, Albert 32, 36, 239, 243, 246; Orpen to 35; Rothenstein to 38
Rutherston, Charles 239, 242, 248

Sadler's Wells, London 17
Salaman, Louise *see* Bishop, Louise
Salaman, Michael 295, 300
Salaman, Michel 17, 30, 31, 32, 33, 246, 247, 295; GJ to 29–30, 33, 34; Ida John to 28; Tonks to 36
Salmond, Gwen xiii, 23, 24–5, 26, 29, 32, 40
Salon des Tuileries, Paris 239
Sampson, John ('Rai') 33; AJ to 89
Sampson, Margaret (*née* Sprunt) ('Meg'), AJ to 89, 137
Samuel, Frederick and Dorothy 247
Sarrilh, General 163
Satie, Erik 124, 202
Schepeler, Alexandra ('Alick') 84
Schopenhauer, Arthur 69
Sculptors' Gallery, New York 224, 226
Segonzac, André de 124, 159, 161, 208, 215, 2
25, 230, 237
Seneca 112
Sérusier, Paul 183
Seurat, Georges 224, 258
The Circus 225, 227
Shakespeare, William 11, 19, 28, 57, 268
Hamlet 122–3
Shaw, George Bernard: Rodin's bust 79
Shute, Winifred (*née* John): childhood 2, 6, 7, 8, 10; relationship with GJ 8; as model for *Landscape at Tenby, with Figures* 9; love of literature 7–8, 11; GJ's portraits 11, 17; studies violin in London 18; drawn by AJ 18; visits AJ and

Ida 33; and the birth of her daughter 162; letters to GJ 38, 77, 103–4, 131, 165; on GJ 13Sickert, Walter 21, 87
Slade School of Art, London 14–17; *see also* Tonks, Henry
Smith, Ada C. 240
Smith, Leah 6
Smith, Mary (*née* Thornton) 5
Smith, Rosina ('Aunt Rose') 6, 103, 131
Smith, Thomas 5; estate 280, 284, 286
Smollett, Tobias 8
Society of Twelve 125
Soudbinine, Monsieur 122
Steer, Philip Wilson 16, 32, 161
Sugo, Henri 145
Swinburne, Algernon 22; descendants 8
'Before the Mirror' 22
Symbolists 22, 27
Symons, Arthur xiv, 172; captivated by GJ's drawings 190; and AJ 190, 201, 208; sends GJ poems 198; with GJ in Paris 193, 200; 'troublesome to be with' 201; increases GJ's interest in poetry 210, 223; invites her to stay 215–16; financial problems 225–6; in contact with GJ 248, 285; on Rodin's drawings 55; on Whistler 26'Faces' 198
Symons, Rhoda 190; friendship with GJ 192–3, 200–1, 208–9, 248, 285; sits to her 216, 219; 'a millionaire's appetite for spending' 225–6

Tenby, Wales 7–9, 103
Tharlow, Fritz 44
Tigre (cat) 78
Times, The 155
Titanic, sinking of the 141–2
Tolstoy, Leon 303
Tonks, Henry xiii, 16, 18–20, 21–2, 32, 36
Transatlantic Review 202
Tum (cat) 211, 227, 232
Turner Art Gallery, Truro 245, 246
Tyrwhitt, Ursula (*née* Tyrwhitt): at the Slade 15, 16; encourages GJ to keep painting 77, 97, 104, 106, 112–13; works in Rodin's studio 91; with GJ in Paris 97–8; longing for financial independence 101; sends GJ Poe stories 103; discouraged in her painting 117; plans to return to Paris 126; views on GJ's paintings 133–4, 135, 164; brief stay in Paris 145; sends GJ war news 155, 161, and clothes 166, 176, 244; exhibits at NEAC 177; sends GJ news 222; misses her in Paris 236; offers to help GJ by selling and buying paintings 238, 244; has not enough work for exhibition 245, 246; writes foreword to Chenil catalogue 247; visits GJ 277–8, 296, 297, 298; travelling 301, 303; sends GJ clothes 303
GJ's letters to xv, 35, 42, 43, 49, 65, 98, 99–100, 104, 106, 110, 114, 117–18, 119, 122, 125, 127, 129, 137, 145, 154, 155, 160, 165, 169, 174, 175, 176, 217, 222, 238–9, 243–4, 260–1, 262, 266–7, 279, 297, 298–300
Tyrwhitt, Walter 278

Valentine (cat) 172, 269, 283–4
Vauxcelles, Louis 100
Veber, 153–4
Verhaeren, Emile 173
Verlaine, Paul 11, 22, 57
Vienna: Meisterwerke Englischer Malerei . . . (exhibition) 252

Villon, Jacques 161
Vuillard, Édouard 23, 41

Walker, Robert: *Locomotive System* 41
Walker, Maynard 278–9, 282, 301
Warren Gallery, London 282
Watkins, Nona 186, 189–90, 198, 208, 217
Waugh, Edna *see* Clarke-Hall, Edna
Waugh, Rosa 21
Westhoff, Clara *see* Rilke, Clara
Westray, Grace 18
Whistler, James Abbott McNeill xiii, 20, 22, 25–7, 53, 54; praises GJ 26
  Nocturne in Blue and Silver 27
  Symphony in White no. 2: The Little White Girl 22, 25
White, Vivien (*née* John) 248, 303
Whiteway, Logic 15–16
Wilde, Oscar 69
Wildenstein Gallery, London 304
Wilson, Miss (schoolmistress) 8, 10
Winter, Mr (at NEAC) 98, 103
Wood, Derwent 167
Woolf, Virginia: *Jacob's Room* 159
Wyndham, George 53

Yashi, Youimoto 133
Yeats, John B. 240
Yeats, John B. 124
Yew Tree Cottage 260–1, 263, 264, 267, 280, 284, 293, 294, 300, 303